Archaeology and Capitalism

One World Archaeology Series
Sponsored by the World Archaeological Congress
Series Editors: Joan Gero, Mark Leone and Robin Torrence

One World Archaeology volumes contain carefully edited selections of the exemplary papers presented at the World Archaeology Congress (WAC), held every four years, and intercongress meetings. WAC gives place to considerations of power and politics in framing archaeological questions and results. The organization also gives place and privilege to minorities who have often been silenced or regarded as beyond capable of making main line contributions to the field. All royalties from the series are used to help the wider work of the organization. The series is published by Left Coast Press, Inc. beginning with volume 48.

Previous volumes in this series, available from Routledge:

Archaeology and Capitalism
From Ethics to Politics

Edited by
Yannis Hamilakis and Philip Duke

**Left Coast
Press** Inc.

Walnut Creek, California

Left Coast
Press Inc.

LEFT COAST PRESS, INC.
1630 North Main Street, #400
Walnut Creek, CA 94596
http://www.LCoastPress.com

ISBN 978–1-59874–270–1 hardcover

Library of Congress Cataloging-in-Publication Data

Archaeology and capitalism/Yannis Hamilakis and Philip Duke, editors.
p. cm. – (One world archaeology series ; 54) Includes bibliographical references and index.
ISBN 978-1-59874-270-1 (hardcover: alk.paper) 1. Archaeology – Social aspects. 2. Archaeology – Moral and ethical aspects. 3. Archaeologists – Professional ethics. 4. Antiquities – Collection and preservation – Moral and ethical aspects. 5. Archaeology – Political aspects. 6. Archaeology – Philosophy. 7. Postcolonialism. 8. Capitalism – Social aspects. 9. Capitalism – Political aspects. 10. Capitalism – Moral and ethical aspects. I. Hamilakis, Yannis, 1966- II. Duke, P. G.
CC175.A724 2007
930.1 – dc22
2007025526

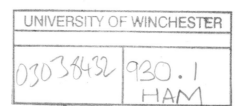
Printed in the United States of America

∞™ The paper used in this publication meets the minimum requirements of American National Standard for Information Sciences—Permanence of Paper for Printed Library Materials, ANSI/NISO Z39.48–1992.

07 08 09 5 4 3 2 1

Contents

List of Illustrations

Figures

Tables

Foreword: Politics Is a Dirty Word, but Then Archaeology Is a Dirty Business

Randall H. McGuire

Thirty years ago the Mexican archaeologists Rebeca Panameño and Enrique Nalda (1979) asked: *Arqueología para quien*? (Archaeology for Whom?) This was and remains a radical question for archaeology. Radical because it implies that archaeology is not a selfless search for knowledge. Instead, the question asserts that archaeology serves the interests of specific social groups. This question is the basic query of an explicitly political archaeology. It is a question that English-speaking archaeologists would take up in a serious way in the 1980s and early 1990s. But since that time, calls for archaeology as political action have gradually faded away. The authors in this book have revived this query and tried to answer it. They argue that archaeology in the West has consistently served the interests of capitalism and this is something that they want to change.

In the English-speaking world, politics is a dirty word. People spurn politics as a grubby business tainted by dishonesty, strong feelings and self-interest. In popular discourse, politics is contrasted with dispassionate, objective science. Many people resist any explicit discussions of politics, because political judgments are emotional and political discussions often acrimonious. People are passionate about politics because they are about what we believe and who we think we are. Political positions necessarily involve moral and ethical attitudes about the world. These attitudes invoke powerful zeal in people. We are taught as young children to exclude politics from polite conversation because politics create tension and hostility between individuals. Politics also have real consequences for peoples' lives. These consequences are often pernicious. People lose their land or their jobs; people starve, die, or are imprisoned. All of this suggests that the safest thing to do is not 'make things political'.

Many archaeologists will view the overt political agenda of this book with alarm and unease. After the political and theoretical turmoil of the later 20th century, these archaeologists look forward to a new century free of theory wars, political struggles and conflicts with descendant communities. In their minds, the codification of ethics, the bureaucratization of conflicts over issues like repatriation, and the mainstream adoption of terms like gender and agency have safely eclipsed the political nature of archaeology. This leaves archaeologists free to go about their business. What they fail to recognize is that none of these actions fundamentally address the feminist, post-processualist, Marxist and Indigenous critiques of archaeology. These actions instead simply gloss over the question of 'archaeology for whom?' More importantly, they leave archaeologists with primary control over how the past is defined, studied and interpreted.

The currently popular concept of archaeologists as stewards of the archaeological record embodies this sidestepping of the political nature of archaeology. A steward is someone who manages someone else's property and/or affairs. A steward is a servant. If archaeologists are stewards, whom do they work for? Or, to put this question another way, *Arqueología para quien*?

Scholars need to recognize that politics may be a dirty word but that archaeology is a dirty business. The authors in this book argue that archaeology began as a bourgeois project embedded in the logic of capital and the fetish of commodities. They clearly show how archaeology has been used to advance imperialistic, colonial, nationalistic and racist agendas in the world. The commodification of archaeology in capitalism manifests itself in many ways from the use of archaeological knowledge to sell Las Vegas casinos, to the conversion of museums and ancient monuments from public teaching tools into entertainment theme parks, to the creation of an archaeological underclass in cultural resource management. Archaeology as a project of Western cultural domination reveals itself in paternalistic attempts to give Indigenous peoples their pasts back and collaborations between archaeologists and US invasion forces to save the 'cradle of western civilization' in Iraq.

Archaeology and Capitalism: From Ethics to Politics effectively reopens a serious discussion of archaeology as political action. It does so by situating the discussion of ethics in the political realm. It does so by advocating a praxis of archaeology that involves knowing the world, critiquing the world, and taking action in the world. It does so by challenging the codified ethics and bureaucratic solutions to conflict that have lulled archaeologists into complacency. But most importantly, it does so by asking the question that we can never fully answer but that we must never quit asking, archaeology for whom?

REFERENCE

Panameño, Rebeca and Enrique Nalda (1979) 'Arqueología para quien?' *Nueva Antropología* 12, 111–124

Acknowledgments

This volume grew out of a symposium titled *An Ethical Archaeology in a Capitalist World* which was held at the 5th *World Archaeological Congress* in Washington, DC in 2003. The participants in the symposium were Alexander Bauer, Shanel Lindsay and Stephen Urice, Pedro Paulo Funari, Francisco Noelli, Martin Hall, Tracy Ireland, George Nicholas, Mark Pluciennik, Nick Shepherd and Alison Wylie. Michael Shanks served as the symposium's commentator. Unfortunately, not all of the participants were able to contribute to this volume, but we are most grateful to them for their stimulating contributions that persuaded us that a volume would be of value. Our gratitude is offered to those contributors whom we subsequently solicited for papers. We are very grateful to Joan Gero for her support of both the initial symposium and this volume, and to Mitch Allen and his production team at Left Coast Press for making the process as painless as possible. We would also like to thank the British Academy and Fort Lewis College for funding our participation in WAC5. The Editors also express their gratitude to the Fort Lewis College Foundation for their generous financial support of the preparation of the index.

PART 1

INTRODUCTION

CHAPTER 1

From Ethics to Politics

Yannis Hamilakis

Why another book on ethics and socio-politics in archaeology? After all, in the last 25 years a good number of them has been produced (eg, Gathercole and Lowenthal 1990; Gero *et al* 1983; Kane 2003; Karlsson 2004; Lynott and Wylie 1995; Meskell and Pels 2005; Pinsky and Wylie 1989; Pluciennik 2001; Scarre and Scarre 2006; Zimmerman *et al* 2003), not to mention many others on looting, repatriation, indigenous archaeologies, and nationalism, which are linked one way or another to ethical and political issues. And this is just what has come out in English (although some of these volumes include contributions from outside the Anglo-Saxon tradition). So why add to the inflation of titles, put further pressures on already struggling academic libraries, and waste world resources? How can we justify the production of this book, beyond the academics' ambitions to publish and further careers, the editors' ambitions to set academic agendas, and the publishers' hopes to compete in the crowded market of academic publishing?

We, the editors and the contributors to this volume, believe that this book does something different. It of course builds on some of the above discussion (and acknowledges its debt to several seminal works on the subject), but it also departs from many of them in significant ways. What makes this book different is its aim and ambition to reframe the discussion on ethics in archaeology by shifting the debate into the field of politics, showing that the ethical and socio-political arenas should not be treated as separate (*cf* Bernstein 1991:9), as is often the case, and proposing that conundrums such as the tension between universal and context-specific ethics can be only dealt with through political praxis (*cf* McGuire *et al* 2005).

The book is divided into four parts, the first being this introduction. The second part questions some of the taken-for-granted assumptions on ethics in archaeology, demonstrating their problems and weaknesses. The third re-examines the debate on ethics indirectly, by looking at the intersection between western archaeology and capitalist economic and social structures. And the fourth takes a prospective view and offers suggestions, through specific cases and examples, on how an ethical-political praxis in archaeology can be achieved. This chapter is more of a programmatic paper and an introduction to the main ideas and motivations behind this book, and not so much an introduction to the specific contents of the volume. That task is achieved with the short introductions for each part. In this chapter, I will start by providing a social and political background for the development of western archaeology, reviewing briefly the debates on ethics and politics to date; I will then proceed to discuss the main problems and pitfalls in these debates and practices, and show how these can be tackled and even avoided if a different framework, based on what I call *the political ethic*, is adopted. I will conclude with some suggestions for future research and debating agendas.

ARCHAEOLOGY AS CAPITALISM

It is now increasingly realised that archaeology as we know and practice it in the modern West is a device of modernity, that is, the constellation of social, economic, cultural and ideological processes that shaped the West in the centuries from the end of the Middle Ages to the present (*cf* Schnapp *et al* 2004; Thomas 2004). The era of modernity reshaped the world, produced the modern individual as we know it (*cf* Foucault 1970), established the ideas and the realities of nation-states, and above all, created the new regime of capitalism. Archaeology as a process of engaging with the material traces of the past and attempting to produce narrative and discourses about them is not of course new, as studies such as the one by Schnapp (1996) have shown. What is new is the regime of western archaeological apparatus that produced a specific set of ideas, discourses and practices in dealing with the material past. It meant the reframing of time and space, the creation of linear, cumulative temporality, and the establishment of a homological link between space and time: As the West, through early colonialism, realised that there was new, previously unknown territory to be conquered and subjugated, in the same way, deeper and longer pasts became available for conquering and colonisation, through the new sciences of geology and archaeology and the ideas of evolution.

But modernity is primarily the era of commodities, the era of equivalence, exchange and capitalism. It is also the era of national imagination, that is, the formation of a new imaginary way of organising space and time, based on homogenisation and easy communication and mobility, essential elements for the development of capital (*cf* Anderson 1991). Archaeology was crucial for national imagination (*cf* Díaz-Andreu and Champion 1996; Hamilakis 2007; Kohl and Fawcett 1995); it could not only provide the material truths necessary to forge a long antiquity for the nation, but it could also generate objects and sites as commodities for (primarily visual) consumption and entertainment by the new middle classes during their newly discovered leisure time. This is what I want to call 'official archaeology' – as opposed to alternative archaeologies such as the pre-modern archaeologies of the West (that may go as far back as prehistory) and the nonwestern archaeologies: the diverse, social engagements with the material traces of the past, and the stories and narratives around them, produced by people outside western modernity. Official archaeology 'rediscovered' sites and ruins, divorced them from the web of daily life, and declared them the object of archaeology; this is what we now call the 'archaeological record' which is meant to be protected, conserved, studied and admired, but primarily from a distance, and mindful of the potential damage that people can cause to it. The ruins that were once experienced through multi-sensory bodily encounters, were the subject of countless stories, and at certain times, such as in the 18th century, the subject of the romantic admiration of westerners who were fascinated by decay and loss (cf Roth et al 1997), now became archaeological monuments. The fence that was often erected around them operated as the symbolic barrier that ended or at least regulated these earlier encounters. Other sites were dug out of the ground – in other words, they were produced anew as archaeological monumental sites (cf Hamilakis 2001). This constructed 'archaeological record' found its way into national mythologies, chronometric timelines, and cultural evolutionist narratives of progress and civilisation.

Alongside these processes, the commodification of these new objects was progressing steadily (cf Kehoe this volume). The early 'antiquities fever' of the 18th and early 19th centuries that gripped antiquarians, diplomats and scholars and led them to pillage the sacred sites of western imagination, especially in the Mediterranean, was an early form of commodification; it transformed objects into valuable and highly desirable commodities; indeed, financial transactions were often involved in their handling. It is worth recalling here Walter Benjamin's observation (as part of his examination of the 19th-century European modernity) that there is a close association between the department store and the museum (2002:415):

> There are relations between department store and museum, and here the bazaar provides a link. The amassing of artworks in the museum brings them into communication with commodities, which – where they offer themselves *en masse* to the passerby – awake in him the notion that some part of this should fall to him as well.

With the establishment of the nation-states in the 19th and early 20th century, antiquities acquired additional value as national icons. Ruins became organised archaeological sites that charged entrance fees, and museums became the regimented exhibition of objects and artifacts to be consumed by the autonomous and highly disciplined gaze (*cf* Bennett 1998); within this framework, these objects and artefacts were often devoid of their physical and experiential properties and became instead abstract equivalences, much like money, that stood for specific time periods, cultures, and ethnic groups. They became the symbolic capital for nations, as well as for a range of groups and communities.

This process of course was far from linear, entangled into a series of tensions such as the one between the role of antiquities as national values and icons, and their commodification as capital, symbolic or otherwise. National imagination wanted them to be venerated almost religiously, as material truths of continuity and the glory of the nation. But nationalism as a worldview originates from the middle class. Capital and commodification are at its base. As a result, antiquities cast as national icons had at the same time to operate as a resource, to be exchanged in the international symbolic economy for financial capital or prestige and national standing (*cf* Hamilakis 2003a, 2007). Other tensions and complications resulted from the diverse forms that western modernity took, often incorporating pre-modern ideas and engaging in a creative dialogue with nonwestern cultures and modernities, for example in areas such as southern and southeastern Europe. As a result, modernist official archaeology can take various guises and forms, and cannot be described as a monolithic construct.

This brief and schematic excursus into the socio-political and economic origins of the discipline of archaeology is meant to remind us that official western archaeology – be it classical, prehistoric, historic or other – is intricately linked with capitalism from its conception and birth. The extreme commodification of archaeology that we have experienced in the last 25 years (especially in countries like USA, UK and Western Europe), and which is thoroughly analysed and critiqued by a number of authors in this book (eg, Silberman, Everill) is simply the most recent and the most aggressive phase of this entanglement.

ARCHAEOLOGY AND THE SOCIO-POLITICAL CRITIQUE

It is well known that culture-history and processual archaeology traditions in official, western archaeology discouraged any explicit reflexive discussion on the politics of origins of western archaeology, and on the ethical and political dimensions of archaeological thinking and practice. This situation changed in the 1980s when a number of processes forced the discipline to confront its own heritage. In Australia, New Zealand and the USA, it was the pressure by indigenous groups who demanded a stop to being treated as the object of western scientific discourse, insisting that their own archaeologies be considered valid and important. As a result, western archaeologists started rethinking their practices, especially in relation to the excavation of human burials.

In Europe, other intellectual and broader social and political processes were under way, the most significant of which were the increasing criticism of the objective and value-free nature of processual archaeology, and the emergence of a number of diverse critical theoretical discourses that are now known as post-processual archaeologies. These discourses, at least at their beginning, emphasised the political character of the archaeological enterprise, and some of its main proponents went as far as to state that archaeology should provide the platform for socio-political action in the present (cf Tilley 1989). At the same time, in the USA and in some European countries, feminist archaeology came into play and challenged the patriarchal nature of the discipline, in terms of both its portrayal of the past and its internal workings and practice. A key event in this early movement of political awareness of archaeology was the foundation of the World Archaeological Congress (WAC) at Southampton, UK in 1986 (cf Ucko 1987). This episode signified a rare moment when a broader socio-political movement, in this case the world anti-apartheid struggle, resulted in a fundamental change in the disciplinary culture of archaeology. WAC was founded on the assumption that archaeology cannot be divorced from the broader political climate, and that values of equality and social justice should be at the centre of archaeological thinking and practice. WAC contributed further to debates on indigenous groups, and on repatriation and reburial of human skeletons and archaeological artefacts. In some of these areas its impact was crucial, in terms of both ideas and practice.

So, where are we today? Where did this early politicisation of archaeology lead? Conventional accounts would respond to this question by pointing to the increased level of writing on the topic as an indication that this move is going from strength to strength, acquiring cumulative weight and disciplinary acceptance and recognition. I contend, however, that the picture is more diverse and somehow less optimistic than it appears. A number of battles have been clearly won and others are still ongoing. For example, the earlier discussions on indigenous issues in archaeology have now given way to an emerging array of *indigenous archaeologies* (eg, Smith and Wobst 2005; Watkins 2001; cf Nicholas and Hollowell this volume). The difference here is significant. Whilst before it was the official, western archaeology that was forced to take into account the grievances of the indigenous groups, the emerging indigenous archaeologies now demand a much more proactive and dynamic role, an agenda-setting role. As we saw above, these alternative archaeologies existed all along and well before the official, western archaeology was established. But now, under the rubric of indigenous archaeologies, these alternative epistemologies and practices claim a central and defining role, alongside the official western archaeology. This hopeful move has the potential of transforming the official western archaeology as well, not only at the level of ideas but also at the level of practice, from data gathering to exhibition and dissemination.

Feminist archaeology has also become more prominent and has achieved some of its goals, especially when challenging patriarchal narratives on the past, although present-day gender inequalities are far from being eradicated (cf Conkey 2005 for a recent review). The looting of archaeological artefacts and its impact have become a major area for discussion and debate (eg, Brodie et al 2001, 2006; Brodie and Tubb 2002; Renfrew 2000) although the dominant archaeological stance on the matter is often monolithic (cf Colwell-Chanthaphonh 2004), ignoring the sometimes deeply felt connections of local people towards the land and the antiquities that come out of it, as well as the economics and politics of 'subsistence looting' for low-income and exploited people (eg, Hollowell 2006; Matsuda 1998). Despite their problems, however, these debates have challenged the commodification of the material past and the impact of the art market. Nationalism has attracted much interest in the last 10 years or so (eg, Atkinson et al 1996; Díaz-Andreu and Champion 1996; Kohl and Fawcett 1995; Meskell 1998), thus drawing attention to the national origins of archaeology but also to the impact of often exclusivist nationalist archaeologies in the past and present, although these writings are often unreflexive, seeing only the nationalism of the 'other' (cf Hamilakis 1996, 2007).

I want to suggest, however, that in addition to the above largely positive and hopeful phenomena, other developments are more worrisome and problematic. Indeed I want to suggest that what has happened in the last 15 years or so is nothing less than the bureaucratisation and instrumentalisation of ethics, and these transformations have resulted in the depoliticisation of ethical debate in archaeology. These are serious contentions, and I do not utter them lightly. The earlier radical calls by prominent advocates of post-processualism for archaeology to be viewed as political action have been toned down and gradually almost disappeared. Since then, most of the focus on theoretical discussion has moved on to interpretative issues having to do with the past, not the present.

Explicitly political archaeologies, of course, continue to exist (such as radical feminism or the Marxist archaeology in the USA, Latin America, or Catalunia; cf McGuire et al 2005), but their impact has been less pronounced. Politics in archaeology, in common with other disciplines, has become primarily the politics of identity, more often than not seen simply in terms of discourse rather than as discursive *and* material power. Some would claim that this is a side effect of the success of post-processualism as an intellectual movement, at least in the UK, some academic pockets in the USA and elsewhere. This success has also meant a success for its advocates, in terms of jobs and positions of influence. As the political project of archaeology inevitably has to start from the interrogation of the power structures internal to the discipline, the move of many of the critics into positions of authority and control within these structures made such a project very difficult. But this is surely an inadequate explanation, despite the fact that it may contain an element of truth. If the political project in archaeology was alive and thriving as it was in the 1980s, it would have produced a much more widespread wave of critics. The explanation therefore needs to be found in other, deeper developments beyond personalities.

My contention is that a more satisfactory explanation can be found in the structural and disciplinary power of professionalisation, and its effect on the ethical debates in archaeology. In the last few years, ethical matters were removed from the arena of conflict in the world, and became a matter of regulation for the professional organisations. While in the 1980s the ethics of doing archaeology were linked to clashes such as the anti-apartheid movement (in the UK), or the earlier civil rights movement and the battles for racial equality (in the USA, *cf* Lynott 2003:22; Zimmerman 1998), in the 1990s ethics were increasingly and primarily a matter for working groups and meetings of the Society for American Archaeology or other such organisations. Whereas in the 1980s the advocates of ethical and political archaeologies were academics (individually, or in groups and forums such as WAC) debating and fighting out of political convictions, in the 1990s the advocates for ethical matters were often academics but increasingly middle and high rank professionals in the cultural resource management (CRM) sector, and operating within the confines of professional organisations.

The establishment of a code of ethics was the next step. The idea was to codify the basic ethical principles that western archaeologists should adhere to in their professional practice. The contentious matters of the day, from reburial and indigenous issues to looting, often became single-sentence principles, after a series of internal debates and compromises. The device of the code and its impact has already become the subject of some penetrating critiques, both in archaeology (Smith and Burke 2003; Tarlow 2000, 2006) and in other cognate disciplines such as anthropology (eg, Pels 1999). These critics point out that the codification of ethics is inscribed within the broader managerial culture of auditing, dominant in western academia at least in the last two decades (*cf* Strathern 2000); they also claim that the logic of the code of ethics relies on the notion of individual morality (taking as its basis the western notion of the autonomous individual person), and it attempts to establish abstract principles of universal applicability. Finally, critics point out that the process of codification closes off and solidifies debate (*cf* Meskell and Pels 2005, esp. Introduction; Pels 1999; and especially Tarlow 2000 for one of the most penetrating and thoughtful critiques).

I am sympathetic to all the above arguments with one slight qualification: I believe that the process of discussion and engagement that precedes the establishment of a code of ethics has the potential to bring into the fore the contentious, difficult, and often swept-under-the-carpet issues of archaeological practice. It can thus be a dynamic and fruitful process (*cf* Wylie 2003:13), although that potential is not always realised. Having said that, unless the codes of ethics and practice are in a constant state of revision and negotiation, the dangers of solidification, stagnation, and ethical complicity are always present. The major weakness of the above critiques on ethics and their codification (in archaeology and anthropology) is that they fall short of suggesting plausible alternatives: alternatives that will reconcile the need to address pressing ethical issues with the need to avoid the risks and the pitfalls of codification; more importantly, to reconcile the need to avoid abstract decontextualised principles based on the notions of western individual morality, with the need to articulate an effective and powerful discourse that does not become paralysed by ethical relativism (*cf* Lampeter Archaeology Workshop 1997).

I believe that there are three fundamental problems that are associated with the phenomenon of the instrumentalisation of ethics. The first is the internalisation of the professionalised ethic, and the notion of professional responsibility: the idea that archaeologists are professionals above everything else, and they should thus adhere to the ethics and principles of their profession. This often means that archaeologists divest themselves of other roles, such as the role of citizen with ethical responsibilities, the role of human being, the role of politically active agent, and so on. These roles, when considered, take secondary place to the primary role, which is the role of the professional archaeologist. Associated with this is the problem of the reliance on a heavily problematic conceptualisation of the nature of archaeological practice. As we saw above, western official archaeology is a recent construction of capitalist modernity, and it carries with it the foundational ideologies of the western middle classes, from the belief in the autonomous individual and the logic of capital and commodity, to the logic of patriarchy and the notion of the disembodied reason.

Moreover, time and again recent discussion has shown (eg, Barrett 1988; Hamilakis 1999; Patrik 1985) that western official archaeology has fetishised an abstract metaphysical entity which it calls the 'archaeological record', and it declares it as its primary object of concern and study. Yet the record as such does not exist, neither in the sense of the intention on the part of past people to leave a record of their actions, nor in the sense of objective reality outside the realm of archaeological practice. What exists is only the fragmentary material traces of the past which are then shaped, reordered, organised, recorded and exhibited by archaeologists as the 'record'. The archaeological process of creating the record is conditioned partly by the ability of these fragments of the past to extend their agency into the present (see below), but it is also significantly constrained by socio-political contexts and practices (colonialism, nationalism and so on) and internal disciplinary regimes, ideas and conditions. The fetish of the 'record' is reminiscent of the fetish of the commodity (as analysed by Marxian thought), a key symptom of capitalism. Given the western archaeology's close links with the logic of the commodity since its inception, this fetishisation is perhaps explainable.

These ideas (especially the role of the archaeological practice in producing the 'record') are now increasingly accepted at the level of archaeological thinking, but they have not influenced discussion on ethics and politics in archaeology which seems still to rely on the ideas of objectivism and positivism. As a result, the professionalised archaeologist now declares as his or her primary professional duty, but also primary ethical responsibility, the care and protection of the archaeological record, as any even cursory look at the codes of ethics of professional organisations can reveal. For example, most (if not all) contributors to a recent important volume on ethics (Zimmerman *et al* 2003) take the notion of the 'record' as given and unproblematic. The primary ethical role of archaeologists, therefore, appears simple according to this logic: It is an issue of doing everything they can within their power to protect, rescue and conserve that record 'for future generations'. The problem with this principle is not simply that it is out of synch with the recent discussion on the social history, the genealogy, and the epistemology and nature of archaeological practice. More importantly, this logic has important ethical and material implications 'on the ground' as I will show below.

Finally, the third problematic aspect of the instrumentalisation of ethics is that the political dimension is almost always absent. It seems that for some, the word *politics* in archaeology is becoming again a dirty word, something to be avoided, something that contaminates, biases and distorts the primary archaeological principles and duties. Politics mess up our work and interfere in what we do, the argument goes. In this logic, therefore, ethics become the decoy that can rescue us from politics, and, once we make sure we comply with the ethical guidelines of our professional organisations, once we have checked the boxes and filled in the forms (along with 'health and safety' forms), then we are okay.

It may sound trivial, but it seems necessary to respond that everything we do in archaeology or in other fields and arenas is political, want it or not. To address the inherently political dimension of archaeology is to address and confront the political means through which it has been constituted as a discipline, to reflect on power structures and dynamics, on power asymmetries, on inequality, inside and outside the discipline. It also means to always ask the question, who is benefiting from our archaeological and other interventions, and at whose expense? What kind of class, gender, ethnic, national or other interests are being promoted by our interventions? This political ethic also constitutes the most profound and penetrating archaeological reflexivity, unlike recent attempts at reflexivity that have ducked the political, and have often failed to go beyond the level of western individual morality or the level of purely archaeological techniques.

I argue that it is this *principle of political ethic* that provides the best antidote to the instrumentalisation and professionalisation of ethical debate. Instrumentalism sees ethics as a tool, as a purely technical device, that can be used to achieve something else, most commonly to continue doing archaeology as normal, to declare that it is 'business as usual', now with the additional advantage of a clear ethical consciousness. I do not wish to deny the good intentions of many archaeologists involved in these procedures; nor that the adoption of ethical principles, even in their instrumentalised form, *may* result in different practices, and at times benefit disadvantaged and persecuted groups and communities. But due to the inherently depoliticised nature of these debates, most of the time they result in generic and vague calls to support and benefit the 'community', the 'people', the 'locals' and so on; they thus implicitly ignore the conflicting interests amongst these diverse groups and take for granted that archaeology and heritage (most often meant in its modernist sense) is good for 'them', only if we could share its benefits with those 'others'. By contrast, the political ethic puts the archaeological enterprise constantly into doubt, asking always the difficult questions, including the most fundamental of all: Why archaeology? These unsettling questions are bound to have unpredictable outcomes and may lead to the abandonment of specific archaeological projects, but then again, who said that archaeology is always a 'good thing'?

I thus contend that it is this political ethic that can provide a way forward and a potential solution to the problems identified by recent critiques of codification and of the managerial view of ethics; it is the same principle, the political ethic, that may potentially help resolve a key dilemma: that of universal versus context-specific and situated ethics.

While, as several authors have suggested, ethical actions and practices are always situated, we need something else if we are to avoid the paralysis of ethical relativism: and that is, politically situated ethics. This does not mean universal and abstract ethics, in fact it means the opposite: It means ethics that take sides, that recognise the contingency and historicity of human action, the nexus that links knowledge and power and produces specific 'regimes of truth' (Foucault 1980). These are also ethics that acknowledge the inequalities and asymmetries of power and the necessity to adopt a stance that sides with certain interests and groups and against others. It is this ethic that moves the debate from the arena of abstract principles within professional structures to the arena of theorised practice. The political ethic is an embedded ethic, and at the same time is a social ethic, an ethic that goes beyond western individuality by recognising the need to address social dynamics (such as class struggle, labour, feminist, green or anti-capitalist movements), and forge alliances with affected groups and people with whom these specific archaeologists share political convictions and goals. I do not suggest that this process is easy, unproblematic and straightforward; in fact it is the most difficult, uncomfortable and risky of the options open to us, but still the one that holds the most promise.

AN ETHICS OF STEWARDSHIP?

Le me illustrate some of these problems and some of the suggested ideas for tackling them by looking at a key concept; a concept that, more than any other, has been at the centre of the archaeological discussions on ethics, that is the concept of stewardship. A look at the codes of ethics and practice of most professional archaeological organisations will show that the primary ethical principle advocated is that of the stewardship of the archaeological record. Here is what the first principle of the Code of Ethics of the Society for American Archaeology (SAA, the largest professional archaeological organisation in the world, which includes academics as well as CRM archaeologists, and plays a key role in the discussion on ethics worldwide) says, under the title of stewardship:

> The archaeological record, that is, *in situ* archaeological material and sites, archaeological collections, records and reports, is irreplaceable. It is the responsibility of all archaeologists to work for the long-term conservation and protection of the archaeological record by practicing and promoting stewardship of the archaeological record. Stewards are both caretakers of and advocates for the archaeological record for the benefit of all people; as they investigate and interpret the record, they use the specialized knowledge they gain to promote public understanding and support for its long-term preservation. (www.saa.org)

The code in which this article forms the most fundamental principle was adopted in 1996, and it was the result of extensive consultation and debate. To my knowledge, this was the first archaeological professional body to adopt this principle. In 1997, the European Association of Archaeologists adopted a similar code, where again the stewardship of the archaeological record forms a fundamental principle (see www. e-a-a.org). It is not my intention here to discuss these codes as a whole (which address many important issues, containing at the same time many contradictions: *cf* Zimmerman 1995), nor even to engage in a broad-ranging discussion on the origins, the biography, the meanings and the effect of the concept of stewardship (which is encountered today in a variety of contexts, from environmental conservation to religion). I only want to interrogate very briefly a specific entanglement of this concept: the association of this idea with ethics, responsibility and advocacy, and the archaeological record (*cf* also Groarke and Warrick 2006; McGuire 1997; Zimmerman 1998 for rare critiques).

If one reads the reports and documents that are associated with the adoption of this principle (eg, Lynott and Wylie 1995) and talks to some of the people who were involved in it, the concept was thought to be an accepted alternative to the concept of ownership. The SAA had to come to terms with the pressing question, Who owns the past? – a question that had acquired a key importance since the challenge leveled at archaeologists from indigenous groups in the USA. At the same time, it had to deal with the increasing commercialisation of the past that took various forms: from the vast sums of money circulated in the market of looted artefacts (sustained by powerful, wealthy collectors and museums) to the pressure of land owners and developers who were (and are) keen to maximise profits and who treat attempts to rescue antiquities as an obstacle. In that sense, declaring that the archaeologist is not the owner of the material past but its steward, and declaring as the primary duty of that steward the care for and protection of that past, solves two problems at once: It sends the message to indigenous groups that archaeologists are there to protect a shared value (indeed the concept of 'shared stewardship' is often employed) rather than claiming exclusive rights of ownership, and it encourages archaeologists to stand up to the destruction of the material traces of the past by developers, looters and others.

Seen in the above light, the principle of stewardship appears to play a dual political role: It counters the logic of private property which is at the basis of capitalist modernity, and it encourages archaeologists to oppose the destruction that results from the ceaseless race for profit. Nevertheless, the concept becomes hugely problematic when its effects 'on the ground' are taken into account. I discussed above how the concept of the archaeological 'record' has been shown to be problematic for archaeology, in that it is an entity not given but constructed by archaeo-logists and others out of the material fragments of the past. For archaeo-logists, therefore, to declare that their primary responsibility is the care and preservation of and advocacy for the record sounds suspiciously self-serving, as some authors recognise (eg, Wylie 2002, 2005). The stew-ardship principle, of course, justifies this duty/task as a mission for the 'benefit of all people', an aim that appears laudable at first. The idea of archaeology as a 'benefit to all people' may have been intended to oppose the notion of purely archaeological interests, or the interests of a few, but in its generality, abstraction and universality, it sounds vacuous and inconsequential. At the end of the day we should not aim at bene-fitting the people who already benefit from inequality and power asym-metry but rather protect the people who suffer from these inequalities and asymmetries. Moreover, given the genealogy and history of the development of official, western archaeology (a genealogy that is not acknowledged in these formulations), why should archaeologists declare themselves the sole advocates of the 'record', and why should official, western archaeology play that role, as opposed to, say, alternative archaeologies, be they indigenous or other (cf Zimmerman 1998)? The concept of shared stewardship, which is meant to establish a collabora-tive mission of care and protection, has attempted to address this last question, but its impact and acceptance is still limited. Furthermore, the implied idea that this responsibility and advocacy aims at preserving the 'record' for future generations (an idea evoked in the passage above by the repeated use of the expression 'long-term') can mean that archae-ologists abrogate themselves of the responsibilities towards the present and towards the living (cf Duke 2003).

Perhaps the most problematic notion in the above formulation is the idea of the 'conservation and protection of the archaeological record'. A discussion on the ethic of conservation and its genealogy in archae-ology is long overdue (cf Ouzman 2006). This ethic has been the cor-nerstone of official, western archaeology since its inception as an autonomous discipline. Perhaps it needs to be reminded that this is not a universally accepted principle and should not be proclaimed as such in an unproblematic manner. A number of groups and people world-wide who practice their own alternative archaeologies do not neces-sarily consider the conservation of the material past as fundamental. Artefacts, sites and material fragments are often living and in a process of constant change and transformation, as the case of the continuous remaking of the Australian aboriginal rock art (one example among many) indicates (cf Mowaljarlai et al 1988). In other contexts such as in some areas in Papua New Guinea, people may want to produce for-getful landscapes, to 'cover the tracks' of their ancestors, rather than expose and preserve them (cf Harrison 2004). In still other cases, the destruction, decay or death of an artefact is part of its biography and is essential if this artefact is to perform its social role within a community, such as to generate remembering and forgetting for example, as in the case of the Melanesian Malanggan figurines (cf Küchler 2002). In the case of the Zhu Botswana rock art, the installing of a shelter to protect rock art from rainwater damage was not deemed necessary according to Zhu adviser Toma, 'because the rock art's authors were gone and the mountain was reclaiming its images' (cited in Ouzman 2006:347). A Zuni spokesman made this point eloquently: 'Everything for ceremonial, religious, and ritual purposes that my culture makes is meant to disintegrate … to go back into the ground. Conservation is a disservice to my culture' (cited in Sease 1998:106; see also Lowenthal 2000, with further discussion).

One could claim, of course, that in my examples there is a living and active relationship between the people who made these artefacts and the artefacts themselves; also that we can know how these people wish the artefacts to be treated and we can thus take these views into account (or better, allow *them* to practice their own alternative archaeology), something we cannot do with the material traces of people long dead. A second objection to my argument could be that destruction due to commercial profit, ethnic or national conflict, is rife today, and the best thing we could do is to protect these traces in the face of greed, national and ethnic hatred, or indifference.

Both arguments are valid, and I do not suggest here that we should declare all attempts at conservation problematic, futile and useless. But it must be remembered that the ethic of conservation is context-specific, seeped in its western origins and linked to the logic of commodity and to identity processes such as colonial and national glorification. Bernbeck and Pollock (this volume) remind us of that important phrase by Walter Benjamin, that there is no document of 'civilisation' that is not at the same time also a document of barbarism and, indeed, conservation in archaeology since the 18th century has always been accompanied by destruction (cf Arrhenius 2003). In other words, archaeologists and others were and are engaging in a selective conservation of some material traces and the erasure and destruction of others. The purification of 'sacred' national sites by archaeologists from their 'barbaric' remnants around them as in the Athenian Acropolis in the 19th century is now well documented (eg, Hamilakis 2003a, 2007). Even the process of excavation today creates a certain selective record (depending on research priorities, techniques and so on) and it eliminates a range of other possible 'records' (that is, alternative material constructions of the past).

In view of the above, therefore, the political ethic approach that I am advocating here should always ask, who wants to conserve and why?

Who wants to destroy and why? What interests are being served today by the destruction or the conservation of the material traces of the past? And furthermore, what are the broader issues at stake for the different communities and groups today, in each context? These questions will help provide context-specific answers to the dilemmas of conservation and protection. In addition, in some cases archaeologists may want to borrow concepts from the green movement and implement a strategy of sustainability (*cf* Lyons 2003:305), but even this principle carries its own problems and should be subjected to political critique rather than seen as a transcendental value.

It is, of course, disingenuous to assume that all archaeologists today will share the same ethical and political views on this and other issues. And this is one of the central fallacies of any attempt by professional archaeological organisations to establish unified codes of ethics and practice. Archaeologists are divided not only by gender, ethnic and national origin (although in the western world, they are overwhelmingly white), but also by rank and, by implication, class, income and hierarchical position. Why should we assume that the managers of major archaeological firms in the CRM sector share the same interests and ideas with the many thousands of low-paid, often itinerant 'diggers' in short-term jobs (*cf* Everill this volume)? This diverse group will necessarily provide equally diverse answers to the above dilemmas, but for the archaeologists who are concerned about social justice and inequality (within and beyond their own context), attitudes towards preservation and destruction, and, by implication, the archaeologists' role and stance in relation to them, will depend on whether equality and social justice are being advanced or whether their archaeological intervention promotes instead commercialisation, class, gender, ethnic or other inequality, or furthers private profit, or operates as the ethical and environmental pretext for the destruction of habitats and communities. The case of prioritising 'rescue' archaeological projects ahead of major 'development' plans is a vivid example of this (*cf* Ronayne, this volume).

Western official archaeology relies on a linear temporality that assumes a radical break between past and present. It also relies on a sharp separation between humans and inanimate things. At the level of archaeological and social thinking, these notions are of course put into doubt by developments such as the anthropology of agency (eg, Gell 1998) and theories of materiality (eg, Brown 2001) which have shown the agency-like properties of objects and things, the archaeology of contemporary life (eg, Buchli and Lucas 2001) and the field of material culture studies, as well as the archaeology of memory that looks at the 'past in the past' – in other words, the reworking of and constant engagement with past material forms (eg, Van Dyke and Alcock 2003).

I want to go one step further and suggest that, as an essential property of materiality is its duration (*cf* Bergson 1988), the material traces initially created in the past embody and re-enact in the present a multi-temporal existence: Their origins lie in the past and they thus carry with them the temporality of the past into that of the present; as such, they are alive, especially when they are implicated in a reciprocal engagement of making and remaking with humans. Archaeologies, both the official one and the alternative ones, deal with the present, not the past; but this is a multi-temporal present, not one that is sharply separated from the past; they also deal not only with the living people who are engaging with these traces today, but also with the material traces of dead people, that is, a projection of their existence into the present.

This thesis has two important implications: firstly, that contemporary people who are engaging with these traces today may have views on their treatment which must be respected, as indigenous archaeologies have been saying for years; and secondly and more importantly, archaeologists, much like anthropologists, engage with living animate and inanimate entities, not dead communities, people and things. They are thus responsible towards the present-day people and to the material traces that may come from the past but continue to live in the present, including the material traces of past people (*cf* Tarlow 2006). This creates a much more complex set of responsibilities but one that is more consistent with nuanced understandings of time, history and materiality, and one that is in tune with widespread beliefs outside western modernity. It also carries a sense of responsibility that prevents archaeologists from treating material things and human remains simply as objects for scholarly study, or creating a distinction between past and present and thus adopting a conveniently escapist view, ignoring present-day people and communities as separate and distant from the past.

Again, the principle of political ethic does not imply that archaeologists and others should always side with these people and communities; they should instead adopt a critical stance towards them, depending on each group's position within the structures of power, views, practices and interests. But this fundamental principle – that we deal with living animate and inanimate entities, not dead people – puts a different light on the notion of stewardship of the record, and brings us much closer to the ethical position of anthropologists and others who have long accepted this principle.

A look at a recent event will help put these ideas into perspective. I refer to the archaeological reactions to the looting of the Baghdad museum and the looting and destruction of archaeological sites following the 2003 US-led invasion and occupation of Iraq. The events are now well known, and I come straight to my point. I claimed elsewhere (Hamilakis 2003b) that, like the apartheid in 1986 (and the subsequent foundation of the World Archaeological Congress), this event represents nothing less than a deep ethical crisis in archaeology that demands serious debate. Archaeologists, both individuals and organisations, before and after the invasion, engaged in a serious and consistent attempt to emphasise the potential dangers and later the losses from looting and destruction. And this is fine; it is their job after all. But several organisations and individuals did more than that: They in fact acted as advisors to the Pentagon and the British Ministry of Defense in providing information and lists of sites to be spared during the bombing of Iraq (cf Stone 2005), an advisory role that may become permanent, so that the invading armies can avoid the embarrassment of looted museums 'next time' (Stone 2005). These advisors thus became 'embedded' archaeologists offering professional expertise without explicitly and publicly questioning (with rare exceptions) the ethical and political justification of their own actions and of the war operations of which they became part. In one of the most extreme expressions of this phenomenon, many major archaeological organisations in the USA signed a letter to the president calling for the rescue of antiquities, in which the rhetoric of the invading countries was completely adopted, and where the invasion was called a 'return to freedom of the Iraqi people'; in another passage the signatories stated that

> [d]uring the fierce fighting of the past few weeks, we were relieved to see that our military leaders and the coalition partners took extreme precautions to avoid targeting cultural sites along with other non-military places. It was also comforting to receive reports that our armed forces have conducted inspections at some of the important archaeological sites. (cited in Hamilakis 2003b)

All this was written when tens of thousands of civilians were killed, and the vast majority of people in the world (including a large proportion within the USA) were opposed to a war that they saw as illegal and immoral and part of a neo-imperial strategy, claims that were vindicated by later events. Leaving aside the adoption of a nationalist rhetoric (when so much has been written recently on archaeology and nationalism), it is clear that archaeologists here feel that in calling for the rescue of antiquities in Iraq they fulfill their duties as the stewards and advocates of the 'record'. Moreover, archaeologists have constructed this 'record' in a highly selective manner, as the production of a list of sites to be protected (as opposed to a holistic approach that sees the whole country, with its living and non-living entities, as heritage to be protected), primarily on the basis of the highly problematic (Eurocentric and racist) rhetoric of the 'cradle of civilisation', prioritising certain ancient Mesopotamian 'firsts' such as writing and urbanisation. Finally, archaeologists have performed an act of symbolic appropriation by declaring this 'cradle of civilisation' as western heritage (*cf* Pollock 2005 for further discussion), justified on the basis of the ethic of stewardship that imposes a western idea of what constitutes the archaeological 'record', heritage, and the sites worthy to be rescued, upon a non-western context.

In the ongoing Iraq war, archaeologists have failed the people of Iraq. The approach of the political ethic would have emphasised the holistic nature of the materiality of heritage, stressing that the human beings who were (and are) being killed daily are the most important agents of this heritage, and that they should thus be the number one priority. It would have also opposed the invasion and the war outright, on the basis of the overwhelming empirical, legal, ethical and political arguments, joining forces with the world anti-war movement. Since 2003 other phenomena, including the undertaking of archaeological surveys and other work with the collaboration and protection of the occupying armies, and the opening of the pages of a major archaeological journal to a US Army officer (where, among other things, he attacks anti-war archaeologists – Bogdanos 2005), testify further to the subjugation of this professionalised archaeology to the dominant structures of power.

AGENDAS OF THE POLITICAL ETHIC: EPILOGUE

In this chapter, I have argued that the debate on ethics in archaeology should adopt an explicitly political approach, what I call the political ethic. It is an approach that not only acknowledges the power dynamics, asymmetries and inequalities both within archaeology and in the broader world, but also takes a political stance in today's battlegrounds and conflicts. It is an approach that is in tune with current theoretical discussion; it recognises that what we call archaeology is only the modernist, western official archaeology, and that a range of alternative archaeologies exist both within and especially outside western modernity. It is a stance that acknowledges the context-specific and situated nature of ethical dilemmas and rejects abstract universalism, but at the same time, rather than adopting an ethical relativism, opts for political values such as social justice and an end to all discrimination and inequality. Finally, it is an approach that embeds ethics into practice but at the same time acknowledges that practice means the adoption of an active stance in today's clashes and battlegrounds. This approach is related to (but not necessarily in full agreement with) various approaches proposed in anthropology (eg, Caplan 2003a, esp. introduction, 2003b), especially within the American Anthropological Association where several voices have called for an activist role for anthropologists, an explicitly political stance, and for the role of the anthropologist as witness (*cf* Scheper-Hughes 1995). In archaeology, this approach is close to the thinking that has defined archaeology as a craft rather than a profession (Shanks and McGuire 1996), and the view that sees archaeology as social praxis (*cf* McGuire *et al* 2005). It also builds on my previous call (Hamilakis 1999, after Said 1994) for the archaeologist to see her/himself not as a steward of the 'record', but as an active intellectual who is involved in the field of cultural production and who maintains her/his critical autonomy and resists professionalisation.

One could argue that there is a danger in this thesis: that the politic ethic may mean the adoption of one specific set of ethics and politics, for example the politics of the author in this case, and/or that it will be difficult to define goals such as 'social justice', even in context-specific situations. First, I have made it clear that the political ethic is a collective rather than an individual ethic, one that is against the notion of western individual morality. The collectivity in this case is one based on shared ideas for the present and the future; these are the ideas of an emancipatory post-capitalist present and future where equality, freedom from all discrimination, and social justice are fundamental. It will mean the alliance with like-minded archaeologists against others, as it will also mean the alliance with some broader groups and collectivities against others. As for the definition of social justice, the concept as I employ it here, while relying on the 19th- and 20th-century major social liberation movements with Marxism being the most prominent, also relates to more recent movements fighting for freedom from all forms of exploitation, based on the constant resistance to hegemonic structures and ideologies, from patriarchy, racism and xenophobia to ruthless neo-liberal capitalism. It is the *articulation* of until recently disparate movements, identity quests, and claims, in a non-totalising but coordinated political discourse and praxis that is the big and difficult challenge for anti-capitalist politics in archaeology and more broadly (*cf* Butler *et al* 2000 esp. 298–301).

The suggested approach could contribute to the reinvigoration of the political project in archaeology. The return of the political (*cf* Hamilakis 2005) and the establishment of the political ethic, however, will not be the work of a single contribution. It is a collective project and should be in constant contact and communication with the movements and groups with which it shares ideas, values, and causes. The essays that follow in this volume are a significant contribution towards the achievement of that goal.

I would like to end with a brief account of some of the many directions that the approach of the political ethic could take. An explicitly political archaeology should address the genealogy of official archaeology as a

device of western capitalist modernity, and interrogate the conservation (and exhibition) ethic and the power dynamics that gave birth and continue to sustain this device. This means not simply the investigation of how, for example, colonialism, nationalism or capitalism have shaped archaeological thinking and practice, but also how archaeological practice itself has contributed and continues to contribute to the reproduction of these ideologies and practices. The chapters by Bernbeck and Pollock, Kehoe, Mourad, Nicholas and Hollowell, and Riggs all deal with these issues. The political ethic should also re-examine the often depoliticised ethical stances adopted by archaeologists and others in major issues, such as repatriation of cultural 'property', reburial and the treatment of the dead, and indigenous issues. Bauer *et al*, for example, point out that we should be asking 'who is benefitting from the restitution of cultural artefacts in each context?', and Shepherd proposes that we should examine the recent exhumations in downtown Cape Town in light of the current political climate and the inequalities and struggles in post-apartheid South Africa. As one of the black activists noted in relation to the burials of black people who were to be exhumed from the now prime real estate land in downtown Cape Town, 'that is a site they have owned for the first time in their lives', thus shifting with a simple phrase the debate on reburial into the arena of past and present ownership, exploitation and destitution.

The adoption of the political ethic also means that a central concern should be the critical exploration of the political economy of the archaeological practice, in the field, in academia, in the museums and in the 'heritage' sector. This does not mean simply discussion and debate on the commodification of material traces of the past by the heritage industry, however important that discussion may be, but also the political economy of doing archaeology in terms of funding and sponsorship, wages and salaries, exploitation and work hierarchies, the politics of academic publishing, the politics of involvement in the neo-liberal capitalist university (*cf* Hamilakis 2004), and the politics of production and reproduction of authority and prestige, be it patronage or selective citation strategies (*cf* Hutson 1998). Why is it, for example, that there is so little discussion on the ethics and politics of sponsorship of archaeological projects by major corporations with questionable environmental and human rights records (Çatal Höyük being the most prominent but hardly the only example – *cf* Hamilakis 1999)? Or on the strategies of major Anglo-American publishers (with the complicity and collaboration of academics) to market ideas of primarily Anglo-American origin and authorship as *the* global – and the only – authoritative agenda-setting voices in the discipline? The chapters by Everill, Funari and Robrahn-González, Silberman, Silverman, and Riggs all address aspects of the political economy of archaeology.

The political ethic in archaeology should attempt to combine the political-ethical arena with the micro- and macro-scale – that is, the micro-politics of a community with the macro-politics of power, from neo-liberal economics to imperialism and neo-colonialism. This is particularly important today when the reinvigorated concept of community archaeology offers much hope (*cf* Marshall 2002), although community archaeology may be in danger of positioning itself as the antidote to macro-politics which are too often seen as irrelevant at the local level. 'Community' of course is not an undifferentiated and homogenous whole but includes many and at times conflicting interests. The political ethic approach asks: Who in the community is benefitting from any community archaeology project, and how are local structures of power implicated in it? For example, how do the alliances and pacts that archaeologists have to make at the local level empower some groups and marginalise others? Importantly, community, especially in view of the recent globalised phenomena, is not a space immune to the macro-scale, and the effects and workings of neo-liberalism, colonialism and nationalism; in fact, the local community is the space where these processes find a direct and explicit expression. A political-ethical approach therefore, should explore the articulations of the macro- with the micro-scale, the local expressions and effects of these broader processes. The chapters here by Saitta, Ronayne, and Gassiot *et al* propose an alternative community archaeology that combines the micro-political with the macro-political, embedding at the same time ethics into practice and in the arena of political struggles of today, from labour rights, to the support of communities displaced by corporate capitalism, to the fight for democratisation.

Finally, the key ethical issue of indigenous rights and claims, an area where most of the recent advances seem to have been achieved, needs to be problematised further from the point of view of the political ethic. Such an ethic, for example, should suggest that we examine indigeny in relation to the severe social problems some of these groups face, in terms of employment, income, educational opportunities and health, and in conjunction with the debate on claims on property, and the right of these groups to establish their own alternative archaeology. The same logic should recognise that indigenous movements against neo-liberal capitalism (such as, for example, the fight against the privatisation of utilities and resources in South American countries) is part of the indigenous struggle for self-determination and a living heritage; they thus deserve consideration and support. At the same time, however, it should be recognised that in some contexts, such as in Europe, for example, the concept of indigenism may acquire exclusivist political connotations, and fuel racism against immigrants and refugees. Finally, the approach of the political ethic recognises that the important postcolonial critique within which indigenous issues are often discussed should neither imply that early colonialist mentalities are dead, nor that neo-colonial practices and projects are non-existent, as the recent imperial wars have reminded us. Nicholas and Hollowell address some of these issues in their contribution.

As Bauman has recognised, the complex realities of late modernity (or postmodernity) at the start of the third millennium, and the subsequent academic deconstructionist projects, have not made the ethical and political questions less relevant; in fact they have made them more relevant and urgent than before (Bauman 1993:250):

> Contrary to one of the most common uncritically accepted philosophical axioms, there is no contradiction between the rejection of (or skepticism towards) the ethics of socially conventionalized and rationally 'founded' norms, and the insistence that it does matter, and *matter morally*, what we do and from what we desist. Far from excluding each other, the two can be accepted or rejected only together.

If archaeologists in the 1980s were radicalised by the struggle against apartheid, today's western archaeologists may wish to reflect on new segregations such as the ones affecting the urban poor, or the millions of economic and political immigrants. If race and gender were the key issues a few decades ago, today class (despite the changes in the industrial structures in the developed world) is emerging yet again as key (*cf* Duke and Saitta 1998), often in close articulation with race, ethnicity or gender; as noted earlier, it is these intersections and articulations that we need to examine urgently today, rather than continuing to treat specific identity quests in isolation and identify politics as a fragmented field (*cf* Conkey 2005). Archaeologists may also wish to consider their ethical and political response to the militarisation of society everywhere, whether it is the bombing of non-western countries or the panoptic surveillance and the imposition of draconian anti-democratic 'terrorism' laws 'at home'. Materiality, time and history – that is, the key concepts of our craft – are at the heart of these social phenomena. Moreover, as we saw in the case of Iraq, militarisation is threatening to engulf (as in the 18th and 19th centuries) the whole western archaeological project. Political-ethical responses are as urgent today as they were 20 years ago. This book does not advance a unified party line, nor is it an evangelical call to arms. It is, however, an academic and political intervention that, through a range of approaches and case-studies, demonstrates the need to repoliticise ethics, that is, to be attuned and attentive to the pain of the other; to be reflexively aware of the knowledge/power nexus; and to accept that the political-ethical dilemmas and decisions will have to be constantly debated in the arenas of today's social clashes and struggles, where archaeologists, like all others, will have to take sides, maintaining at the same time their critical autonomy from professionalisation, institutions, and structures of power.

ACKNOWLEDGMENTS

I would like to thank the following people for discussions, feedback and bibliographic suggestions: Ran Boytner, Meg Conkey, Phil Duke, Claire Lyons and Randy McGuire; thanks are also due to the series editors, to Ginny Hoffman for the copyediting, and to two anonymous readers for their perceptive comments. None is to blame for the views expressed here.

REFERENCES

Anderson, B (1991) *Imagined Communities*, London: Verso (2nd edition)

Arrhenius, T (2003) *The Fragile Monument: On Conservation and Modernity*, Stockholm, Doctoral Dissertation, School of Architecture KTH

Atkinson, JA, Banks, I and O'Sullivan, J (eds) (1996) *Nationalism and Archaeology*, Glasgow: Cruithne Press

Barrett, J (1988) 'Fields of discourse: Reconstituting a social archaeology', *Critique of Anthropology* 7, 5–16

Bauman, Z (1993) *Postmodern Ethics*, Oxford: Blackwell

Benjamin, W (2002) *The Arcades Project*, Cambridge, MA: The Belknap Press of Harvard University Press (translated by Eiland, H and McLaughlin, K)

Bennett, T (1998) 'Pedagogic objects, clean eyes, and popular instruction: On sensory regimes and museum didactics', *Configurations* 6, 345–371

Bergson, H (1988) *Matter and Memory*, New York: Zone Books

Bernstein, RJ (1991) *The New Constellation: The Ethical/Political Horizon of Modernity/Postmodernity*, Cambridge: Polity

Bogdanos, M (2005) 'The casualities of war: The truth about the Iraq museum', *American Journal of Archaeology* 109, 477–526

Brodie, N, Doole, J and Renfrew, C, (eds) (2001) *Trade in Illicit Antiquities: The Destruction of the World's Archaeological Heritage*, Cambridge: The MacDonald Institute for Archaeological Research

Brodie, N and Tubb, KW (eds) (2002) *Illicit Antiquities: The Theft of Culture and the Extinction of Archaeology*, London: Routledge

Brodie, N, Kersel, M, Luke, C and Tubb, KW (eds) (2006) *Archaeology, Cultural Heritage and the Trade in Antiquities*, Gainesville: University Press of Florida

Brown, B (2001) 'Thing theory', *Critical Inquiry* 28, 1–22

Buchli, V and Lucas, G (eds) (2001) *The Archaeology of Contemporary Past*, London: Routledge

Butler, J, Laclau, E and Zizek, S (2000) *Contingency, Hegemony, Universality: Contemporary Dialogues on the Left*, London: Verso

Caplan, P (ed) (2003a) *The Ethics of Anthropology: Debates and Dilemmas*, London: Routledge

—— (2003b) 'Anthropology in the new world (dis)order', keynote speech given at the Conference of the Anthropologists of Southern Africa, University of Cape Town, 24 August

Colwell-Chanthaphonh, C (2004) 'Those obscure objects of desire: Collecting cultures and the archaeological landscape in the San Pedro Valley of Arizona', *Journal of Contemporary Ethnography* 33, 571–601

Conkey, M (2005) 'Dwelling at the margins, action at the intersection? Feminist and indigenous archaeologies, 2005', *Archaeologies: The Journal of the World Archaeological Congress* 1, 9–59

Díaz-Andreu, M and Champion, T (eds) (1996) *Nationalism and Archaeology in Europe*, London: UCL Press

Duke, P (2003) 'Touring the past: Archaeology and tourism in a capitalist world', paper presented at the 5th World Archaeological Congress, Washington DC, June 2005

Duke, P and Saitta, D (1998) 'An emancipatory archaeology for the working class', *Assemblage* 4 (http://www.shef.ac.uk/assem/4/)

Foucault, M (1970) *The Order of Things: An Archaeology of the Human Sciences*, New York: Pantheon Books

—— (1980) *Power/Knowledge* (edited by Gordon, G), New York: Pantheon Books

Gathercole, P and Lowenthal, D (eds) (1990) *The Politics of the Past*, London: Unwin Hyman

Gell, A (1998) *Art and Agency: An Anthropological Theory*, Oxford: Oxford University Press

Gero, J, Lacy, D and Blakey, M (eds) (1983) *The Socio-politics of Archaeology*, Amherst: Department of Anthropology, University of Massachusetts (Research Report Number 23)

Groarke, L and Warrick, G (2006) 'Stewardship gone astray? Ethics and the SAA', in Scarre, C and Scarre, G (eds) *The Ethics of Archaeology: Philosophical Perspectives on Archaeological Practice*, Cambridge: Cambridge University Press

Hamilakis, Y (1996) 'Through the looking glass: Archaeology, nationalism and the politics of identity', *Antiquity* 70, 975–78

—— (1999) 'La trahison des archéologues? Archaeological practice as intellectual activity in post-modernity', *Journal of Mediterranean Archaeology* 12(1), 60–79

—— (2001) 'Monumental visions: Bonfils, classical antiquity and nineteenth century Athenian society', *History of Photography* 25(1), 5–12 and 23–42

—— (2003a) 'Lives in ruins: Antiquities and national imagination in modern Greece', in Kane, S (ed) *The Politics of Archaeology and Identity in a Global Context*, Boston: Archaeological Institute of America

—— (2003b) 'Iraq, stewardship and the "record": An ethical crisis for archaeology', *Public Archaeology* 3, 104–111

—— (2004) 'Archaeology and the politics of pedagogy', *World Archaeology* 36, 287–309

—— (2005) 'Whose world and whose archaeology? The colonial present and the return of the political', *Archaeologies: The Journal of the World Archaeological Congress* 1, 94–101

—— (2007) *The Nation and Its Ruins: Antiquity, Archaeology, and National Imagination in Greece*, Oxford: Oxford University Press

Harrison, S (2004) 'Forgetful and memorious landscapes', *Social Anthropology* 12, 135–51

Hollowell, J (2006) 'Moral arguments on subsistence digging', in Scarre, C and Scarre, G (eds) *The Ethics of Archaeology: Philosophical Perspectives on Archaeological Practice*, Cambridge: Cambridge University Press

Hutson, S (1998) 'Strategies for the reproduction of prestige in archaeological discourse', *Assemblage* 4 (http://www.shef.ac.uk/assem/4/4hudson.html)

Kane, S (ed) (2003) *The Politics of Archaeology and Identity in a Global Context*, Boston: Archaeological Institute of America

Karlsson, H (ed) (2004) *Swedish Archaeologists on Ethics*, Lindome, Sweden: Bricoleur Press

Kohl, P and Fawcett, C (eds) (1995) *Nationalism, Politics, and the Practice of Archaeology*, Cambridge: Cambridge University Press

Küchler, S (2002) *Malanggan: Art, Memory and Sacrifice*, Oxford: Berg

Lampeter Archaeology Workshop (1997) 'Relativism, objectivity and the politics of the past', *Archaeological Dialogues* 4, 164–198

Lowenthal, D (2000) 'Stewarding the past in a perplexing present', in Avrami, E, Mason, R and de la Torre, M (eds) *Values and Heritage Conservation*, Los Angeles: The Getty Conservation Institute

Lynott, M (2003) 'The development of ethics in archaeology', in Zimmerman, L, Vitelli, KD, and Hollowell-Zimmer, J (eds) *Ethical Issues in Archaeology*, Walnut Creek, CA: AltaMira Press and the Society for American Archaeology

Lynott, M and Wylie, A (eds) (1995) *Ethics in American Archaeology: Challenges for the 1990s*, Washington, DC: Society for American Archaeology

Lyons, C (2003) 'Archaeology, conservation and the ethics of sustainability', in Papadopoulos, J and Leventhal, R (eds) *Theory and Practice in Mediterranean Archaeology: Old World and New World Perspectives*, Los Angeles: The Cotsen Institute of Archaeology, UCLA (Cotsen Advanced Seminars 1)

Marshall, Y (ed) (2002) *Community Archaeology*, London: Routledge (World Archaeology 34(2))

Matsuda, D (1998) 'The ethics of archaeology, subsistence digging, and artifact looting in Latin America: Point, muted, counterpoint', *International Journal of Cultural Property* 7, 87–97

McGuire, R (1997) 'Why have archaeologists thought the real Indians were dead and what can we do about it?' in Biolsi, T and Zimmerman, L (eds) *Indians and Anthropologists: Vine Deloria, Jr, and the Critique of Anthropology*, Tucson: University of Arizona Press

McGuire, R, O'Donovan, M and Wurst, LA (2005) 'Probing praxis in archaeology: The last eighty years', *Rethinking Marxism* 17, 355–372

Meskell, L (ed) (1998) *Archaeology Under Fire: Nationalism, Politics and Heritage in the Eastern Mediterranean and the Middle East*, London: Routledge

Meskell, L and Pels, P (eds) (2005) *Embedding Ethics: Shifting Boundaries of the Anthropological Profession*, Oxford: Berg

Mowaljarlai, D, Vinnicombe, P, Ward, G and Chippindale, C (1988) 'Repainting of images on rock in Australia and the maintenance of Aboriginal culture', *Antiquity* 62, 690–696

Ouzman, S (2006) 'Why "conserve"? Situating Southern African rock art in the here and now', in Agnew, N and Bridgland, J (eds) *Of the Past for the Future: Integrating Archaeology and Conservation*, Los Angeles: The Getty Conservation Institute

Patrik, L (1985) 'Is there an archaeological record?', in Schiffer M (ed) *Advances in Archaeological Method and Theory 8*, New York: Academic Press

Pels, P (1999) 'Professions on duplexity: A prehistory of ethical codes in anthropology', *Current Anthropology* 40, 101–136

Pinsky, V and Wylie, A (eds) (1989) *Critical Traditions in Contemporary Archaeology*, Cambridge: Cambridge University Press

Pluciennik, M (ed) (2001) *The Responsibility of Archaeologists: Archaeology and Ethics* (Lampeter Workshop in Archaeology 4), Oxford: Archaeopress (BAR S981)

Pollock, S (2005) 'Archaeology goes to war at the newsstand', in Pollock, S and Bernbeck, R (eds) *Archaeologies of the Middle East: Critical Perspectives*, Oxford: Blackwell

Renfrew, C (2000) *Loot, Legitimacy and Ownership*, London: Duckworth

Roth, M with Lyons, C and Merewether, C (1997) *Irresistible Decay: Ruins Reclaimed*, Los Angeles: The Getty Research Institute

Said, E (1994) *Representations of the Intellectual*, New York: Pantheon Books

Scarre, C and Scarre, G (eds) (2006) *The Ethics of Archaeology: Philosophical Perspectives on Archaeological Practice*, Cambridge: Cambridge University Press

Schnapp, A (1996) *The Discovery of the Past*, London: British Museum

Scheper-Hughes, N (1995) 'The primacy of the ethical: Propositions for a militant anthropology', *Current Anthropology* 36, 405–440

Schnapp, J, Shanks, M and Tiews, M (eds) (2004) *Archaeologies of the Modern*, Special issue of *Modernism/Modernity*, 11(1)

Sease, C (1998) 'Codes of Ethics for conservation', *International Journal of Cultural Property* 7, 98–115

Shanks, M and McGuire, R (1996) 'The craft of archaeology', *American Antiquity* 61, 75–88

Smith, C and Burke, H (2003) 'In the spirit of the code', in Zimmerman, LJ, Vitelli, KD and Hollowell-Zimmer, J (eds) *Ethical Issues in Archaeology*, Walnut Creek, CA: AltaMira Press and the Society for American Archaeology

Smith, C and Wobst, MH (eds) (2005) *Indigenous Archaeologies: Decolonising Theory and Practice*, London: Routledge

Stone, P (2005) 'The identification and protection of cultural heritage during the Iraq conflict: A peculiarly English tale', *Antiquity* 79, 1–11

Strathern, M (ed) (2000) *Audit Cultures: Anthropological Studies in Accountability, Ethics and the Academy*, London: Routledge

Tarlow, S (2000) 'Decoding ethics', *Public Archaeology* 1, 245–259

—— (2006) 'Archaeological ethics and the people of the past', in Scarre, C and Scarre, G (eds) *The Ethics of Archaeology: Philosophical Perspectives on Archaeological Practice*, Cambridge: Cambridge University Press

Thomas, J (2004) *Archaeology and Modernity*, London: Routledge

Tilley, C (1989) 'Archaeology as socio-political action in the present', in Pinski, V and Wylie, A (eds) *Critical Traditions in Contemporary Archaeology*, Cambridge: Cambridge University Press

Ucko, P (1987) *Academic Freedom and Apartheid: The Story of the World Archaeological Congress*, London: Duckworth

Van Dyke, RM and Alcock, S (eds) (2003) *Archaeologies of Memory*, Oxford: Blackwell

Watkins, J (2001) *Indigenous Archaeology*, Walnut Creek, CA: AltaMira Press

Wylie, A (2002) *Thinking from Things: Essays in the Philosophy of Archaeology*, Berkeley: University of California Press

—— (2003) 'On ethics', in Zimmerman, LJ, Vitelli, KD and Hollowell-Zimmer, J (eds) *Ethical Issues in Archaeology*, Walnut Creek, CA: AltaMira Press and the Society for American Archaeology

—— (2005) 'The promises and perils of stewardship', in Meskell, L and Pels, P (eds) *Embedding Ethics*, Oxford: Berg

Zimmerman, L (1995) 'Regaining our nerve: Ethics, values and the transformation of archaeology', in Lynott, M and Wylie, A (eds) *Ethics in American Archaeology: Challenges for the 1990s*, Washington, DC: Society for American Archaeology

—— (1998) 'When data become people: Archaeological ethics, reburial, and the past as public heritage', *International Journal of Cultural Property* 7, 69–86

Zimmerman, L, Vitelli, KD and Hollowell-Zimmer, J (eds) 2003 *Ethical Issues in Archaeology*, Walnut Creek, CA: AltaMira Press and the Society for American Archaeology

PART 2

ETHICS IN QUESTION

Philip Duke

As Alexander Bauer, Shanel Lindsay and Stephen Urice point out in this volume, historically archaeology has concentrated on the *discovery* of the past and distanced itself from the *policy*, as it were, of who owns the past and how it is used. Policy only recently has become a focus of scrutiny in the discipline. The subsequent debate that this scrutiny has engendered will continue to evolve, as contemporary mores change and as new academic, social and political factors take stage. And it will remain incumbent upon archaeologists to engage in a constant and continuing interrogation of the assumptions that underlie how best to make archaeology a truly ethical and emancipatory practice. The papers in this section introduce the reader to the multi-faceted nature of this interrogation and thus adumbrate the papers that follow.

The papers all are united by the common position that archaeology's most fundamental responsibility – the heart of its ethical commitment – is not to that nebulous concept of 'the past', with its material remnants. Nor is its fundamental responsibility to science and objectivity. Rather, archaeology's primary, perhaps only, responsibility is simply to contemporary people. Nick Shepherd examines how the controversy between ownership of an early Colonial cemetery in Cape Town is rooted in, amongst other issues, the idea that archaeology should be scientific (a legacy of processualism) and that our interpretation of the past will have a universal relevance (a legacy of cultural resource management). Yet the vexing question of who constitutes *the people* lies at the hub of any subsequent discourse. Charles Riggs exposes the problems of trying to serve different constituencies in his analysis of the archaeology of the American Southwest. Moreover, even in cases where the *people* might at first blush appear obvious there are unintended consequences. Bauer *et al* ask whether returning material to a nation-state promotes nationalist perspectives and thereby runs the risk of closing down alternative discourses. Shepherd's discussion of the politics of the excavation of the early Colonial cemetery shows how local interests were pitted against those of the state.

Moreover, what does it mean 'to give the past back to the people'? Was it ever archaeologists' in the first place? The paternalism that still exists in too many quarters of archaeology is exposed in all of the papers as strong and objectionable: something along the lines of 'we'll write your past for you, and that way you'll feel better for having your peculiar history recognized. Aren't we nice?' However, what if the recipient group doesn't want it, an irony exposed in Shepherd's chapter? In this instance the local community did not want the cemetery to be relocated and memorialized; rather, they vehemently lobbied simply for it to be left alone, and for development – the cause of the controversy in the first place – simply to be denied planning permission.

Bauer *et al* further our understanding of repatriation by contextualizing it within the framework of wider theoretical contradictions. They ask whether repatriation, the return of material to a *single* community, contradicts the notion that culture is fragmented and fluid, not normative in the sense, say, of a single nation-state, a reading that is almost inevitably taken from the very word *repatriation*. Moreover, if artefacts have their own *social lives*, can they ever be returned to their original owners with their original meanings intact? Does their existence within a contemporary framework of cultural meanings vitiate this possibility? Finally, they ask whether cultures actually need all artefacts to be returned in order to ensure their own cultural *survival*?

Of course, despite all our best efforts thus far, archaeology still remains a remarkably paternalistic enterprise. As George Nicholas and Julie Hollowell point out, the discipline still holds most of the cards when it comes to determining how the past is studied and what past is constructed. Riggs demonstrates that despite the passage of such laws as NAGPRA and despite the embrace of politically correct terms such as *Ancestral Pueblo* over *Anasazi*, traditional power structures still dominate; the essentially colonialist nature of the discipline has been merely glossed over; a pig with lipstick is still just a pig.

So, how do we construct an ethically responsible archaeology? Nicholas and Hollowell hint at the creation of a true applied archaeology; not the middle-class pap of cultural resource management, but one rather that focuses on the solution of real problems suffered by real communities. They offer us nine ways already existing in the discipline that may provide a way to recognize other worldviews without abandoning the *craft* of archaeology. Their point, that we cannot simply abandon archaeology as a *discipline*, leads us to further issues raised by Bauer *et al*; ie, do we ignore the fact that archaeologists might entertain different ethical standards in different circumstances? If Western people 'loot' sites when they are not scientifically trained, why are non-Western peoples not accused of the same crime whenever they treat sites in the same manner? Should indigenous groups be allowed to do whatever they want with *their* sites, a question that brings us back to the ownership of the past?

As I noted at the beginning of this introduction, an ethically informed archaeology can never rest on any laurels it happens to have been awarded. These papers show us some of the issues that need to be examined if a truly ethical and emancipatory archaeology is to be achieved, and they expose the great amount of work that still lies ahead.

CHAPTER 2

When Theory, Practice and Policy Collide, or Why Do Archaeologists Support Cultural Property Claims?

Alexander A. Bauer, Shanel Lindsay and
Stephen Urice

CONTEMPORARY ARCHAEOLOGY AND REPATRIATION

Archaeologists who advocate export controls and the return of cultural property to their countries of origin tend to do so for one or both of the following reasons. First, they hope that such policies will serve to counteract and discourage the illicit looting and destruction of archaeological sites that feed the antiquities market. But in the more than three decades since the UNESCO Convention of 1970, it is not at all clear that the increase in controls and repatriation has stemmed the looting (see Renfrew 2001). Second, archaeologists explain support of return for moral reasons: to make amends for past injustices committed through colonial and imperial practices and to empower the groups whose property has been taken. This view is increasingly held by archaeologists and anthropologists and is called in a recent essay by Elezar Barkan (2002:17) a 'prime moral issue in the international community'. He continues:

> Control of one's patrimony is seen as a mark of equality and has become a privileged right in today's world. Restitution of cultural property, therefore, occupies a middle ground that can provide the necessary space in which to negotiate identities and a mechanism to mediate between the histories of perpetrators and victims. (Barkan 2002:16–17)

Indeed, current policy supporting return fits well within contemporary 'postcolonial' criticism of the Western hegemonic power structures that have dominated global politics in general and anthropological research in particular since the field's inception. Some archaeologists endorse this view partly out of respect for cultural diversity and partly in sympathy for less-powerful and non-Western groups against the appropriation and 'pillaging' of their culture by Westerners. And when anthropologists mount the rare challenge to repatriation efforts, international or domestic, such as in the celebrated 'Kennewick Man' case (Harding 2005), it causes tension within the discipline (see recently Watkins 2004; Zimmerman 2005).

Problems emerge, however, when these latter 'morality-based' reasons are examined in the context of contemporary anthropological theorizing about culture and cultural rights. For one, the notion of 'retaining' or 'returning' culture assumes that culture can both be partitioned and alienated in the first place (Weiner 1992; Welsh 1997). It ignores the point widely recognized in anthropology that cultural meanings shift among contexts and that prioritizing some sort of 'original' cultural meaning over all others may be simplistic and reductionist. Second, the fact that support for embargoes and repatriation in practice often means supporting nation-states motivated by a desire to use the archaeological record in creating a national identity makes archaeologists' support difficult to reconcile with simultaneous critiques of nationalism. The distinct possibility that materials belonging to indigenous groups and other disempowered minorities will not be under their control in such circumstances raises the question, In whose possession would the objects best serve to advocate their rights?

Here, we examine how archaeologists' support of export regimes and repatriation policies in light of contemporary theorizing about culture and cultural rights risks undermining the field's own theoretical program and larger ethical goals. In particular, we discuss this problem in light of the two sets of assumptions just mentioned: first, that return restores the integrity of a culture and/or the object belonging to it, and second, that return corrects injustices and effects support for disenfranchised groups. We then take as an example the recent US support of Peru's cultural property claims to illustrate the contradiction at the heart of this view, ie, that return does not necessarily achieve the ends or benefit the groups archaeologists hope it will. Finally, and by way of explanation, we suggest that archaeologists support return for reasons of political economy that usually go unacknowledged or are explicitly avoided in most academic discourse, and we consider theoretical and practical risks in continuing to maintain these positions.

Assumption 1: National Control Maintains the Integrity of a Culture and/or the Object Belonging to it

One of the most often cited reasons for supporting retention or the return of cultural material to another country or group is that the object naturally 'belongs' there. The very word 'return' implies an 'original' state, to which both the material and the culture may be restored through that return. This is the perspective that underlies the policies following the UNESCO 1970 Convention, as well as claims for the return of particular objects such as the Parthenon/Elgin Marbles (Merryman 1986, 2005; Prott 2005).[1]

An immediate problem with this view, at least insofar as anthropological thinking is concerned, is that it is based on an essentialist concept of culture long critiqued within the discipline (Handler 2003). Is culture a set of specific objects and traditions that do not change, or is it dynamic, fluid, and continually developing in new ways, with new material manifestations, or at least new understandings of old ones? If culture is the latter, then a given object is not what makes that culture whole, if 'whole' is even attainable.

Is it accurate to say that a culture is somehow 'diminished' or not 'whole' when it lacks a specific object? More than that, since we do not make similar assertions about our own, modern Western culture, what is it that distinguishes between the two? For example, when the London Bridge was moved to Arizona, neither English nor London's cultures ceased to exist, even though one of its most recognizable landmarks had been taken away. When the World Trade Center collapsed, New York City's cultural identity was not diminished. On the contrary, to a degree New Yorkers developed a greater sense of pride and community despite the loss to its skyline. We are not condoning either the theft, displacement, or destruction of cultural property, which many export laws and repatriation efforts are aimed at remedying; we simply raise the question to what degree other cultures have the same capacity to survive such losses. Put another way, assuming that other cultures are less resilient than Western ones is not only inaccurate, but may be seen as replacing one form of paternalism with another. Anthropologists working in Papua New Guinea and elsewhere in the Pacific have demonstrated that for some cultures objects are more effective at maintaining cultural identity when kept in circulation (Leach 2003), raising the possibility that the retention of objects (at least in some sort of state-managed depot) is in some cases antithetical to cultural well-being.

Similar problems arise when arguing that repatriation restores the integrity of the object being returned. Anthropologists and archaeologists uniformly posit that objects taken unscientifically out of context cease to be meaningful. But this general claim ignores the now widely accepted view that objects themselves have 'social lives' (Appadurai 1986) and develop new meanings in new contexts. In fact, accepting that the life of material culture does not just 'stop' when appropriated into Western contexts (which, again, is a view that maintains a paternalistic regard for 'authenticity'), we should at least recognize the contemporary theorizing that the movement of artifacts – and even looting – constitutes another re-use, or 'cultural-transform' to use Michael Schiffer's (1976) term, in the life history of an object (Kopytoff 1986). As Hamilakis (1999) points out in his study of the life history of the Parthenon/Elgin Marbles, the removal of the sculptures from Athens by Lord Elgin was only one episode in a long and complex history of individual, community and national relationships with the objects, including those that have emerged as a result of their removal and subsequent installation in the British Museum.

A similar point is made by Gavin Lucas (2001) when he rightly observes that excavation is not really 'destruction' but the 'transformation' of a site, albeit a dramatic one. His regard for excavation as part of, rather than separate from, prior social engagements with an archaeological site parallels our contention here that we should not separate contemporary activities from similar ones conducted in the past, or by non-Western groups. Archaeologists study the removal and re-use of materials in the past as part of their endeavor, but contemporary removal of material from a site is called 'looting' and rarely studied as a social phenomenon (but see Hollowell-Zimmer 2003; Matsuda 1998; Migliore 1991; Staley 1993). True, looting is usually conducted purely for monetary gain, causes the extensive destruction of sites and archaeologically important data, and is occurring on a scale unprecedented in earlier times, all of which may condemn it as morally wrong. But our point here is the disjunction between morality and epistemology. Do we similarly condemn the undocumented digging up of material by 'indigenous' groups for their own re-use, or is this still to be considered an 'authentic' or 'primary' cultural use of an object? The loss of historical information due to looting is undeniably a tragedy, and archaeologists are right to mitigate such loss however possible. But to claim that a looted object ceases to be meaningful denies the validity of any way of 'knowing' that is not in line with Western 'scientific' archaeological discourse. In other words, is looting as much a tragedy for local communities as it is for archaeologists? While in many cases the answer may be yes, this question is worth asking. As Larry Zimmerman (2000 [1995]:72) points out with regard to the 'stewardship principle' at the heart of the Society for American Archaeology's ethics code, this view

> seems to hinge on a unilateral declaration of the 'archaeological record as a public trust'... Were I a member of a group of nonarchaeologists, I might have a very different view, especially if I saw the heritage as the intellectual property of my people or if I saw the artifacts and their sale as a normal way to make a living.

One case where the assumption might hold that an object and culture are 'whole' only when together, occurs in cases meeting what Merryman

(1988:495*ff*) calls the test of 'essential propinquity'. The essential propinquity standard asserts that there are indeed objects so necessary to the existence of a culture and its practices, that without the object the culture ceases to function fully. In Merryman's view, few objects meet this standard, and he cites the Afo-a-Kom sacred to the Kom of Cameroon as a rare example. This case illustrates the importance some objects have for a social group's identity and continuing cultural practices, but at least in anthropological terms it is appropriate to ask whether the absence of such objects truly effects the end of a culture. Rather, we suggest that what is at issue in most cases is not this loss of cultural identity, not the essentialist cultural designation of a disputed object; rather, the issue is one of fundamental respect (Shapiro 1998).

Assumption 2: Support for Export Controls and/or Repatriation Efforts Puts Right Past Injustices and Offers Support to Traditionally Disenfranchised Groups

The second assumption that tends to shape anthropological and archaeological views on the movement of cultural property is that support for policies such as export controls or repatriation is morally right with respect to the living communities that feel most closely connected to it (eg, Barkan 2002). This is to make amends for past injustices and offer both support and respect (as well as the prospect of monetary gain, in some cases) to groups disenfranchised by the loss of the property and their disempowered political status. From the standpoint of an ethically engaged archaeology, these aims are significant and at best provide what Barkan (2002:17) calls the 'necessary space in which to negotiate identities and … mediate between the histories of perpetrators and victims'. Repatriation can and should promote dialogue about contested and often unsavory histories, with the aim of moving toward reconciliation and respect among individuals and communities. Such a pragmatic goal underlies the two most significant policy developments affecting museums at the end of the 20th century: NAGPRA and the restitution of 'Holocaust Art' (see AAMD n.d.; Nason 1997). These policies, one enacted through legislation, the other through codes of practice, are both aimed at returning objects directly to individuals or groups that maintain a close connection to them, and thus are not the kinds of policies we wish to criticize here.

In contrast are the cases of export controls and international repatriation efforts undertaken by nation-states, which largely enjoy the support of archaeologists for moral reasons, but often without a more careful consideration of their ethical and political impacts. These efforts typically follow one of two patterns: one, there may be a call for the return of specific objects, such as the Parthenon/Elgin Marbles or the Rosetta Stone, which in some circumstances may promote the kind of positive dialogue mentioned above. Italy's recent return of the Aksum Obelisk to Ethiopia may prove to be such a case. A second method nation-states use to reclaim objects internationally is through the ratification of treaties or other legislation to prevent further movement of cultural property, such as the recently renewed Memorandum of Understanding (1997) between Peru and the United States, which prohibits the import of any cultural material from Peru dating before 1532.[2]

Support for repatriation policies of either kind raises epistemological contradictions that anthropologists and archaeologists have generally ignored, issues that are implicated by the very terms 'patrimony' and 'repatriation'. First, the notion of patria, which forms their root, calls to mind many of the same assumptions regarding a 'normative' view of culture raised earlier. When we are confronted with the duty to return an object, it is not always clear what the object's actual 'homeland' is, particularly since borders and cultures tend to change over time. A simplistic understanding of patria as 'nation' may not adequately address the needs of cultural minorities or groups outside current national borders. To whom, for example, should we return an important medieval Armenian artifact, if the site it is from now lies in Turkey?[3] Cases such as these, hypothetical or real, should encourage us to think more carefully about what 'repatriation' accomplishes, and consider defining it more broadly than where an object resides. This broader definition is precisely what NAGPRA attempts to do with its provisions to prioritize 'affiliation' over geography.[4]

The issue of control leads us to a second point regarding the term patria. Namely, it is the relationship of patria to nationalism that is even harder to reconcile with the post-colonial stance of a discipline equally skeptical of nationalist programs. Many cultural property policies – either to reclaim specific objects or to enact and enforce national 'patrimony' laws prohibiting export – are undertaken by nations seeking to retain their cultural heritage (Merryman 1988). While important reasons exist for respecting such efforts, it is equally important to identify and understand the unanticipated and perhaps less beneficial ramifications, such as promoting nationalist perspectives and inhibiting the development of alternative discourses (the complexities of this conundrum are nicely illustrated in McIntosh et al 1996 [1989]). In some cases (as in the Peru example below) these efforts result in the state's ownership and control over cultural materials most closely affiliated with indigenous groups largely disempowered within their own country. Unquestioning support for the return of objects and for national patrimony laws thus have the potential to undermine rather than secure the rights of the groups archaeologists intend to help.

REPATRIATION FOR WHOM? THE CASE OF PERU

Archaeologists' support of other nation's patrimony laws are most difficult to understand when such legislation fails to serve the best interests of groups culturally linked to the material in question. Most modern nation-states include multiple ethnic groups whose diverse traditions contribute to the nation's cultural patrimony. But it is rare for all such groups to share political power. Thus it is common that a nation declares itself owner or steward for the nation's entire cultural patrimony even while it ignores, disenfranchises, or oppresses its own minority populations. Peru may serve as an example, although other countries, including the United States, could be equally illustrative. We choose Peru because the USA and Peru, with support of the Cultural Property Advisory Committee, a national advisory group which includes archaeologists, recently renewed their Memorandum of Understanding (MoU) which creates an embargo on the import into the USA of all Peruvian material dating before 1532 A.D. and selected material dating between 1532 and 1821 (MoU 1997).

At first glance the MoU may seem a good approach for discouraging the US market in Peruvian antiquities: It makes US policy explicitly supportive of Peru's cultural patrimony laws, which, inter alia, declare all such cultural material property of the state. The question that emerges, however, is whether Peru's domestic laws and policies serve the best interests of the indigenous communities whose ancestors created and used the very cultural property that modern-day Peru has nationalized. The history of indigenous rights in Peru suggests that these laws and policies do not (Poole 1994a; Strong 1992). 'The thrust of both past and present [Peruvian] governments ... has been to integrate "the Indian" into the national culture as a modern Peruvian "Western" man' (Sharp 1972:230). Even the movement known as *Indigenismo*, which sought to reclaim the past greatness of pre-Hispanic culture for the sake of the groups that continued to exist, all but died out by the 1950s in the face of urban migration and the Peruvian government's assimilation policies (Coggins 2002:111). To cite one example, on 24 June 24 1969, which had been the annual holiday celebrating Peru's indigenous past, the government passed the Agrarian Reform Law, eliminating the word *indio* from the national vocabulary (Poole 1994b:20). Cultural diversity was no longer to be recognized, and only a single, national Peruvian culture was to remain. In recent years, the Peruvian government has paid little attention to indigenous groups, in effect ignoring their continuing presence, and the indigenous populations continue to be disproportionately poor and underserved (see eg, Coggins 2002; Psacharopoulos and Patrinos 1996). Relevant to the arguments here, Peru's 1929 patrimony law (Law 6634) vests ownership of all pre-Columbian objects in the government of Peru, preventing existing indigenous groups from curating what is arguably their heritage on their own terms.

One may legitimately ask why the Peruvian government would be so anxious to retain and control the cultural legacy of the communities its policies have so effectively marginalized. As put into practice, Peru's assimilation policies have enabled the government to co-opt the cultural legacy of indigenous groups for nationalistic benefit; Peru's patrimony laws effectively function to support a multibillion-dollar tourism industry, the benefits of which are not shared with indigenous communities (Silverman 2002; for a similar example from Egypt, see Meskell 2000). The 1929 vesting law thus enables the government to use these objects to develop a sense of national identity, as well as benefit from them monetarily, without either financial or cultural regard for its indigenous communities.

A different situation is presented by Peru's recent request that Yale University return artifacts in its collection gathered from Machu Picchu by Hiram Bingham. Over the course of three expeditions in 1911, 1912, 1915, Peru claims that Bingham brought back some five thousand objects, some in contravention of Peruvian laws at the time, and others as temporary loans.[5] Peru is now asking for the objects back, and given that most if not all of the site's most important pieces are half a world away, it seems a reasonable request for archaeologists to support, particularly if laws were violated. This case may demonstrate that repatriation is often justifiable and in some cases not only an important mechanism for redress but also a proper remedy for an illicit act. But even in those situations, the question arises whether return is all we should hope for or expect. In cases where repatriation is supported on moral or legal grounds, should supporters of repatriation not use the opportunity to push for greater justice? In the case of Machu Picchu, for example, it is worth asking what kind of rights or economic benefits might be forthcoming to neighboring communities upon the objects' return, and pushing for such policies in exchange for archaeologists' support.

Peru is not alone in claiming national ownership of cultural objects within its borders, and actively seeking the return of those outside. Many nations have similar patrimony laws and domestic policies, and the United States has concluded agreements with several to help enforce them internationally. The question for archaeologists is whether we should continue to support such laws, policies, and international agreements. If other nations' cultural patrimony laws fail to benefit indigenous communities linked to the material purportedly protected, and if those nations' domestic policies explicitly or implicitly minimize cultural diversity, what is the rationale for supporting those laws and policies?[6] Where state interests are representing national sentiment as a whole, it may be difficult to criticize such action. But at best, repatriation should be aimed at opening the space for debating political asymmetries and injustices, both in the past and present.

WHAT'S AN ARCHAEOLOGIST TO DO?

Obviously we do not suggest that repatriation is never warranted or that there are not important grounds for supporting export controls. But as legal scholar Paul Bator concluded over 20 years ago, there are also tangible benefits to maintaining cultural materials in circulation (Bator 1982). Most broadly, recognizing the value and meanings that cultural products have for a variety of communities – nations and decent groups as well as those across the globe without so 'direct' a claim – may act to encourage respect for cultural diversity and for cultural dynamics such as hybridity and creativity (Sen 2004). Indeed, most anthropologists have little trouble supporting acts of resistance such as the counter-appropriation of Western objects in the developing world, which in a general sense is just the ascription of value to other cultures' products, confirming the notion that groups culturally unrelated to those products nevertheless have valid interests (Brown 2005; Madhavi Sunder, personal communication).[7] Nor are we saying that there are not occasions when the United States or other governments should appropriately work in concert with the world community to staunch crises in the looting of archaeological materials. What we are saying is that blind support of blanket repatriation requests and export controls from other nations deserves more careful analysis, including an assessment of the requesting government's own commitment to its minority and indigenous groups.

This conclusion brings us back to the question we pose in the title of this paper: In light of the potential negative effects of repatriating materials to other nation-states in some cases, why do archaeologists rarely critically examine such claims? While colonialist discourses about the past hidden in a cloak of objectivity may be countered by local, politically contextualized 'nationalist' ones, supporting the latter may only serve to 'exchange one set of limiting conditions with another' (McIntosh *et al* 1996 [1989]:189). To walk the fine line between these two poles requires replacing discourses of objectivity with ones that respect differences in worldview and ways of knowing the past. But while relativism has taught us to question the authority of science, it is equally problematic to cede authority (and also possession of objects) based on *any* single way of knowing, whether nationalist or colonialist, or even 'indigenous', 'non-Western', and those of 'descendant communities'.

Clearly there are dangers in going down this road, and we would need to proceed carefully. But as Joe Watkins (2003:132) remarks in a recent essay, what is at issue is not really ownership as much as control over the presentation of the past. This is what makes NAGPRA both so difficult to deal with and yet potentially so productive: Its attempt to balance interests forces all parties to communicate and work toward compromise and sharing control.

We suggest that archaeologists need to question critically support for cultural property claims, particularly those from nation-states. Most of us now accept that our work operates in a political context. With that realization comes the obligation to examine the political impact our work and support of other nations' laws and policies have. As Anne Pyburn (2003b:289–290) points out, 'Here is where the serious housework needs to come in, because gender equality, nation building, economic development, and ethnic pride are not programs that can be built on good intentions'. By discussing frankly and openly the merits of any specific claim, we will strengthen our ability as a profession to promote the end results – support for indigenous communities, support for cultural diversity, support for repatriation in appropriate circumstances – better than we are now accomplishing. Put another way, we need to examine carefully our 'nice' approach to the policies of the nation-states whose claims we are supporting:

> [archaeologists should not] try to 'be nice' to the locals, at least not without some subtle understanding of what is the local definition of 'nice'… It is nice to be in good standing with the national governments where we work; it is not nice to let the local authorities use the project vehicle to transport political prisoners. (Pyburn 2003a:170; see also Kohl 1998:240–241)

CONCLUSION

Contemporary archaeological attitudes tend to favor the retention and return of cultural property to other nations in accordance with their patrimony laws. Part of the rationale for this support has been a desire to help historically disenfranchised groups (re-)claim their heritage, although in some cases the laws clearly do not achieve these ends, but rather serve to further disenfranchise these groups within their own countries. The current archaeological position, well intended though it may be, must thus be re-evaluated and more critically examined, and may further illustrate why all archaeologists must strive to be more fully aware of the particular political and social contexts in which they work.

Beyond this, it is important that we take a critical look at the assumptions underlying archaeologists' support of certain cultural property policies because the current view risks undermining its own theoretical position. What is at issue is not simply a matter of resolving an epistemological inconsistency. Rather, there are important 'real world' implications at stake. Theoretical 'purity' or consistency may deserve to be cast aside for the sake of greater ends. As Robbins and Stamatopoulou (2004) point out, the irony that the concepts of 'culture' and 'ethnicity' are being deconstructed by academics just as ethnic groups are beginning to assert themselves politically is not lost on indigenous activists. Such 'strategic essentialism' has an important place in political discourse. However, cultural property claims require careful scrutiny and evaluation on a case-by-case basis. In situations where indigenous or minority groups are disenfranchised (or worse) by national governments, supporting repatriation or national retention policies may undermine efforts to protect those groups' efforts for greater recognition, autonomy, and control of their cultural heritage. Those situations may present an opportunity where the archaeological community may have a valuable tool for fighting cultural and human rights abuses by more critically assessing the nation-states' claims.

Second, our support for policies that benefit the kinds of nationalist agendas we also criticize is an incompatibility that does little to enhance our credibility outside the discipline. It has been said, likely many times, that there are as many definitions of culture as there are scholars of the subject, and policymakers, who probably do not find this diversity so endlessly entertaining, might not agree with any of them. But while we archaeologists and anthropologists may resent the fact that our concept of 'culture' has been expropriated and subsequently misunderstood by policymakers (Brown 2004), some of the blame surely must lie with us: In cases such as those involving national patrimony policies, when we become involved in issues of policy we ignore our own arguments. By doing so, we do more than aid in maintaining simplistic views of culture in policy; worse, we risk relegating our academic discussions to irrelevance.

The damage done to our ethical goals is thus twofold. There is the specific point that our support for repatriation may not benefit those we hope it will, particularly those disempowered groups whose heritage, once returned, may be co-opted into dominant nationalist discourses. On a more general level, however, is the fact that our failure to adequately scrutinize such inconsistencies in our own views undermines our ability to productively engage in policy debates. This is a problem we must consider seriously, as it has implications for all issues we hope to raise in the public sphere, now and in the future.

ACKNOWLEDGMENTS

We wish to thank Michael Brown, Philip Duke, Yannis Hamilakis, and Niklas Hultin, and two anonymous reviewers for their thoughtful comments on earlier drafts of this paper. As usual, we are to blame for the views expressed as well as any errors of fact.

NOTES

1. As observed by Shapiro (1998), among others, the very name one decides to use for the sculptural frieze now housed in the British Museum is seen to imply on which side of the debate one falls.
2. The import of selected material dating between 1532 and 1821 is also prohibited (MoU 1997). See discussion later in this paper.
3. Though a rare example, the Taliban's destruction of the Bamiyan Buddhas illustrates what can happen when a nation controls the fate of material important to a minority constituency or extra-national group.
4. 25 U.S.C. § 3002(a) et seq. Another interesting development worth noting is UNESCO's recent decision to recognize the first multi-national 'World Heritage' site, the 'Frontiers of the Roman Empire World Heritage Site' (Jilek 2004).
5. Parsons, Claudia, 'Peru to sue Yale for Inca treasure 'theft'', The Scotsman, 5 March 2006 (http://scotlandonsunday.scotsman.com/international.cfm?id=332772006).
6. Interestingly, at the time of revising this paper, the Peoples' Republic of China made a request to the United States to enter into an MoU similar in scope to Peru's. At the Cultural Property Advisory Committee's public hearing on the request, a large number of the objections raised focused on China's poor record respecting and safeguarding minority culture and rights, most notably that of Tibet. The final decision is pending.
7. What Bator (1982:31–32) called 'a general interest in the breakdown of parochialism' can be more fully understood to encompass the recognition that cultures are not static, 'normative' entities but continually re-form and renegotiate their existence through daily practices, which includes responding to new circumstances brought about by, and enacted through, the circulation of culture through the world (see Urban 2001).

REFERENCES

AAMD (n.d.) Art museums and the identification and restitution of works stolen by the Nazis, New York: Association of Art Museum Directors, www.aamd.org/pdfs/Nazi%20Looted%20Art.pdf

Appadurai, A (ed) (1986) *The Social Life of Things: Commodities in Cultural Perspective*, Cambridge: Cambridge University Press

Barkan, E (2002) Amending historical injustices: the restitution of cultural property – an overview, in Barkan, E and Bush, R (eds), *Claiming the Stones/Naming the Bones: Cultural Property and the Negotiation of National and Ethnic Identity*, Los Angeles: Getty Research Institute

Bator, PM (1982) *The International Trade in Art*, Chicago: University of Chicago Press

Brown, MF (2004) 'Heritage as property', in Verdery, K and Humphrey, C (eds), *Property in Question: Value Transformation in the Global Economy*, Oxford: Berg

—— (2005), 'Heritage trouble: recent work on the protection of intangible cultural property' *International Journal of Cultural Property* (12) 40–61

Coggins, C (2002) 'Latin America, Native America, and the Politics of Culture', in Barkan, E and Bush, R (eds), *Claiming the Stones/Naming the Bones: Cultural Property and the Negotiation of National and Ethnic Identity*, Los Angeles: Getty Research Institute

Hamilakis, Y (1999) 'Stories from exile: fragments from the cultural biography of the Parthenon (or "Elgin") Marbles', *World Archaeology* 31, 303–320

Handler, R (2003) 'Cultural property and culture theory', *Journal of Social Archaeology* 3, 353–365

Harding, S (2005) '*Bonnichsen v. United States*: Time, place, and the search for identity', *International Journal of Cultural Property* 12, 247–261

Hollowell-Zimmer, J (2003) 'Digging in the dirt, ethics and "low-end looting"' in Zimmerman, LJ, Vitelli, KD and Hollowell-Zimmer, J (eds), *Ethical Issues in Archaeology*, Walnut Creek, CA: AltaMira Press

Jilek, S (2004) 'Session and working party – the frontiers of the Roman Empire: defining a World Heritage Site', Annual Meeting of the European Archaeological Association, Lyon, France

Kohl, PL (1998) 'Nationalism and archaeology: on the constructions of nations and the reconstructions of the remote past', *Annual Review of Anthropology* 27, 223–246

Kopytoff, I (1986) 'The cultural biography of things: commoditization as process, in Appadurai, A (ed), *The Social Life of Things: Commodities in Cultural Perspective*, Cambridge: Cambridge University Press

Leach, J (2003) 'Owning creativity: cultural property and the efficacy of custom on the Rai coast of Papua New Guinea', *Journal of Material Culture* 8, 123–144

Lucas, G (2001) 'Destruction and the rhetoric of excavation', *Norwegian Archaeological Review* 34, 35–46

Matsuda, D (1998) 'The ethics of archaeology, subsistence digging, and artifact "looting" in Latin America: point, muted counterpoint', *International Journal of Cultural Property* 7, 87–97

McIntosh, RJ, McIntosh, SK and Togola, T (1996 [1989]) 'People without history', reprinted in Vitelli, KD (ed), *Archaeological Ethics*, Walnut Creek, CA: AltaMira Press

Merryman, JH (1986) 'Two ways of thinking about cultural property', *American Journal of International Law* 80, 831–853

—— (1988) 'The retention of cultural property', *U.C. Davis Law Review* 21, 477–513

—— (2005) 'Cultural Property Internationalism', *International Journal of Cultural Property* 12, 1–29

Meskell, LM (2000) 'The practice and politics of archaeology in Egypt', in Cantwell, AM and Friedlander, E (eds) *Ethics and Anthropology: Facing Future Issues in Human Biology, Globalism, and Cultural Property*, New York: New York Academy of Sciences

Migliore, Sam (1991) 'Treasure hunting and pillaging in Sicily: acquiring a deviant identity', *Anthropologica* 33, 161–175

MoU (1997) Memorandum of understanding between the Government of the United States of America and the Government of Peru concerning the imposition of import restrictions on archaeological material from the prehispanic cultures and certain ethnological material from the colonial period of Peru. 52 Federal Register 31713

Nason, JD (1997) 'Beyond repatriation: cultural policy and practice for the twenty-first century', in Ziff, B and Rao, PV (eds), *Borrowed Power: Essays on Cultural Appropriation*, New Brunswick, NJ: Rutgers University Press

Poole, D (ed) (1994a) *Unruly Order: Violence, Power, and Cultural Identity in the High Provinces of Southern Peru*, Boulder, CO: Westview

—— (1994b) 'Introduction: anthropological perspectives on violence and culture – a view from the Peruvian high provinces', in Poole, D (ed), *Unruly Order: Violence, Power, and Cultural Identity in the High Provinces of Southern Peru*, Boulder, CO: Westview

Prott, L (2005) 'International Movement of Cultural Objects', *International Journal of Cultural Property* 12, 225–248

Psacharopoulos, G and Patrinos, HA (eds) (1996) *Indigenous People and Poverty in Latin America*, Avebury: Brookfield

Pyburn, KA (2003a) 'Archaeology for a new millennium: the rules of engagement', in Derry, L and Molloy, M (eds), *Archaeologists and Local Communities: Partners in Exploring the Past*, Washington, DC: Society for American Archaeology

—— (2003b) 'We have never been postmodern: Maya archaeology in the ethnographic present', in Golden, CW and Borgstede, G (eds) *Continuities and Changes in Maya Archaeology: Perspectives at the Millennium*. New York: Routledge

Renfrew, AC (2001) 'Foreword', in Brodie, N, Doole, J and Renfrew, C (eds), *Illicit Antiquities: The Destruction of the World's Archaeological Heritage*, Cambridge: McDonald Institute for Archaeological Research

Robbins, B and Stamatopoulou, E (2004) 'Reflections on culture and cultural rights', *South Atlantic Quarterly* 103, 419–434

Schiffer, MB (1976) *Behavioral Archaeology*, New York: Academic Press

Sen, A (2004) 'How Does Culture Matter?', in Rao, V and Walton, M (eds), *Culture and Public Action*, Stanford: Stanford University Press

Shapiro, D (1998) 'Repatriation: a modest proposal', *NYU Journal of International Law and Politics* 31, 95–108

Sharp, DA (ed) (1972) *U.S. Foreign Policy and Peru*. Austin: University of Texas Press

Silverman, H (2002) 'Touring ancient times: the present and presented past in contemporary Peru', *American Anthopologist* 104, 881–902

Staley, DP (1993) 'St. Lawrence Island's subsistence diggers: a new perspective on human effects on archaeological sites', *Journal of Field Archaeology* 20, 347–355

Strong, S (1992) *The Shining Path: Terror and Revolution in Peru*, London: Harper Collins

Urban, G (2001) *Metaculture: How Culture Moves through the World*, Minneapolis: University of Minnesota Press

Watkins, J (2003) 'Archaeological ethics and American Indians', in Zimmerman, LJ, Vitelli, KD and Hollowell-Zimmer, J (eds), *Ethical Issues in Archaeology*, Walnut Creek, CA: AltaMira Press

—— (2004) 'Becoming American or becoming Indian? NAGPRA, Kennewick and cultural affiliation', *Journal of Social Archaeology* 4, 60–80

Weiner, AB (1992) *Inalienable Possessions: The Paradox of Keeping-While-Giving*, Berkeley: University of California Press

Welsh, PH (1997) 'The power of possessions: the case against property', *Museum Anthropology* 21, 12–18

Zimmerman, LJ (2000 [1995]) 'Regaining our nerve: ethics, values, and the transformation of archaeology', in Lynott, MJ and Wylie, A (eds), *Ethics in American Archaeology* (2nd Edition), Washington, DC: Society for American Archaeology

—— (2005) 'Public heritage, a desire for a "White" history for America, and some impacts of the Kennewick Man/Ancient One decision', *International Journal of Cultural Property* 12, 263–272

CHAPTER 3

Ethical Challenges to a Postcolonial Archaeology: The Legacy of Scientific Colonialism

George Nicholas and Julie Hollowell

In recent decades, archaeologists have responded to internal dialogues and external critiques by facilitating greater involvement of descendant peoples and other source communities in many aspects of archaeology. Although significant changes have occurred, substantial ethical challenges remain. While most archaeologists are nominally in favor of a more equitable archaeology, in reality they still hold the power in terms of the actual production and interpretation of archaeological knowledge, access to or use of data, and the capital derived from these processes. The very idea of sharing power appears threatening to some because it means a radical re-visioning of ethical responsibilities and research paradigms and altering deep-seated notions about scholarly privilege, intellectual property, and control over the production of knowledge (Ames 2003:171; Conkey 2005; Joyce 2002; Meskell and Pels 2005; Nicholas and Bannister 2004; see also Harding 1998). On the other hand, members of descendant communities,[1] who understandably experience their own anxieties over losses of cultural knowledge, have challenged the relevance of archaeology to their needs and beliefs, sometimes seeking to amend historical power imbalances through exclusionary practices, restrictions on access to sites or the information derived from them. At the same time, archaeology often occupies an ambivalent or subordinate position in relation to political and economic interests (Hamilakis 1999; Schmidt 2005).

Given these challenges, the search for more ethical and equitable relationships calls for acknowledging and addressing *real* differences among diverse interests in objectives and motivations for doing – or not doing – archaeology, recognizing what an archaeology that seeks greater equity entails or looks like, and determining ways to get there. Previously, we have considered the importance of negotiated practice and intellectual property rights to a postcolonial archaeology

(Nicholas and Hollowell 2004). Here we focus on archaeology's legacy of scientific colonialism as an essential challenge archaeologists face in creating more ethical research paradigms. We describe key aspects of the production of knowledge that must be intentionally transformed for archaeology to become postcolonial and refer to examples of epistemological approaches and engagements between archaeologists and descendant communities that move toward this possibility. At the same time, we consider the reverse of this power imbalance – the idea that there may well be limits to how far archaeologists (or anyone) should go to accommodate variable interpretations of the past.

WHY ARCHAEOLOGY IS NOT YET POSTCOLONIAL

Worldwide, members of descendant communities have viewed archaeology as a colonialist enterprise – just another tool of oppression that objectifies the past and disenfranchises them from their own histories (eg, Deloria 1969; Langford 1983; Thomas 2000; Watkins 2000; for counter-examples, see Dongoske *et al* 2000; Kuwanwisiwma 2002). Many archaeologists decry such statements as politically driven, pointing out that their work has not only increased knowledge of human history, but helped restore cultural traditions in the wake of epidemics, warfare, or forced acculturation. Nonetheless, nationalist, imperialist, and colonialist traditions have figured prominently in archaeology's development (Trigger 1984:356–357), and the end of these relationships does not concur with the so-called end of colonial eras.

Historically, archaeology has served the needs of the nation-state and those in positions of power and privilege. Archaeologists often work as technicians of the state, under a system of 'governmentality' (Pels 1997; Smith 2004:68–74). The idea that archaeologists are specially appointed stewards of the 'archaeological record' – a concept that they themselves created (Hamilakis 1999) – for the benefit of all people comes with an implicit presumption of privilege justified by appeals to intellectual and scientific authority (see Wylie 2005). In actuality, public access to the material and intellectual results of archaeological research remains limited, and in most contexts 'held in the public trust' means 'owned and managed by the state' for particular state interests and purposes.

Larry Zimmerman (2001:169) has used the term *scientific colonialism* to describe the historical relationship between archaeologists and Indigenous peoples. The concept emerged from ethical dilemmas raised by Project Camelot (Galtung 1967:295–302) and refers to situations in which knowledge is extracted and produced or processed elsewhere, without benefits returning to those at the source. A major feature of scientific colonialism is claiming an unlimited right of access to data extracted from a 'colony'. Another is the export of data (or people) to one's own territory for processing into profitable goods such as articles, books or PhDs:

> Researchers typically not only claim property rights over the knowledge they produce, but also proprietary rights over the subject matter – the field of raw data – from which they extracted their knowledge. This conceptual paradigm continues to be imposed upon the world – as a type of vestigial colonialism – long after the decline of those imperial regimes that gave rise to it in the first place. (Ames 2003:171)

The result is an asymmetrical production and distribution of knowledge about the 'colony', one that excludes people at the source from participating in the most creative or rewarding aspects of research (Galtung 1967:297). This describes all too well the uneven history of many relationships between archaeologists and communities where they have worked.

Descendant populations are well aware of the scientific colonialism that persists in archaeology. As Yellowhorn (2002:77) notes:

> Archaeological theory was constructed by imperial interests within a colonial regime for a settler population to study a past to which they had contributed nothing. Their explanations are unimpressive to Indians because the authors cater to an audience that is culturally distant from the data they observe. Indians see little of themselves or their ancestors when they review those theories so they perceive little gain by giving archaeology any consideration.

Indeed, archaeology continues to operate in contexts where Indigenous peoples are marginalized and subordinated to dominant structures and policies (Watkins and Ferguson 2005:1372), and the best intentions for collaboration[2] may never entirely escape the legacy of colonialism.

Sites, objects, and interpretations of the past are also sources of cultural capital that can be converted to economic, social, political or intellectual resources (Bourdieu 1977). Archaeologists, the state and, more recently, the heritage industry have been the primary beneficiaries of capital created from reconstructing the pasts of others, but very little of this returns to those at the source. For their part, Native Americans and other Indigenous peoples[3] have been subjected to untold social and emotional distress regarding the extent to which others have disturbed ancestral sites or profited from and abused their cultural capital (Brown 2003; Nicholas 2005).

In his seminal work, *Reinventing Anthropology* (1974), Del Hymes stated that for anthropology to survive, it had to deal with its legacy of scientific colonialism. To this end, anthropologists a generation ago initiated steps such as publishing in the host country or in the local language, training local researchers, and providing communities with reports of their work. Hymes (1974:49–50) calls these *courtesies* – they are not enough. Though there has long been an ethical responsibility not to conduct research that could be injurious to others, less recognized is the obligation to find ways that knowledge received in working with individuals or communities also benefits those at the source. Professional codes of ethics do not automatically provide guidance in meeting these challenges, since most have been constructed on the basis of exclusivity, to distinguish one group's definitions of appropriate behavior in contrast to non-professionals (Meskell and Pels 2005; Pels 1999). Research guidelines or protocols developed by Indigenous groups, such as those published by the Australian Institute for Aboriginal and Torres Strait Islander Studies (2000), may be far more helpful here.

In sum, reversing scientific colonialism may well be the primary ethical challenge facing archaeology and other research disciplines. Embedded in the concept itself are the seeds of how to cultivate more equitable and post-colonialist relationships.

MOVING TOWARD A POSTCOLONIAL ARCHAEOLOGY

Postcolonialism, according to philosopher of science Sandra Harding (1998:15–17), simultaneously embraces and defines a temporal era, a political condition, relationships between the once-colonized and the colonizer, and many forms of critical counter-discourse by or about the colonized. In all of its manifestations, postcolonialism identifies a stance that is not monolithic, but diverse and situational – an active intervention that emerges from particular histories, interrogates the status quo, and moves consciously toward decolonization politically, intellectually and economically. Underlying postcolonial critique is an ethical commitment to address and transform relations of inequality or oppression, wherever and in whatever form they exist.

Archaeology, with its materialist biases and time depth, has obvious contributions to make to understanding the processes and aftermaths of colonialism and its alternatives (Gosden 2004; Kristiansen and Rowlands 1998). Postcolonial perspectives emerged in archaeology from studies of colonial sites, the unearthing of alternative histories, critiques of processualism, reflection on the ethics of practice, calls for repatriation, and the emergence of multivocal, subaltern, and world-systems approaches (Gosden 2001; Rowlands 1998). They were pushed further by Aboriginal desires to reaffirm relationships and claims to the past, both materially and intellectually (Lilley 2000; Nicholas and Andrews 1997; Watkins 2000). Today once-marginalized groups are publicly reclaiming archaeological pasts, 'reshaping them in local terms that do not describe them as a variant of food production, urbanism or the origins of the state' (Rowlands 1998:332, cited in Conkey 2005), rejecting ways archaeology was employed against them (Hamilakis 2002), and discerning how archaeologists can work with and for them (see Ferguson 2003; Smith and Wobst 2005). The post-processual turn in archaeology is decidedly postcolonial in its embrace of multivocality and attention to social and interpretive contexts. The multifaceted economic and political roles that archaeology and interpretations of the past play in the world today make it all the more critical to examine and address ethical challenges facing a postcolonial archaeology (*cf* Pluciennik 2001; Zimmerman *et al* 2003).

This chapter is concerned with locating postcolonialism in archaeological practice, identifying approaches and epistemologies that move beyond the 'tradition' and legacy of scientific colonialism. Those working on this terrain agree that such a shift necessitates a comprehensive transformation in the structure of research practices and the very conceptual frameworks that guide the research process (Conkey 2005; Harding 1998; Marshall 2002; Riggs, this volume), combined with greater accountability to archaeology's multivalent role in broader fields of cultural production (Hamilakis 1999). To meet these challenges, archaeology, in whatever form it exists, must confront two key features of scientific colonialism, both of which have significant implications for theory, practice and ethics: first, the lack of standing given to alternative worldviews and ways of meaning-making, and second, inequities in relations of power and the distribution of research benefits.

Acceptance of Other Worldviews

Acceptance of alternative worldviews and histories as valid forms of meaning-making is one of the greatest challenges faced by archaeology and by sciences in general (Harding 1998; Wylie 1995). Archaeologists have tended to 'see the past as "being lost" if not archaeologically investigated' (Zimmerman 1990:414). The postcolonial critique goes as follows:

> Archaeologists have, in general, treated indigenous societies as something of the past and not deemed the opinions and values of their living descendants valid or relevant to a history of that people's homelands. The traditional indigenous version of these people's own history has been relegated to a minor auxiliary role as 'mythical', or 'ethnohistory', a curiosity not to be confused with so-called objective truth. (Allison 1999:279)

Oral histories have been widely used by archaeologists, but primarily to supplement or corroborate their own findings and seldom, until recently, as valid histories in their own right (Bernardini 2005; Echohawk 2000; Thomas 2000, chapter 23; Whitley 2002; but see Mason 2005).

Today we are more aware than ever that the very nature of scientific knowledge is shaped and legitimized to a large extent by the relations of power and hierarchy that define and demarcate a 'discipline' (Collins 1999:276; Conkey 2005; Harding 1998; Kuhn 1962). Archaeology carries the baggage of a scientistic/eurocentric worldview, one that implies that with 'better science' we come closer and closer to a more accurate interpretation of the past (Harding 1998:3). But if we define 'science' in more inclusive terms, as 'any systematic attempt to produce knowledge about the natural world' (Harding 1998:10), the boundaries between Western and non-Western sciences start to dissolve. Ethically, then, a postcolonial archaeology entails decentering a scientistic approach to allow for other ways of knowing and doing as valid alternatives. For example, Saitta (this volume) discusses how the interweaving or *convergence* of diverse standpoints and knowledge systems, rather than competition, can act as a method of evaluating truth-claims, thereby expanding and strengthening the field of possibilities for both theory and action.

When archaeology overrules or discounts traditional or Indigenous epistemologies, experiences, or worldviews, it in effect challenges the credibility of community values, histories, and explanations in a world whose dominant paradigm is overwhelmingly biased toward competing ideas, replicability, and measurable proof. Accepting alternative worldviews also includes acknowledging and remembering the particularities of colonial histories, the uneven experiences of decolonization, and the myriad forms that postcolonialism takes in different parts of the world (Pagán-Jiménez 2004).

Moreover, archaeology is bereft without embracing other ways of meaning-making. Archaeologists who described their work to community members in Brazil's Reserva Uaça as 'the study of things left behind in the ground' later realized that local people used a very different term, one that did not convey a false sense of dissociation or abandonment. In their eyes and minds, archaeology was 'reading the tracks of the ancestors' (Green *et al* 2003:377).

Inequitable Relations of Power

A second defining aspect of scientific colonialism is the asymmetrical power relationship between archaeologists and descendant communities concerning who controls, who benefits, and how control and benefits are shared. One challenge involves de-centering professional – particularly 'first world' – archaeologists as *the* producers of knowledge about the past and, in general, making archaeology a more inclusive, less predatory venture (Appadurai 2002). Archaeologists are experts of certain technologies and techniques (Shanks and McGuire 2000), but others have their own objectives and may perceive the benefits of archaeology very differently.[4] Descendant communities have every right to challenge the ethics of an archaeology that deals with their heritage but is irrelevant to their needs. Since the knowledge archaeologists produce depends in large part upon what questions and interests they bring to the research process, the issue of who gets to define these is critical. What counts as 'evidence' or is deemed 'significant' often represents a contest between differing interests and concerns (Battiste 2000; Shepherd, this volume; Smith 1999). How concepts such as *preservation, curation, mitigation, ownership* or *management* are defined, or 'culture' and 'periods' are named, or jargon and technical terms are used has much to say about the locus of power and control in the production and distribution of knowledge. When archaeologists find themselves in situations where they must defer to Native languages or practices, it places them in a very different relationship.

Post-processual methodologies (Hodder 2000; McDavid 2002), museologies (Kreps 2003; Peers and Brown 2003), and critiques of archaeological stewardship (Groarke and Warrick 2006; Wylie 2005) signify changing notions of accountability and control, but the 'scientific' standpoint often retains a position of power that affects relations and the economy of knowledge.

Regardless of how inclusive archaeology may become, a postcolonial ethic must contend with the fact that archaeology's stakeholders are certainly not equal in terms of power or capital. Typically, those closest to the source of extracted data have little control over the means of production or access to potential benefits, and often they are the ones most lacking in political and economic capital. Addressing these inequities requires not only a conscious reworking of the production of archaeological knowledge and practice but exposing the implicit and explicit interests that archaeology serves and analyzing the 'very systems of muting and suppression' that work within *and* outside of the discipline to preserve vestiges of colonialism (Conkey 2005:20). So much of archaeology today occurs in collusion with the state that many claim archaeological expertise has become a tool of 'governmentality', primarily serving and legitimating state interests (Smith 2004), a relationship that places obvious constraints on the possibility of a postcolonial archaeology.

Major imbalances also exist in access to and distribution of resources, status, and capital available to archaeologists in different regions of the world, often as the result of the historical position of archaeology in nationalist and institutional structures. In more and more cases, such as in Eritrea today (Schmidt 2005), archaeological concerns take a back seat to more powerful nationalist and capitalist interests, with some communities, after weighing their benefits, siding in favor of land development over conservation.

Anne Pyburn (2003:171) cautions that archaeologists often read the gap between themselves and local people as cultural, when it is really a matter of unequal economics and life chances. Matsuda (1998:93) describes this from the perspective of rural Central Americans:

> Every year, the archaeologists dig up the artifacts and take them away. The next year they come back with more money, people, and equipment. They talk of our ancestors with reverence, but treat us, their descendants, like ignorant peasants... The excavations are often run like plantations, where we are exploited... We are never asked what we think and there is no chance for advancement. The artifacts represent money and power to archaeologists and art historians. That is how they make their upper-class living.

These are discomforting thoughts for most archaeologists, but, as Green *et al* (2003:369) note, 'the task of understanding and exposing the relations of power in the production, circulation and consumption of archaeologically-produced knowledge requires a willingness to engage with that which is by definition contested'. Inevitably, postcolonial archaeologies are embedded in a matrix of unequal global, national, and intracommunity power relations over which individuals have little control. The structural inequalities that permeate most social relations can undermine attempts to facilitate genuine participation and equitable forms of exchange. Thus archaeology must not only transform its own research relationships, but confront its role in the construction of social concepts of *race, indigeneity, identity, culture,* and *progress* and its complicity in perpetuating global inequities in the distribution of economic and social capital (Hamilakis 1999).

In sum, a postcolonial archaeology necessitates new ways of doing archaeology that emerge from negotiated practice, return benefits of research to those at the source, and engage researchers with community needs and goals that may lie well beyond the frame of a traditional project. Along with this comes greater accountability to the ethical and political consequences of differing interpretations and a heightened sense of responsibility for how knowledge is handled and produced.

DECOLONIZING METHODOLOGIES

Much discussion about postcolonialism within archaeology and other disciplines has remained at the level of theory, critique, and textual representation (Pagán-Jiménez 2004). A lingering challenge is not simply whether archaeology is willing to critique the relationships and processes that sustain scientific colonialism – many voices within the discipline have already tackled this – but whether intentional 'decolonizing methodologies' and new or hybrid forms of more equitable and ethical practice follow. Linda Tuhiwai Smith (1999) has outlined some basic principles for decolonizing research methodologies from her perspective as a Maori researcher and educator (see also Mihesuah 1998). These recognize and declare the rights of descendant communities to:

- share in the processes of archaeological knowledge production and choose how to do so;
- use archaeological information to construct their own narratives and alternative histories that may enrich or disagree with archaeological knowledge; and
- benefit from knowledge that comes from research conducted in their communities and its production into various forms of capital.

These statements apply equally well to archaeology and any form of research with or by colonized populations, and they correspond directly to the ethical challenges discussed above. Smith also reminds archaeologists that descendant communities have their own stories to tell, which include histories of Western research from the perspectives of the colonized. Most importantly, she emphasizes that a postcolonial archaeology is obligated to do more than simply deconstruct Western scholarship or dismantle scientific colonialism; it must offer ways of doing research that contribute to the needs and survival of communities and individuals.

Several research approaches in archaeology incorporate decolonizing principles at some level. They include: community-based archaeology; applied anthropology; Indigenous archaeologies; feminist archaeologies; Marxist archaeology; and ethnocritical and ethics-based approaches. This is not an exhaustive list, nor are these discrete entities in practice, but varied ways of meeting some of the ethical and practical challenges of postcolonial transformation in archaeology. Indeed, perceiving them as separate camps carries a risk of marginalizing the issues, when, at this juncture, the discipline can no longer avoid the elephant in the room.

There is nothing intrinsically 'good' or inherently 'postcolonial' about any of these approaches, but they each offer a philosophical foundation that has the potential to provide essential support for transformative, postcolonial practice. In their review of gender in archaeology, Meg Conkey and Joan Gero (1997:416) discuss how the underlying assumptions of different theoretical approaches directly influence empirical findings, analysis, interpretation, and practice. The same is true for postcolonial perspectives, and here we are interested in some of the common implications or guidelines for practice that can be drawn from the various approaches briefly discussed below.

Community-Based Archaeologies

The tradition of community archaeology developed out of collaborative work with Indigenous communities in Australia and New Zealand and embraces a wide range of approaches and methodologies, some less – or more – colonialist in practice than others (Derry and Malloy 2003; Field *et al* 2000; Marshall 2002). The common element is the community's greater degree of control over the production of knowledge and objectives of research (see Gosden 2001:245–249). In its most inclusive form, a community invites an archaeologist to do work they want accomplished (eg, Pyburn 2003; Smith *et al* 2003). Especially moving, from a postcolonial standpoint, are instances where historic enemies or perpetrators and victims of colonialism (eg, slave owners and slaves; some NAGPRA negotiations) come together through archaeology over 'memories that hurt' (McDavid 2002; Bernbeck and Pollock, this volume). Catherine Dowdall and Otis Parrish (2002) offer an exceptional example of community-based postcolonial practice in the context of cultural resource management in which archaeologists from the California Department of Transportation worked closely with members of a Kayasha Pomo community to develop hybrid, situational practices (some quite controversial) based on Kayasha worldview and values, which at the same time satisfied agency mandates. The case study itself is written in a collaborative format.

Postcolonial community-based archaeology also requires negotiating equitable and appropriate terms for sharing local knowledge and the tangible and intangible products of research. Sometimes these terms are spelled out in local protocols or research agreements, but often they are embedded in local beliefs about appropriate behavior. An important aspect of Claire Smith's work in Australia is talking with people in the community where she works about rules outsiders should follow when they visit or work on Aboriginal land (Smith *et al* 1995:37). Community leaders reserve the right to censor aspects of her research that they find distressing or offensive, but censoring is minimized since Smith designs her research in consultation with community members and negotiates the intellectual property rights before hand (Smith 1996:96).

Questions about who *really* represents 'the community', how to make decisions, and who benefits are critical in this context (Marshall 2002:215). This is particularly the case when community archaeology entails developing a site for tourism or economic development (eg, Ardren 2002; Rowan and Baram 2004). Capitalist ventures can end up funneling profits to elite or outside interests, promoting an essentialized or idealized past, and generating other ethical dilemmas (Kohl 2004; Mortensen 2006). On the other hand, there are examples of archaeotourism that truly benefit local residents, such as in Agua Blanco, Ecuador, where community members once known for looting now profit from a local museum and giving tours of unspoiled sites (Howell 1996; McEwan *et al* 2006).

Leslie and David Green and Eduardo Neves (2003) explicitly set out to explore postcolonial research ethics in a participatory community-based project in Brazil's Reserva Uaça. They designed research questions and practices to involve the community in the production of knowledge, but once in the field, their good intentions required significant rethinking and reworking. Ethnographic methods helped them learn what questions were important to local residents – securing a livelihood, the rapid loss of traditional skills and knowledge about the landscape, and fears that outsiders would take their lands away. Redesigning their research practices to promote more balanced relations of power meant attending to a host of issues including the influence of the project on local social dynamics; the creation of an effective community decision-making process; the uneven empowerment of individuals; and local versions of history and identity that sometimes essentialized or opposed archaeological accounts. Though time-consuming and ethically challenging, the researchers found that the approach 'compelled the rethinking of the production of archaeological knowledge ... [and] challenged notions of heritage, ethics, historiography, practices of research and assumptions about community participation' (Green *et al* 2003:393).

Applied Anthropology

Applied anthropology struggles with a weighty colonialist legacy as a result of its association with top-down notions of development, yet applied anthropology can offer examples of postcolonial archaeological practice (see Shackel and Chambers 2004).

In the American Southwest, the Hopi and Zuni have developed a distinctly postcolonial model of research that TJ Ferguson (2003) calls 'reciprocal archaeology' or 'anthropological archaeology', and that treats archaeology as applied anthropology. Whereas traditional archaeology uses (and privileges) scientific studies to create knowledge with the goal of informing further research and theory, these tribes have constructed a more reciprocal and inclusive model of knowledge production; one that integrates *all* subfields of anthropology (and any other useful disciplines), with the primary goal of providing benefits to the tribe and community. Ethnographic data play a major role, since much of this work proceeds from the present to the past, tracing land use and social identity back through time, filling gaps in local histories along the way – essentially turning the direct historical method on its head. Epistemologically, this integrated approach to archaeology greatly expands the evidence that can be brought to bear on interpretations of the past, creating a 'synergistic effect', further heightened by the tribal community's demand for relevance (Ferguson 2003:142–144).

Indigenous Archaeologies

The example above also falls under the heading of Indigenous archaeology, a term used to describe both the engagement of Indigenous peoples in the process of archaeology and the development of non-Western approaches to the past (eg, Davidson *et al* 1995; Nicholas 2007; Nicholas and Andrews 1997; Swidler *et al* 1997; Watkins 2000). McGuire (2004:1) suggests that the concept arose from attempts to make archaeology 'something other than a colonialist practice where the conquerors define the heritage of the conquered'. In many places, from Polynesia to Africa, archaeology has gained importance as Indigenous communities seek to expand and deepen alternative local histories, recognizing the role these can play in transforming the consciousness and identity of once-colonized peoples (Lelevai 2003; Schmidt 2005).

Although Indigenous archaeology has been most visible in the guise of educational initiatives, collaborations, and community-based projects, its more significant contributions may well be in the development of alternative epistemological approaches. Eldon Yellowhorn, a Peigan (Blackfoot) archaeologist, endorses an 'internalist' archaeology, closely guided by cultural traditions. Archaeological explanations begin from Blackfoot histories, customs and practices. Data are interpreted in light of these traditions and, more generally, through Blackfoot identity and worldview. Rather than employ such culturally empty terms as 'Archaic' or 'Historic', a more meaningful culture history discusses time in terms of 'Dog Days' or 'Horse Days' (Yellowhorn 2002:235). The result is an archaeology that enriches and validates traditional history and provides a meaningful bridge between communities and their heritage.

Feminist Epistemologies

Feminist scholarship has produced a substantial body of literature and a range of strategies representing postcolonial paradigms (see Conkey and Gero 1997; Harding 1998, 2004; Mihesuah 2003; Spector 1993; Spencer-Wood 2000). Situated multivocality, tolerance, critical pedagogy, transparency in the production of knowledge, recognition of the political nature of archaeology and the power differentials it represents, the hallmarks of feminist approaches are to a large degree synonymous with postcolonial ethics, since they are partially cut from the same cloth. Feminist epistemologies typically begin from the standpoints of those whose voices have been marginalized, silenced, or otherwise dismissed. 'A willingness to consider other ways of knowing' (Wylie 2000:xviii) lies at the very heart of feminist epistemology and methodologies.

Feminists Marsha Hanen and Jane Kelley (1989) argue for using multiple-working hypotheses versus nomological-deductive reasoning, because this pushes archaeologists toward alternative and *unanticipated* conclusions. Such an approach not only promotes post-positivist philosophies of science, but also strengthens positivist ones.

In a recent review article, Meg Conkey (2005) discusses how working from an intersection of feminist and Indigenous approaches can offer insights that compel archaeologists to re-examine their categories, concepts and perspectives on the past. She points out that it is not a matter of simply adding Indigenous concerns to feminist theory, or vice versa, but about reconceptualizing and reformulating research as part of a continuous reflexive process.

Marxist Archaeology

It is not surprising that feminist, Indigenous, and Marxist approaches all embrace postcolonial archaeology so easily, since they emerge from an ethical commitment to addressing inequities among those who have been the subjects and objects of colonialism. With its focus on power relations and emancipation, Marxism, as both an epistemology and a means for social change, offers a way for archaeologists to analyze inequalities in past socio-political systems and in the contemporary world, as well as ways archaeologists continue to control and benefit from archaeological knowledge (Kristiansen and Rowlands 1998; McGuire 1993; McGuire and Reckner 2003; Patterson 2003; RATS 2003). We may talk and critique and theorize about ethical dilemmas or decolonization, but unless we take action, little will change. As a Marxist archaeologist, McGuire sees *praxis* – theoretically informed action – as the basic ingredient for an ethical postcolonial archaeology. A commitment to praxis

> allow[s] communities other than the middle classes to define the interests
> and questions of archaeology … to critically and empirically examine
> these questions, to arrive at knowledge that will transform the political
> struggles of our world, both in terms of advancing non-bourgeois inter
> ests and in critically assessing the interests and beliefs of the commu
> nities that archeologists work with. Such a praxis of archaeology stands
> the best hope of contributing to a change in society for the collective good
> of a majority of human beings. (McGuire 2004:18–19)

Ethics-Based Approaches

Another fertile field for postcolonial archaeology derives from approaches informed by various ethics frameworks, which move far beyond the adverse obligation to simply 'do no harm'.[5] Saitta (this volume), for example, describes an emancipatory archaeology anchored in pragmatist ethics that emphasizes the responsibility of creating affirmative relationships based on mutual needs and power sharing.

The work of Colwell-Chanthaphonh and Ferguson (2004) with four Native groups affiliated with Arizona's San Pedro Valley exemplifies an ethics-driven methodology, rooted in the philosophy of virtue ethics. Working from culture-based ideals of virtuous conduct and moral integrity, they developed a research process in which participants shared power, responsibility, and value for the work, even when they perceived very different benefits from doing archaeology. An ethic of collaboration was explicitly promoted by working with research assistants and cultural advisors representing each tribe to establish culturally appropriate research frameworks that incorporated Native terminology, oral traditions and interpretations. The project's hybrid methods and non-dichotomous thinking helped erase boundaries between researcher and researched, expert and lay – another hallmark of postcolonial research.

An Ethnocritical Archaeology

Larry Zimmerman's (2001) discussion of an 'ethnocritical' archaeology describes a distinctly postcolonial epistemology, one that asks archaeologists and descendant groups to acknowledge their differences in both ways of knowing and positions of power, and to use the tools and histories available to them in constructing their own versions of the past – versions that then can be shared, critiqued, and strengthened through the inclusive understanding offered by both (or many) points of view. An ethnocritical approach asks scholars and others involved to work at the margins of their own understandings of the world and to share in producing more contextualized, transparent, and transrelational constructions of the past.

How would this look in practice? Perhaps two accounts would stand together, in a format that allows them to interweave yet maintain integrity, along with a narrative of how each was produced. Critical scrutiny of the research process is built-in to an ethnocritical approach, making latent colonialism easier to identify. Dowdall and Parrish's (2002) work with the Kayasha Pomo, Saitta's pragmatist approach (this volume), the virtue ethics of Colwell-Chanthaphonh and Ferguson (2004), and many feminist practices show a strong connection to ethnocritical epistemology. Other examples surely exist, yet to be identified as such.

Defining New Agendas

Acceptance of other worldviews and more equitable relations in the production of knowledge are key elements of all of the approaches described above. While archaeology may never be truly postcolonial, its practitioners can work to make it *less* colonialist by aspiring to a postcolonial ethic and sharing examples of what this looks like in practice. The main ethical challenges involve inclusivity, a shift in power, and greater equity in all aspects of archaeological practice – in who defines when and why archaeology is valuable, what counts as evidence, whose worldviews and interpretations matter, who develops the questions and objectives of research, and in concepts of preservation, curation and management. Though we can – and should – look at examples of good practice and commonalities among successful approaches[6] (see Watkins and Ferguson 2005), there is no how-to book to follow. The agendas and designs of postcolonial archaeological practice are situational and will depend on context, requiring case-by-case consideration. Indeed, some warn that importing practices and hybrid approaches into other contexts without careful consideration is simply another form of colonialism (Pagán-Jiménez 2004). Postcolonial practice is not simply about adding enrichment activities or new forms of public outreach but about reconceptualizing every aspect of the research process – from project design and research questions to the production and distribution of knowledge and capital.

The ethical and practical challenges of turning postcolonial research ideals into practice cannot be overestimated. Foremost is the time and commitment required to understand community needs and dynamics and to build and maintain respectful relationships and reciprocal research designs. Incorporating principles of informed consent and benefit-sharing, which already play a critical role in other research disciplines (Laird 2002; Rosenthal 2006), raises complex questions about who has the authority to give consent and how benefits will be shared. Most funding agencies do not include these practices (or other postcolonial practices) in their budgets, timelines, or agendas.

One of the defining characteristics of a postcolonial archaeology is a research design that fits the needs of those affected by the study or those from whom data are extracted. There is no reason that the objectives or benefits need to be or should be the same for all interested parties. Indigenous communities, for example, are interested in a range of things that archaeology can do for them – from documentation for repatriation or land claims, recovering ancestral histories, generating teaching resources, protecting sites or forms of knowledge, and monetary benefits, to other less expected things (see Colwell-Chanthaphonh and Ferguson 2004:6–7). A postcolonial perspective makes room for both mutual and distinctively different objectives within the same project, guided more by an ethic of reciprocity than sharing. This also holds for other stakeholders, whether governments, land developers, biotech firms, private landowners, tourism companies, antiquities dealers, universities, or media interests such as the Discovery Channel.

Finally, by accepting the experiences of others as valid and meaningful, postcolonial approaches call attention to the particularities of history and the uneven and varied ways that colonialism and its repercussions are lived and experienced throughout the world. In many places, archaeology still operates under extreme colonialist or oppressive regimes. In these and other locations, local expressions of archaeological practice have defied disciplinary centricities and created their own hybrid and meaningful forms of practice (see Pagán-Jiménez 2004). These voices need to be heard, as they expand our vision of what a postcolonial archaeology can be. They also point to new roles for ethnography that make direct and indirect contributions to postcolonial archaeological practice. Post-processual archaeologies have long made use of ethnography as a reflexive and dialectic method of throwing new light (and casting new shadows) on archaeological methods and modes of production. Distinctly postcolonial roles for ethnography include giving voice to other ways of knowing or interacting with the past and contextualizing and interpreting perspectives on archaeology and its interventions (see Breglia 2006; Edgeworth 2006; Hollowell and Nicholas 2007; Meskell 2005). The existence of case studies that serve as rich illustrations and vital examples of postcolonial practices and archaeologies is to a great extent due to these new turns in ethnography.

THE DANGER OF GOING TOO FAR

In spite of a commitment to postcolonial ethics, there are questions as to whether one can go too far and end up subverting good intentions or objectives. Here we identify some areas of concern, recognizing that each of these questions needs consideration on a situational basis.

One danger in working with subaltern or marginalized groups is unintentionally co-opting their voices (see Bernbeck and Pollock, this volume; Zimmerman 2001). Many Aboriginal persons tend to defer to an 'expert', sometimes at the expense of their own views.[7] On the other hand, Watkins and Ferguson (2005) point out that archaeologists can actually *use* the discipline's privileged position to help re-enfranchise Indigenous and other groups by involving them, consulting with them, and sharing expertise. The very topics archaeologists choose to research and write about, and how they choose to write about them, have power to both construct and deconstruct epistemological walls and power inequalities (Conkey 2005; Smith 1999; Smith and Wobst 2005).

Archaeological projects also generate rivalries for jobs, monies, or status that have wider social repercussions. In Brazil, Green *et al* (2003:382) avoided some of this by rotating people through jobs, but wage labor still created problems: 'If a person has an agenda of becoming a power-player in local society, participation in a project such as ours becomes a means to an end that can be disruptive to local social relations'. At the same time, archaeologists working closely with a community risk becoming pawns of factionalism. Even the most ethical collaborative projects can be jeopardized by a change in archaeological personnel or tribal officials because arrangements are so dependent on the trust established between individuals. The same is true at the level of the state, where political interests can infiltrate, stifle, or even put an end to archaeology.

This raises two larger, but related, issues: first, that of atoning for the historical legacy of colonialism, and second, the collusion of archaeology with essentialist representations of the past. As Ruth Phillips (2003:165) warns, 'there is a double danger ... that legitimate modes of explanation [or of research] will be dismissed along with oppressive constructs. That is, of trading one set of exclusionary practices for another'. An archaeology that becomes a source for a descendant community's – or nation's – identity can unintentionally reinvent and reinforce essentialisms and claims of exclusivity or ownership (see Bauer *et al*; Bernbeck and Pollock, this volume). Avoiding this pitfall requires carefully navigating a middle ground between various versions or histories, while trying to avoid the danger of contributing to essentialist or repressive cultural notions.

Some contend that a postcolonial standpoint – one that gives credence or special consideration to alternative, divergent, and previously marginalized accounts and worldviews alongside those of science – necessarily weakens objectivity and cultivates rampant relativism. But this is only the case if one accepts accounts uncritically, when all knowledge claims are certainly not equally valid (Harding 1998:18–19). Knowledge claims can be scrutinized and evaluated according to standards of good science (defined broadly), common sense, and critical thinking; standards such as internal coherence, consistency, explanatory power, reliability, contextual depth (match with other local evidence) and breadth (application to other situations), correspondence, and consequences (McGuire 2004; Wylie 2004; Zimmerman 2001).[8] A *critical* multivocality is not only ethical, it submits archaeological interpretations to other critiques, forcing them to be more robust (J. Cunningham, personal communication e-mail, 28 April 2005). Without this, postcolonial practice would lapse into hyperrelativism and lose its ethical grounding. Should then the claims of some interests, due to their standpoint (eg, as a cultural descendant or a member of a particular affected community) be given more or less consideration than others? Perhaps yes, in light of their experience or positioning, but *all* accounts and standpoints should be subject to standards of 'robust reflexivity' (Harding 1998:20–21; Wylie 2004). The real question then becomes what historical processes, relations of power, moral arguments, or other social or psychological mechanisms maintain and legitimize particular standpoints (Wylie 2004), and what path archaeology should take among these.

McGuire (2004) insists that there will be a place for archaeologists in a postcolonial context, as long as a critical self-scrutiny exists. In fact, he advocates that archaeologists must retain the 'authority of their craft' and remain independent of interests or causes that do not correspond to knowledge derived from the craft of archaeology. Feminist epistemology would suggest, however, this may be impossible to achieve. The craft of archaeology is certainly not immune to its own biases, and its scientist and bourgeois roots predispose archaeology and its particular systems of meaning-making to blind spots and hegemonies. We would caution that alternative or Indigenous methodologies, like all standpoints and methodologies, need critical evaluation and scrutiny. Not only can they be restrictive or exclusive (eg, Smith's [1999] argument that the only valid knowledge of a people is produced by themselves), they may also be produced by those in a position of relative privilege or power.

SEEKING REFLEXIVE EQUILIBRIUM AND ENLIGHTENMENT

Archaeologists today are challenged with reconciling the objectives and values of multiple stake- and rights-holders with those of archaeology at a meaningful level. The delicate task is to find an equitable balance between the (at times seemingly incommensurable) objectives of archaeologists and those of descendant communities. Archaeologists have demonstrated that it is possible (and desirable) to share control, accommodate community interests, and still do good archaeology. Another looming ethical challenge for a postcolonial archaeology, less developed in this chapter but no less important, is that of navigating the responsibilities of archaeology and archaeologists in broader political and economic contexts. Transforming research to overcome the legacy of scientific colonialism will go a long way in providing examples of ethical practice for these wider circles.

The connection between an epistemological foundation that respects alternative ways of knowing and a postcolonial work that rebalances and transforms relations of power lies in research that includes the questions, experiences, and objectives of traditionally disenfranchised stakeholders. Postcolonial archaeologies (whether Marxist, feminist, Indigenous or other) recognize that our interpretations are historically and politically situated, and are given meaning by worldview. By giving serious consideration to other ways of knowing and making significant changes toward more equal relations of power in the research process, archaeology as a discipline begins to engage in a production of knowledge that is a more equitable endeavor, grounded in both principles of archaeological science and Indigenous knowledge. These steps have enormous implications for both archaeological practice and theory and stand to make archaeology a richer, more robust and ethical way of making meaning from the past that also contributes to a more humanitarian future.

NOTES

1. We share Dean Saitta's definition (this volume) of a 'descendant community' as a non-homogenous, self-identified group encompassing those who, regardless of background, identify with a particular past or locale through shared traditions, proximity, or collective memories. This is distinct from a narrower concept of 'descendants' as individuals with ancestral or familial links to the archaeological record.
2. In archaeological contexts, 'collaboration' is a term of broad usage and equally broad meaning, which can range from little more than what is required for 'working together' to relationships in which decision-making and power are truly shared. See Watkins and Ferguson 2005.
3. We caution that the term *Indigenous* does not bestow automatic privilege or a particular ethical standpoint. In some cases, immigrant populations are the ones oppressed and exploited by Indigenous groups that hold essentialized or racist attitudes (see Hamilakis 2005).
4. This is certainly not unique to archaeology. Murray Wax's 1991 study found that members of Native American communities perceived the research of outsiders in very different and sometimes incommensurable ways.
5. For example, the Precautionary Principle (Bannister and Barrett 2001) embodies a 'when in doubt, err on the side of caution' ethic whereby precautions are proactively taken to prevent damage or harm, even when scientific evidence cannot predict the consequences.
6. Some of the terms and principles that describe a postcolonial ethic for archaeology, gleaned from the approaches and examples in this text, include the following: inclusive, non-predatory, respectful, situated, emancipatory, transparent, critical, reciprocal, hybrid, particularistic, contextualized, dissolving dichotomies (observer/observed; expert/lay; science/myth; subject/object), challenging official versions and the status quo, benefit-sharing, honoring multiple voices, exposing hegemony, democratized, self-scrutinizing.
7. This is not limited to Indigenous peoples, but is far more widespread, linked to the image/power of archaeologists as knowing scientists.
8. For an in-depth discussion of relativism in archaeology, see Lampeter Archaeology Workshop 1998.

REFERENCES

Allison, J (1999) 'Self-determination in cultural resource management: indigenous people's interpretation of history and of places and landscape', in Ucko, PJ and Layton, R (eds), *The Archaeology and Anthropology of Landscapes*, London: Routledge

Ames, M (2003) 'How to decorate a house: the renegotiation of cultural representation at the UBC Museum of Anthropology', in Peers, L and Brown, AK (eds), *Museums and Source Communities*, London: Routledge

Anyon, R and Ferguson, TJ (1995) 'Cultural resource management at the Pueblo of Zuni', *Antiquity* 69, 919–930

Appadurai, A (2002) 'The globalization of archaeology and heritage', *Journal of Social Archaeology* 1, 35–49

Ardren, T (2002) 'Conversations about the production of archaeological knowledge and community museums at Chunchucmil and Kochol, Yucatan, Mexico', *World Archaeology* 34, 379–400

Australian Institute for Aboriginal and Torres Strait Islander Studies (2000) *Guidelines for Ethical Research in Indigenous Studies* [http://www.aiatsis.gov.au/data/assets/pdf_file/2290/ethics_guidelines.pdf, last accessed 24 September 2007]

Bannister, K and Barrett, K (2001) 'Challenging the status quo in ethnobotany: a new paradigm for publication may protect cultural knowledge and traditional resources', *Cultural Survival Quarterly* 24, 10–3

Battiste, M (ed) (2000) *Reclaiming Indigenous Voice and Vision*, Vancouver: UBC Press

Bernardini, W (2005) 'Reconsidering spatial and temporal aspects of prehistoric cultural identity: a case study from the American Southwest', *American Antiquity* 70(1): 31–54

Bourdieu, P (1977) *Outline of a Theory of Practice*, Cambridge: Cambridge University Press

Breglia, L (2006) 'Complicit agendas: ethnography of archaeology as ethical research practice,' in M Edgeworth (ed), *Ethnographies of Archaeological Practice: Cultural Encounter, Material Transformations*, Lanham, MD: AltaMira Press

Brown, M (2003) *Who Owns Native Culture?* Cambridge, MA: Harvard University Press

Collins, PH (1999) 'Moving beyond gender: intersectionality and scientific knowledge', in Ferre, MJ, Lorber, J and Hess, B (eds), *Revisioning Gender*, Thousand Oaks, CA: Sage

Colwell-Chanthaphonh, C and Ferguson, TJ (2004) 'Virtue ethics and the practice of history: Native Americans and archaeologists along the San Pedro Valley of Arizona', *Journal of Social Archaeology* 4, 5–27

Conkey, MW (2005) 'Dwelling at the margins, action at the intersection? feminist and indigenous archaeologies', *Archaeologies* 1, 9–80

Conkey, MW and Gero, J (1997) 'Programme to practice: gender and feminism in archaeology,' *Annual Review of Anthropology* 26, 411–437

Davidson, I, Lovell-Jones, C and Bancroft, R (eds) (1995) *Archaeologists and Aborigines Working Together*, Armidale: University of New England Press

Deloria, V, Jr (1969) *Custer Died for Your Sins: An Indian Manifesto*, London: MacMillan

Derry, L and Malloy, M (eds) (2003) *Archaeologists and Local Communities: Partners in Exploring the Past*, Washington, DC: Society for American Archaeology

Dongoske, K, Aldenderfer, M and Doehner, K (eds) (2000) *Working Together: Native Americans and Archaeologists*, Washington, DC: Society for American Archaeology

Dowdall, K and Parrish, O (2003) 'A meaningful disturbance of the earth', *Journal of Social Archaeology* 3, 99–133

Echohawk, RC (2000) 'Ancient history in the New World: integrating oral traditions and the archaeological record in Deep Time', *American Antiquity* 65, 267–90

Edgeworth, M (ed), (2006) *Ethnographies of Archaeological Practice: Cultural Encounters, Material Transformations*, Lanham, MD: AltaMira Press

Ferguson, TJ (2003) 'Archaeological anthropology conducted by Indian Tribes: traditional cultural properties and cultural affiliation', in Gillespie, S and Nichols, D (eds), *Archaeology Is Anthropology*, Washington, DC: American Anthropological Association

Field, J, Barker, J, Barker, R, Coffey, E, Coffey, L, Crawford, E, Darcy, L, Fields, T, Lord, G, Steadman, B and Colley, S (2000) 'Coming back: Aborigines and archaeologists at Cuddie Springs', *Public Archaeology* 1, 35–48

Galtung, J (1967) 'After Camelot', in Horowitz, I (ed), *The Rise and Fall of Project Camelot: Studies in the Relationship between the Social Sciences and Practical Politics*, Cambridge, MA: MIT Press

Gosden, C (2001) 'Postcolonial archaeology: issues of culture, identity, and knowledge', in Hodder, I (ed), *Archaeological Theory Today*, Cambridge: Polity Press

—— (2004) *Archaeology and Colonialism: Cultural Contact from 5000 BC to the Present*. Cambridge: Cambridge University Press

Green, LF, Green, DR and Neves, EG (2003) 'Indigenous knowledge and archaeological science: the challenges of public archaeology in the Reserva Uaça', *Journal of Social Archaeology* 3, 366–398

Groarke, L and Warrick, G (2006) 'Stewardship gone astray? ethics and the SAA,' in Scarre, C and Scarre, G (eds), *The Ethics of Archaeology: Philosophical Perspectives on Archaeological Practice*, Cambridge: Cambridge University Press

Hamilakis, Y (1999) 'La trahison des archéologues? archaeological practice as intellectual activity in postmodernity', *Journal of Mediterranean Archaeology* 12, 60–79

—— (2002) '"The other Parthenon": antiquity and national memory at Makronisos', *Journal of Modern Greek Studies* 20, 307–338

—— (2005) 'Whose world and whose archaeology? The colonial present and the return of the political,' *Archaeologies* 1, 94–101

Hanen, M and Kelley, J (1989) 'Inference to the best explanation in archaeology', in Pinsky, V and Wylie, A (eds), *Critical Traditions in Contemporary Archaeology: Essays in the Philosophy, History and Socio-politics of Archaeology*, Albuquerque: University of New Mexico Press

Harding, S (1998) *Is Science Multicultural? Postcolonialisms, Feminisms, and Epistemologies*, Bloomington: Indiana University

—— (ed) (2004) *The Feminist Standpoint Theory Reader*, New York: Routledge

Hodder, I (ed) (2000) *Towards Reflexive Methodology in Archaeology: The Example at Catalhöyük*, Cambridge: McDonald Institute for Archaeological Research

Hollowell, J and Nicholas, GP (2007) 'A critical assessment of ethnography in archaeology', in Castañeda, Q and Matthews, C (eds), *Ethnographic Archaeologies*, Lanham, MD: AltaMira Press

Howell, C (1996) 'Daring to deal with huaqueros,' in Vitelli, KD (ed), *Archaeological Ethics*, Walnut Creek, CA: AltaMira Press

Hymes, D (1974) 'The use of anthropology', in D Hymes (ed), *Reinventing Anthropology*, New York: Vintage Books

Joyce, R (2002) 'Academic freedom, stewardship and cultural heritage: weighing the interests of stakeholders in crafting repatriation approaches', in Fforde, C, Hubert, J and Turnbull, P (eds), *The Dead and Their Possessions: Repatriation in Principle, Policy, and Practice*, London: Routledge

Kohl, P (2004) 'Making the past profitable in an age of globalization and national ownership: contradictions and considerations', in Rowan, Y and Baram, U (eds), *Marketing Heritage: Archaeology and the Consumption of the Past*, Walnut Creek, CA: AltaMira Press

Kreps, CF (2003) *Liberating Culture: Cross-cultural Perspectives on Museums, Curation, and Heritage Preservation*, New York: Routledge

Kristiansen, K and Rowlands, M (eds) (1998) *Social Transformations in Archaeology: Global and Local Perspectives*, New York: Routledge

Kuhn, T (1962) *The Structure of Scientific Revolutions*, Chicago: University of Chicago

Kuwanwisiwma, LJ (2002) 'Hopi understanding of the past: a collaborative approach', in Little, B (ed), *Public Benefits of Archaeology*, Gainesville: University of Florida Press

Laird, S (ed) (2002) *Biodiversity and Traditional Knowledge: Equitable Partnerships in Practice*, London: Earthscan

Lampeter Archaeology Workshop (1997) 'Relativism, objectivity and the politics of the past', *Archaeological Dialogues* 164–184

Langford, R (1983) 'Our heritage – your playground', *Australian Archaeology* 16, 1–6

Lelevai, P (2003) 'History and archaeology in 'Uvea (Wallis Island), Western Polynesia: among tradition, myth and science', in Sand, C (ed), *Pacific Archaeology Assessments and Prospects*, Le Cahiers de l'Archéologie en Nouvelle-Calédonie 15

Lilley, I (ed) (2000) *Native Title and the Transformation of Archaeology in the Postcolonial World*. Oceania Monographs 50, University of Sydney

Marshall, Y (2002) 'What is community archaeology?', *World Archaeology* 34, 211–219

Mason, RJ (2005) *Inconstant Companions: Archaeology and North American Indian Oral Traditions*, Tuscaloosa: University of Alabama Press

Matsuda, DJ (1998) 'The ethics of archaeology, subsistence digging, and artifact "looting" in Latin America: point, muted counterpoint', *International Journal of Cultural Property* 7(1):87–97

McDavid, C. (2002) 'Archaeologies that hurt; descendants that matter: a pragmatic approach to collaboration in the public interpretation of African-American archaeology', *World Archaeology* 34, 303–314

McEwan, C, Silva, M-I and Hudson, C (2006) 'Using the past to forge the future: the genesis of the community site museum at Agua Blanca, Ecuador', in Silverman, H (ed), *Archaeological Site Museums in Latin America*, Gainesville: University Press of Florida

McGuire, R (1993) *A Marxist Archaeology*, San Diego: Academic Press

—— (2004) 'Knowledge claims in a politically committed archaeology', AAA Conference paper (www.AnthroCommons.com)

McGuire, R and Reckner, P (2003) 'Building a working class archaeology: the Colorado Coal Field War Project', *Industrial Archaeology Review* 25, 83–95

Meskell, L (2005) 'Archaeological ethnography: conversations around Kruger Park,' *Archaeologies* 11, 81–100

Meskell, L and Pels, P (eds) (2005) *Embedding Ethics*, Oxford: Berg

Mihesuah, D (1998) 'Introduction', in Mihesuah, D (ed), *Natives and Academics: Discussions on Researching and Writing about Native Americans*, Lincoln: University of Nebraska Press

—— (2003) *Indigenous North American Women: Decolonization, Empowerment, Activism*, Lincoln: University of Nebraska Press

Mortensen, L (2006) 'Structural complexity and social conflict in managing the past at Copán, Honduras', in Brodie, N, Kersel, M, Luke, C and Tubb, KW (eds), *Archaeology, Cultural Heritage, and the Antiquities Market*, Gainesville: University Press of Florida

Nicholas, GP (2005) 'The persistence of memory; the politics of desire: archaeological impacts on Aboriginal peoples and their response,' in Smith C and Wobst HM (eds), *Decolonizing Archaeological Theory and Practice*, New York: Routledge

—— 2007 'Indigenous archaeology', in Pearsall, D (ed), *Encyclopedia of Archaeology*, Oxford: Elsevier

Nicholas, GP and Andrews, TD (eds) (1997) *At a Crossroads: Archaeology and First Peoples in Canada*, Burnaby, BC: Simon Fraser University Archaeology Press

Nicholas, GP and Bannister, KP (2004) '"Copyrighting the past?": emerging intellectual property rights issues in archaeology', *Current Anthropology* 45, 327–350

Nicholas, GP and Hollowell, J (2004) 'Intellectual property rights in archaeology?' *Anthropology News* 45, 6, 8

Pagán-Jiménez, JR (2004) 'Is all archaeology at present a postcolonial one? constructive answers from an eccentric point of view', *Journal of Social Archaeology* 4(2):200–13

Patterson, TC (2003) *Marx's Ghost: Conversations with Archaeologists*, New York: Berg

Peers, L and Brown, A (eds) (2003) *Museums and Source Communities*, London: Routledge

Pels, P (1997) 'The anthropology of colonialism: culture, history and the emergence of western governmentality', *Annual Review of Anthropology* 26, 163–183

—— (1999) 'Professions of duplexity: a prehistory of ethical codes in anthropology', *Current Anthropology* 40, 101–136

Phillips, R (2003) 'Community collaboration in exhibitions: toward a dialogic paradigm', in Peers, L and Brown, AK (eds), *Museums and Source Communities*, London: Routledge

Pluciennik, M (ed) (2001) *The Responsibilities of Archaeologists: Archaeology and Ethics*, Archaeopress, Oxford. Lampeter Workshop in Archaeology 4, BAR S981

Pyburn, A (2003) 'Archaeology for a new millennium: the rules of engagement', in Derry, L and Malloy, M (eds), *Archaeologists and Local Communities: Partners in Exploring the Past*, Washington DC: Society for American Archaeology

RATS (2003) 'Abstracts of the radical archaeological theory symposium', Binghamton University, New York, www.finder.binghamton.edu/abstracts.htm (accessed 1 July 2007)

Rosenthal, JP (2006) 'Politics, culture and governance in the development of prior informed consent in indigenous communities', *Current Anthropology* 47(1): 119–142

Rowan, Y and Baram, U (eds) (2004) *Marketing Heritage: Archaeology and the Consumption of the Past*, Walnut Creek, CA: AltaMira Press

Rowlands, M (1998) 'The archaeology of colonialism', in Kristiansen, K and Rowlands, M (eds), *Social Transformations in Archaeology: Global and Local Perspectives*, New York: Routledge

Schmidt, PR (2005) 'Teaching revolutionary archaeology: African experiments in history making', *Archaeologies* 1(2):46–59.

Shackel, P and Chambers, E (eds) (2004) *Places in Mind: Public Archaeology as Applied Anthropology*, New York: Routledge

Shanks, M and McGuire, R H (2000) 'The craft of archaeology', in Thomas, J (ed), *Interpretive Archaeology: A Reader*, London: Leicester University Press

Smith, C (1996) 'Situating style: an ethnoarchaeological study of social and material context in an Australian Aboriginal artistic system', unpublished Ph.D. Dissertation, University of New England

Smith, C, Willika, L, Manabaru, P and Jackson, G (1995) 'Barunga rock art', in Davidson, I, Lovell-Jones, C and Bancroft, R (eds), *Archaeologists and Aborigines Working Together*, Armidale, New South Wales: University of New England Press

Smith, C and Wobst, HM (eds) (2005) *Decolonizing Archaeological Theory and Practice*, New York: Routledge

Smith, L (2004) *Archaeological Theory and the Politics of Cultural Heritage*, London: Routledge

Smith, LT (1999) *Decolonizing Methodologies: Research and Indigenous Peoples*, London: Zed Books

Smith, L, Morgan, A and van der Meer, A (2003) 'The Waanyi women's history project: a community partnership project, Queensland, Australia', in Derry, L and Malloy, M (eds), *Archaeologists and Local Communities: Partners in Exploring the Past*, Washington, DC: Society for American Archaeology

Spector, J (1993) *What This Awl Means: Feminist Archaeology at a Wahpeton Dakota Village*, St. Paul: Minnesota Historical Society Press

Spencer-Wood, SM (2000) 'Strange attractors: feminist theory, nonlinear systems theory, and their implications for archaeological theory', in Schiffer, MB (ed), *Social Theory in Archaeology*, Salt Lake City: University of Utah Press

Swidler, N, Dongoske, K, Anyon, R and Downer, A (eds) (1997) *Native Americans and Archaeologists: Stepping Stones to Common Ground*, Walnut Creek, CA: AltaMira

Thomas, DH (2000) *Skull Wars: Kennewick Man, Archaeology, and the Battle for Native American Identity*, New York: Basic Books

Trigger, B (1984) 'Alternative archaeologies: nationalist, colonialist, imperialist', *Man* 19, 355–370

Watkins, J (2000) *Indigenous Archaeology*, Walnut Creek, CA: AltaMira

Watkins, JE and Ferguson, TJ (2005) 'Working with and working for indigenous communities', in Maschner, HDG and Chippindale, C (eds), *Handbook of Archaeological Methods, vol. II*, Walnut Creek, CA: AltaMira

Wax, ML (1991) 'The Ethics of Research in American Indian Communities,' *American Indian Quarterly* 15, 431–456

Whitley, PM (2002) 'Archaeology and oral tradition: the scientific importance of dialogue', *American Antiquity* 67, 405–416

Wylie, A (1995) 'Alternative histories: epistemic disunity and political integrity', in Schmidt, P and Patterson, T (eds), *Making Alternative Histories: The Practice of Archaeology and History in Non-Western Settings*, Santa Fe: School of American Research

—— (2000) 'Foreword', in Dongoske, K, Aldenderfer, M and Doehner, K (eds), *Working Together: Native Americans and Archaeologists*, Washington, DC: Society for American Archaeology

—— (2004) 'Why standpoint matters', in Harding, S (ed), *The Feminist Standpoint Reader*, New York: Routledge

—— (2005) 'The promises and perils of stewardship', in Meskell, L and Pels, P (eds), *Embedding Ethics: Shifting Boundaries of the Anthropological Profession*, Oxford: Berg Press

Yellowhorn, EC (2002) 'Awakening internalist archaeology in the aboriginal world', unpublished PhD Dissertation, McGill University

Zimmerman, LJ (1990) '"This has bothered me for 500 years": the impact of concepts of time and the past on the Reburial issue', in Klesert, A and Downer, A (eds), *Preservation on the Reservation: Native Americans, Native American Lands, and Archaeologists*, Navajo Nation Papers in Anthropology 26

—— (2001) 'Usurping Native American voice', in Bray, T (ed), *The Future of the Past: Native Americans, Archaeologists, and Repatriation*, New York: Garland Press

Zimmerman, LJ, Vitelli, KD and Hollowell-Zimmer, J (eds) (2003) *Ethical Issues in Archaeology*, Walnut Creek, CA: AltaMira

CHAPTER 4

Cultural Sensitivity, Science and Ethical Imperatives: Contemporary Archaeology in the Southwestern United States

Charles R. Riggs

INTRODUCTION

Today it is impossible to engage in fieldwork or scholarly writing regarding the southwestern United States without seriously considering the Native American point of view. Though some archaeologists continue to resent this new cooperative relationship with tribes, most view this as a positive step, one that is mutually beneficial to scholars and tribes alike. There remains, however, a wide gulf between the practice of archaeological research and our ability to be culturally sensitive. Much of this gap comes from a deeply engrained colonialist mindset that continues to dominate not only our interpretive frameworks, but the very terminology we employ.

Each academic term I am reminded of the chasm between Native American views of the past and those of the academy as I teach introductory anthropology and archaeology courses and upper-division classes in Southwest and North American Prehistory to a student body that is, on average, anywhere from 18 to 20 percent Native American (on one occasion, Native American enrollment in a class was 60 percent). As I try to expound on A.V. Kidder's contributions to Southwest archaeology or on the intricacies of the many versions of the Hohokam chronology, I am invariably struck by how alien many of these concepts must seem to the very people in my class whose ancestors created the archaeological record I have spent my career trying to understand. Over the semesters, I have increasingly tried to visit the oral histories of the tribes affiliated with these prehistoric groups, and have found that there is often good archaeological support for the oral histories that I have read. These experiences have very much shaped my views not only of the prehistory of the Southwest, but of my own role as a scientist and educator. Fortunately, my own self-journey is informed also by a shift in the attitudes of my colleagues toward being more respectful to the peoples we study.

The passage of the Native American Graves Protection and Repatriation Act (NAGPRA) in 1990 marked the culmination of a growing concern in the United States over historic properties and Native American rights (Fine-Dare 2002). As a result of this legislation, the products of archaeological research have been brought increasingly onto the radar screen of Native Americans. It is important to note that our laws and ethical guidelines now marginalize (as they should) that portion of society engaged in looting and other types of vandalism, and have addressed the wrongs of our predecessors with regard to human remains and burial goods. The problem, as I see it, comes not in archaeologists' ability to adhere to the guidelines regarding responsible scientific procedure, but rather in adhering to what are contradictory guidelines regarding scientific ethics on one hand and cultural sensitivity on the other. As I demonstrate below, Southwest archaeologists today continue to use colonialist terminology and models to explain the prehistory of the southwestern United States, despite NAGPRA's and our own ethical codes' emphasis on cultural sensitivity.

These often contradictory ethical codes are a large component of the problem. Monolithic statements of ethics are, by nature, subject to multiple interpretations because ethics, not unlike the remainder of archaeological discourse, are contextualized in contemporary political discourse. Below I delve into some of the continuing sensitivity issues that I regard as problems in contemporary southwestern archaeology, as it has been practiced since the 1980s.

ETHICAL GUIDELINES AND THEIR CONTRADICTIONS

Serving as ethical and political barometers for archaeology are the Society for American Archaeology (SAA) and the American Anthropological Association (AAA), both of which have specific ethical guidelines regarding not only how archaeologists proceed in the course of research, but in matters of respect for subject groups and how they should disseminate their results to the public. If we are faced, as we are in the Southwest, with a diversity of interest groups, then these professional organizations must address, and do address, the interests of these groups. The ethical code of the SAA is encapsulated in its mission statement (www.saa.org/aboutSAA/103strat.html), which reads:

> The mission of the Society for American Archaeology is to expand understanding and appreciation of humanity's past as achieved through systematic investigation of the archaeological record. The society leads the archaeological community by promoting research, stewardship of archaeological resources, public and professional education,

and the dissemination of knowledge. To serve the public interest, SAA seeks the widest possible engagement with all segments of society, including governments, educators, and indigenous peoples, in advancing knowledge and enhancing awareness of the past.

The ethical guidelines of the AAA echo those above, but make explicit the responsibility of the researcher to the pursuit of science as well as to their subject matter, assigning primary importance to the concerns of the subject groups over the acquisition of knowledge and the publication of research results. Regarding science, the AAA guidelines state:

> Anthropological researchers bear responsibility for the integrity and reputation of their discipline, of scholarship, and of science. Thus anthropological researchers are subject to the general moral rules of scientific and scholarly conduct. (www.aaanet.org/committees/ethics/ethcode.htm)

The SAA ethical code is all but silent on the subject of scientific responsibility, stating simply in Principle No. 8 that

> [g]iven the destructive nature of most archaeological investigations, archaeologists must ensure that they have adequate training, experience, facilities and other support necessary to conduct any program of research they initiate in a manner consistent with the foregoing principles and contemporary standards of professional practice. (www.saa.org/aboutSAA/committees/ethics/principles.html)

Both organizations place more importance on the treatment of their subject matter than on that of scientific research, a further testimony to the influence of NAGPRA and other preservation laws on the conduct of archaeological research in North America. Regarding research about other cultures, the AAA ethical guidelines state:

> Anthropological researchers have primary obligations to the people … they study and to the people with whom they work. These obligations can supersede the goal of seeking new knowledge. (www.aaanet.org/committees/ethics/ethcode.htm)

The SAA guidelines, as stated in Principle No. 2, are less specific:

> Responsible archaeological research, including all levels of professional activity, requires an acknowledgement of public accountability and a commitment to make every reasonable effort, in good faith, to consult actively with affected group(s), with the goal of establishing a working relationship that can be beneficial to all parties involved. (www.saa.org/aboutSAA/committees/ethics/principles.html)

The conundrum comes not from adhering to any of these principles alone, but from trying to adhere to all of them. Often, scientific research is at odds with respect for other cultures. The AAA guidelines are quite clear regarding which should take precedence, whereas the

SAA guidelines make no such statement. As I demonstrate in the examples below, archaeologists and Native Peoples living in the South west, as in the rest of the world, have different ideas about their past. More to the point, Native Americans recognize and have been vocal about the distinction between science and beliefs:

> The scientific imperative presumes an unqualified right to suspend social ethics and cultural taboos in the name of a greater good: objective discovery. In the name of objective discovery, empiricism distinguishes for us between ... grave robbery and archaeology. Unfortunately this notion amounts to an ethical blank check for visits to Indian Country. (White Deer 1997:39)

As this statement implies, archaeology in the Southwest, just as in the rest of North America, has a dubious history when it comes to respecting the wishes of its primary subject matter. Fortunately, NAGPRA has opened up a necessary dialogue between archaeologists and Native Americans, which has eliminated the more blatant issues regarding respect for human remains.

It is my contention, however, that we still have work to do. As the examples below demonstrate, much of the recent archaeological literature of the Southwest remains replete with models that are frankly colonialist and Eurocentric in nature. Despite (and perhaps because of) the ethical statements quoted above, western models of warfare (Wilcox et al 2001); frontier models (Herr 2001); and Eurocentric social complexity models (Gregory and Nials 1985; Rice 1990; Upham 1982; Wilcox 1993), to name just a few, still enjoy prominence in southwestern literature. It is, without doubt, a lasting byproduct of 19th-century colonialism – wherein wealthy antiquarians viewed Native Americans at best as wards to be looked after and at worst as an inferior group with no rights – and which was responsible for laying the foundations upon which southwestern archaeology continues to rest. The extent to which we try to remedy this problem, I fear, will continue to remain an issue in American archaeology, as some contemporary examples will make clear.

EXAMINING THE PROBLEM: SOME EXAMPLES

> Some archaeologists suggest that this issue [Native American beliefs and scientific inquiry] is akin to debates between scientists and creationists, but there is a major difference, because in archaeology and the associated issues of repatriation and reburial, we are dealing with 'archaeological colonialism'. Pasts created by archaeologists have been imposed on Indian pasts without a chance for debate. (Zimmerman 1997:53–54)

As the foregoing statement indicates, one problem with the practice of archaeology in the United States is a perception by Native Americans that they have no say in the production of their own past. I suggest that the issue goes far beyond the problems associated with burials and repatriation to the central core of our discipline. I could provide dozens of examples of recent archaeological studies in the Southwest that demonstrate the continuing insensitivity among archaeologists, but in the interest of brevity, I will focus on just a few, which I have separated into terminological issues and interpretive issues.

Terminological Issues

Any recent visitor to Mesa Verde National Park will no doubt note that the first thing they are told, as they take one of the ticketed tours of Cliff Palace or Balcony House, is that archaeologists no longer use the term *Anasazi* to refer to the ancestors of the modern pueblo builders out of respect for the wishes of the Hopi Tribe, preferring instead the more generic term *Ancestral Pueblo*. They are told that this is because Anasazi is a Navajo word meaning 'ancient enemies'. What tourists are not told, however, is that the term Anasazi does not necessarily mean 'ancient enemies', but rather has a number of possible meanings including also 'ancient people', 'old people', 'alien ancestors', and 'enemy ancestors'. Furthermore, they are not informed that many archaeologists have refused to abandon this traditional term, which they correctly view as nothing but an anglicized version of a Navajo word with vague meaning, but which in English refers simply to the pre-Columbian dwellers of the Colorado Plateau region (Walters and Rogers 2001).

Whereas this example suggests that some archaeologists and government agencies are attempting to uphold one component of their ethical responsibilities – the Native Americans' point of view (or more specifically, a small yet vocal subset of Native Americans) – this particular example of terminological manipulation seems little more than lip service to a recently empowered Hopi tribe. I suggest that not only does it not solve the problem of archaeologists' insensitivity to Native concerns, it actually does more damage than good to all, including the Hopi tribe. From the point of view of a tourist, it is nothing but another example of the archaeological community trying to confuse and complicate the southwestern past, in this instance, by eliminating a term that is well entrenched in the popular and scientific literature. From the point of view of the modern Hopi, this kind of behavior does a disservice by glossing over the important intra-cultural differences (ie, the 'footprints') within the pre-Columbian archaeological record (Riggs 2005). Perhaps even more insidious, it draws attention away from the still persistent problem of not effectively adhering to the ethical guidelines of both the SAA and the AAA, specifically those guidelines related to respect for subject cultures.

Masked by this issue is, in my opinion, a much more serious terminological matter that has not been addressed. Deeply entrenched terminology in the literature includes a number of culturally insensitive terms. The most striking example in the Southwest, as in other parts of the New World, is the terminology used in our three part-division of prehistory conforming to an old, a middle, and a new stone age. What Old World archaeologists call the Paleolitihic, New World archaeologists call the Paleoindian or 'ancient/primitive Indian' period. The following Mesolithic period is referred to as the Archaic, or 'no longer useful or efficient' period. Finally, the Neolithic period, which in the Southwest includes the Anasazi culture, is referred to as the Formative period, implying that this stage was important or somehow influential in the development of the character of the indigenous inhabitants of the United States. Unlike the use of the term Anasazi, which is derived from a Navajo word with unclear or multiple meanings, these words are perfectly acceptable, unambiguous English terms (see Webster's 2004), but which are loaded with colonialist baggage. A cynically minded person, for example, might point out that if we were to take these terms literally, the Paleoindian-Archaic-Formative sequence suggests that it was not until the coming of Europeans that indigenous Americans were finally instructed in what it means to be on the same intellectual footing with Europeans.

Herein is where our dilemma lies. Do we adhere to the guidelines of the SAA and AAA, which suggest that we should change these culturally insensitive terms, or do we argue that their deep entrenchment in the literature makes them so difficult to change that we would violate our own ethics relating to scientific knowledge and clear communication to the public? I have no answer to this question other than to say that if we can change Anasazi, why not change Paleoindian, Archaic, and Formative as well? It would certainly make my job as an educator in a classroom of 20 percent Native American students that much easier. At the same time, however, there is merit to the idea that, as unfortunate as the terms may seem today, they are the monikers with which we have reconstructed southwestern prehistory and therefore should not be changed simply because it might be politically fashionable to do so.

Interpretive Issues

Unfortunately, the problem of cultural insensitivity does not end with our terminology. Even with the rise of 'modern archaeology' and the attendant laws and ethical codes, the problem of insensitivity continues to impact our interpretive frameworks. Once again, I could easily trace the history of this problem back to the colonialist beginnings of the discipline, but in the interest of time, I pick up the thread in the mid-1980s and restrict my discussion to a couple of more recent examples.

Modern Southwest archaeology's Eurocentrism is well illustrated by the research conducted at Chavez Pass Pueblo, or Nuvakwewtaqa, an ancestral Hopi community dating predominantly to the 14th century A.D. The original controversial study (Cordell *et al* 1987; Downum 1986; Feinman *et al* 2000; Graves 1987; McGuire and Saitta 1996; Plog 1985; Reid 1999; Reid *et al* 1989; Upham 1982; Upham and Plog 1986), has been reexamined in a number of recent publications (Feinman *et al* 2000; McGuire and Saitta 1996; Reid and Whittlesey 2005). Only a few understand that the failing of the Chavez Pass researchers was not a theoretical one (McGuire and Saitta 1996), but rather one of methodology (Reid and Whittlesey 2005) and scientific ethics (Downum 1986). To add to the many critiques of the Chavez Pass study, I suggest that its greatest shortfall was a complete disregard for the views of the Hopi tribe regarding their own history.

Chavez Pass archaeologists suggested that the ancestral Hopi community of Nuvaqueotaka was controlled by a group of managerial elites with centralized control over the trade of valued polychrome ceramics and agricultural surpluses:

> Following the theme of world-systems and the economic organization that those models suggest, I have analyzed data from Nuvaqueotaka ... in relation to the attributes suggested by a port-of-trade model to provide a perspective on political and economic organization at the local level. Data from Nuvaqueotaka suggest the presence of a centralized decision-making organization that not only managed local construction and agricultural activities but also played an important role in the regional economic network. (Upham 1982:200)

Furthermore, these elites coerced labor from the people (Plog and Upham 1983; Upham 1989) as if the Puebloans' ancestors had suddenly found themselves in the Tigris-Euphrates or Nile River valleys at the dawn of Western Civilization. The irony of this model in its full expression is that its proponents suggested that it was Western colonialism that had erased the Pueblos' abilities to engage in such colonial types of endeavors:

> While Pueblo ethnographies are valuable to the extent that they provide information on groups of people whose ancestors occupied many of the sites studied by archaeologists, there is little basis for employing models of Pueblo social or political structure in archaeological interpretation. Periods of Spanish, Hispanic and Anglo domination, coupled with settlement dislocation and population loss, resettlement and population concentration, the loss of native lands ... have combined to alter the precontact structure of Pueblo societies. (Upham and Plog 1986:237)

There is no doubt that Western colonialism severely affected Pueblo societies, but to reject ethnography completely can serve only archaeologists, not their subject matter. In fact, as demonstrated below, there is a great deal to be gained from indigenous knowledge of the past (Anyon *et al* 1997). In the case of Nuvaqueotaka, it is scarcely possible to find scholarly writing that demonstrates such a blatant disregard for Native American beliefs regarding their own past. To make matters worse, all of the field work conducted by the Chavez Pass camp was funded by federal tax dollars in the form of grants from either the National Science Foundation or the National Forest Service, which manages the property on which Chavez Pass is located (Upham 1978). Yet the data from these excavations, which would allow archaeologists, Native Americans, and the public to evaluate the claims of the researchers, remain unpublished except for a handful of journal articles and a single monograph (Upham 1982).

Looking at this interpretation in a post-NAGPRA era, it is perhaps easy to criticize, but the Hopi have always had their own interpretation of the history of Chavez Pass and its place in their culture. In Hopi oral history, the story of Chavez Pass is recounted in the following way:

> After many years they [the Palatkwapi Clans] departed from Hohokyam and moved on to another place, Neuvakwiotaka, which is now known as Chaves Pass, and there they remained for a long time. And later on, after many harvests at Neuvakwiotaka, they moved on to the Little Colorado River near where the present town of Winslow stands. (Courlander 1971:72)

The contrast in these two accounts highlights the extent to which a Western colonialist model was imposed on a non-Western culture. A more recent discussion of this very same prehistoric community demonstrates how archaeologists need not engage in such insensitive behavior. Recently, using architecture and ceramic analysis, Bernardini (2005) has examined the archaeological evidence for Hopi migration histories focusing specifically on Chavez Pass as well as a number of other villages and has concluded that there is a great deal of archaeological support for Hopis' understanding of their own clan migration histories.

With regard to the original Chavez Pass world systems model, it is difficult to imagine why an archaeologist would formulate such a Western view of an indigenous, non-Western past, and with such disregard for the subject culture's history. The Chavez Pass model of social complexity, though formulated before the passage of NAGPRA and the active involvement of Native Americans, was an indication of the insensitive attitudes of archaeologists working in the Southwest. Despite being put forth in the middle and late 1980s, the fact that this model is still being revisited in the literature (Feinman *et al* 2000; McGuire and

Saitta 1996; Reid and Whittlesey 2005) indicates its continued influence on southwestern archaeology. This case points out that many archaeologists continued to be unconsciously steeped in the colonialist notions of the late 19th century as late as the final years of the 1980s. Sadly, this attitude, though not as blatant, continues to persist despite the passage of NAGPRA and its attendant influence on our professional ethical guidelines.

More recently, one can turn to the literature of the Southwest and see a number of colonialist and Eurocentric-sounding models purporting to 'explain' some facet of southwestern prehistory. In the 1980s and early 1990s managerial elites with coercive power suddenly appeared all over the Southwest, whether they controlled trade routes along the Mogollon Rim of central Arizona (Lightfoot 1984) or they lived atop platform mounds and managed complex irrigation systems in the Phoenix area (Gregory 1987; Wilcox 1991).

In the late 1990s Western notions of the Native American past continued to be espoused by southwestern archaeologists, who began to talk about a 'Chaco Frontier' (Herr 2001), or to debate the importance of endemic warfare (LeBlanc 1999; Wilcox and Haas 1994) and institutionalized cannibalism (Turner and Turner 1999) as factors in shaping the development of southwestern society, oftentimes with little or no systematically derived archaeological proof, or perhaps without consideration for the very real possibility of equifinality of the evidence (Walker 1993).

Perhaps the most extreme expression of this type of thinking relates to interpretations of the Chacoan state. In Wilcox's (1993) view, the large great houses in Chaco Canyon were the facilities from which elites managed the polity growing at Chaco Canyon with its standing armies:

> An organized force of 500 to 1,000 warriors, organized into squads and larger divisions, could have been housed at Chetro Ketl or Pueblo Alto and would have been a sufficient force to make the proposed system work. (Wilcox 1993:84)

and network of roads for dispersing these armies as if they were Roman legions, marching against their subjects to extract tribute:

> In the early 1000's, this polity, I infer became a tribute demanding polity (or state) that began to advance against its populous, agriculturally successful neighbors to the south and southwest. (Wilcox 1993:81)

Once again, the Hopi view of their history as it relates to Chaco Canyon is rather more prosaic and decidedly non-Eurocentric:

> Thus Yupköyvi [Chaco] became a gathering place for clans who had stopped at what might be called staging areas some distances away. Among the initial clans to settle in the Chaco landscape were the Parrot

and Katsina clans. Later, the Eagle, Sparrowhawk, Tobacco, Cottontail, Rabbitbrush, and Bamboo clans arrived. (Kuwanwisiwma 2004:45)

Furthermore, other Puebloan peoples share similar beliefs regarding the canyon:

What we do know is that waves of people came and went from the [Chaco] Canyon, as they did throughout the Southwest. Our present-day pueblo belief system seems applicable here. It tells us that because we now dwell in the fourth world, where we know not only the stable earth but also the movement of the sun, moon, stars, and clouds, we know that movement is a desirable part of living. (Swentzell 2004:51)

The archaeologists above would no doubt defend their theories and methods by saying that they are producing a scientific, objective view of the past. This is, of course, part of what the SAA and AAA dictate that we do as professionals. Should this mean, however, that we have the freedom, under the same set of ethical standards, to promote theories of an indigenous southwestern past that are not only alien to Native Peoples and their belief systems, but in some cases are downright offensive? It seems to me, for example, that telling the Hopi or Zuni that any of their ancestors lived on the margins of a 'Chaco Frontier' will only reinforce their perceptions of a dominant colonialist society serving its own ends at their expense.

Did individuals living in the Southwest in the 1000s and 1100s actually live on the margin of a Chaco Frontier? Did some achieve status by controlling trade routes to the extent that they had coercive power over others? Did they march in legions against their neighbors? Or did groups of various size move across the landscape in what Bernardini (2005) refers to as 'serial migrations', leaving what the Hopi call 'footprints' in the form of ruined pueblos, rock art, and burials (Ferguson and Anyon 2002; Kuwanwisiwma 2004)? Clearly the 'Chaco Phenomenon' represents something larger and more complex than what is retained in Puebloan oral history, but where and how do we draw the lines between science and oral history? Should all of our interpretations ultimately derive from Hopi or other tribal oral history? Of course not. But where is the middle ground and is it always in the same place for each archaeological situation?

For now, I can offer no answers, but can only suggest that there is a serious problem wherein insensitivity is deeply ingrained in Southwest archaeology; to the extent that even our terminology and models, albeit unintentionally, continue to reflect our colonialist past. Add to this the ongoing problem of advertising ourselves as scholars by latching on to currently fashionable models and ideas to produce marketable dissertation or paper topics, and we have a recipe for perpetuating this insensitivity.

We have to ask ourselves as scholars of a past not our own if these fashionable ideas are ways of deriving realistic interpretations of the past or if they are ways to make a living in an expanding discipline that is tightly controlled by legislation and is increasingly competitive, as academic programs slash their budgets and eliminate positions. Perhaps the Southwest is, as A.V. Kidder long ago indicated, a 'sucked orange', leaving archaeologists no new information to discover, but rather only new ways to reprocess the same old data. I suggest that all of these forces are operating in the Southwest to some extent, as they undoubtedly are in the archaeologies of other culture areas. I am not, by the way, suggesting that the archaeologists promoting these models are intentionally trying to disrespect Native American beliefs. Instead, it seems that the contradictions between science and belief, between empiricism and respect will continue to play out in the discipline, as they undoubtedly should. I suggest here only that we be mindful of our subject matter and realize that the past we attempt to explain here in the Southwest is definitively not a Western past and is probably not knowable through explanations derived from the paradigms of Western science.

Given the current political climate in the post-NAGPRA era, it is only through the continued participation of archaeologists and the indigenous peoples we study that we will be able to survive as a discipline. With this in mind, there are several recent studies in southwestern archaeology that suggest that the situation is not entirely hopeless.

OTHER CONTEMPORARY APPROACHES AND THE ROLE OF ORAL TRADITION

> By respecting the value of Native American Oral traditions, archaeologists will lay a foundation for Native Americans to respect the values of scientific knowledge and for scientists to respect the values of oral traditions in ways that do not demean either approach to understanding the past. (Anyon *et al* 1997:85)

It is clear that not everything we as scientists wish to explain about the past will be found in the oral traditions of Native Americans, just as it is true that Western notions of time, space, and ideology are ill-suited to offer explanations of a Native American past. There are, however, places at which we can come together in our attempts.

Deriving from the post-processual critique (Hodder 1986; Shanks and Tilley 1987), several southwestern archaeologists have recently applied landscape approaches to understanding pre-Columbian material culture (Van Dyke 2000; Whittlesey 1998, 2003; Zedeno 2000).

The attractiveness of these approaches is that they inherently recognize the importance of place in the belief systems of southwestern cultures (Basso 1996). For example, the Hopis' belief in the footprints of their ancestors in the form of archaeological sites, shrines, and sacred landmarks (Ferguson and Anyon 2002) is not only accommodated by this type of approach, but provides the archaeologist a framework within which to understand and perhaps explain the distribution of archaeological sites in a given region, without resorting to Western notions of optimal foraging or managerial elite centers.

Tangentially related to the trend toward landscape archaeology in the Southwest is the revitalization of what can best be described as a direct-historical set of inquiries, not unlike those conducted by Cushing and Fewkes in the late 19th century (Willey and Sabloff 1993:57). I refer here to the growing importance of migration studies in the Southwest. Initially based on the writings of David Anthony (1990) who studied migration among Copper-Age populations around the Black Sea using a push-pull model derived from population geography, recent migration studies in the Southwest attempt to integrate the views of the Native American groups, whose migration history (footprints if you will) they seek to delineate (Bernardini 2002, 2005; Lyons 2003). Missing from these models are heavily Eurocentric notions and in their place are testable hypotheses about where the modern Puebloans believe they have come from, derived in large part from dialogs with living Pueblo informants and oral histories. If we recall from the discussion above Bernardini's (2005) reanalysis of Chavez Pass data, it is easy to see how archaeologists can build bridges between Western science and oral traditions.

CONCLUDING THOUGHTS

In closing, I recognize that we are still left with the question of how to address these conflicting ethical guidelines. If there were a single solution to the problem, then there would be no need to craft an essay such as this one. For now, I can only suggest that the beliefs of indigenous peoples are a good starting point – a place to discover ideas to be tested that are not foreign to our subjects. From here we can incorporate other ideas, but ideas that are respectful to those whose past we wish to discover. After all, archaeology is a probabilistic science and unless a particular approach to understanding the past has a high probability of being the only correct interpretation, why inflict it upon an indigenous past when other avenues may be available? Overall, the guidelines for proceeding should be informed by compassionate and inclusive explanations rather than by dispassionate objectification of the past.

REFERENCES

Anthony, DW (1990) 'Migration in archaeology: the baby and the bathwater', *American Anthropologist* 92, 895–914

Anyon, R, Ferguson, TJ, Jackson, L, Lane, L and Vicenti, P (1997) 'Native American oral tradition and archaeology: issues of structure, relevance, and respect', in Swindler, N, Dongoske, K, Anyon, R and Downer, A (eds), *Native Americans and Archaeologists: Stepping Stones to Common Ground*, Walnut Creek, CA: AltaMira Press

Basso, K (1996) *Wisdom Sits in Places*, Albuquerque: University of New Mexico Press

Bernardini, W (2002) 'The Gathering of clans: understanding ancestral Hopi migration and identity', unpublished PhD dissertation, Arizona State University

—— (2005) *Hopi Oral Tradition and the Archaeology of Identity*, Tucson: University of Arizona Press

Cordell, LS, Upham, S and Brock, SL (1987) 'Obscuring patterns in the archaeological record: a discussion from southwestern archaeology', *American Antiquity* 52, 565–577

Courlander, H (1971) *The Fourth World of the Hopis: The Epic Story of the Hopi Indians as Preserved in their Legends and Traditions*, Albuquerque: University of New Mexico Press

Downum, CE (1986) 'Potsherds, provenience, and ports of trade: a review of the evidence from Chavez Pass', paper presented at the Fourth Mogollon Conference, Tucson, Arizona

Feinman, GM, Lightfoot, KG and Upham, S (2000) 'Political hierarchies and organizational strategies in the Puebloan Southwest', *American Antiquity* 65, 449–470

Ferguson, TJ and Anyon, R (2002) 'Hopi and Zuni cultural landscapes: implications of history and scale for cultural resources management', in Weinstein, L (ed), *Native Peoples of the Southwest: Negotiating Land, Water, and Ethnicities*, Westport, CT: Bergen & Garvey

Fine-Dare, KS (2002) *Grave Injustice: The American Indian Repatriation Movement and NAGPRA*, Lincoln: University of Nebraska Press

Graves, MW (1987) 'Rending reality in archaeological analysis: a reply to Upham and Plog' *Journal of Field Archaeology* 14, 243–249

Gregory, DA (1987) 'The morphology of platform mounds and the structure of classic period Hohokam sites', in Doyel, DE (ed), *The Hohokam Village: Site Structure and Organization*, Glenwood Springs, CO, Southwestern and Rocky Mountain Division of the American Association for the Advancement of Science

Gregory, DA and Nials, FL (1985) 'Observations concerning the distribution of Classic Period Hohokam platform mounds', in Dittert, A and Dove D (eds), *Proceedings of the 1983 Hohokam Symposium*, Arizona Archaeological Society Occasional Paper 2, Phoenix

Herr, SA (2001) *Beyond Chaco: Great Kiva Communities on the Mogollon Rim Frontier*, Anthropological Papers of the University of Arizona 66, Tucson: University of Arizona

Hodder, I (1986) *Reading the Past: Current Approaches to Interpretation in Archaeology*, Cambridge: Cambridge University Press

Kuwanwisiwma, LJ (2004) 'Yupköyvi: The Hopi story of Chaco Canyon', in Noble, DG (ed) *In Search of Chaco: New Approaches to an Archaeological Enigma*, Santa Fe: SAR Press

LeBlanc, SA (1999) *Prehistoric Warfare in the American Southwest*, Salt Lake City: University of Utah Press

Lightfoot, KG (1984) *Prehistoric Political Dynamics: A Case Study from the American Southwest*, DeKalb: Northern Illinois University Press

Lyons, PD (2003) *Ancestral Hopi Migrations*, Anthropological Papers of the University of Arizona 68, Tucson: University of Arizona Press

McGuire, RH and Saitta, DJ (1996) 'Although they have petty captains, they obey them badly', *American Antiquity* 61, 197–217

Plog, FT (1985) 'Status and death at Grasshopper: the homogenization of reality', in Thompson, M, Garcia, MT and Kense, FJ (eds), *Status, Structure, and Stratification: Current Archaeological Reconstructions*, Calgary: University of Calgary

Plog, FT and Upham, S (1983) 'The Analysis of Prehistoric Political Organization', in Tooker, E and Fried, M (eds), *The Development of Political Organization in Native North America*, Washington, DC: American Ethnological Society

Reid, JJ (1999) 'The Grasshopper-Chavez Pass debate: existential dilemmas and archaeological discourse', in Whittlesey, SM (ed), *Sixty Years of Mogollon Archaeology: Papers from the Ninth Mogollon Conference, Silver City New Mexico, 1996*, Tucson: SRI Press

Reid, JJ, Schiffer, MB, Whittlesey, SM, Hinkes, MJ, Sullivan, AP, Downum, CE, Longacre, WA and Tuggle, HD (1989) 'Perception and interpretation in contemporary Southwestern Archaeology: comments on Cordell, Upham, and Brock', *American Antiquity* 54, 802–814

Reid, JJ and Whittlesey, SM (2005) *Thirty Years into Yesterday: A History of Archaeology at Grasshopper Pueblo*, Tucson: University of Arizona Press

Rice, GE (1990) 'Variability in the development of Classic Period elites', in Rice, G (ed), *A Design for Salado Research*, Roosevelt Monograph Series No. 1, Anthropological Field Studies No. 22, Tempe: Arizona State University

Riggs, CR (2005) 'Late Ancestral Pueblo or Mogollon Pueblo? an architectural perspective on identity', *Kiva* 70, 323–348

Shanks, M and Tilley, C (1987) *Re-Constructing Archaeology: Theory and Practice*, Cambridge: Cambridge University Press

Swentzell, R (2004) 'A Pueblo Woman's Perspective on Chaco Canyon', in Noble, DG (ed) *In Search of Chaco: New Approaches to an Archaeological Enigma*, Santa Fe: SAR Press

Turner, CG, II and Turner, JA (1999) *Man Corn: Cannibalism and Violence in the Prehistoric American Southwest*, Salt Lake City: University of Utah Press

Upham, S (1978) 'Final report on the archaeological investigations at Chavez Pass Ruin: the 1978 season', Manuscript on file at the Coconino National Forest, Flagstaff, Arizona

—— (1982) *Polities and Power: An Economic and Political History of the Western Pueblo*, New York: Academic Press

—— (1989) 'East meets West: hierarchy and elites in Pueblo society', in Upham S, Lightfoot, K and Jewett, R (eds), *The Sociopolitical Structure of Southwestern Societies*, Boulder: Westview Press

Upham, S and Plog, FT (1986) 'The interpretation of prehistoric political complexity in the central and northern Southwest', *Journal of Field Archaeology* 13, 223–238

Van Dyke, RM (2000) 'Chacoan ritual landscape: the view from Red Mesa Valley', in Kantner, J and Mahoney, NM (ed), *Great House Communities Across the Chacoan Landscape*, Anthropological Papers of the University of Arizona 64, Tucson: University of Arizona Press

Walker, WH (1993) 'Puebloan witchcraft and the archaeology of violence', paper presented at the annual meeting of the Society for American Archaeology, St Louis, April 18

Walters, H and Rogers, HC (2001) '"Anasazi" and "Anaasází": Two Words, Two Cultures', *Kiva* 66, 317–326

Webster's Dictionary of the English Language, 2nd Encarta Edition (2004), New York: Bloomsbury Press

White Deer, G (1997) 'Return of the sacred: spirituality and the scientific imperative', in Swindler, N, Dongoske, K, Anyon, R and Downer, A (eds), *Native Americans and Archaeologists: Stepping Stones to Common Ground*, Walnut Creek, CA: AltaMira Press

Whittlesey, SM (1998) 'Archaeological landscapes: a methodological and theoretical discussion', in Whittlesey, SM, Ciolek-Torrello, RS and Altschul, JH (eds), *Vanishing River: Landscapes and Lives of the Lower Verde River; The Lower Verde Archaeological Project*, Tucson: SRI Press

—— (2003) *Rivers of Rock: Stories from a Stone-Dry Land; Central Arizona Project Archaeology*, Tucson: SRI Press

Wilcox, DR (1991) 'Hohokam social complexity', in Crown, PL and Judge, WJ (eds), *Chaco and Hohokam: Prehistoric Regional Systems in the American Southwest*, Santa Fe: SAR Press

—— (1993) 'The evolution of the Chaco polity', in Malville, JM and Matlock, G (eds), *The Chimney Rock Archaeological Symposium*, USDA Forest Service General Technical Report RM-227, Fort Collins, CO: USDA Forest Service

Wilcox, DR and Haas, J (1994) 'The Scream of the Butterfly: Competition and Conflict in the Prehistoric Southwest', in Gumerman, G (ed), *Themes in Southwest Prehistory*, Santa Fe: SAR Press

Wilcox, DR, Robertson, G, and Wood, JS (2001) 'Organized for War: The Perry Mesa Settlement System and its Central Arizona Neighbors', in Rice, G and LeBlanc, S (eds), *Deadly Landscapes: Case Studies in Prehistoric Southwestern Warfare*, Salt Lake City: University of Utah Press

Willey, GR, and Sabloff, JA (1993) *A History of American Archaeology* (3rd edition), New York: Freeman Press

Zedeno, MN (2000) 'On what people make of places: a behavioral cartography', in Schiffer, MB (ed), *Social Theory in Archaeology*, Salt Lake City: University of Utah Press

Zimmerman, LJ (1997) 'Remythologizing the relationship between Indians and archaeologists', in Swindler, N, Dongoske, K, Anyon, R and Downer, A (eds), *Native Americans and Archaeologists: Stepping Stones to Common Ground*, Walnut Creek, CA: AltaMira Press

What Does It Mean 'To Give the Past Back to the People'? Archaeology and Ethics in the Postcolony

Nick Shepherd

Our earth is full of skeletons.
Breyten Breytenbach, Dog Heart: A Memoir (1999:21)

INTRODUCTION

I want to begin with a question that takes us to the heart of a tangled issue: What does it mean 'to give the past back to the people'? To ask this is to pose a question with an ethical slant. In the first place it raises an issue of ownership: In order to give the past back, it must first of all be yours to give. In the second place, it implies a conception of 'the people', who stand in a separate relationship to both the givers of the past and to 'the past' itself. In the third place, it raises the question of the format in which the past is to be returned. The 'pastness' of the past means that that which is to be returned is not the thing-in-itself but something standing in for the past, usually through a metaphoric or metonymic relation: a set of texts, a pile of bones, a patch of ground, a body of memories, certain rituals of enactment. More generally, to frame one's practice in terms of a wish 'to give the past back to the people' implies a proprietorial attitude towards the past. When uttered by an archaeologist it implies notions of 'stewardship' of the 'archaeological record', and connects us with a set of phrases and intentions which have become part of a commonplace language for discussions of ethics in archaeology: to 'build bridges', to 'consult stakeholders' and 'descendant communities', to recover 'hidden histories', to 'democratise the past'.

As an opening move in thinking ethically about archaeology in the postcolony, I want to suggest that many of these formulations need to be placed in doubt. In a paradoxical way (paradoxical because they seem to be well intentioned), they set limits on ethical action, obscure more than they reveal, excuse forms of unreflexive behaviour and dis-enable certain types of engagement. More particularly, they elide key questions of ownership and agency. In the case of my starting formu-lation, the wish 'to give the past back to the people' frequently over-looks the telling of a prior story of dispossession. By placing 'the people' in the passive relation of the receivers of a gift of 'their past', it also elides the alternative possibility, that they may wish actively to take it back. Furthermore, that they may wish to repossess their (mul-tiple) pasts in forms unanticipated by the limiting discourse of cul-tural resource management.

My case study concerns the exhumation of an early colonial burial ground in central Cape Town, South Africa, in 2003–2004. It makes a useful study for the purposes of thinking through issues of ethics in archaeology. Not only has it been the most publicly contested instance of archaeological work in South Africa in the period since 1994, but South Africa itself has historically been an important site for thinking through the issue of ethical action in archaeology, most significantly in the events around the formation of the World Archaeological Congress in the mid-1980s (Ucko 1987). More generally, the events of my case study have their unfolding in the context of a prevailing debate in post-apartheid society around issues of truth, reconciliation and restitution, at the heart of which lie a number of fundamentally ethical questions: How do we atone for the wrongs of the past? What is a just basis for the formation of a common society which includes perpetrators, victims and beneficiaries?

TIME-LINE PRESTWICH STREET: MAY 2003–JULY 2004

Green Point is a part of Cape Town strategically located between the central business district and the new waterfront development at Cape Town's harbour. For much of the 17th and 18th centuries, it lay outside the formal boundaries of the settlement, a marginal zone which was the site of the gallows and place of torture (situated on a prominent sand dune). It was also the site of a number of graveyards, including the graveyards of the Dutch Reformed Church and the military, and of numerous undocumented, informal burials. Those buried outside the official burial grounds would have made up a cross-section of the underclasses of colonial Cape Town: slaves, free blacks, artisans, fish-ermen, sailors, maids, washerwomen and their children, as well as executed criminals, suicide deaths, paupers, and unidentified victims of shipwrecks (Hart 2003). In the 1820s Green Point was subdivided and sold as real estate, in time becoming part of the densely built urban core. In the late 1960s and early 1970s black and Coloured residents of Green Point were forcibly removed and relocated to the bleak townships of the Cape Flats (a series of events which have entered popular imagination via the fate of the residents of District Six, on the other side of the city). Green Point is currently undergoing a process of rapid gentrification, driven by skyrocketing property prices. For many former residents this means that even as the political space has opened up in which they might reacquire property in the city centre, so they face new forms of economic exclusion.

In mid-May 2003, in the course of construction activities at a city block in Green Point bordered by Prestwich Street, human bones were discovered. The developer notified the South African Heritage Resources Agency (SAHRA) in accordance with the newly passed National Heritage Resources Act (Act No. 25 of 1999), and construction was halted. Also in terms of the Act, the developer appointed the Archaeology Contracts Office (ACO), a University of Cape Town (UCT) affiliated contract archaeology unit to do the archaeological investigation. The ACO applied for and was issued a permit by SAHRA for a 'rescue exhumation of human remains'. The act provides for a 60-day notification period and for a public consultation process. Antonia Malan, a UCT-based historical archaeologist, was appointed to run the public consultation process, which she did in the name of the Cultural Sites and Resources Forum (CSRF), an advocacy organisation with a track record of involvement in heritage issues.

On 11 June, exhumation of the bodies began. Seven weeks later, on 29 July, a public meeting was held at St Stephen's Church in central Cape Town. At this point the remains of approximately 500 individuals had been exhumed. Most bodies were shallowly buried, without grave markers or coffins. Earlier burials were intercut by later ones. The site was fenced with wire-link fencing and was open to public view. Estimates of the total number of bodies stood at 1,000 (up from an initial estimate of 200), on the 1,200-square-metre site. In the mean time, a Special Focus Reference Group (SFRG) had been set up, mainly of UCT-based archaeologists and human biologists. Malan and the SFRG framed the agenda for the public meeting in terms of consultations regarding the relocation of the bodies and the memorialisation of the site. Judith Sealy, an archaeologist in the SFRG, presented a proposal in which she envisaged reinterment of the bodies 'in individual caskets, in a crypt or mausoleum'. This would be a place where 'one could honour the dead' while allowing 'access to the skeletons for careful, respectful, scientific study, by bona fide researchers' (Sealy 2003).

The response was immediate, vociferous and angry. The minutes of the meeting record '[a] general feeling of dissatisfaction, disquiet and disrespect' (Various 2003a). Questions were asked as to why the demolition permit had been approved without the requirement of an archaeological survey, why the exhumations had continue through the 60-day notification period, and why the first public meeting had come so late in the process. Opposition to the exhumations came from several quarters: community leaders, many of whom had been active in the struggle against apartheid; Christian and Muslim spiritual leaders; academics from the historically black University of the Western Cape; heritage-sector NGOs; and Khoisan representatives. Zuleiga Worth, who identifies herself as a Muslim Capetonian, said, 'I went to school at Prestwich Street Primary School. We grew up with haunted places; we lived on haunted ground. We knew there were burial grounds there. My question to the City is, how did this happen?' The minutes also record comments by a number of unnamed individuals:

> Woman at back: On what basis does SAHRA decide on exhumation? Issues of African morality and African rights...
>
> Man in green shirt: Developer contacted SAHRA and did marketing strategy for this evening. I don't buy these ideas... Archaeologists can go elsewhere to dig...
>
> Rob (Haven Shelter [a night shelter for homeless people]): Many questions come from black people who hang around the site. Why are white people, and white women, scratching in our bones? This is sacrilege...
>
> Zenzile Khoisan, leaving hall: Stop robbing graves – stop robbing graves! (Various 2003a)

On 1 August 2003, SAHRA announced an 'interim cessation' of archaeological activity on the site until 18 August, to allow for a wider process of public consultation. This was later extended to 31 August. On 16 August the CSRF convened a second public meeting, and also collected submissions by telephone, email and fax (Various 2003b). Just over 100 submissions were collected. Mavis Smallberg from Robben Island Museum said 'my strong suggestion is to cover up the graves ... Apart [from] the recently renamed Slave Lodge, there is no other public space that respectfully marks or memorialises the presence of slaves and the poor in Cape Town society ... Only scientists are going to benefit from picking over these bones – of what purpose and use is it to the various communities to which the dead belong to know what they ate 150 years ago or where they came from?' Imam Davids wrote on behalf of the Retreat Muslim Forum to say '[we] view the work and approach of the CSRF, based at UCT, with dismay ...'

Kerry Ward, a historian from Rice University, proposed the transformation of the Slave Lodge into a museum of slavery with an archaeological laboratory: 'I think it would be fascinating to have a working archaeological laboratory in view of the public, perhaps with glass-fronted laboratories, where the public can watch ongoing research as it takes place'. The Slave Lodge is one of the oldest buildings in Cape Town, and was originally constructed to house the slaves of the Dutch East India Company. During the apartheid period it was converted into the South African Cultural History Museum, a shrine to settler histories at the Cape (indigenous pasts were represented up the road at the Natural History Museum). Adolph Faro was among a number of people who phoned in with '[stories] of bones when [he was a] schoolboy at Prestwich Primary'. A comment by the UCT-based human biologist Alan Morris is logged as follows: 'Members of public/prominent academics (especially UWC) suggested development stop and site is made into memorial. They have totally misjudged the reason for having a public process. NOT opportunity to control development of the city, but IS opportunity to join process of memorialisation ... don't let pseudo-politicians benefit at [the expense of the people of Cape Town]' (Malan 2003).

The developer submitted a report to the CSRF, via the project facilitator, Andre van der Merwe, 'to provide the developmental perspective'. Many of the luxury apartments that comprised the residential development had been pre-sold. At the time of commencement of construction, R21 million' worth of sales contracts had been concluded and were at risk due to the delay. As well as carrying the costs of the delay, the developer was also paying for the archaeological work and the public consultation process. The report expressed the hope for 'a sensible solution' (van der Merwe 2003).

On 9 August, the synod of the Cape Town diocese of the Anglican Church, under the leadership of Archbishop Njongonkulu Ndungane, the successor to Desmond Tutu, unanimously passed a resolution condemning the exhumations and calling for the 'appropriate institutions and organisations to be guided by African values and customs with regard to exhumations, burials and cemeteries', and for '[our] government, through its heritage agency ... to maintain the integrity of the site as that of a cemetery'. On 25 August the CSRF submitted their final report to SAHRA on the public consultation process. Between 25 and 29 August, SAHRA convened a series of 'Special Focus Group' meetings with 'interested and affected groups'. According to the minutes, a meeting with UCT-based 'archaeologists and academics' was 'fuelled by strong sentiment about the public's perception of archaeology. The point was raised that the public seemed to think all archaeologists wanted to do was to dig up bones ... [It was felt that this] was part of the perception and general sentiment that demonized the discipline' (SAHRA 2003). At a meeting with the Cape Metropolitan Council, it emerged that the delegation of powers between SAHRA and the City was in question, and that the City was 'acting illegally on some of [its] duties' (SAHRA 2003b).

On 29 August, SAHRA convened a third public meeting at St Andrew's Church in Green Point 'to wind up the public participation process' (SAHRA 2003a). The verbatim transcript of the meeting records a number of comments from the floor. An unnamed respondent said: 'There is this kind of sense that it is a *fait accompli*. There were 60 days. The 60 days are over, now it's will the developer be kind enough to us. Now to me this is not about the developer. This is about those people lying there and the people that were part, historically, of that community ... [The interests of the developer] must be of secondary importance. The same with the archaeologists as well ... [T]hey have a social responsibility first before they have a responsibility towards the developer'.

Another respondent said,

> [T]here are multiple implications for this burial ground and its naked openness in the centre of the city... Genocide is about the destruction of memory. The destruction of memory involves the destruction of all possible connections to even established family trees... Now I think that in this city there's never been a willingness to take up that issue as part of a project of centuries long that was about... destruction of human communities that were brought from across the globe... This is an opportunity to get to the bottom of that and time means different things to different people, institutions, stakeholders. Time for the dead – we need to consider what that means. (SAHRA 2003a:17–18)

Michael Wheeder, who was later to play a central role in the Hands Off Prestwich Street Ad Hoc Committee, said:

> Many of us of slave descent cannot say 'here's my birth certificate'. We are part of the great unwashed of Cape Town... The black people, we rush into town on the taxis and we need to rush out of town. At a time many decades ago we lived and loved and laboured here. Nothing [reminds us of that history] ... and so leave [the site] as a memorial to Mr. Gonzalez that lived there, Mrs. de Smidt that lived there. The poor of the area – the fishermen, the domestic workers, the people that swept the streets here. Memorialise that. Leave the bones there... That is a site they have owned for the first time in their lives *het hulle stukkie grond* (they have a little piece of ground). Leave them in that ground. Why find now in the gentility of this new dispensation a place which they have no connection with? (SAHRA 2003a:18–19)

Mongezi Guma, one of the facilitators of the meeting, said in his closing remarks: 'How do we deal with the intangibles of people's lives that were wasted? ... [This is not just about] an individual or family. It is not just about that. It is about people who got thrown away literally... I'm trying to move SAHRA away from simply a legalistic decision'.

On 1 September, despite a clear weight of opinion opposed to the exhumations at the third public meeting, Pumla Madiba, the CEO of SAHRA, announced a resumption of archaeological work at the site. In a statement to the press, she said: 'Out of respect the skeletons will be moved … Many of the people who objected were highly emotional and did not give real reasons why the skeletons should not be relocated' (Kassiem 2003). A feature of the period leading up to the announcement appears to have been a growing anxiety on the part of SAHRA over the cost of expropriation, and the possibility of legal action on the part of the developer. A leaked internal memo to SAHRA's Archaeology, Palaeontology, Meteorite and Heritage Object Committee (the permit-issuing committee in this case) expresses the concern that, should the site be conserved as a heritage site it would have 'disastrous consequences for the developer who will presumably appeal against the decision and may instigate litigation against SAHRA and the city'. The committee is informed that it is 'imperative that a responsible decision be made by SAHRA and the city … The matter is urgent, as the apartments in the development have been presold and every delay means that the expenses are increasing' (PPPC 2003).

On 4 September, the Hands Off Prestwich Street Ad Hoc Committee (HOC) was launched. At this point opposition to the exhumations shifted outside the officially mandated process of public consultation, to civic society and the politics of mass action. On 12 September, the Hands Off Committee lodged an appeal with SAHRA calling for a halt to the exhumations and 'a full and extended process of community consultation'. The appeal document notes that '[for] a large section of Cape Town's community, whose existence and dignity has for so long been denied, the discovery and continued preservation of the Prestwich Street burial ground can symbolically restore their memory and identity'. It continues: '[The] needs of archaeology as a science seem to have been given precedence over other needs: the needs of community socio-cultural history, of collective remembering and of acknowledging the pain and trauma related to the site and this history that gave rise to its existence'. In opposing the exhumations it argues that '[exhumation] makes impossible a whole range of people's identifications with that specific physical space in the city. Such a removal echoes, albeit unintentionally, the apartheid regime's forced removals from the same area' (Various 2003c).

The 23rd of October was set as the date for a tribunal hearing to consider the appeal. In the run up to the hearing, the Hands Off Committee organised regular candlelit vigils at the Prestwich Street site on Sunday evenings. A billboard was erected outside St George's Cathedral, a symbolic site of anti-apartheid protest, with the slogan: 'Stop the exhumations! Stop the desecration!' Lunchtime pickets were held in the city centre. On 19 November the SAHRA-convened Appeals Committee handed down a written ruling. The excavation permit awarded to the ACO was revalidated and the rights of the developer upheld. The Hands Off Committee reconvened as the Prestwich Place

Project Committee to launch an appeal directly to the Minister of Arts and Culture. A letter of appeal was lodged with the Ministry on 12 January 2004. Supporting documents call upon the Minister to expropriate the site and 'to conserve Prestwich Place as a National Heritage Site' and a site of conscience (PPPC 2003). By this stage all of the human remains on the original site had been exhumed and were in temporary storage in Napier House, a building on the adjacent block, itself to be demolished as part of the Prestwich Place development. During the SAHRA appeal process, the ACO had applied for permits to disinter human remains believed to occur under West Street and the adjacent block containing Napier House. This was expected to result in the exposure of a further 800 to 1000 bodies.

On 21 April 2004 – Freedom Day in South Africa – the remains were ceremonially transferred from Napier House to the mortuary of Woodstock Day Hospital, on the other side of the city. Some of the bones were carried in procession through the city centre in 11 flag-draped boxes, one for each of the official language groups in the country. Muslim, Christian and Jewish religious leaders blessed the remains in a ceremony at the site prior to the procession. The *Cape Times* of 30 April 2004 reports frustration among researchers interested in the bones. The pending minister's tribunal was preventing them 'from beginning anthropological studies to work out the demographic information of each skeleton'. It quotes Jacqui Friedling, a physical and forensic anthropology doctoral student: 'It's become politicised and because of that there have been unnecessary delays... Science is held captive until these two groups can sort out their problems' (Neuwahl 2004).

On 22 July, the developer was informed that the appeal to the minister had been dismissed. Terry Lester of the PPPC was reported to be 'deeply saddened'. He said, 'We're acting the whore in this instance, bowing down to the god of development and selling a segment of our history' (Gosling 2004).

'HIDDEN HISTORIES' AND RIVAL LANGUAGES OF CONCERN

Clearly the events around the Prestwich Street exhumations constitute a complex playing out of social and political interests, forces, values and ideas. Coming 10 years after the democratic transition of 1994, they serve to capture many of the conflicts and debates in post-apartheid society, to explore its fault lines, to point up its unresolved tensions and antagonisms. There are a number of ways of framing these events, although in keeping with the complexity of post-apartheid contexts, each needs to be qualified and explained. At one level they appear as a conflict between the forces of memory and the forces of modernisation, development and urban renewal. At another level they appear as a conflict between the forces of civil society, expressed through People's Power and the politics of mass action, and various state agencies and institutions of governance (SAHRA, Heritage Western Cape, the Office of the Minister). At one point in the third public meeting, Pumla Madiba, CEO of SAHRA, said, 'I think we are moving slowly away from the culture of mass meetings and rallies. We are getting into dealing with issues head-on'.

A third way of characterising the conflict would be in terms of a dispute over the role of the sciences in post-apartheid society. In fact, it was not so much pro- or anti-science (as some of the protagonists suggested), as a dispute over notions of social accountability in the sciences, and the different interests for whom knowledge is produced. A feature of the Prestwich Street dispute was the manner in which this was expressed as conflict between universities (the historically white University of Cape Town versus the historically black University of the Western Cape), and between disciplines (archaeology versus history). A full account of these oppositions would need to take on board the different institutional histories of the two universities, and the different historical trajectories of the disciplines of archaeology and history in South Africa. A key difference between these disciplinary histories has been the relative openness of part of the discipline of history to engaging with prevailing social and political contexts, whether through the Marxist and revisionist histories of the 1970s, the People's History movement of the 1980s, or the strong public history school which emerged in the 1990s.

A notable feature of the research process around Prestwich Street is what we might call the 'archaeologising' of the remains. Particularly notable was the absence of social historians on the SFRG, and the lack of systematic oral historical research despite the obvious leads given by Zuleiga Worth and others who spoke of their memories of growing up in the area. More generally, discussions of the scholarly and scientific value of the burial site were consistently framed in terms of the archaeological and physical anatomical value of the human remains, just as it was archaeologists who were invited to give expert opinion, write proposals and sit on panels and platforms.

A fourth way of framing the events is in terms of issues of race and identity, and of local, regional and national concerns and interests. It is relevant, for example, that nearly all of the archaeologists working on the site and involved in the public consultation process, as well as nearly all of the members of the SFRG and key facilitators from the CSRF, are white. It is also relevant that the majority of the members of the Hands Off Committee and the Prestwich Place Projects Committee are Coloured (to use an apartheid racial designation denoting a complex amalgamation of *mestizo* identities with the descendants of Khoisan groups, people imported as slaves from the Dutch possessions at Batavia, and others), and that the CEO of SAHRA and the Minister of Arts and Culture are black (or African, to use a current designation)[1]. However, rather than finding in these events a simple fable of racial antagonism, I would argue that they represent a complex convergence between slave histories, Coloured identities, and regional 'Cape' politics on the one hand, in tension with national heritage priorities articulated in terms of 'Africanisation' and accounts of essentialised black African cultural histories, on the other. It is the kind of complexity in which the New South Africa abounds, and which has seen the convergence between new (black) and historical (white) elites, and the continuing marginalisation of black and Coloured working classes, as was arguably the case at Prestwich Street.

Ethically speaking, there are a number of ways of framing the events around the Prestwich Street exhumations. In the first place they might be framed in terms of an ethico-legal concern with the nature of the legislation governing archaeology and heritage practice. Approached from this perspective, the events reveal key areas of weakness in the legislation. The first is the provision whereby the developer pays the costs of the archaeological work and the public consultation process, a practice which embeds a conflict of interest in the process (at least from the perspective of the archaeological contractor). The second is a lack of detail in the legislation around the nature and extent of the public consultation process, and of the procedures to be followed in the case of deadlock. Rival interpretations of the requirements of the public consultation process lay at the heart of the appeals mounted by the Hands Off Committee (even – or especially – the language differs; it is notable how what is framed as a public 'consultation' process by the pro-exhumation lobby, becomes in the hands of the anti-exhumation lobby, a public 'participation' process).

A third area of concern is the requirement that interested parties demonstrate 'direct descent' in order to play a meaningful role in the fate of a human burial. In the violently socially disruptive contexts of colonialism and apartheid, one of whose effects was to break ties between settled communities of people and a given landscape (including sites of burial), and in the context of the selective nature of the colonial archive, the possibilities of demonstrating direct descent are severely curtailed for whole classes of people. Moreover, it is precisely the most marginalised, disadvantaged and at risk, those who are arguably most in need of restitution and legal protection who – by definition – have the least chance of demonstrating direct descent. In the case of the Prestwich Street exhumations, this was no abstract set of disruptions. Apartheid-forced removals, as recently as the late 1960s and early 1970s, served substantially to disrupt any sense of community identification with the site, just as they served to fragment and disperse a community of memory.

A further way of approaching these events is from the point of view of existing ethical guidelines and statements of best practice within the discipline of archaeology itself. One of the striking features of the long and contested process of archaeological work at the site, and of the many press releases and official statements from SAHRA, UCT, the CSRF and from individual archaeologists and contractors is the absence of reference to internationally accepted protocols and statements of best practice regarding the archaeological treatment of human burials (the Vermillion Accord and the World Archaeological Congress's First Code of Ethics are cases in point), and of comparative legislation and statements of ethics (like NAGPRA, and the many statements of ethics of professional archaeological bodies). Even more striking in its way was the absence of reference on the part of archaeologists to probably the most directly comparable case study internationally, the African Burial Ground in New York, even though – in another of the ironic conjunctures attached to the case – the reinterment of bodies from the African Burial Ground coincided in time with the disinterment of bodies from the Prestwich Street site.

In fact, what I want to do, ethically speaking, is more particular. That is, to situate these events in the context of the emergence of what we might term rival languages of concern. Through the course of events at Prestwich Street, a clear polarisation emerges, with those arguing for exhumations doing so on the basis of the scientific value of the remains as a source to access 'hidden histories'. The proposal circulated by the SFRG at the first public meeting states: 'These skeletons are also – literally – our history, the ordinary people of Cape Town, whose lives are not written in the official documents of the time. They did not leave possessions or archives. If we want to recover their history, then one of the most powerful ways to do so is through the study of their skeletons' (Sealy 2003). In this case the semantic slide from 'our history' to 'their history' is instructive precisely in that it elides issues of agency and ownership. A number of tropes emerged and were recycled by archaeologists throughout the process. At the second public meeting, Belinda Mutti argued in favour of exhumation 'to give history back to the people'. Liesbet Schiettecatte argued that '[leaving] bones leaves information unknown. Studying them brings them back to life ...' Mary Patrick argued to '[continue the] exhumation – otherwise half a story is being told' (Various 2003b). At a public level this desire to 'give history back to the people' and 'bring the bones to life' was mediated by the technical discourse of cultural resource management, with its rituals of 'public consultation', and its circumscribed notions of value, need and interest. The double valency given to notions of 'respect' and 'dignity' by SAHRA and others had its counterpart in a pragmatic language focused on 'real issues', 'responsible decisions', and the fact that 'life must go on'.

In opposition to this discourse, the Hands Off Committee emphasised the language of memory and personal reminiscence. They sought to articulate an alternative set of values (African values, spiritual values) and alternative notions of space and time (the notion of the site as a heritage site or a site of conscience; and in one memorable intervention, the notion of 'time for the dead'). They insisted on recalling a more recent past of apartheid and forced removals, as well as a deep past of slavery and colonialism. More generally, they sought to insert the events at Prestwich Street into a prevailing debate in post-apartheid society around notions of truth, reconciliation and restitution (a debate which had its most public expression in the workings of the Truth and Reconciliation Commission). If the aim of the first language of concern was closure and containment, then the second aimed at openness. The events became a 'learning moment' (as the Hands Off Committee put it), potentially an opportunity to reconfigure public space in the city and to articulate new identities based on the recall of shared histories.

Building on this, it is possible to observe a number of instructive convergences in the events around Prestwich Street. The first is a convergence between the practices of troping that I have described and a positivist conception of archaeology as science, resulting in the production of observable data and 'information'. The notion of history that emerges – the history that is to be 'given back to the people' – becomes severely curtailed, as essentially archaeological data relating to the provenience of the burials and physical, chemical and anthropometric measurements of the bones themselves. A second convergence is between the discourse of cultural resource management and a political strategy of containment. Particularly instructive in this case, I would argue, was the manner in which the language and practices of CRM actively discouraged the emergence of radically new identities and refigurings of the public sphere, through a narrowed conception of need, interest, value, and the mechanics of public participation. The notion of 'heritage' that emerges is itself narrowed and ambivalent, internally divided between the promise of individual restitution and reconciliation, and the practice of restricted access and bureaucratised control.

Each of the protagonists in the events around Prestwich Street can be understood to have acted out of a complex mix of motivations and interests, framed in terms of these rival languages of concern. Understanding the position taken by the majority of archaeologists in this dispute means understanding something of the deep historical divide between archaeology and society in South Africa. Two episodes are of particular relevance in this regard. The first was the shift in the late 1960s and early 1970s towards Americanist archaeological theory, and the New Archaeology in particular. Coinciding with a period of economic growth in South Africa and the rapid creation of jobs within the discipline, the conception of archaeology as a 'hard' science, consciously distanced from the distractions of politics and society, was key to reconciling the potentially explosive nature of its subject matter with its position as part of the cultural apparatus of a modernised apartheid state (Shepherd 2003). Martin Hall has shown how the archaeology of the Southern African Iron Age, substantially accomplished around this time, was tightly packaged in a technical language which effectively placed it out of reach of African Nationalist and liberationalist idealogues (Hall 1990).

The second significant shift was the advent of cultural resource management and 'contract archaeology' in the late 1980s in South African archaeological circles, and its embrace as 'the future of South African archaeology' (as Hilary Deacon put it in an editorial in the *South African Archaeological Bulletin*) (Deacon 1988). This meant that archaeology entered the period of social and political upheaval of the 1990s with a ready-made conception of 'archaeological heritage', and a technical – and apparently neutral – language for conceptualising the relation between archaeology and society. One of the effects of this shift was to entrench an already established division between the discipline of archaeology and a prevailing lively set of discussions around public history, popular memory and reconceptualised notions of social accountability. Given this history, the considerable contemporary fallout from the events around the Prestwich Street exhumations is, first and foremost, a testimony to the failure of the discipline to engage. South African archaeology finds itself limited – I would say fundamentally limited – not only by a tradition of unaccountable practice, but also by the failure to develop an adequate conception of the relation between science and society, or the demands and dynamics of scholarship in a context of social transformation.

CONCLUSION

If we understand ethical practice to involve, in its deepest sense, a thoroughgoing notion of social accountability, then the central requirement for an ethical archaeology in the postcolony becomes clear. That is, to think through the relation between archaeology and society in all of the complexity and detail demanded by its context, and to develop forms of practice adequate to this conceptualisation. Not 'to give the past back to the people', 'to tell the full story', 'to bring the bones to life', but more modestly: to give to the discipline an adequate conception of its own history; to not stand in the way of public negotiations around heritage, access and social accountability; to agree to revisit unexamined notions of science and society; to acknowledge the validity of rival claims to the sanctity and significance of the remains of the dead; to agree to give up a little after having benefited from so much.

While I was revising this paper for publication, I received in the mail a brochure for the new upmarket residential development to be located on the Prestwich Street site. *The Rockwell* (as it is to be called) will consist of 103 'New York-style apartments', priced in the range R950,000 to R3,5 million. In the words of the brochure: 'Situated in trendy De Waterkant, *The Rockwell* will be one of the most impressive architectural statements in Cape Town, infusing the surrounding area with heart and soul ... The feeling is upmarket. The lifestyle is cosmopolitan. The crowd is young and trendy' (Anon. 2005). With a design approach described as 'a mix of old-school character and modern free-thought', the most overt historical point of reference is New York's jazz era of the 1920s and '30s. This is because, the brochure explains, '[at] the turn of the previous century they did design right. Not only because it was classical in form and function. Not only because it was the birth of a new age and an explosion of fresh ideas. But because they did it with soul. It was the beginning of a new era ... And with this era came the music, the freedom of spirit and the romanticism. It is in this spirit that *The Rockwell* was conceived' (Anon. 2005). The images that accompany this editorial form a kind of pastiche of the young, the trendy and the cosmopolitan – Moet and Chandom champagne, espresso coffee, sushi, a gleaming health club, and a hot tub – all of it (one assumes) a long way from Mr Gonzalez and Mrs Smidt and *hulle stukkie grond*.

How are we to make sense of this? Postmodern irony? The kind of playfulness and pastiche that follows from a global free-for-all? Certainly there is a strand of Cultural Studies that would attempt to validate such imaginings, or at least take them seriously as signs of a new historical freedom and consumer choice. In fact, in telling the story of Prestwich Street I want to suggest that we need to resort to a prior language of global capital manipulations and structural inequalities, a language more in tune with the intention of this book. In my reading it is difficult to see *The Rockwell* and its cynical cancellation of prior histories as anything other than a catastrophic failure for heritage management and discourses of reconciliation and restitution in post-apartheid society. For South African archaeology, the challenges all lie ahead.

ACKNOWLEDGMENTS

My thanks are due to a number of people for assistance in the research process: Noeleen Murray for frequent, enlightening discussions; Antonia Malan for making available the archive of the Cultural Sites and Resources Forum; Ciraj Rasool for drawing my attention to the 'archaeologising' of research at Prestwich Street; and Janine Dunlop for her exemplary research assistance. Financial support was received from the National Research Foundation and the Project on Public Pasts.

NOTE

1. It should be noted that each of these terms is contested and carries a specific history of usage and denotation. My distaste for the practices of racial classification and my understanding that notions of race are bankrupt as social scientific designations is weighed against the fact that history forces these terms on us as analytical categories in the present context.

REFERENCES

Anon. (2005) *The Rockwell: Luxury De Waterkant Living*, Cape Town: Dogon Gavrill Properties

Deacon, HJ (1988) 'Guest editorial: What future has archaeology in South Africa?', *South African Archaeological Bulletin* 43, 3–4.

Gosling, M (2004) 'Exhumation of Prestwich Street skeletons has been given go-ahead, says developer', *Cape Times*, 23 July, p. 1

Hall, M (1990) '"Hidden history": Iron Age archaeology in Southern Africa', in Robertshaw, P (ed), *A History of African Archaeology*, London: James Currey

Hart, T (2003) *Heritage Impact Assessment of West Street and Erf 4721 Green Point, Cape Town*. Prepared for Styleprops 120 (Pty) Ltd, December 2003, Cape Town: University of Cape Town

Kassiem, AE (2003) 'Slaves' skeletons to be relocated', *Cape Times*, 3 September, p. 6

Malan, A (2003) Prestwich Place: Exhumation of Accidentally Discovered Burial Ground in Green Point, Cape Town [Permit no. 80/03/06/001/51]: Public Consultation Process 9 June to 18 August 2003. Cape Town: Cultural Sites and Resources Forum

Neuwahl, J (2004) 'Prestwich Place bones could provide a "whole mixed bag of answers" say scientists', *Cape Times*, 30 April

PPPC (2003) *Submission to DAC Tribunal*, Cape Town: Prestwich Place Project Committee

SAHRA (2003a) *Minutes of South African Heritage Resources Agency Public Consultation Meeting held on 29th August 2003 at St Andrew's Presbyterian Church, Somerset Rd, Green Point Cape Town*, Cape Town: South African Heritage Resources Agency

—— (2003b) *Minutes. Prestwich Place Burial Ground: Meeting between SAHRA, HWC, City Council and Department of Public Works*, Cape Town: South African Heritage Resources Agency

—— (2003c) *Minutes. Prestwich Place Burial Site: Meeting with Archaeologists and Academics*, Cape Town: South African Heritage Resources Agency

Sealy, J (2003) *A Proposal for the Future of the Prestwich Street Remains*, Cape Town: University of Cape Town

Shepherd, N (2003) 'State of the discipline: science, culture and identity in South African archaeology, 1870–2003,' *Journal of Southern African Studies* 29, 823–44

Ucko, PJ (1987) *Academic Freedom and Apartheid: The Story of the World Archaeological Congress*, London: Duckworth

van der Merwe, A (2003) *Report submitted as part of the Public Submission Process, August 2003*, Cape Town

Various (2003a) *Minutes of first public meeting held at St Stephen's Church, Riebeeck Square, Cape Town on 29 July 2003*, Cape Town: Cultural Sites and Resources Forum, University of Cape Town

—— (2003b) *Minutes of second public meeting held at Alexander Sinton High School, Crawford on 16 August 2003*, Cape Town: Cultural Sites and Resources Forum, University of Cape Town

—— (2003c) *Substantiation of Appeal submitted by the Hands Off Prestwich Street ad hoc committee*, Cape Town: Hands Off Prestwich Street ad hoc committee

PART 3

ARCHAEOLOGY IN CAPITALISM, ARCHAEOLOGY AS CAPITALISM

Philip Duke

This section focuses on the inevitable nexus between capitalist practice and contemporary archaeology. Although the discipline has since its inception been embedded in Western ideology and by extension Western capitalism, global economic – as well as ideological – changes that have occurred since the collapse of the Warsaw Pact (some of them to the point that capitalism is viewed by many as the *only* economic system now viable) have sharpened the effects of capitalist practice on how archaeology is conducted, on who conducts it, and on what sort of past is ultimately produced. The papers in this section examine the sharpening of this relationship and what it means, not at the level of abstract theorising, but rather for the active production and consumption of archaeological knowledge. A number of themes are explored by the authors of this section.

The first theme concerns the marketing of archaeology within a capitalist economic context. The roots of this run deep in the discipline, as Alice Kehoe's paper makes abundantly clear. Kehoe shows that archaeology, from the Renaissance onward, has been deeply implicated in providing a past that would charter and legitimise global capitalist expansion. Archaeology in the service of the state is not something that just happened. It is what we have always been about; some of us are just better at ignoring that essential fact than others. As Kehoe points out, the marketing of heritage had many ethical problems, and not just in the use of archaeological knowledge to sell Las Vegas casinos. Even in situations that would at first blush avoid what Kehoe calls the 'pandering to vulgar partialities', such as the marketing of indigenous archaeology through tribal museums, etc., we are not home free. For, as Kehoe points out, the very idea of marketing an indigenous group's past is permeated with Western ideology, since the concepts of museums and archaeology itself are not indigenous to First Nations. Tamima Mourad's chapter is a sobering and frankly frightening exposé not just of how Near Eastern archaeology has since its inception been inculcated in the imperialist project of that region (Breasted's archaeological work was both archaeological and virtually military in nature), but also how archaeologists were part of the invasion and occupying forces currently in Iraq. Mourad forces us to ask whether such archaeologists can legitimately claim the rights and protections of *civilians* when they are so actively involved in military ventures.

The second theme explores the nature of the relationship between capitalism and the (mis)representation of the past at publicly accessible archaeological sites and museums. As Neil Asher Silberman points out in his chapter, the last 25 years have seen the radical transformation of the physical structures of public presentation at the very time when academic archaeology has increasingly concerned itself with issues of ideology, multivocality and narrative representation. Silberman's point is that these sites have become so entangled into local, national and global economic systems that their traditional role as public educational tools has become subordinate to their economic potential as venues for leisure-time entertainment. Archaeologists often primarily play the role of content providers and run the risk of losing *control* of these sites altogether. Silberman's paper implicitly asks us whether we can have it both ways – both to be supported by 'economically sustainable' heritage and to remain aloof from active critique and/or involvement with this economically driven process. He concludes that archaeologists, as individuals and as a discipline, must begin actively to acknowledge the potency of market forces and capital investment in the transformation of the historical landscape.

A naked example of the (mis)representation of the past is provided by Helaine Silverman's analysis of two museums in Cuzco, Peru, each one of them purportedly narrating the same history but each of them offering divergent versions. The Museo Inka is a public university museum with barely enough funds to keep its doors open. It is a community-oriented museum and its exhibition script presents the *longue durée* of Peruvian history down to its present-day inhabitants. In contrast, the Museo de Arte Precolombino (MAP), a privately (and lavishly) funded institution created for the upscale tourist market, represents a neocolonialist version of history; it 'implies a finite end to Andean creativity with the Inkas being replaced by the Spanish colonial regime'. Cuzco's inhabitants are not linked to their past and thereby they are denied the chance to claim physical and narrative space in either the museum or, by extension, the city itself.

The third theme played out in this section is the impact of capitalism on the *management* of archaeological practice. Paul Everill's paper uses the case of *rescue* archaeology in Great Britain today. As that country has increasingly embraced a neo-liberal economic model, archaeology has increasingly been driven by market forces. This is seen in the tension between professional goals for particular projects and the need to meet often unrealistic deadlines and budget. The result is often a decline in the quality of results. At the same time, Everill argues that archaeology has not been able to overcome traditional biases against both field archaeology in particular and so-called manual labour in general. His paper reveals the continuance of the virtual disdain that some academics hold for field archaeologists, and perhaps vice-versa; Paul Bahn's (1989:15) brilliant aphorism that 'field archaeologists dig up rubbish, theoretical archaeologists write it down' is a misperception that may unfortunately be as commonly held today as it was 20 years ago. Everill also suggests that in Britain there is still a bias against so-called manual labour, and field archaeologists, despite their holding required degrees, are treated as something other than real professionals.

The dangers of archaeology's exposure to capitalism, the latter expressed in development projects, is further explored in Pedro Paulo Funari and Erika Robrahn-González's chapter. Their study focuses on Brazil and the emergence of archaeology as an increasingly important component in the creation and maintenance of heritage. On the one hand, their paper documents many of the same negative effects as Everill's, including the destruction of archaeological sites as a result of some archaeologists' not following basic ethical standards or the lack of control over fieldwork by understaffed and ill-equipped heritage agencies. On the other hand, Funari and Robrahn-González concede that capitalism, when properly regulated, can help lead to a better understanding of the past and involve communities in the interpretation of the archaeological past in ways that were not possible before. Like Everill, they expose the potential dissonance between CRM archaeology and academic archaeology, and question whether the importation of interpretive models from developed capitalist countries is appropriate for Brazil. Solutions to these problems are offered in both papers. Everill, for example, argues that only a strong union coupled with the reintegration of rescue archaeology into a strong, centrally organised governmental unit can help overcome the problems of CRM in Britain. Similarly, Funari and Robrahn-González hold out hope that the strengthening of state archaeological institutions will continue to foster the necessary cooperation between developers, archaeologists and local communities. It is noticeable that both place their faith in stronger governmental participation.

REFERENCE

Bahn, P (1989) *Bluff Your Way in Archaeology*, Horsham: Ravette Books Ltd

British Commercial Archaeology: Antiquarians and Labourers; Developers and Diggers

Paul Everill

INTRODUCTION

In the UK, as elsewhere, the replacement of governmental funding for 'rescue' or 'salvage' excavations by developer funding – and the related competitive tendering for work (known as 'bidding' in the USA) – during the 1980s has led to significant changes in the experiences of site staff. Despite the fact that a degree is now insisted upon by most archaeological units when employing new staff, pay and conditions of employment remain substantially below what one might expect for a graduate career. Many within the profession agree that pay, conditions and the sheer number of jobs have consistently improved since the effective 'privatisation' of contract archaeology, yet there is a deeply held belief that competitive tendering is also actually preventing the sort of substantial improvements that would adequately reflect the skill, education and dedication of staff. In this paper I aim to investigate the changes in UK professional field archaeology that have been propagated by its increasingly commercial nature, and in doing so provide a specific case study within the broader, global context represented by other papers in this volume. I will provide a brief historical background to the evolution of British professional field archaeology, before discussing some of the contemporary concerns of site staff that have been illuminated by a number of internal and external surveys. I will also draw upon examples from the early years of field archaeology and a related profession to demonstrate that the employer-employee relationship is, even now, not far removed from that of antiquarian and labourer.

THE GROWTH OF DEVELOPER-LED ARCHAEOLOGY

Prior to the Second World War, 'rescue' archaeology, as it became known, was almost unheard of. If construction workers found archaeological material it would be sent to a museum or university, and occasionally an academic or interested amateur would sift through the spoil heaps at construction sites in order to obtain artefacts or bones. During the war the large-scale construction of military installations required a governmental response, and the first recognisable, centrally funded 'rescue' projects took place. The widespread redevelopment of historic towns and cities throughout the 1950s and 1960s led to the formation of local and regional archaeological societies who occasionally managed to negotiate some time ahead of construction work to undertake the excavation of remains, but during the 1960s it became clear that these volunteers could not keep pace with the destruction of the archaeology. So, in 1971, RESCUE: The British Archaeological Trust was formed in an attempt to address this rapid destruction of the archaeological resource. High on their list of priorities was the need to get far greater government subsidies to support the work of 'rescue' archaeologists ahead of large-scale development projects. For a number of years RESCUE was successful and these subsidies were increased, though the financial support available from government, via the Historic Buildings and Monuments Commission, still fell well short of the figure required. At around this time the Manpower Services Commission (MSC) was created. It was a response to the economic troubles of the early 1970s, and from 1974 it provided jobs and training for the long-term unemployed. Archaeology, with its high labour requirements, was ideally suited to this and featured heavily in the Community Programmes run through the MSC from 1980.

> The Community Programme (CP) is designed for adults of 25 and over who have been unemployed for 12 of the preceding 15 months, (and have been unemployed in the 2 months preceding the start of the project), and for people aged 24 and over, who have been unemployed for 6 months previously. (Green 1987:28)

By 1986 the MSC provided funding of £4.8 million for archaeology, compared to £5.9 million from the Historic Buildings and Monuments Commission (Crump 1987), and in September 1986 there were 1,790 individuals employed on archaeological projects through the CPs. On top of the dependence archaeology developed for MSC funding, there were a number of side effects to this relationship.

> Ironically, one positive 'spin-off' from MSC involvement in archaeology is that volunteer rates may have gone up in some areas to bring them into line with CP wages. Also, as site safety is one of the areas monitored by MSC, standards have to be rigorously maintained. The provision of safety clothing and foul weather gear by MSC also marks an improvement except where unscrupulous sponsors spend this part of the 'capitation grant' on machine time and volunteers. (Crump 1987:45)

There were also some criticisms of the effect that the MSC was having, both on archaeologists and the unemployed that it was designed to help. The old 'circuit' had been replaced by CP projects, and there were concerns that recent graduates were finding it harder to find work in archaeology. There were also concerns that the average CP wage of £67 a week meant that the CP workforce was not encouraged to have a commitment to the project and supervisors spent as much time policing the site as excavating it (Crump 1987).

There is no doubt, however, that MSC funding was vital to archaeology, and when the commission was scrapped in 1987 it left a huge hole. During the 1980s the relationship between archaeological units and developers had become more solid, and the void left by the MSC was to become increasingly filled by funding from developers. This relationship was to become an integral part of the future of professional archaeology after 1990. The 21st of November of that year witnessed the resignation of Margaret Thatcher as Prime Minister and the launch of Planning Policy Guidance Note 16 as part of the Town and Country Planning Act (Wainwright 2000). PPG16 was carefully worded to place no extra financial burden on local authorities and was, of course, only 'guidance' rather than statutory, but it still forms the cornerstone of current commercial, contract archaeology in the UK. It states, for example that

> it would be entirely reasonable for the planning authority to satisfy itself before granting planning permission, that the developer has made appropriate and satisfactory provision for the excavation and recording of the remains. Such excavation and recording should be carried out before development commences, working to a project brief prepared by the planning authority and taking advice from archaeological consultants. (DoE 1990, paragraph 25)

With the 'polluter pays' principle thus enshrined (Graves-Brown 1997), British contract archaeology rapidly became a very commercial venture, with a number of units willing and able to work outside of the areas that they had traditionally been restricted to. This of course had huge implications for the maintenance of regional expertise in the field, and since 1990 a number of the older county council-based units have suffered at the hands of the many, more mobile, private units that have sprung up. In 2005 there were 121 contracting units (including those based within county councils, universities, and those established as trusts) employing approximately 2,100 archaeologists.

THE DIGGERS

As previously mentioned, a degree is now almost a prerequisite for the employment in contract archaeology of new site staff. Yet even in 1987, with the profession still very much in its infancy, it was clear that

> few, if any, of the [degree] courses were really seen, by those on them, as providing the necessary background for archaeological employment. One major factor in this was argued to be the perceived conflict between an archaeology degree as a general academic education and as an archaeological training. Put crudely, some archaeology degrees have little or no value for a student rash enough to want to follow a career in archaeology in Britain. (Joyce *et al* 1987:v)

This situation has never been universally addressed – despite the efforts of a small number of universities to provide high-quality practical courses – and the junior field archaeologist has become, by virtue of the system, not an inheritor of the world of the educated and respected archaeologists of old, but merely an enthusiastic labourer to be trained and moulded in the workplace. When Shortland (1994) discusses how geologists in the field defined themselves, not through their perceived origins as 'gentlemen amateurs', but almost unconsciously through their roots in mining, it throws up an interesting question. How do commercial field archaeologists define themselves? Perhaps it is through their perceived or actual roots; through the relationships they develop on site – both with their colleagues and with those 'others' with whom they share their workplace – and certainly through their perceptions of their position within the commercial environment. Field archaeologists of the past defined themselves in opposition to the labourers on their site, whether they be culturally separate through nationality as in, for example, Woolley's (1930) work in Mesopotamia, or through class as on any of the large field projects run in the UK which utilised large numbers of workmen. This relationship was class-based and often imperialist. The modern British commercial archaeologist might be described as having more in common with the scaffolders and bricklayers of a large construction site, dressing the same (all being required to wear the same Personal Protective Equipment [PPE], often only being distinguishable by the colour of their hard hats or the logo of their respective employer on their high-visibility vests). Perhaps, in the same way as Shortland's geologists, commercial archaeologists see their roots lying more squarely with the labourers of the large-scale research digs than with the educated 'gentlefolk'.

Internal Surveys of the Profession

A number of surveys have been undertaken on the archaeological profession in the UK since the late 1970s. Prime amongst these was the work of RESCUE. Spoerry (1992, 1997) synthesises some of this earlier data when writing about the 1990–1991 and 1996 surveys. The total number of curatorial and rescue archaeologists in 1978–1979 was estimated to be about 1,600, of which 663 were 'permanent' posts. By 1986–1987 the total figure had grown massively, due in no small part to the Manpower Services Commission, to 2,900, though only about 600 of these were permanent. By 1990–1991 the end of the MSC saw numbers drop to about 2,200 archaeological staff, though permanent posts had risen to 860. The 1996 survey indicated an overall figure of 2,100 jobs and suggested that the profession had achieved a certain stability. In terms of pay, the surveys indicate that '[i]n 1990–91 three quarters of archaeological staff were paid less than £12,000 p/a. In this same period the national average salary (both sexes) was about £13,200 p/a' (Spoerry 1992:19). If one looks at the figures, however, and removes the permanent posts that most likely do not represent 'site staff', then in actual fact over three-quarters were earning less than £10,000 in that period. 'In 1995–6 just over three-quarters of archaeologists were paid less than £16,000 pa, when the national average earnings (both sexes) was about £17,500 pa' (Spoerry 1997:6). One can again safely assume that archaeologists in the field were well below even that figure.

In 1999 the Institute of Field Archaeologists, English Heritage and the Council for British Archaeology published a survey of organisations in the UK that employed professional archaeologists. The results were published in the booklet 'Profiling the Profession' (Aitchison 1999). There were seven initial Objectives behind the undertaking of the study (Aitchison 1999:ix):

1. To identify the numbers of professional archaeologists working in Britain
2. To analyse whether the profession is growing, static or shrinking
3. To identify the range of jobs
4. To identify the numbers employed in each job type
5. To identify the range of salaries and terms and conditions applying to each job type
6. To identify differences in employment patterns between different geographical areas
7. To help those seeking to enter the profession

The survey identified 349 relevant organisations, which were divided into 10 categories including 'Archaeological Contractors' and 'Other Commercial Organisations', but also university departments, local government staff and independent consultants. Of the estimated 93 contracting organisations, employing approximately 30% of the total archaeological workforce, 51 responded to the postal questionnaire. This questionnaire required each unit to give details of their work and their staff as it stood on 16 March 1998. There was some disbelief amongst the staff of commercial organisations when the published results demonstrated that the average salary for all full-time archaeologists was £17,079. This figure is clearly skewed by the inclusion of academic staff, consultants and other more highly paid members of the profession. However this relative distortion of results becomes particularly relevant in comparison with other related occupations.

In Table 6.1 the archaeological profession occupies a place above construction industry workers but below the managers and other related specialists. However closer inspection reveals that had 'Builders, building contractors' been put together with 'Managers in building and contracting' – in the same way that archaeologists had been lumped together – their average salary would well exceed that of archaeologists. The organisers of the survey could justifiably argue that their aim was not to specifically study any one group within the profession but to provide an overall picture. It is interesting, however to look at the information relating directly to those employed within the commercial sector of archaeology in March 1998 (see Table 6.2).

Data from the follow-up survey, published in 2003 (Aitchison and Edwards), do show an encouraging rise in the average full-time salaries over the preceding five years (Table 6.3). However, this is against a backdrop of substantial increase in other sectors that actually sees a relative fall for the entire archaeological profession in terms of salaries (Table 6.4). These figures would seem to suggest that the contracting organisations have been experiencing a period of growth and increased profit, which has been reflected in the salaries of staff. This is perhaps in contrast to the rest of the archaeological profession, which saw a far smaller wage increase in the same period.

Table 6.1 Archaeologists' full-time salary compared to other occupations in the UK in 1998 (Aitchison 1999)

Profession	Average Gross Earnings
University and polytechnic teaching professionals	£30,179
Civil, structural, municipal, mining and quarrying engineers	£28,286
Architects	£25,882
Town planners	£25,887
Managers in building and contracting	£25,689
Building, land, mining and 'general practice' surveyors	£24,495
Draughtspersons	£19,745
Scientific technicians	£19,641
Librarians and related professionals	£19,010
Archaeologists	**£17,079**
Road construction and maintenance workers	£16,904
Construction trades	£15,512
Builders, building contractors	£15,345
Other building and civil engineering labourers not elsewhere categorised	£13,843

Table 6.2 Average archaeological salaries in the UK in 1998 (Aitchison 1999)

Position	Average Full-Time Salary	Temporary Contract	Permanent Contract
Site Assistant	£10,094	73%	27%
Supervisor	£12,830	53%	47%
Finds Officer	£14,966	25%	75%
Project Officer	£15,060	43%	57%
Project Manager	£19,434	30%	70%
Director	£22,629	29%	71%
Average of all	**£15,835.5**		

Table 6.3 Average archaeological salaries in the UK in 2003 (Aitchison and Edwards 2003)

Position	Average Full-Time Salary	Increase since 1998	Temporary Contract	Permanent Contract
Site Assistant	£12,140	20.26%	82%	18%
Supervisor	£14,290	11.38%	41%	59%
Finds Officer	£18,422	22.42%	35%	65%
Project Officer	£18,049	19.85%	17%	83%
Project Manager	£22,433	15.43%	12%	88%
Director	£27,148	19.97%	14%	86%
Average of all	**£18,747**	**18.22%**		

Table 6.4 Archaeologists' full-time salary compared to other occupations in the UK in 2003 (Aitchison and Edwards 2003)

Profession	Average Gross Earnings	Increase since 1997/98
University and polytechnic teaching professionals	£34,791	15%
Architects	£34,426	33%
Managers in building and contracting	£33,924	32%
Civil, structural, municipal, mining and quarrying engineers	£31,527	12%
Building, land, mining and 'general practice' surveyors	£30,275	24%
Town planners	£27,064	5%
Draughtspersons	£23,227	18%
Scientific technicians	£23,157	18%
Librarians and related professionals	£22,728	18%
Road construction and maintenance workers	£20,183	19%
Builders, building contractors	£19,277	26%
Archaeologists	**£19,161**	**12%**
Construction trades	£18,809	21%
Other building and civil engineering labourers not elsewhere categorised	£17,455	26%

There are also interesting statistics relating to age and gender within contracting organisations which demonstrate the relative youth of the profession (77% are aged between 20 and 40 in 1998 and 66% in 2002) and the under-representation of females in the commercial workplace. There is also a significant female domination of the 'Finds Officer' roles (see Table 6.5) as discussed in Cane *et al* (1994).

The 2003 study of the Archaeology Labour Market (Aitchison and Edwards 2003) also included for the first time data on disabled employees and on the ethnic diversity of the profession. This demonstrated that there is actually very little diversity at all, with 99.34% of archaeologists being white (compared to 92.1% nationally), while only 0.34% of staff were defined as disabled (compared with 19% of the total working population).

The Invisible Diggers

The data for my doctoral thesis, which was a study of the current situation in UK contract archaeology, was obtained by conducting extensive, qualitative interviews with commercial archaeologists, by undertaking a period of 'participant observation' within a commercial unit, and through an online survey which was to provide demographic information, but also test opinions across the profession. The quantitative data from my 'Invisible Diggers' website contradicts some of the IFA figures and provides an alternative view of the profession to that provided by previous studies.

Rather than contacting units and asking for data, I instead specifically advertised for respondents in *The Digger* – an anonymously produced, free newsletter that discusses and confronts many of the issues faced by site staff – and online at David Connolly's 'British Archaeological Jobs Resource' (BAJR) – a free-to-use job service started in 1999 that now receives several thousand hits a week. By the

Table 6.5 Gender differentiation within the archaeological profession in the UK (Data taken from Aitchison 1999, and Aitchison and Edwards 2003)

Position	Male (1998)	Female (1998)	Male (2002)	Female (2002)
Site Assistant	69%	31%	67%	33%
Supervisor	57%	43%	66%	34%
Finds Officer	27%	73%	36%	64%
Project Officer	68%	32%	69%	31%
Project Manager	79%	21%	77%	23%
Director	75%	25%	72%	28%
Average of all	**62.5%**	**37.5%**	**64.5%**	**35.5%**

time I closed it down in June 2005, my online survey had received responses from an estimated 15.67% of UK site staff, producing results with a margin of error of 5.4% at 95% confidence. Interestingly, 77% of my respondents were aged between 20 and 40, which is identical to the IFA's figures from the 1998 survey but significantly larger than the IFA's most recent figure of 66%. It may be that younger staff were more motivated to take part in my survey, though I strongly suspect that this is also a reflection of an under-representation of the under 40s (and more particularly the under 30s) in the 2002 IFA study. Although my results suggest that 35.56% of site staff are female – almost identical to the IFA's 2002 figure of 35.5% – the results, as shown in Figure 6.1, indicate that actually there are more female than male staff in the 21–25 age group. The number of female contract archaeologists falls at a fairly constant rate from the early twenties to the mid-thirties before beginning to level off. The figures for male staff, by contrast, fall off most markedly from the early forties.

In terms of experience in the field, Figure 6.2 demonstrates the noticeable fall in staff numbers after five years (which correlates to the number leaving the profession in their late twenties – shown in Figure 6.1). This is also borne out in my qualitative interviews with current and ex-contract archaeologists that indicate that staff become disillusioned with the pay, conditions of employment and the general level of respect they receive. After about five years' experience there is a widespread tendency to re-examine their careers, and this is when

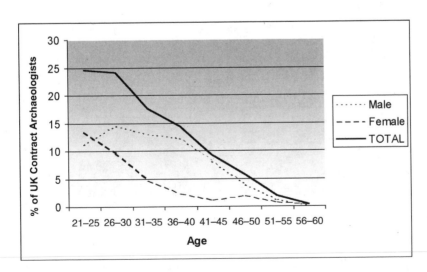

Figure 6.1 Gender differentiation across the age groups of UK archaeologists. Data from the 'Invisible Diggers' project.

many opt to leave the profession in favour of a more stable, better-paid career – despite still having a passion for archaeology. It is interesting, however, to note the obvious increase, against the general trend, at the 16–20-year experience bracket which I believe is directly related to the influx of staff through the MSC in the mid- to late 1980s and the fact that a significant number of this body of people have managed to maintain employment and their interest in the job, despite the obvious difficulties that are associated with it.

A View From Outside the Profession

In 2003 the All-Party Parliamentary Archaeology Group (APPAG) published its first report entitled 'The Current State of Archaeology in the United Kingdom'. Formed in 2001, APPAG advertised for 250-word submissions from organisations and individuals with an interest in archaeology, receiving 267 submissions in total. It also questioned representatives from certain key bodies at a number of committee sessions. The published report was detailed and wide-ranging, with a large number of recommendations – not least that an absence of one, clear, non-governmental lobby group has created a confusing muddle of different voices that results in little being achieved. However, in Part 3, section B, the topic of 'Archaeology as a Career' is discussed. It is essential to quote large sections here as this

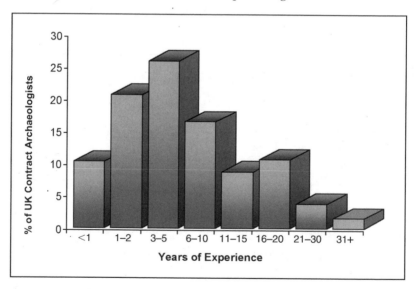

Figure 6.2 Field experience amongst UK archaeologists. Data from the 'Invisible Diggers' project.

represents the single most important analysis of the profession by an external body.

28. The submissions emphasised the plight of archaeologists as insecurely employed, poorly paid and generally itinerant, as demonstrated by Aitchison's report *Profiling the Profession* (1999). This is in large part due to the effects of the system of competitive tendering... A mobile casual workforce is inevitably excluded from training opportunities where they do exist. The absence of proper training prohibits promotion to more secure senior posts. There is no clear career development path and, in most cases, neither universities ... nor employers appear to consider it their role to prepare archaeologists for professional practice. This is largely due to external financial pressures, with developer funding dominating and contributing sums approaching £75 million per annum; but it is also because archaeology only has a weak professional structure.

29. Although archaeology is a graduate profession this is neither reflected in the career opportunities nor in remuneration. Often those who work in excavation units are treated as site technicians who simply record archaeological deposits rather than as archaeologists who are capable of interpreting them. The current fragmentation of the profession is already exacerbating those problems...

31. ... Training is vital if archaeology is to achieve high professional standards and it needs to be linked to career development, providing benchmarks for salaries which reflect the true worth of the multifarious skills of the profession.

Recommendation

32. There is an urgent need to improve pay and conditions for employment in field archaeology so that they are commensurate with graduate entry level in allied professions such as local authority planning officers, civil engineers and university lecturers... In the longer term, the current fragmented commercial unit system which has resulted from competitive tendering should be replaced with a more stable regional, or more local framework of archaeological organisations. (APPAG 2003:14)

FIELDWORK AS 'LABOURING'

Although most of the problems in contemporary British contract archaeology can be put down to the commercial marketplace that now drives it, I believe that there is another reason behind the treatment of site staff. In many respects it seems as though junior staff, ie, those who actually undertake the physical work on site, are being stripped of individuality by the process of excavation and the deferred interpretation of sites and, furthermore, are being completely removed from the process of knowledge production.

In many ways, site assistants are completely interchangeable – he or she is not a person but a digging machine and although some assistants may be more efficient than others, their 'local knowledge' or personality is

> often ignored and certainly never mentioned in any contemporary manuals on fieldwork. (Lucas 2001:9)

This form of physical invisibility is created by a sense of 'interchangeability'. Site assistants become depersonalised on site, and feel overlooked and disenfranchised by their managers and professional body, the Institute of Field Archaeologists. Shapin (1989) makes a similar observation concerning scientific technicians, who are often almost completely overlooked. Using the historical example of Robert Boyle's laboratory, Shapin highlights the huge number of skilled technicians and assistants who worked there – often unsupervised – who were rarely referred to by Boyle in his writing. However, 'the role of technicians was continually pointed to when matters did not proceed as expected. In such circumstances, technicians' labor (or rather, the incompetence of their labor) became highly visible' (Shapin 1989:558).

This attitude towards skilled staff is seen in archaeological work from its earliest years. When, for example, Cunnington and Colt Hoare embarked on their fieldwork in Wiltshire at the turn of the 19th century, the former, charged with managing the day-to-day activities, took on local labourers. Contemporary practice was to leave the labourers to the hard work and to receive the finds from them afterwards.

> Cunnington from the first wanted more than this, though he never thought it necessary to be present all the time. He did the next best thing, however, and within a few years had trained two skilled diggers, Stephen and John Parker, on whom he and Hoare might rely to report where and how the finds were made as well as make them. (Cunnington 1975:13)

In an extremely socially stratified age, the Parkers became renowned and widely respected for their skill – despite their effective status as 'mere' labourers. In 1807 Colt Hoare's friend Iremonger was preparing to excavate barrows near Winchester, Hampshire. He had already invited Colt Hoare to join him when he wrote to him again at the end of June.

> You will I trust not think me guilty of great intrusion in requesting the assistance of your Wiltshire labourers on this occasion, for my Hampshire men have disgraced themselves by their exorbitant demands; and I am confident the expenses of their journey will be amply repaid by their superior skill and alacrity. (Cunnington 1975:107)

The death of William Cunnington in 1810 marked the end of their archaeological career and the Parkers presumably returned to their previous lives. John Parker however, as an old man, was able to give General Pitt-Rivers information about a barrow he excavated for Cunnington and Colt Hoare. To the end of his life, and beyond, he and his father would remain unsung heroes of the early years of archaeological excavation because of their status. I believe, however, that there is still very much a culture of 'labouring' within contemporary, contract archaeology not least because the unit archaeologists have been disenfranchised by the system – a system of management codified by 'The Management of Archaeological Projects (MAP2)', published by English Heritage in 1991 – which separates the excavation, interpretative and post-excavation elements. It is commonplace, and often accepted today, that the very people who are excavating archaeological features will have no say in their interpretation or integration into the overall site. In terms of the production of knowledge, the prime motivation for conducting fieldwork, junior site staff are treated as little more than labourers.

My research has shown that professional archaeology is not alone in its current predicament. In an article in *The Garden: Journal of the Royal Horticultural Society*, a student at the RHS Gardens at Wisley comments on the situation.

> Many people never consider horticulture as a possible career. Perhaps this lack of encouragement is related to the fact that most horticulturalists earn unacceptably low wages. For example, a gardener is unlikely to earn more than £12,000 in the first year of a new job, whilst most head gardener positions attract about £18,000. Compare this with the average UK wage of around £24,000, take into account the training and experience such a position requires, and something is seriously wrong – even when the employer provides accommodation. The benefits of a healthy, relatively stress-free lifestyle are small compensation, but the profession is not always as idyllic as we might like. Gardeners work outside in all weathers, for long hours, often doing monotonous or physically demanding tasks. But for those with passion, interest and commitment, the opportunities are there. Horticulture is often a vocation more than a career, followed by people who would not want to do anything else, however poor the pay. (Fitzgerald 2003:797)

The parallels with contract archaeology are clearly very striking. Tim Hughes (personal communication), the Head of Training at the Royal Horticultural Society Garden at Wisley, puts the current situation down to a number of factors. Although horticulture is a broad umbrella, like archaeology, and covers a number of quite varied professions from laboratory-based sciences to hard and soft landscaping, the professional gardeners are in much the same position as professional archaeologists. Trainees at Wisley Gardens start at £11,000, while a Junior Gardener earns £14,000. Despite this, Mr Hughes has seen an increase in people in their 30s leaving lucrative jobs in the City to retrain as gardeners. He puts this down to a lifestyle choice and the perception of gardening as a low-stress, healthy profession which outweighs the low wages in the minds of many people.

Mr Hughes also raised another interesting point with regard to the perception of gardening as a career. Traditionally, career advisors at school, when dealing with children who were perhaps weaker academically, would point them towards a 'land-based' career. Equally, archaeology may be glamorised in the minds of the public through its media profile, but the actual physical act of excavation remains subject to some historic prejudices. Ask someone to name a famous historic gardener and their answer would most likely be one of the renowned designers of large private gardens. The hands-on, physical gardeners were generally servants. Even today advertisements for gardening positions at private houses often include family accommodation and the possibility of domestic work in the main house for their partner. So it seems that even qualified and experienced gardeners are often still seen as part of the system of servitude when it comes to pay and conditions. To quote Tim Hughes, 'Working with your hands and working with the land is still seen as labouring', and this is equally applicable to field archaeologists.

The combined effects of commercial values (including the separation of excavation from interpretation), inadequate fieldwork training in universities, and what might be described as a 'labouring subculture' amongst many site staff result in something that many do not consider to be a 'proper job'. During my research I have conducted qualitative interviews with a number of British commercial archaeologists, including one who had recently been appointed a county archaeologist (this is a curatorial post responsible for monitoring commercial archaeology – see Cumberpatch and Blinkhorn [2001] for a discussion on how archaeological responsibilities have been fragmented under a commercial system). Having spent 22 years working his way up the profession, he had a number of interesting insights into it.

> P19: But it has to be said you're not going to get rich as an archaeologist. It's a lifestyle choice. Doesn't mean you have to be underpaid to do it, but be realistic. There are only so many counties in Britain. There are only so many units in Britain, so there are only x amount of jobs. It cannot expand exponentially. It's at saturation point as it is so I would say to 85% of diggers, you know, accept it. Enjoy your three or four years as a digger, or five years as a digger. Use it, have a good life, smoke lots of drugs, drink lots of drink, get off with either women or men or both. Go abroad. And then get a proper job. If you're lucky and really want to be an archaeologist for the rest of your life then you'll make it. I mean, 22 years I waited to get where I am and who knows how long I'll be an archaeologist. I mean I'm never going to give it up. Absolutely not.

Starting as a digger himself, P19 had also seen first-hand how the profession had changed since the early 1980s. Believing that standards had declined, he apportioned the blame equally between poor university training, the failure of commercial units to invest in their staff and a change in attitude amongst diggers, perhaps resulting from their own feeling of disenfranchisement.

> P19: Managers I think have got more to manage. A lot more paperwork, a lot more worries. Health and Safety. Risk Assessments … Spot checks. The digger, strangely for the digger, like we discussed before, diggers … really a lot has not changed, in as much as dreadlocks, ripped clothes, army combats are *de rigueur*. The one thing that has changed is they don't seem to have the interest and the confidence anymore. Because, again we go back, they come out of university and they have not a 'scooby doo' about how to dig a site and they never learn, because not at any point does a contracting unit have time to say 'hey, this is how we do it' or 'go and learn some blah, blah.' It's 'Can you do it?' 'No.' 'Right, forget it. Get him. Can he do it? Yes he can. Right.' Engage with the past and *then* you're worth your money. Until then I'm afraid you're a person who digs holes … slowly.

CONCLUSION

It seems clear that in embracing a capitalist marketplace, having previously missed the opportunity to establish a national framework with regional units in the 1970s (Wainwright 2000), 'rescue' archaeology in the UK has become a profession that bears more similarities to the antiquarian activities of Sir Richard Colt Hoare than a modern profession that accurately reflects the skills, training and dedication of the archaeologists and other specialists employed within it. There is also a widespread concern amongst archaeologists that competitive tendering is resulting in some units undertaking low quality work, or even damaging the archaeology – cutting corners to meet targets and deadlines that are unachievable otherwise.

In the UK today, by far the vast majority of archaeological sites are excavated by commercial units ahead of development projects. In many cases the quality of the work is of the highest standard, and yet this is because of the professionalism of the supervisors and site staff who refer to themselves, disparagingly and with some humour, as merely 'diggers'. Many academic archaeologists sneer at these endeavours, failing to appreciate the skill of people who, even in their mid-twenties, have accumulated more field experience than could be achieved in a career's worth of summer seasons on site. It is a sad fact of contemporary archaeology that commercialisation and privatisation have almost universally disenfranchised the archaeologists who ply their trade within that system.

Increased unionisation is one way forward. Over the last several years many of the larger units have recognised the trade union

'Prospect' and it is hoped that a national pay agreement can be established in the future, with discussions between Prospect, the IFA and the Standing Conference of Archaeological Unit Managers (SCAUM) currently planned. There is also the recently established *Diggers Forum*. It is hoped that this can provide a focal point for archaeologists and specialists below management level, with the aim of instigating real change within the profession. It can only be hoped that organisations like 'Prospect' – and the other trade unions including 'Unison' which represents many county council-based archaeologists – *The Digger* newsletter, the BAJR website and *Diggers Forum* can work together to shift the emphasis away from the current profit-driven one toward one that is both ethical and fair for the archaeologists employed within the profession in the UK.

It is also important that the issue of training be adequately addressed. If units are to insist on university-level education, then there desperately needs to be a dialogue between the employers and academics resulting in the kind of fieldwork training that is so desperately lacking currently. Failing that, perhaps archaeology, like gardening, should be more widely available as non-degree-level courses that deal almost entirely with site-based skills, though it may not be beneficial to further fragment the discipline along these lines. I firmly believe that the university system, which is sadly now also subject to commercial pressures as never before in the UK, has overlooked its responsibility to prepare archaeology students for a career in archaeology in its rush to provide 'transferable skills' to those with no real interest in the subject. The training of archaeologists should not cease, however, once they have graduated. It is just as important that commercial units take their responsibilities seriously in this issue and look beyond the short-term contracts they offer their staff. Instead they should collectively consider the universal benefits of providing 'on the job' training and specialist courses, etc. Unfortunately, in the cutthroat commercial environment, this is often seen as an avoidable expense (along with improving wages for staff) which makes it harder for them to undercut their competitors.

There also needs to be a recognition amongst some site staff that, as in all professions, a graduate archaeologist must spend a certain amount of time learning their trade on the job before earning extra responsibility. Equally, it is unlikely that a graduate archaeologist will ever earn as much as a graduate engineer or architect because of the way in which society values those professions and the perceived 'end product'. Such comparisons are ultimately useless in a capitalist society. There is, however, no reason why unit staff could not be paid a substantial amount more than they currently are to reflect the level of skill and training required.

The only wide-reaching solution I can see to the current imbalances in contract archaeology would be to create a state archaeology service, administered and managed through regional offices and funded by a tax on developers that was proportional to the construction work they were undertaking (this is really only a refinement of the existing 'polluter pays' system, but would allow greater flexibility when administered centrally rather than per job and per unit). Within this framework, national pay scales, job grading and continuous training could be put in place. The work undertaken would utilise one, universally recognised recording system to agreed standards of excavation, interpretation, illustration, analysis and publication. Archaeologists would be able to move around between regional offices, when the demand was higher elsewhere, without losing the sick pay and holiday entitlement that they had earned and without, in all probability, suffering long periods of unemployment. Furthermore regional offices would support, and indeed encourage, the kind of local archaeological expertise that was once commonplace but is rapidly becoming a victim of commercial pressures. Only when archaeology is no longer undertaken for profit will it become a truly profitable endeavour for all concerned.

REFERENCES

Aitchison, K (1999) *Profiling the Profession: A Survey of Archaeological Jobs in the UK*, York: CBA, EH and IFA

Aitchison, K and Edwards, R (2003) *Archaeology Labour Market Intelligence: Profiling the Profession 2002/3*, Bradford: Cultural Heritage National Training Organisation

APPAG (2003) *The Current State of Archaeology in the United Kingdom – First Report of the All Party Parliamentary Archaeology Group*, London: APPAG

Cane, C, Gilchrist, R and O'Sullivan, D (1994) 'Women in archaeology in Britain: three papers', in Nelson, MC, Nelson, SM and Wylie, A (eds) *Equity Issues for Women in Archaeology*, Arlington: American Anthropological Association (Archaeological Papers of the American Anthropological Association 5)

Crump, T (1987) 'The role of MSC funding in British archaeology', in Mytum, H and Waugh, K (eds), *Rescue archaeology – What's Next? Proceedings of a Rescue Conference held at the University of York, December 1986*, York: Department of Archaeology, York University (University of York Monograph 6)

Cumberpatch, C and Blinkhorn, P (2001) 'Clients, contractors, curators and archaeology: who owns the past?' In Pluciennik, M (ed), *The Responsibilities of Archaeologists: Archaeology and Ethics*, Oxford: Archaeopress (Lampeter Workshop in Archaeology 4, BAR S981)

Cunnington, R (1975) *From Antiquary to Archaeologist: A Biography of William Cunnington 1754–1810*, Aylesbury: Shire Publications

DoE (Department of the Environment) (1990) *Planning Policy Guidance Note 16: Archaeology and Planning*, London: HMSO

English Heritage (1991) *The Management of Archaeological Projects (second edition)*, London: English Heritage

Fitzgerald, C (2003) 'Why choose horticulture as a career?' *The Garden: Journal of the Royal Horticultural Society* 128, 796–797

Graves-Brown, P (1997) 'She who pays the piper … archaeology and the polluter pays principle', *Assemblage* 2, www.shef.ac.uk/~assem/2gb2.html

Green, F (1987) 'MSC: their involvement in archaeology', in Joyce, S, Newbury, M and Stone, P (eds) *Degree, Digging, Dole our Future? Papers Presented at YAC '85*, Southampton: Southampton University Archaeology Society

Joyce, S, Newbury, M and Stone, P (eds) (1987) *Degree, Digging, Dole our Future? Papers Presented at YAC '85*, Southampton, Southampton University Archaeology Society

Lucas, G (2001) *Critical Approaches to Fieldwork: Contemporary and Historical Archaeological Practice*, London: Routledge

Shapin, S (1989) 'The Invisible technician', *American Scientist* 77, 554–563

Shortland, M (1994) 'Darkness visible: underground culture in the golden age of geology', *History of Science* 32, 1–61

Spoerry, P (1997) 'The Rescue Survey 1996: Some Preliminary Results', *Rescue News* 72, 6–7

—— (1992) *The Structure and Funding of British Archaeology: The Rescue Questionnaire 1990–1*, Hertford: RESCUE

Wainwright, G (2000) 'Time please', *Antiquity* 74, 909–943

Woolley, Sir L (1930) *Digging Up the Past*, Harmondsworth: Penguin Books

CHAPTER 7

Ethics, Capitalism and Public Archaeology in Brazil

Pedro Paulo A. Funari and
Erika M. Robrahn-González

INTRODUCTION

Archaeology, in the last few decades has moved away from a positivist, processual understanding of society and the discipline itself. The aim of knowledge of the past 'as it really was' – *wie es eingentlich gewesen*, to use the words of Leopold von Ranke (in Funari 2003a:12) – proved to be too ambitious and the discipline turned its attention to ethics and politics. It is no coincidence that this move was going on just as globalisation was introduced as a new catchword to describe capitalism. Since the start, globalisation appeared as both an opportunity and a menace to nature and society. Karl Marx (1973:74) had already mentioned the powerful forces of capitalism:

> The discovery of America, the rounding of the Cape, opened up fresh ground for the rising bourgeoisie. The East-Indian and Chinese markets, the colonization of America, trade with the colonies, the increase in the means of exchange and in commodities, generally, gave to commerce, to navigation, to industry, an impulse never before known, and thereby, to the revolutionary element in the tottering feudal society, a rapid development.

The American continent was, therefore, from the beginning of the modern era, at the heart of the capitalist expansion (Orser 2004). However, it was only with the digital revolution that capitalism spread to everyday life in remote areas. The issues arising from this situation are varied, and worry not only critics of capitalism, but also those who consider it inevitable. Joseph Stiglitz (2002), a famous economist, Nobel Prize winner and adviser to President Bill Clinton, stated:

> I believe that globalization – the removal of barriers to free trade and the closer integration of national economies – can be a force for good and that it has the potential to enrich everyone in the world, particularly the

poor. But I also believe that if this is to be the case, the way globalization has been managed, including the international trade agreements that have played such a large role in removing those barriers and the policies that have been imposed on developing countries in the process of globalization, need to be radically rethought.

Capitalism has menaced diversity, both in nature and in culture. Archaeology is directly linked to the overwhelming power of capital to protect or to destroy the archaeological record. In this chapter, we will introduce the reader to Brazil and its archaeology and then produce several examples of the challenges archaeologists face. Capitalism regulated by heritage legislation has produced new opportunities to the archaeological work, but ethical issues are particularly important in this new context.

BRAZILIAN SOCIETY AND ARCHAEOLOGY IN HISTORICAL PERSPECTIVE

Archaeology and capitalism in Brazil must be understood in its specific historical context. Brazil as a nation state has always been linked to capitalism, from the arrival of the Portuguese in the 15th century. However, it has also been characterized by patriarchal, even feudal features, so much so that an understanding of archaeological resource management in Brazil must be placed within the context of the country's complex geography and historical development. Brazil is a large country (8,511,965 square km); its Atlantic coastline reaches 7,408 km. Almost the entire country has a tropical or semi-tropical climate: In the north there is the heavily wooded Amazon Basin covering half the country; the northeast region is semi-arid scrubland; a large *serrado* (savannah) area stretches to the south; and semi-tropical vegetation exists from São Paulo State in the south up to the Pampa in Rio Grande do Sul State.

The inception of archaeological university research (1950s–1964) coincided with Brazil's longest period of democracy (1945–1964). The leading humanist Paulo Duarte established academic archaeology. Due to his friendship with Paul Rivet, director of the Musée de l'Homme, Paris, France, Duarte created the Prehistory Commission at São Paulo State University in 1952. Duarte pushed for legal protection of the Brazilian heritage, and as a result of his efforts the Brazilian Congress enacted a federal law (3537/57, approved as law 3924 in 1961) protecting archaeological sites. To this day, it is still the only explicit federal law on the protection of archaeological heritage.

The military period (1964–1985) changed the situation. The Americans Clifford Evans and Betty Meggers were able to set up a National Program of Archaeological Research, known by its acronym

PRONAPA. The Program was sponsored by the Smithsonian Institution in Washington, and by Brazilian institutions such as the National Research Council (CNPq). In the period between 1965 and 1971, PRONAPA trained Brazilian archaeologists and carried out surveys and excavations throughout the country, with few resulting publications. The new authorities used the supposed lack of funds to undermine the project of scholarly archaeology as proposed by Duarte. He was expelled from the University of São Paulo in 1969, and the Institute of Prehistory he created was subjected to restrictions. Archaeology suffered then a lot, as a result of authoritarian trends inside the profession. However, democracy (from 1985 onwards) favoured the flourishing of archaeology, and this freedom led to the development of a variety of new activities regarding archaeological resources. Interpretive books have been published, as well as a greater number of articles in scholarly journals, for the first time not only in Brazil but also abroad.

Capitalism and Archaeological Heritage in Historical Perspective

Archaeological resources have been the subject of several government bills, the first comprehensive one in 1936, prepared by the leading intellectual, Mário de Andrade. It was concerned with both ethnological as well as archaeological resources, specifically monuments, artefacts (such as pottery, lithics, cemeteries, shell middens, and rock art), landscapes (rivers, fauna, caves and even traditional paths) and folklore. In January 1937 the Brazilian Heritage body, 'Serviço Histórico e Artístico Nacional', was established in order to protect, preserve and publicise heritage. The bill 511/36, originally proposed by Mário de Andrade, was being discussed in the Congress in November 1937 when a coup closed the parliament. In that same month, President Vargas, now as a dictator, published the bill as a decree, 'decreto-lei n. 25/37', which is still in force. A new penal code was also issued, in 1940, which for the first time punished the destruction of cultural resources, including archaeological ones. From 1940, the Brazilian Heritage body established a register of protected sites and archaeological collections. In 1948, in Paraná State, a law was passed protecting Spanish and Jesuit settlements, with a protected surrounding area of 100 hectares, resulting in the later establishment of the heritage parks of Vila Rica, Santo Inácio and Ciudad Real. Several judges and other officials have also tried to protect shell middens in different areas of the country.

The Commission for Prehistory was established in 1952 by Paulo Duarte. It was instrumental in fostering a bill for the purpose of protecting archaeological sites, approved by Congress in 1961 as Law 3924/61.

The law deals with 'archaeological and prehistoric monuments' and establishes that they are protected by law and should be preserved; they are to be controlled by the State and are not subject to the general rules of private property. Archaeological sites in general are considered monuments. It is thus forbidden to destroy these sites, and their economic use is not allowed. The sites are considered as property of the Federal State. The law also mentions archaeological excavations and the need to create a register of sites controlled by the Brazilian Heritage body. The same law also mandates the production of an archaeological report and to carry out the necessary arrangements for the storage of the archaeological material.

The restoration of civilian rule in 1985 led to a growing activity of state assemblies and town councils, free to legislate on a wide range of subjects, not least resource management. Several states introduced legislation protecting archaeological sites and establishing state registers of monuments and archaeological collections. This has been particularly the case of states with strong archaeological activities, like São Paulo and Rio Grande do Sul. Town councils also introduced legislation to that effect, and several municipal administrations introduced town Heritage offices. Urban archaeology has thus been developing and there has been a flurry of interest in archaeological resources. A new primary school syllabus, introduced in the 1990s, emphasizes the importance of learning, in a local context, so that the town becomes the starting point for understanding social life. Thus, archaeology can play a special role, enabling schoolchildren to know that natives inhabited their town in prehistoric times. Furthermore, material evidence from the historic period has also been used to show that the picture given by documents is biased and that blacks, natives, people of mixed complexion, immigrants, migrants and poor people in general, usually underrepresented in official documents, left material evidence now recovered by archaeology. Local primary school textbooks are now introducing archaeological evidence in order to give the children a more complex view of the past, enabling them to better understand present-day contradictions in society.

Capitalism, Archaeology and the Participation of the Public

The technological revolution of the last two decades led to a huge spread of archaeological information, and Brazil was very much affected by this process. Thanks to the enactment of national, state and municipal heritage legislation, archaeology has been involved in development projects throughout the country. The main ethical issue, though, is related to the inclusion of the public in archaeological practice and discourse. We understand the public as comprising not only local inhabitants, ethnic communities and pupils, but also the general public who read magazines and enjoy popular science programmes on radio and television. The inclusion of this ethical consideration is still in its infancy in Brazil, however, as most of the heritage legal constraints refer to bureaucratic procedures rather than the spreading of knowledge and the interaction between archaeologists and the public.

It is now well accepted that archaeology and education are inextricably linked, and that the past is often represented as a mirror of the dominant groups in a given society. Both education and archaeology deal with the manipulation of present and past to forge identities useful for people in power, and archaeologists and educators have been active promoters of critical approaches. Archaeologists have been pointing out that 'silent majorities' are represented in the material record and that archaeologists must increasingly take into account the interests of native people and of ordinary people in general. Archaeology and education intersect particularly in museums, classrooms and textbooks.

The Challenges of Capitalism to Archaeology in Brazil

Capitalism challenges an ethical archaeological practice in Brazil, as elsewhere, on several grounds. First and foremost, capitalist greed is at the heart of the large-scale natural and human destruction. In the Amazon rain forest, the destruction of the natural resources is a major challenge, and the advance of capitalist endeavours also directly affects traditional communities. There are similar trends in capitalist plunder elsewhere on the planet, but the uniqueness of the rainforest makes this threat a special one, as is acknowledged both by the Brazilian government and by several international institutions. Archaeologists face an ethical dilemma, however. Heritage legislation, enacted as a result of the democratic struggle, requires that all major development projects pay for a comprehensive archaeological survey, including rescue and salvage actions. Even if the law is not enforced in several cases, due to the short-term benefits to capitalist enterprises, there are several instances when archaeologists are dully employed to carry out the fieldwork. In a poor country, ordinary archaeologists face a daunting task just to survive; as a result, capitalist enterprises can count on hiring unemployed archaeologists who are under pressure to sign reports, usually stating that there are no archaeological sites in the area (Funari 2001). There are thus plenty of opportunities for a collusion of interests between archaeology and capitalist development.

The employment conditions for archaeologists within the capitalist system are thus quite inadequate. Public universities, museums and heritage institutions employ a number of archaeologists, but wages are not encouraging, even in the most prestigious institutions. The development of private archaeological trusts in this context is a mixed blessing. On the one hand, private trusts usually pay adequately for archaeologists, so that there are scores of young archaeologists interested in participating in fieldwork and laboratory in those private companies. As large firms are under pressure by the Brazilian Heritage body to produce reports on their activities, they are usually honest and enable archaeologists to get important experience. On the other hand, there is no official policy enforcing the publication of archaeological reports and the inclusion of community interests and concerns. This means that most reports remain unpublished and thus inaccessible to other scholars and to the communities and society at large. Initiatives aimed at including people's interests are at the discretion of private firms, and only those working in close collaboration with public institutions develop public archaeology programmes (Funari 2004). We discuss an example of this move below in order to show some features of those joint ventures.

For archaeologists themselves, contract archaeology may be a very invigorating first experience, and they can contribute, to some extent, to challenging the most aggressive and destructive aspects of capitalist policies. However, given that these are private enterprises and often not linked with public institutions, they are not necessarily an option for a long-term job. Middle-aged or older archaeologists, with their invaluable experience, are not so prone to accept the hard conditions offered by those firms (*cf* Everill, this volume).

In a very unequal society, such as Brazil's, with aristocratic patriarchal features, the elites use archaeology to foster upper-crust mores and values, and are able to control public institutions and individuals who inherited their positions thanks to their loyalty to dictatorial rule. Capitalist values and so-called bourgeois niceties are hailed, and non-capitalist values in society are disregarded, not least the different features of people's social identities (Funari 2002). Slavery and its consequences, the exploitation of native Brazilians, among others, are subjects neglected by local elites who prefer to consider themselves, since the heyday of slavery in the 19th century, as capitalists, and thus agents of progress. Another consequence for archaeology is also the importation of foreign interpretive models, perhaps adequate in understanding developed capitalist countries, but distant from Brazilian realities.

Archaeologists who oppose capitalism face restrictions in using archaeology for emancipatory aims. There are several examples of archaeological projects (including underwater research) whose goal is to study such subjects as slave resistance, slave trade, local identities and native Brazilian heritage. However, critical approaches may be charged with being ideological, as if pro-capitalist interpretations were neutral (Funari 2003b). Outside academia, in anti-capitalist social movements, archaeology is just beginning to play a role, mostly through its potential as a counterweight to conservative worldviews. Native Brazilian and Former Slave Runaway descendants' movements now work in close relationship with archaeologists in order to foster their interests against capitalist expansion.

If we compare the situation in Brazil with that in the developed capitalist world, we should stress the differences. Whilst archaeological trusts are closely monitored in most cases in the West, in Brazil the state is incapable of monitoring both capitalist endeavours and heritage salvage actions. The most important difference, though, is perhaps the fact that capitalism in Brazil is deeply intertwined with aristocratic ethos and traditions, the elites being at the same time patriarchal and capitalist. Ordinary people, Native communities and several other local groups are usually only partially affected by capitalism, and this is a huge difference with the conditions in the West. Archaeological commodification is only partial in Brazil and this opens opportunities for alternative actions, in contrast to capitalist trends in the West. Archaeologists can thus play an important role in engaging in a dialogue with those non-capitalist outlooks and traditions.

PUBLIC ARCHAEOLOGY AND SOCIAL SUSTAINABILITY

In Brazil, as well as in many different countries, archaeology remained for a long time restricted to academic research and/or to high school teaching, leaving to a team of non-archaeologists (including treasure hunters, amateurs, and looters) the mission of distorting archaeological features and interpretations.

As observed above, however, in the past few years Brazilian archaeologists have begun to introduce a public archaeology agenda, such as education, and this includes interaction with the community (including indigenous societies), and the protection and preservation of archaeological resources. They started to assume their social responsibility in linking the experience of the past to the present, and improve the future. On the other hand, since in Brazil public archaeology has been mostly linked with contract research, its discussion and practice is associated with a major goal: the definition of tools and strategies towards socio-environmental sustainability in a capitalist context.

Since the United Nations Conference on Environment and Development held in Rio in 1992, 'sustainable development' has become an important keyword for a political rhetoric involving quality of life, conservation of natural resources and a sense of obligation to future generations. Although the discussion was initially to do with natural sciences and the analysis of economic growth, the broader issue is social, historical and cultural: the viability of the relationships between society and nature over long periods of time (Becker *et al* 1999:1–6).

Therefore, the discourse on sustainability is basically social and linked to issues like social justice and political regulation. Archaeologists can contribute significantly to this process by improving community cohesion, by building links between the present and the past, by preserving history and tradition, and by valuing cultural heritage (see Becker and Jahn 1999; de Vries 2003; Little 2002; McManamon 2000). This leads, however, to ethical issues concerning, from one side, the fundamental differences between social groups in understanding and valuing the past, and from the other side, the intellectual ethnocentricities that often dominate archaeologists' attitudes.

In fact, as stated by Smith and Ehrenhard (2002:123), we do not have one public to consider, but many, each one with a singular sociocultural history and different interests in the events of the past. Although the question 'What is to be socially sustained?' will never find a commonly agreed answer, we may reach a consensus on the effective participation of the community in archaeological research, based on a non-hierarchical way in which methods and interpretations are allowed to interact (see Faulkner 2000, for an experience of 'democratic archaeology').

This is a particularly sensitive question in Brazil, a country formed not only by an enormous diversity of local historical and cultural contexts, but also by a stratified social structure, where a great deal of the population has no access to critical resources, including education. For this reason, the recent practice of public archaeology in Brazil is a stimulating challenge. We present below an example, based on our shared experience from central Brazil, and place the challenges capitalism poses to Brazilian archaeology in a wider international setting.

Public Education and Citizenship: An Experience with an Amazonian Border Community

The Peixe-Angical Dam Archaeological Rescue Program, located at the middle valley of the Tocantins River, on the southern border of the Amazonian basin with the Brazilian Central Plateau[1], was initiated in 2001. The project was organised under the auspices of a legal injunction, relating to archaeological and environmental protection during the construction of a huge hydroelectric dam. The private company building the dam paid for, but had no interference in, the project, which was run by a team of professional archaeologists who were fully responsible for the work. Paid by a private company, but fully autonomous, as established by law, all the participants were keen to follow a public archaeology approach. During the first three years, research focused on the survey and excavation of almost 120 sites located in the future lake area, following the schedule of construction. During this period, great attention was given to the knowledge of the history and cultural traditions of the involved community, trying to evaluate specific strategies for actions, in partnership with that community. Thus, informal interviews and discussions with more than 300 families occurred, in which the researchers tried to contextualize their own historical and cultural perspectives.

At Tocantins, as in Brazil in general, the local communities were the result of the destruction of native indigenous communities by Portuguese and later Brazilian colonisation, compounded by the introduction of enslaved Africans. This mixed picture is further aggravated by the fact that several towns in the region are extremely recent (after 1960) as a result of the opening of the Belém-Brasilia highway. People from different regions of the country had settled there, creating a heterogeneous community without a common history. This, however, offered an opportunity for the community to create new, non-capitalist features and traditions, such as their varied parties and festivities.

In this context, archaeological heritage was considered as something that would contribute to bringing together the different components of the community. The geographical setting offered the opportunity to discuss with them their common interests. This way public archaeology tried to build links inside the communities in the present, through the vestiges of the past. As McManamon mentions (2000:32), physical remains help to assure us there really was a past, a link between before and the present, illuminating the process of history and memory.

The symbolic value of archaeological resources was also stressed, as was the care that must be taken when studying these resources, and that the non-renewable nature of archaeological remains makes clear the irreplaceable value of their land. Contrary to capitalist ideology, land is interpreted as a cultural asset, not as a monetary one. The preservation of archaeological remains is considered in this context as part of their own strategy to foster their own, non-capitalist values.

Amongst the different actions taken by the archaeologists working with the population, the 'Week of Archaeology' distinguished itself. It was carried out in all three towns in the Peixe-Angical Dam area, and it involved 3,782 students registered in state schools (children in school age as well as adults in alphabetisation programmes). The conception and organisation of the event had been made possible through a partnership between the archaeologists, the community and the construction company. This stage involved six months of work, including the definition of the expectations of the community, the alternatives of action, and the events proper of 'Week of Archaeology' itself. Thanks to the public archaeology aims of the project, the community played a vital role in these activities. The diversity within the community featured prominently, and their non-capitalist, traditional social strategies were fully taken into account. Local potters were integrated in several workshops in order to explore the traditional, non-capitalist way of understanding pottery manufacture, use and symbolism. Tradition at the grass roots level is understood as a collective asset, as common cultural creation. It is thus anti-capitalist at its heart, as tradition refers to collective aims and aspirations, not to individual capitalist mores and ethos (Funari and Pelegrini 2006). Archaeological fieldwork, as a collective endeavour, proved a catalyst in their understanding that their own communal lifestyles are important in science, in opposition to popular capitalist ideology, which stresses the individual.

As one of the preparatory activities, a qualification course focusing on Archaeology and Public Education was planned to include all teachers (reaching 120 people). In parallel, the donation to the libraries of each of the schools of sets of books with critical approaches was aimed at allowing the continuity of community study and reflection. At the end of the course a participation certificate was awarded, signed by the Centre for Strategic Studies in Public Archaeology of the Campinas University (UNICAMP), a valid document enabling local teachers to have access to better positions. All the teachers took part in the preparatory meetings and activities, and during Archaeology Week, 15 archaeologists acted with teachers, educators, local artisans and others to produce a whole week of critical activities. The archaeologists included some senior scholars, but most were undergraduate or graduate students. The aim was to foster their own identities, empowering them in their fight to defend their own local, non-capitalist interests and perceptions of the world.

Classes, drawings, expositions, poems, strolls in the historical downtown areas, craftworks, dances, singings and tricks had been developed with all the students. Archaeological sites were set up at each one of the schools, which enabled the students, during one day, to experience the daily routine of research. After one week of intense activities, the community held a closing party, where presentations of traditional dances not practiced for years were performed: People rediscovered festive clothes, remembered songs and re-congregated old groups. The parties were organised by the community itself, and were a way of reinforcing their traditional, popular symbolism, so far removed from the global capitalist mores.

To the great satisfaction of the team, Archaeology Week still continues to have an impact on the everyday activities of the city, almost one year after its execution. The schools, together with the students, applied the subjects of archaeology and cultural historical heritage to different disciplines such as writing, mathematics, historical research, art, and many others. The teachers passed on the experience and the materials used during the event to schools in other cities, which had requested kits and relevant material. The pottery craftworks of the city, which were restricted before to only one woman, now have new apprentices, and the price of the products tripled in a few days due to an increase in demand and interest.

The Peixe-Angical Dam Archaeological Rescue Project continues. The citizenship experience, based on the free expression of the community in its diversity and its willingness for preservation, constitutes the basic element of this project. Archaeology can play an important role in fostering people's concerns and their anti-capitalist traditions and actions, even when working with private companies. The true challenge is to spread this critical approach; public institutions can play an essential role in this task. A report on the project has been written and sent to the Brazilian Heritage body, and is soon to be published. Two further remarks are worth mentioning, relating to this public archaeology activity. First and foremost, it is still an exception in Brazil to include such critical public approaches in mandatory archaeological fieldwork, hence its discussion in this chapter. Secondly, this case study, and its uniqueness, highlights the difficulties and limitations of such an anti-capitalist approach, for it is much easier to carry out a so-called academic, scientific, positivist fact-finding mission, when it is supposedly completely detached from present-day society, ignoring in effect the interests of ordinary people and communities (*contra* Prous 2006:12).

CONCLUSION

Capitalism is not the only force binding together Brazilian society. Most social scientists agree that Brazil is a society with a strong patriarchal background, and patronage and personal relations are at the heart of its vastly unequal income distribution. Capitalism functions within this traditional framework. CRM (cultural resource management), a typical capitalist scheme to deal with the archaeological heritage, works in Brazil in its local, specific context. This explains both the success of private archaeological enterprises and the fact that ethical compromises are left to the discretion of each individual firm. Several private archaeology activities have been criticized, for such things as the absence of scholarly reports and the lack of public monitoring. This can lead to several ethical issues. On the one hand, capitalist greed can lead to the destruction of archaeological heritage, when archaeologists do not follow basic ethical standards, and the heritage institutions are not equipped to check and monitor fieldwork practice. On the other hand, capitalism, regulated and controlled by heritage institutions and the judiciary, can contribute to a better understanding of the past. Initiatives that include the participation of the population are now more and more frequent, and the collaboration of private and state institutions to foster public awareness is also increasing. But at the end of the day, we cannot avoid the major ethical issue: who benefits from archaeological work?

ACKNOWLEDGMENTS

We owe thanks to the following colleagues: Barbara Little, Walter Alves Neves, Charles E. Orser Jr., and Anna Curtenius Roosevelt. We received institutional support from the National Research Council (CNPq), the São Paulo State Science Foundation (FAPESP), the World Archaeological Congress and the University of Campinas, São Paulo, particularly its Centre for Strategic Studies (NEE/UNICAMP). The ideas are our own and we are therefore the only ones responsible for them.

NOTE

1. This project is also headed by Dr Paulo De Blasis (de Blasis and Robrahn-González 2003).

REFERENCES

Becker, E, Thomas, J and Stiess, E (1999) 'Exploring uncommon ground: sustainability and the social sciences', in Becker, E and Jahn, T (eds) *Sustainability and the Social Sciences*, Paris: UNESCO/ISOE/Zed Books

Becker, E and Jahn, T (1999) *Sustainability and the Social Sciences*, Paris: UNESCO/ISOE/Zed Books

De Blasis, PA and Robrahn-González, EM (2003) 'Dam contract archaeology in Brazil: some prospects and a case study at the Amazonian border', *International Workshop on Cultural Heritage Management and Dams*, BID

de Vries, B (2003) *In Search of Sustainability: What Can We Learn from the Past?* Paper for the International Symposium on World System History and Global Environmental Change, Lund University, Sweden

Faulkner, N (2000) 'Archaeology from below', *Public Archaeology* 1, 21–33

Funari, PPA (2001) 'Public archaeology from a Latin American perspective', *Public Archaeology* 1, 239–243

—— (2002) 'Class interests in Brazilian archaeology', *International Journal of Historical Archaeology* 6, 209–216

—— (2003a) *A Antiguidade Clássica: a Historia e a Cultura a Partir dos Documentos*. Campinas: Ed.Unicamp (2nd edition)

Funari, PPA (2003b) 'Dictatorship, democracy, and freedom of expression', *International Journal of Historical Archaeology* 7, 233–237

—— (2004) 'Public archaeology in Brazil', in Merriman, N (ed) *Public Archaeology*, London: Routledge

Funari, PPA and Pelegrini, S (2006) *Patrimônio Histórico e Cultural*. Rio de Janeiro: Jorge Zahar Editor

Little, BJ (2002) 'Archaeology as a shared vision', in Little, BJ (ed), *Public Benefits of Archaeology*, Gainesville: University Press of Florida

McManamon, FP (2000) 'Archaeological messages and messengers', *Public Archaeology* 1, 5–20

Marx, K (1973) *On Society and Social Change*, Chicago: Chicago University Press

Orser, CE (2004) *Historical Archaeology* (2nd ed.), Upper Saddle River, NJ: Pearson

Prous, A (2006) *O Brasil antes dos Brasileiros, A Pré-História do nosso País*. Rio de Janeiro: Zahar

Smith, GS and Ehrenhard, JE (2002) 'Protecting the past to benefit the public', in Little, BJ (ed), *Public Benefits of Archaeology*, 121–129, Gainesville: University Press of Florida

Stiglitz, J (2002) *Globalization and Its Discontents*, New York: Norton

CHAPTER 8

An Ethical Archaeology in the Near East: Confronting Empire, War and Colonization

Tamima Orra Mourad

As a child does with his or her toys, Western culture quite often investigates what it is destroying, from alien peoples and cultural heritages to landscapes and material resources.
- Mario Liverani (2005:221)

INTRODUCTION

'The 'E' and the 'I' words, empire and imperialism, are back in fashion' (Arrighi 2005:23). The words have not come back in use due to the 'American unipolar age' (*cf* Valladão 1993), an era that started much earlier with the collapse of the Soviet bloc in 1989, and which initiated the decade of 'globalisation'. Rather, what started the neo-imperial programme occurred in 2001, when the Bush neo-conservative administration, answering to the catastrophe of September 11, launched the Project for a New American Century, ie, a new imperial programme (Arrighi 2005:23). The sudden reappearance of imperialism made all the difference to the international geopolitical scenario, especially in Near Eastern politics where the daily lives of civilians were affected and countless deaths of Afghan and Iraqi civilians resulted. It also made a difference to Near Eastern archaeology. In this article I explore the history of imperial strategies of expansionism that have historically involved archaeologists and the use of archaeological remains to control new territories, to glorify empire, inform intelligence and military strategies, and secure colonies and provinces in the Near East. I am not implying here that expansionism and the exploitation of annexed territories along with their peoples is exclusive to capitalism. Rather, I explore the features of empires that ruled the Near East during the 19th century and how they influenced the role of archaeologists.

I concentrate on three periods of colonization, in order to gain an understanding of the legacies of archaeologists in our present-day situation: (1) the Ottoman Empire and semi-colonial European in-filtration; (2) the Mandate period starting in post-World War I; and (3) the recent invasion and colonization by American and British coalition forces. Looking back on the development of Near Eastern archaeology, we can understand how and when archaeologists began to play political roles as representatives of their countries' interests. At the same time that we understand the ethical context surrounding the development of archaeology as an academic discipline, we will note the formulation of international laws on conduct during warfare.

Immediately following the invasion of Iraq (Mesopotamia, the 'cradle of civilisation'), its archaeological sites gained unprecedented attention and media coverage. Destruction of sites, looting and the illicit sales of antiquities became headlines, and archaeologists were invited by the media to report the destruction of or damage to archaeological sites. Some journals, such as *National Geographic Magazine*, hosted expeditions to Iraq in conjunction with the US army (Hamilakis 2003:105). But archaeological expertise was not limited to the popular media. Archaeologists also visited the Pentagon to point out risks to local museums and to provide the geographical coordinates of sites (*cf* M. Gibson interview in *Archaeology*, 56(4), July–August 2003; and Hamilakis 2003 for critique). Peter Stone, chief executive officer of the World Archaeological Congress, advised military intelligence, as did Roger Matthews, former director of the British School of Archaeology in Iraq, who in return was offered 'a superior post in the coalition administration, as a cultural advisor to the Ministry of Culture' (a position that was declined[1]). While some archaeologists who have given information to military intelligence still question whether such posture is ethical, others have argued that '[t]he military needs to create a civilian cultural authority board' (Victor Hanson 2003, cited in Hamilakis 2003).

The writing of this article was thus prompted by contemporary world events and the need to reconsider the role of archaeologists during wartime. Above all, it is an effort to clarify the civilian status of archaeologists during both national and international conflicts, as defined by the Geneva protocols and conventions. Clearly archaeologists have a social role, and the knowledge we produce should be made public, not only for academics but for society in general. The circulation of archaeological knowledge does not itself jeopardize our status as civilians, intellectuals, academics, and scientists. What changes our status from civilians to combatants, according to the Geneva conventions and protocols, is our association with armies, armed forces, militias or armed individuals during war or armed conflicts. Such associations endanger our cred-ibility as civilians, intellectuals, academics, and scientists; and our role as social scientists becomes automatically questionable.

To understand the archaeologist's role in the history of imperialism, we must first contextualize the specific geopolitical situation in which we find ourselves. I do not suggest that any individual archaeologist should necessarily adhere to right- or left-wing politics or programmes. What I propose in this article is that we should maintain our civilian status during times of conflict and dissociate ourselves from the agents of war; otherwise, our involvement with such agents would imply a status shift from civilian to combatant. Before defining a new ethical parameter, however, we must understand what exactly is meant by neo-imperialism, where we stand, and how we got to this position.

Briefly, what is promoted by the media as a 'benevolent empire' (Kagan 2003) is backed by a military supremacy, a desire for economic hegemony (including the strategic control of petroleum) and technological domination. Despite the use of the old term 'empire', it does not necessarily have the traditional elements of empire, such as direct dominion, centralized power, and territorial occupation. Instead, the neo-conservative empire is about being the only sovereign country; the current US administration has set itself beyond international legality as evidenced in its refusal to sign the Kyoto protocol, its rejection of the International Court of Justice, and its ignoring of the United Nations' decisions on the military intervention in Iraq. In short, sovereign is the one who decides the exceptions (paraphrased from Valladão 1993, in Moita 2005). There is no need for occupation. Rather, there is a global militarization made possible by the worldwide deployment of soldiers and the network of global surveillance made possible by satellite technology. Instead of imperial tribute, there are new economic instruments such as the control of natural resources abroad (oil and gas) and strategic raw materials (guaranteed by the presence or threat of military intervention), and the imposition of economic policies made feasible through the adoption of neo-liberal policies, such as those outlined by the 'Washington Consensus' and adopted by the World Bank, IMF, and World Trade Organisation, all under the influence of the White House. These new characteristics, stressed by Moita (2005), are sufficient to initially explain the financial, technological, and military supremacy of the neo-empire. In the end, the empire functions in the exercise of coercion behind a façade of democracy.

The empire is supra-national, capitalist, and portrayed as democratic, as in the words of the former director of the US Central Intelligence Agency: 'We also have to realize who we are. We are not a race or a culture or a language. We are the creatures of the fourth US President James Madison's Constitution and his Bill of Rights. We can never forget that' (Woolsey 2003:8)[2]. The empire, benevolent in appearance (Kagan 2003), may not be in fact: 'When democracy becomes an empire, it is evidently no longer democratic in relation to the country where it interferes … But the internal democracy of the Imperial-state cannot be immune to the imperial logic implemented overseas' (Moita 2005). If we consider that 'democracy' is to be exported (and, if necessary, imposed), the Near East is at the top of the list of priorities because of the presence of oil:

> If we want to be successful in this long war, we will have to take on this issue of democracy in the Arab world. We will have to take on the – and I would use the word 'racist'– view that Arabs cannot operate democracies. We will need to make some people uncomfortable. (Woolsey 2003:9)

Archaeology in the Near East developed in these same crossroads of imperial hegemony, serving respective empires in their attempts at territorial, social, and political control of strategic zones of natural resources, commerce, transportation, and military control since the 19th century (Larsen 1994:29). Archaeology is always involved when it comes to colonial or imperial control of the Near East; archaeology developed at the core of the relationship between capitalist advancements and the cycle of dispossession, appropriation and annexation of territories. Consequently, archaeology and archaeologists have become instrumental to imperial advancements (Liverani 2005:223–243).

HISTORICAL BACKGROUND

In order to understand the role of archaeologists in the modern geopolitics of war in the Near East, it is imperative to understand how the facets of the *metier* came together in the mid-19th century. The interference in the Near East reflected a general need of the industrial powers for raw materials and craftsmanship (Liverani 1994:5). There was an increasing concern with local geography and topography, and the need for accurate maps of the harbours for safe navigation and anchorage, a well as the location of wells for water supply. There also was an interest in roads for the movement of armies and trade goods. Archaeologists became servants to empires, as capitalist agents, diplomats and intelligence officers. In the past, this led to the development of field projects and the creation of museum collections in Europe and in present-day Turkey. Orientalists and archaeologists were hired for such positions as geographers, diplomats, trade agents and translators. They offered their services to their respective consulates in return for payments that would guarantee the continuation of their research. As orientalists had knowledge of local languages and traditions, they became accessories to European interference in the Near East. As stated by Wesseling (2001:74), a great stimulus to Orientalism came from colonialism, where 'the training of civil servants became part of the European university education in the 19th century'. The curriculum included courses on languages, colonial administration, and imperial and colonial history, all of which were equally important for their careers. Orientalists became the emissaries of emperors and their regimes.

European powers such as France, Britain, Germany and Russia competed for the control of Levantine markets while they also shared fears regarding the Islamic front of the Ottoman Empire, a direct threat to Christianity. Europeans regarded the Near East in a collective projection, the *Orient Chrétien*, an imagined affinity between a Christian Europe and peoples, toponyms, and civilizations mentioned in the Bible, the Mesopotamian, Egyptian, Greek, Roman and Byzantine civilizations, and the Crusader past. At the same time, the Islamic past, Arab history and Turkish conquests were ignored. Islam as a unifying factor was (and still is) viewed as a threat to any hegemonic power. 'Islamophobia' in the 19th century led to a disregard for the Islamic past and its remains. In our latest experience, during the invasion of Iraq, full attention was given to what was considered as part of the 'cradle of civilisation' construct, yet Islamic remains were given a subordinate position.

The portrait of the Near East as the 'Cradle of Western Civilisation', and at present as the 'homeland of Chaos', with Islam at its core, is not a novelty. According to Larsen (1995:233), ever since the 19th century the socio-political atmosphere in the Near East has been regarded as undemocratic and despotic, in contrast with the West. It has served the marketing strategy of empires to interfere, infiltrate or invade the Near East at different times with overt 'benevolent' concerns and excuses. Among the most common are the institution or re-establishment of law and order, modernization in order to 'remedy stagnant or retrograde aspects of society', the civilizing of what is regarded as 'barbaric' through educational systems, and the dethroning of despotic rulers or leaders, replacing them with local ones, preferably not less tyrannical but subservient to foreign needs. Throughout the 19th century, Levantine princes, pashas and governors were appointed and controlled by the Ottoman Sultan, and every so often deposed and executed whenever it satisfied the goals of the Ottoman governmental programme. During the mandate period (1919–1945), lines of new states were drawn, and the local elites were educated at local universities and abroad to take charge of the newly created states. The post-colonial experience no longer involved direct rule and control of natural resources, but rather indirect influence over local regimes. Such characteristics can be understood even in today's neo-imperialist tendencies:

> As we undertake these efforts in the Middle East and elsewhere, occasionally by force of arms but generally not, generally by influence, by standing up for brave students in the streets of Tehran, we will hear

people say, from President Hosni Mubarak's regime in Egypt or from the Saudi royal family, that we are making them very nervous. And our response should be, 'Good. We want you nervous. We want you to change, but realize that now, for the fourth time in a hundred years, the democracies are on the march. And we are on the side of those who you most fear: your own people'. R. James Woolsey (2003:9), former Director of the Central Intelligence[3]

Throughout antiquity the Levant was the 'isthmus' of the network of trade that encompassed the Mediterranean, the Levantine coast, and Asia. Throughout antiquity the historical sequence of conquests of the Levantine coast illustrates the constant interests of expanding local and foreign empires. Yet despite the fact that the investigation of archaeological finds was not a novelty to local intellectuals and historians in earlier centuries (cf El Daly 2005), it was only starting in the 19th century that empires found a growing need to unearth and collect material vestiges of the past; in fact, it became a fashion and a mania as European traders infiltrated the Ottoman Empire. Near Eastern archaeology, as it evolved during the 19th century, should be recognized as an extension of industrial capitalism.

In the case of the Near East, under Ottoman rule, European semicolonial control of the territory was guaranteed through the agreements made with the Sublime Porte to modernize the empire. This strategy led the French, British and Germans to compete for and to exercise power and control over the territory, initially through the construction of roads, railroads and the Suez Canal, and subsequently, by the end of the 19th century, of telegraph lines. From a technical perspective, archaeology benefited from this territorial control, not only because archaeological sites were used as landmarks in maps, but also because there was an exploration of human and natural resources, and as a consequence archaeological finds were to be explored and exploited. Besides biblical references to the Near Eastern antiquity and landscape, small finds and ruined monuments, were given new meaning in representing expansionist political and economic control. Near Eastern archaeology as a discipline developed within these parameters and involved a similar cycle of observation, recording, classification, control, and appropriation. From a financial perspective, archaeological remains were treated like all resources found in the soil and subsoil: as assets having set market prices, to be sold as historical landmarks, souvenirs or decorative pieces.

The archaeologist/orientalist thus produced a discourse, here regarded as an artefact, intended to fulfil political purposes that were changed, upgraded or abandoned in regard to contemporary semicolonial, colonial, and imperialist circumstances. Archaeological discourse could be bought, sold or sponsored, and served the purposes of career promotion. Orientalism was aimed at the same strategies of imperialism: the perception, recording, classification and control of both past and living cultures and populations; and measuring and justifying degrees of cultural superiority/inferiority, diversity/uniformity, development/stagnation, civilization/barbarism, ancestral/non-lineal, antiquity/modernity, dynamism/lethargy. The orientalist persona was an extension of the colonizing agency, as an extension or mimesis of colonizing policies of empires; archaeology could not be regarded separate from other local assets. The Near East was not only the 'Cradle of Western Civilisation'; it was also the 'Cradle of raw materials for western industrialisation'. Although the theoretical and methodological perspectives in the field of Near Eastern archaeology have considerably changed, the geopolitical status of the Near East as a disputed region for its natural resources, such as oil, has not. The region still attracts foreign interference, as in the case of the invasion and war in Iraq. As archaeologists were used as mediators between empires and overseas interests in the past, they still have this potential role today; and whenever necessary archaeologists are invited to play it.

ARCHAEOLOGY CELEBRATING CONQUEST AND CIVILIZATION: PROPAGANDA, GLAMOUR, IMPERIALISM

The concept of the 'cradle of civilisation' encapsulates the prerequisites of a civilized past that would promote 19th-century European powers. Imperial expansion was concerned not only with present conquests; rather, it was also concerned with a competition between past imperial powers and *their* conquerors. It was ultimately about the awareness, conquest and control of what was conceived of as a 'civilised' past. As archaeologists, philologists, antiquarians and diplomats dug the past, they also involved themselves in contemporary issues as they represented their respective governments. They notoriously opposed Islam, and at a symbolic level regarded themselves as new conquerors surmounting past conquerors. Napoleon I and his invasion of Egypt in 1798 started the mania for emulating rulers and conquerors of antiquity as means of demonstrating his own power (*cf* Liverani 1994:4). The cycle consisted of the intervention of foreign armies in local conflicts – an investment justifiable due to local markets and resources – and the investigation of the past, and the subsequent removal of surviving remains. Archaeological remains became the personal passion of rulers, but they also served other purposes, as evidenced by the collections made by Napoleon III which are now housed in the Louvre. Napoleon III was particularly fond of archaeology.

Beyond his personal passion, archaeology also served a socio-political function for glorifying hegemony. Archaeological remains were valued as art, for their 'beauty' and for their decorative purposes – to adorn his palaces, even personal chambers and chapels. As to the socio-political function of archaeology, it served as a way to fabricate the past – according to the people whom he hired to narrate the past.

In contrast, the *British Museum* was not linked so closely to the idea of industrialization. Rather than functioning as a *bureau*, as was Napoleon's Louvre, the British Museum was more akin to a bank. During the 19th century, it expended generous amounts of money on fieldwork and invested noteworthy sums of money for the purpose of building its collections. The museum's reputation escalated in pace with the diversity of its collections; what James Henry Breasted would later characterize as the 'scholastic Bank of England' (Breasted 1945:85). In England, archaeologists became public figures as exemplified by men like Henry Austen Layard who was greeted in public as a hero for unearthing Nimrud. Archaeological remains adorned spaces, celebrated capitalism and promoted archaeologists. Artefacts were valued for their market value, sold rather than collected. Such relationships are still present in our behaviour. Vestiges of the past functioned efficiently as symbols of emperors and empires, diffused to the public as images of the predominance of the empire, another legacy that has survived to our day.

Thus today, when an archaeologist suggests shooting a looter, as during the 2003 invasion of Iraq and the subsequent looting of museums and sites (*cf* Kennedy 2003 in Hamilakis 2003), this is not about punishing a thief who robbed the 'cradle of civilization'; more exactly, it demands retribution for a raider of the actual empire. Throughout the recent invasion of Iraq, sites and monuments were celebrated as landmarks of conquest, and their preservation and survival celebrated as testimonies to military accuracy: 'Somebody in the US government deserves positive credit for sparing the archaeological sites from bombing' (H. Wright in an interview by Vedantam 2003). As archaeology was spared for the purpose of celebrating empire, it was dehumanized, and the loss of human life and the conditions of local populations were regarded as secondary to the preservation of the sites. Should archaeologists give information that was collected for academic and scientific purposes to assist armies? In a way, sites are to be preserved while human lives are shoved into the category of collateral damage. To what extent have archaeologists maintained a constructive academic-social role?

This association between archaeologists and foreign armies fighting in the Near East is not a novelty. By the early 20th century, the cradle of civilization had been militarized and upgraded as the 'bridgehead' in military terms: 'a forward position held by advancing troops in enemy territory, serving as a basis for further advances'. As we shall see, this is the significance of the Cradle/bridgehead to the neo-imperialist geopolitical aims.

THE NEAR EAST AS THE BRIDGEHEAD OF ASIA MINOR: ARCHAEOLOGISTS AS POLICY-MAKING AND MILITARY THINK TANKS

James Henry Breasted's *The Bridgehead of Asia Minor* describes a combination of strategies to secure control over the great bastion of western Asia. It was conceived and delineated as war strategy for a navy having its home in the Atlantic; it was a plan drawn for the United States and Great Britain. Historically, the bridgehead overlapped and combined strategic zones of natural resources, commerce, transportation and military control, a stronghold for Eastern Mediterranean rule which buttressed the Persian, Macedonian, Roman, and Turkish conquests of the Suez and Egypt. The whole arrangement gravitated around the control of transportation, communication and a safe location for troops, in order of the Suez (which gave access to the Red Sea) and to secure control over Asia Minor and access to the Persian Gulf. Within this framework, the Baghdad railway was implicated in 'fundamental questions of the inter-oceanic, intercontinental strategic of this world struggle – a strategic demanding an outlook so spacious that it is only bounded by the planet itself'. Although these words seem to echo today's news, this piece of foreign policy was outlined by Breasted in a 1918 article discussing the tactical 'dos' and 'don'ts' to sweep off Germans and Turks, but also demarcating sections of land to be divided as mandated territory and that were crucial to gaining and maintaining the hegemony in the region.

Breasted represented America and sided with England. He had long studied the war campaigns of antiquity and was at the time considered most qualified to give advice to guide military commanders. He was particularly convinced that there was a need to take over a 'highway', a territorial patch broad enough to be strategically defensible:

> An army advancing upon the Suez from Asia inevitably comes from the north, and having the desert on the one hand and the eastern shores of the Mediterranean on the other, it marches southward for over four hundred miles down relatively narrow cultivable fringe between the desert and the sea. This contracted avenue between sea and desert is strategically like a four-hundred-mile prolongation of the Isthmus of Suez northward. Together with the isthmus it forms a long link like the handle of a

dumb-bell between Asia and Africa – a link nearly five hundred miles long. On this long bridge Palestine is in the south, while Syria occupies the northern portion. Every army moving against Suez must transverse almost the entire length of this narrow five-hundred-mile corridor, and access to it can be gained only in the region bordering on the southeast corner of Asia Minor. Without passing the southeastern corner of Asia Minor, it is impossible to attack the Suez, and it is this fact which so enormously increases the strategic importance of Asia Minor. (Breasted 1918:676)

The bridgehead, or the handle of the dumb-bell described above, is precisely what he had academically coined the 'Fertile Crescent' two years earlier, a scientific version of the 19th century's 'cradle of civilization' (Figure 8.1). The concept gained scientific credibility through diffusionist explanations that situated it as the place of the rise of civilizations. It also involved a highly racist discourse, arguing that civilization was an exclusive achievement of the 'Great White Race'[4], and that the 'Negroid' and 'Mongoloid' races played no part in the 'rise of civilisation' (Breasted 1916:130–131). Breasted became a military celebrity, and his work began to be used as military strategy. As soon as America entered the First World War, Colonel Theodore Roosevelt consulted Breasted as a war strategist (Breasted 1945:232–233).

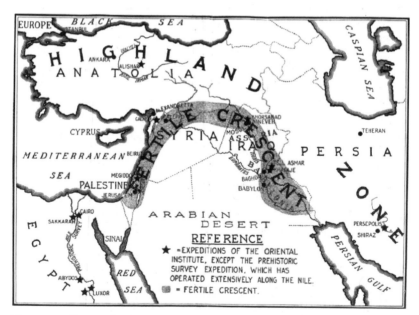

Figure 8.1 Breasted's 'Promising Fertile Crescent', and research headquarters. Source: Breasted, JH, *The Oriental Institute*, Chicago: University of Chicago Press, 1933.

The mistakes of antiquity dictated mistakes not to be made by the powers fighting the war. And, in this case, Breasted proved to be useful to the British Mediterranean fleet as well:

> 'You know, for you have very fully written of it,' Allenby said, 'how Thutmose III crossed Camel Ridge, riding through the pass to meet the enemy in a chariot of shining electrum. We had our book with us, and we had just read the account of it, so we knew the dates: Thutmose went through on the 15th of May over 3,000 years ago, and on the same day I took Lady Allenby for the first time to see the battlefield where we beat the Turks, and like Thutmose III, we also went through in a chariot of shining metal – for our machine had wheels of aluminium and was all covered with polish [sic] metal. So she saw the scene of victory on the anniversary of the earliest known battle there, and also approached it in a chariot of glittering metal. I wanted her to see it, for as I have told you before, I took my title from there – Allenby of Megiddo – because it was a cavalry operation which broke the Turkish line, and I am a cavalry officer.' (Breasted 1945:311–312)

Past glories were translated into the present with the same magnificence, splendour, and radiance. Breasted was glorified by military officials and by the British archaeologists working in the region. Like Breasted, archaeologists were not undertaking fieldwork activities; they had come to a halt due to the war. Unlike Breasted, they were working for military intelligence – among them Gertrude Bell, Hogarth, Sir Leonard Wooley and T.S. Lawrence (of Arabia) – in order to control the growing nationalist movement so that it would be an instrument to rival France, at the same time that it was held under the limits tolerated by the British and American forces. These archaeologists were to become instrumental in imperial policy-making think tanks:

> The British Empire has become a great and sacred international trust, with responsibilities of vital importance for all mankind. With a high sense of the moral obligations involved in these responsibilities, British statesmen have everywhere met them with a fidelity, efficiency, and success, marred chiefly by the treatment of Persia, which rebuffed some of us very grievously for a time. But that is happily passed, and to-day the British Empire furnishes the basic organization for policing the world. It [the Bridgehead or Fertile Crescent] must be supported and strengthened at every point *strategically requiring it* [italics in the original]. (Breasted 1918:677)

Interestingly, the British played the same geopolitical role as the United States today. Breasted also defended the British in the possession and control of the 'Fertile Crescent', just as the coalition forces invest in the control of the region today. A further remark contrasting past and present geopolitics is that France is left out of the war and conquest exercise – whether willingly or involuntarily:

> France already has great responsibilities in northern and western Africa. Let her therefore have western Africa from Morocco to Cameroon and

the Congo, with such present neutral holdings there may require.
(Breasted 1918:678)

Breasted's article on the bridgehead to Asia Minor concluded with the
suggestion that the Near East required European intervention; otherwise, local disturbances would endanger world peace, exactly the same
excuses used nowadays by the coalition forces. To solve the Near
Eastern question it was important to promote the 'political education
of Eastern nationalities, divided into independent groups on the basis
of geographical and economical considerations – reinforced by historical development' (Breasted 1918:678). What was suggested as 'political education of Eastern nationalities' was clearly nationalism for
state formation – a field where archaeologists had proven to be particularly useful.

Archaeologists assisted by both providing nationalist discourses
with 'scientific content' – recuperating the *'beaux titres ancestraux'* – and
by implementing them in educational systems such as universities
(*cf* Contenau 1926:261 for an example of this programme). There was a
race for identity. Where the archaeological past was imposed as ancestry, ancestry was equated with ethnicity, and ethnicity was equated
with political identity; in other words, nationalism. Breasted's 'fertile
crescent' became a symbol for the Arab nationalist movement in the
1950s (*cf* Mourad 2003). The political movements that were once motivated in the mandated states, as Breasted mentioned, turned out to be
uninteresting to the modern-day scenario of international interests in
the region. These nationalist views of the past, constructs of 'previous
empires', today vex the 'neo-empire':

> There are really three movements in the Middle East that are essentially
> at war with the west, with modernity, with the western Europe and the
> United States and our allies. They are, first of all, the fascists, a term that
> I use advisedly because the Arab nationalist movements of Syria – until
> recently Iraq and Syria – and Libya and other such groups in the
> Middle East are effectively modelled on the fascist parties of the 1920s
> and the 1930s. They are structured like them, and are similarly anti-
> semitic [*sic*]. They are fascists and there is no reason to mince words.
> (Woolsey 2003:6–7)

This exasperation with Arab nationalist movements justified the 2003
invasion of Iraq, a strategic part of the 'fertile crescent'. Syrian troops
were whisked out of Lebanon. Elsewhere in the crescent, Israel and
Jordan are on good terms, Iran has been blacklisted, Egypt, Saudi
Arabia, and Turkey intimidated. 'The war is essentially, similar to the
Cold War. This is the origin of the phrase World War IV, which Professor
Eliot Cohen came up with in America shortly after September 11 2001,
to characterize the parallels between this war and what he called World

War III – the Cold War' (Woolsey 2003:6). He 'pacifies' us by explaining that 'Nonetheless it is not hopeless. It is the best path to peace, since democracies do not fight one another. They fight dictatorships and dictatorships fight each other, and democracies sometimes pre-empt against dictatorships, but they do not fight one another' (Woolsey 2003:9). In this 'democratic' bullying game, are we archaeologists to take on the legacies of the last world wars and steward the new 'World War IV' by hiding behind archaeology? If the 'creatures of the fourth US President James Madison's Constitution and his Bill of Rights' are to declare war, and invade, are archaeologists to steward 'democratic archaeology', empire, military advancements? Are we to celebrate savage capitalist advancements? Are we to celebrate industrialization again, the industry of weapons and destruction?

CONCLUSION: ON ETHICS

All of us live in a society, and are members of a nationality with its own language, tradition, historical situation. To what extent are intellectuals servants of these actualities, to what extent enemies? The same is true of intellectuals' relationship with institutions (academy, church, professional guild) and with worldly powers, which in our time have co-opted the intelligentsia to an extraordinary degree. The results are, as Wilfred Owen put it, that 'the scribes on all the people shove/And bawl allegiance to the state'. Thus in my view the principal intellectual duty is the search for the independence from such pressures. Hence my characterizations of the intellectual as exile and marginal, as amateur, and as the author of a language that tries to speak the truth to power. (Said 1994:xv–xvi)

Before addressing academic dignity and intellectual integrity, seriously jeopardized whenever we serve empires, regimes or armed forces, I wish to call attention to the fact that the Near East should not be regarded as the only target of the New American Programme launched in 2001, 'unipolar age', 'World War IV', 'benevolent empire' or whatever people choose to call it. As a reminder, in 2001 the number of American soldiers sent abroad reached a total of 254,788 (Moita 2005). The reason for keeping the troops overseas is not to dispatch them into conflict but to intimidate the rest of the world. It is a form of expressing sovereignty by exception, as stated above, by not implementing international agreements or UN decisions, and by refusing to sign international treaties. We must not regard Iraq – or the 'axis of evil'– as an isolated case. It is, of course, unknown if such troops will be called into action, but in case they do, we must remember that the United States is not a signatory of the Hague Convention – it is therefore highly probable that archaeologists will be invited again to assist military strategies. And, in this case, what are we to do? How are we to deal with our academic social role? Are we to collaborate with the structures of war and put our civilian status at risk? Are we to directly collaborate and place our knowledge, constructed for academic purposes, at the service of armed forces, armed individuals, and militias? Are we to seek and find opportunity in disaster as suggested by Matthews (2003:1)? Are we to leave behind the dilapidated and problematic history of the discipline of archaeology, leaving it unquestioned (as suggested by Matthews 2003:1)? Are we to assist armies, war and imperial aims?

Throughout this chapter I have attempted to illustrate a socio-political process of the services provided by orientalists to empire, rulers, armies, and so on. It is very common for those who oppose the critique of imperialism and capitalism to dismiss the discussion on orientalism as a separation between East and West. Orientalism was not about a cleavage. It was about intellectuals serving the empire, and ultimately it was about business and self-promotion. It is not about intellectuals who lost their intellectual freedom; it is about intellectuals who made it subordinate to imperialism. Orientalism, therefore, has nothing to do with being an easterner or westerner. Orientalism is a political posture towards empire, where an intellectual offers himself as its instrument or agent, and serves the empire. The socio-political history of the discipline elucidates circumstances, characteristics, classifications; paradigms that should be dropped and postures that we must change. These insights are not only essential for fighting orientalism in times of peace and war, but also for confronting problems in the discipline that resulted from its links to empire, colonialism and nationalism.

And what about times of war? The history of the Geneva conventions and protocols dates back to 1864, when they were first created to set limits to war behaviour. They consist of a body of conventions and protocols that define the status of personnel involved in war and conflicts, define weapons and their legality, list and define war crimes and the rights, duties and proper treatment of armed forces, and define the status of combatants, civilians and mercenaries. It is therefore imperative to classify the status of individuals during times of conflict so that their rights, duties and treatment are defined. It is also important to investigate these definitions in order to distinguish possible roles for archaeologists during war. I believe that it is necessary to briefly review the status of combatants, civilians and mercenaries as defined by the Geneva conventions and protocols, before proposing any parameter for archaeologists.

A combatant is not only a uniformed soldier. He (she) can be considered within this category if classified as a fighter, carrying arms while preparing for, or during an attack (Protocol I, Art. 44, Sec. 3).

Compliance with structures of war also sets the individual in the category of combatant; and the only exceptions to this rule are religious and medical personnel. They must wear uniforms, and they may carry arms and use them in case they are attacked illegally. Despite their function and their uniform and the fact that they are armed, they are still considered civilians. Another exception was recently made for journalists as a category that deals with providing information for the public in general. It is only recently, since the adoption of the 1977 Protocols, that journalists were recognized as civilians, as unarmed individuals, non-combatants and non-compliant with the structures of war. Before that, they were considered civilian members of the military, they often wore uniforms, and could be taken as prisoners of war. The distinction between the civilian and the combatant must also be made visually clear. Combatants must wear uniforms and must carry their weapons openly making their category recognisable. Identification is fundamental so that both civilians and combatants receive protection. The only exception to this protection is made to mercenaries, who are identified as soldiers who are not nationals and who receive higher pay than the local soldiers. If the archaeologist is to directly advise armed forces, individuals and militias, what will be our status? In the case of war in Iraq, considering what was stated by Hamilakis (2005), that 'some archaeologists "embedded" themselves in the US and UK military structures prior and during the invasion', how are we to classify the status of these archaeologists?

I personally adopt the humanitarian concept that I am an intellectual. I classify myself as a civilian and therefore automatically as a non-combatant, non-compliant with armies, above all when they by-pass internationally ratified laws or organizations. I adopt the civilian ethic as defined by Slim (2005:482):

> a belief that all of us, no matter what side we are on, have a greater common identity as human beings than the particular identities that war bestows on us as 'enemies' or 'allies'. Belief in the idea of the civilian turns, therefore, on issues of personal identity and social relationship. It requires us to allow people a fundamental and vulnerable human identity that is not determined by their immediate relationship with the politics, economics or social structure of war. Their human value transcends their social connections with the war.

In order not to leave it as a meta-naïve label, I further quote (2005:498):

> The power of the civilian identity, therefore, is not to reduce this person to some sort of naïve cliché of a harmless victim, but to affirm him [her] as like us: non-innocent in many ways; bound by circumstance and the power of others, and reliant on mercy. As an unarmed enemy he [she] is a complex phenomenon that demands our restraint rather than murder.

I do not deny that we as archaeologists or private citizens hold political views and critique world order and events, yet our direct involvement with war structure involves a shift in our social role and status. The role of civilian informs our relationship with stewardship. Instead of regarding ourselves as stewards of material culture, and their physical integrity, we should regard ourselves as stewards of the informational content of material culture. Whenever we ask ourselves for whom are we preserving the past, we should answer for civilians, local communities and the public, and not for armies. We should safeguard the history of human experience, promoting and celebrating human diversity and existence, instead of providing historical advice for armies. We should question the fragrance of 'democracy', which trespasses universal human rights and which evaporates to leave us with the harsh reality of at least a hundred thousand dead in Iraq, with torture in Abu Ghraib, with deaths in Afghanistan. It is time to redefine ourselves as civilians and to realize that when activities in Iraq or Afghanistan are advertised as benevolent, humanity is the victim.

ACKNOWLEDGMENTS

I wish to thank Yannis Hamilakis for the invitation to write an article for this volume, and Philip Duke for his careful reading and heavy editing of the initial draft. I owe immense thanks to a number of friends for reading and/or commenting on this article (before it was heavily edited), among them: Pedro Paulo Funari, Fekri Hassan, Janes Jorge, Ana Elisa Campos Salles, Ana Elisa Cascão, and Wei He. I dedicate this article to the memory of my father, Abdul Halim Youssef Mourad, who would have loved to share this dedication with all the civilians, those who are victims of crimes of war. I should at this point stress that any faults or errors remaining in this article are entirely my responsibility.

NOTES

1. Personal correspondence, London, April 21, 2004.
2. Taken from his address at the Political Risk Conference held in June 2003, at the Royal Institute of International Affairs, London.
3. Taken from his address from the Political Risk Conference held at the Royal Institute of International Affairs, June 2003.
4. The 'Great White Race' was divided into the Nordic type, Alpine type, and Mediterranean type (Breasted 1933:130–131).

REFERENCES

Arrighi, G (2005) 'Hegemony unravelling – 1', *New Left Review* 32, 23–80
Breasted, C (1945) *Pioneer to the Past*, New York: Charles Scribner's Sons

Breasted, JH (1916) *Ancient Times: A History of the Early World*, Boston: Ginn
—— (1918) 'The Bridgehead of Asia Minor', *The Nation*, 106, 676–678
—— (1933) *The Oriental Institute*, Chicago: University of Chicago Press
Contenau, G (1926) 'Le Congrès International D'Archéologie de Syrie-Palestine', in *Syria*. Paris: Librairie Orientaliste Paul Geuthner
El Daly, O (2005) *Egyptology: the Missing Millennium: Ancient Egypt in Medieval Arabic Writings*, London: UCL Press
Hamilakis, Y (2003) 'Iraq, stewardship and the "record": an ethical crisis for archaeology', *Public Archaeology* 3, 104–111
—— (2005) 'Whose world and whose archaeology? the colonial present and the return of the political', *Archaeologies: The Journal of the World Archaeological Congress* 1, 94–101
Hanson, V (2003) 'Postbellum thoughts', *The National Review*, 9 May
Kagan, R (2003) *Of Paradise and Power: America and Europe in the New World Order*, New York: Alfred A. Knopf
Kennedy, M (2003) 'Kill looters, urges archaeologist'. *Guardian*, 9 July
Larsen, MT (1994) 'The appropriation of the Near Eastern past: contrasts and contradictions', in *The East and the Meaning of History*. International Conference (23–27 November 1992), Rome: Bardi Editore
—— (1995) 'Orientalism and Near Eastern archaeology', in Miller, D, Rowlands, M and Tilley, C (eds) *Domination and Resistance*, London: Routledge
Liverani, M (1994) '*Voyage en Orient*. The origins of archaeological surveying in the Near East', in *The East and the Meaning of History*. International Conference (23–27 November 1992), Rome: Bardi Editore
—— (2005) 'Imperialism', in Pollock, S and Bernbeck, R (eds) *Archaeologies of the Near East: Critical Perspectives*, Oxford: Blackwell
Matthews, R (2003) 'Year zero for the archaeology of Iraq', *Papers from the Institute of Archaeology* 14, 1–6
Moita, L (2005) 'A Propósito do Conceito de Império', *Nação Defesa* 110, 9–32
Mourad, TO (2003) *Shattering the Myths of Archaeological Ancestries in Lebanon: Identity, Nationalism and Neglected Stratigraphies*, unpublished M.A. thesis. Department of History and Archaeology: American University of Beirut
Said, E (1994) *Representations of the Intellectual: The 1993 Reith Lectures*, New York: Pantheon Books
Slim, H (2005) 'Why protect civilian? innocence, immunity and enmity in war', *International Affairs* 79, 481–502
Valladão, A (1993) *Le XXIe Siècle Sera Américain*, Paris: Éditions la Découverte
Vedantam, S (2003) Worst looting may be in remote parts of Iraq, *Washington Post*, 12 June
Wesseling, H (2001) 'Overseas history', in Burke, P (ed) *New Perspectives on Historical Writing*, University Park: Pennsylvania State University Press
Woolsey, JR (2003) 'At war for freedom', *The World Today* 59, 6–9

CHAPTER 9

Archaeology within Marketing Capitalism

Alice B. Kehoe

INTRODUCTION

Malinowski observed,

> Immediate history, semi-historic legend, and unmixed myth flow into one another, form a continuous sequence, and fulfill really the same sociological function... [T]he really important thing about the myth is its character of a retrospective, ever-present, live actuality... It is clear that myth functions especially where there is a sociological strain, such as in matters of a great difference in rank and power, matters of precedence and subordination, and unquestionably where profound historical changes have taken place.... [M]yth serves principally to establish a sociological charter. (Malinowski 1954:126, 144)

In the same vein, Hayden White argued that

> in the nineteenth century ... historical reflection ... serve[d] as the very paradigm of realistic discourse ... constituting an image of a *current* social praxis as the criterion of plausibility by reference to which any given institution, activity, thought ... can be endowed with the aspect of 'reality'. (White 1987:101–102, my italics)

Archaeology, from its beginnings in the Renaissance and early-modern science, provided trappings of a past to charter a present of capitalist expansion. Its first phase, deployed by mercantile capitalism, produced pure white marble forms of youths and women and columned temples, exemplars of exalted taste unsullied by blood, sweat, or tears. Its second phase, serving industrial capitalism, turned to anonymous quantities of mundane tools, flint blades and potsherds, to chart the rise of civilisation through technological progress. The final third of the 20th century's massive decline in manufacturing employment – humans replaced by robotic programs, and jobs for humans primarily in assembling components or serving the wealthier – necessarily must elicit a newer sociological charter.

Globalisation is touted as a New Thing, a claim that would have surprised those anatomically modern humans migrating out of Africa onto the rest of the planet. Coca-Cola and McDonald's are icons of the global now, as if tobacco, sugar, tea, coffee and cotton, not to mention biface blades, worked copper, iron and ceramics, had not been their predecessors. What is much newer is enshrinement of the marketing concept, the creation of consumers 'increasingly reliant upon the market for the provisioning of their needs and wants' (Applbaum 2004:256n4). This form of capitalism focuses not upon mercantile transactions, not upon production, but upon manipulating consumers, persuading millions to always carry brand-name bottles of water and buy labeled Happy Meals.

Archaeologists are shifting gears to come up with tangible pasts to charter marketing capitalism. 'The new marketing idea is to break the wall, burn the roof and towers that historically limited the marketing imagination' (Applbaum 2004:208). Results include heritage programs, eco-tourism, public education in archaeology, and forensic archaeology. From the standpoint of marketing capitalism, research topics such as gender-in-archaeology, 'settler', 'colonial', slave-quarter, brothel, industrial and other facets of historical archaeology, indigenous archaeology, landscape archaeology, and so on parallel marketing's fragmentation of the individual into a set of identities each demanding materialisation via costumes, grooming preparations, food, leisure activities, furnishings – for example, a professional who is a 'suit' at work, in 'sweats' to work out in a health club, 'casual punk' in a bar, 'suited up' for scuba diving or cycling, 'jammies' for Sunday morning lazing at home, 'sexy' for romantic evenings. In other words, modernity's ideology elevating the individual self has hypertrophied into the individual as a bundle of alternate selves determined by calendar day and clock time, each of them flagged by purchased commodities. Where the rationalisation of the economy through mercantile capitalism looked for embodiments of classical logic in Greek statuary and architecture, and industrial capitalism looked for quantities of mundane artifacts, marketing capitalism looks for construction of pasts as multitudinous as the needs it fosters in consumers.

MULTIPLE PASTS

'Multiple pasts' is not a postmodern notion. Collingwood (the only practicing field archaeologist who was also a first-rank professor of philosophy) taught:

> The historical past is the world of ideas which the present evidence creates in the present. In historical inference we do not move from our present world to a past world; the movement in experience is always a movement within a present world of ideas... [H]istory is not the past as such. (Collingwood 1956 [1946]:154)

Stuart Piggott warned us to distinguish between the real past, which is virtually infinite, encompassing every microbe, every change in every crystal; the known past; and the wished-for past, whether 'the glory that was Greece' or 'nasty, brutish and short' Paleolithic lives (Piggott 1981:187, crediting Glyn Daniel for unpublished remarks). Chartering myths conjure up wished-for pasts: A touching (or infuriating) case is the picture of matriarchal earth-mother amazons worshipping The Goddess, allegedly revealed by Marija Gimbutas's research and expounded to 'empower' contemporary women (Eller 2000).

Nationalism notoriously produces wished-for pasts (Kehoe 1992:5; Malina and Vasíček 1990:25–26, 63–64; Schnapp 1996:291, 295, 303; Trigger 1984). The Nazis' Aryan myth chartering their genocide campaigns is a satanic example (Arnold 1990). Denmark's fostering of archaeology immediately following its disastrous defeat in the Napoleonic War perfectly illustrates Malinowski's observation that 'profound historic change' provokes chartering myths (Kristiansen 1981, 1985, 1993). American archaeology perniciously supported, and was confined by, Manifest Destiny ideology (Kehoe 1998:83; Kennedy 1994). Archaeology in the service of the state is characteristic of the profession (Fowler 1987; see also White 1973:136).

Marketing archaeology has an equally long history. Schnapp describes Christian Thomsen, pioneering curator of the Danish National Museum, as 'a self-taught businessman ... who did not hesitate ... to organize, mobilize and convince ... the public [which] crowded his museum' (Schnapp 1996:301). A century after Thomsen, in 1929, New York state archaeologist Arthur C. Parker spoke to a national conference urging states to support archaeology, explaining that in addition to civic responsibility toward their resources and the promulgation of knowledge, states should realise that *'Archaeological remains are monumental exhibits. –* The marking of prehistoric Indian sites and their protection from promiscuous digging would ... attract the attention of the sight-seeing public' (quoted in O'Brien and Lyman 2001:22, emphasis in original). And at the end of the twentieth century, a commentator on archaeology in the Southeast noted that even university departments had come to depend upon 'popular attractions, such as the University of Alabama's museum at Moundville, successfully combin[ing] research with tourism and public education' (Sassaman 2002:237).

Thirty years after its founding in 1879, the Archaeological Institute of America was discombobulated by enthusiasts from western states who wanted their donations to support local projects rather than, as requested, Classical archaeology at Delphi. Charles Lummis in Los Angeles and Edgar Hewett in Santa Fe built archaeological societies through attracting local business boosters. Lummis called his vision, culminating in the Southwest Museum in Los Angeles, the 'western idea', that newer cities in the West needed to construct identities incorporating their unique histories, however brief, and elements of Spanish and American Indian cultures of the region. In 1905, Lummis chose to use what he termed 'modern business methods' to reach, en masse, consumers of heritage events, and soon after, Hewett in New Mexico copied Lummis's methods (Snead 2002).

What the 21st century faces is a shift from the modern ideal of a wholly dominant centralised state to the postmodern conceptualisation of the state as mosaic, varied elements existing within the frame of the state. 'Identity politics' foregrounds diversity in targeting voting blocs, to the point of seeking possible emergent constituencies (as when, in 2003, fans of Democratic presidential candidate Howard Dean were labeled 'Deaniacs' and viewed as a likely bloc even after Dean withdrew his candidacy). Recognising, even celebrating, diversity opens up new markets. Ethnic foods, music, and religious edifices multiply consumer opportunities and niches for marketing. Archaeology is called upon to validate, ie, to charter, diverse communities within the territory.

The most blatant employment of archaeology, speaking broadly, is in Las Vegas where boosterism most extravagantly exceeds taste. Caesar's Palace hotel and casino (see book cover) and some of the quickie wedding chapels pay hunky surfers to stand around in short, Roman-style kilts and, if a nuptial couple wishes, attend the wedding ceremony; one can add a bare-chested man labeled 'King Tut' to add Egyptian mystique. At the opposite pole, though not necessarily physically very distant, are New Agers making pilgrimages to sites alleged to emanate primordial power. Stonehenge has been described as 'a center of popular resistance to the market-driven values of modern society' (Del Giudice and Porter 2001:5). As with the plastic medicine men equipped to process credit-card payments for participation in their 'traditional American Indian' ceremonies[1], marketing brings the customers to the sites. New Age magazines carry a lot of advertising.

ETHICAL ISSUES WITH MULTIPLE PASTS

Marketing heritage has many ethical pitfalls. The eternal bugaboo of splitters versus lumpers rears up over how much consumers ought to know, need to know, are willing to bother knowing from presentations of archaeological matters. Practitioners are challenged by the discipline's stance as science, versus marketers' focus on what sells. Who owns the past in our fragmented societies? Indigenes' descendants? Colonisers' descendants? Entrepreneurs? Politics influences what pasts are selected to be investigated, as well as which are foregrounded in the public. One approach to evaluating ethical issues is to analyse presentation of the heritage as narrative. Proponents of this approach emphasise that it includes 'frames, rhetoric, interpretation [both participants' and customers' meaning-making], public discourse … and collective identity' (Davis 2002:4). Narrative here includes 'expressive symbols, music, film, rules, rituals, histories, sacred places' in addition to its verbal component (Davis 2002:10). Narratives are constrained by cultural practices, expectations and also prohibitions arising from audiences' socialisation; at the same time that they cannot be too outré, they should contain a small surprise or sentimental note to make the narrative a memorable experience. A pitfall in heritage marketing is the temptation to draw customers by titillating them with corpses or gold – eg, a 2004 traveling exhibit titled 'Quest for Immortality: Treasures of Ancient Egypt'. The narrative here panders to a mass market eager to see (other people's) death, gold, and a mystery (why did Egyptians make extraordinarily elaborate and wealthy tombs?). Highlighting these standard lures allows the host museum to charge visitors $11.50 to see the special exhibit, on top of regular museum entrance at $7.00. Is it right to pander to lurid vulgar taste, thereby earning money to support a great natural history museum, when as anthropological archaeologists we think the public should learn more about everyday life and commoners' lots, to compare and contrast with their own lives?

Indigenous archaeology would seem to answer the issue of pandering to vulgar partialities. Tribal museums are designed to inspire community members and impress tourists. Some, like the Makahs' museum in Washington State, showcase the results of archaeological excavations, in this case the buried village at Ozette. Other chapters in this volume discuss indigenous archaeologies more fully; suffice it here to cite James Clifford's presentation of the Alutiiq exhibit and catalog *Looking Both Ways: Heritage and Identity of the Alutiiq People* (Clifford 2004). Thanks to *Current Anthropology*'s solicitation of comments, readers see that even Clifford's nuanced analysis missed (or avoided) some contentious points. Replying to the commentators, Clifford acknowledges slighting 'the nitty-gritty: the money trail, institutional interests, structural pressures, social processes of inclusion and exclusion … changes in the policy of institutions such as the Smithsonian … personal agendas (intertwined idealism and bureaucratic realism) … [and] different evaluations of "success" by participants and outsiders' (Clifford 2004:26). Such a litany of concerns makes it clear that we cannot side-step issues simply by bowing to 'native leaders' or even 'native elders'. From the perspective of the marketing concept, every endeavor toward indigenous archaeology or museum has a marketing aspect, usually several categories of consumers are simultaneously targeted, and the very idea is fraught with Western ideology because neither archaeology nor museum (as cabinet of curiosities or secular education) is indigenous to First Nations.

Looking at archaeology and its products from the standpoint of capitalists' marketing concept, Jorvik in England may be emblematic: Discovered during construction of a shopping mall intended to revitalise a downtown commercial zone, the foundations of Danelaw York were then vivified by 're'-constructing a village, complete with troll-faced manikins, underneath mall level and running little trains around it for ticket-buying tourists to gawk at 'Viking York'. While the Viking Centre sells itself as authentic, complete with an ambience sound tape of people speaking Old Norse, for tourists the experience is similar to a Disneyland theme-park ride, complete with a shop to wend through before reaching the exit. Jorvik draws huge numbers to its shopping mall, and its profits helped finance other archaeology in York. Being literally inextricable from the shopping mall, and presented as its forerunner with workshops and wharves, Jorvik became a beacon for other cities seeking to capitalise on mandated salvage archaeology, turning rough sow's ears into silk purses (Renfrew and Bahn 1996:534).

Was the enterprise ethical? No one was harmed, and much money has been earned by enticing tourists to the center of York and entertaining them with a simulacrum slice of 'their' past. Proponents believe the simulated archaeological excavation and lab through which tourists pass between the 'village' and the shop promote a positive attitude toward, and interest in, archaeology. But to what end? Increasing jobs for archaeologists? In a broader context, an economy where the college business is a significant segment marketed as the means to white-collar careers, requires increasing jobs for college graduates. Proliferating employment in fields such as counseling, surveys and evaluation research, and motivational workshops is welfare for the middle class, dutifully degreed and too numerous to be accommodated in earlier-established professions. Proliferating local museums and cultural resource management accomplishes this end, too. Heritage workers produce chartering myths for the identities utilised in identity politics. No one is harmed, and masses of people who must be consumers (because no one in North America can live off the land today [Feit 1989:85–92]) earn the wherewithal.

But archaeology is supposed to be a science seeking irrefutable interpretations of real data. Records of the past exist and materialise memories and documents. 'Cogito, ergo sum homo': to be human is to be cognizant of being and temporality. Pursuing a scientific archaeology, we need to be particularly careful to distinguish between syntagm, the actual detritus as it lies, and paradigm (model) (Kehoe 1998:143, 229).

Linking the two are chains of signification. The crux of ethical archaeology is meticulous exposure, recording, archiving and publishing corpora of data, that is, syntagms as they existed. They are given meaning through labeling and reference to models; labels are normally conventional, taught to students by practitioners, and models are usually ethnographic analogies. It cannot be overemphasised that labeling is a critical exercise, too often applied without serious attention to its tendency to bias interpretation: for example, conventionally labeling a triangular, sharp biface 'projectile point' slants interpretation toward men's activities, whereas attention to asymmetry of the blade's long sides would suggest it was a kitchen knife, calling up pictures of domestic life and women's activities. Paradigms embody precedent and corollary postulates, another source of bias; if an archaeologist working in Scandinavia premised, without thinking about it, that knapped flint tools are prehistoric, the archaeologist might interpret a medieval site as prehistoric (Knarrström 2001:108–111). It takes longer to juxtapose alternate working hypotheses in order to avoid facile conformist conclusions; but that's the trouble with ethics, it's not generally the convenient path.

Syntagm and paradigm correspond to Gibbon's exposition of realist philosophy distinguishing '*intransitive* objects of knowledge, the real things and structures, mechanisms and processes, events and possibilities of the world which are for the most part quite independent of us and invariant to our knowledge of them' (Gibbon 1989:144) from '*transitive*' knowledge affected by data, methods, and paradigms 'available to the science of the day' (*ibid*). The infinite minutiae of the vast real past are largely beyond our powers of observation, but more influential is the processing structure of the human brain, categorising sense impressions into fuzzy sets (Lakoff 1987:176, 337). Multiple pasts are inevitable.

The difference between Gordon Childe (eg, 1958) and Gimbutas is not fact versus fantasy, nor patriarchy versus feminism. Childe looked at the breadth of Eurasia for patterns of societal changes from harvesting from the wild to producing for markets, while Gimbutas puzzled the meanings hypothesised to have been intended by Neolithic artisans. On the other hand, the difference between James B. Griffin and Erich von Däniken is between readily replicable observations (in the University of Michigan's Ceramic Repository) and assertions at odds with all our knowledge of organisms and physics. Clear enough, until California Goddess worshippers made Gimbutas an avatar of their deity, and Griffin's hard-nosed empiricism drowned under Michigan's Socialist Labor party line (Kehoe 1998:122–127, 183–185). We have multiple pasts, multiple ideologies, multiple career strategies stretching all the way to psychic romance writing.

CONCLUSION

Michael Herzfeld describes 'archaeology *as a social practice*' that can powerfully impact upon people's lives when marketing entrepreneurs manipulate archaeological representations to draw tourists (Herzfeld 1992:76–77, his italics). For Crete, Greece's national Archaeological Service designates buildings 'Venetian' if they fit the preferred segment of Crete's multiple pasts, 'Turkish' if less attractive. Exteriors of 'Venetian' houses cannot be altered, 'Turkish' houses don't matter. (Herzfeld states that the actual ages of houses are not significant.) In a refinement of the marketing concept, needs and wants of one weak class of consumers, poor villagers, are ignored as marketers advertise a 'traditional, historic' Crete to affluent consumers abroad (Herzfeld 1992:76–77). Archaeology as a social practice is prone to edit out, even destroy, data from less-valued phases of the past, and value, as in Crete, is likely to be set according to tourist marketing. When subway construction in downtown Mexico City hit the Aztec Templo Mayor, an archaeological zone was decreed and the remnants exposed and stabilised to become a Tourist Draw Mayor. That at least a dozen discernible earlier and later occupation levels were in the stratigraphy fell out of the picture (Lopez Wario 1993). Treasuring the Templo Mayor affirms Mexico City's centrality to the Mexican nation, once and future capital of empire. Multiple pasts are, as Herzfeld observed, produced by politico-economic strategies *assisted* by archaeologists.

The Society for American Archaeology celebrated its fiftieth anniversary in 1985. Patty Jo Watson, assigned to discuss 'Archaeological Interpretation', counted several degrees of skepticism among her colleagues, causing her to 'view with alarm contemporary moves toward denial of the real past or of access to it' (Watson 1986:452). She referred to 'contemporary sociopolitical forces' in only one sentence, that they 'inevitably warp and distort our perceptions of all alien social processes, present or past' (Watson 1986:450). Consumers of archaeology products were, to her, professional and avocational archaeologists and 'the interested lay public' (Watson 1986:444). First Nations, archaeological tourism, sites as shrines (New Age or older), and archaeology as business apparently were not yet on the horizon for mainstream leaders of the profession such as Watson. In the 1990s, these became hammer-blows against mainstream's premised 'real past' (not Piggott's real past, a Kantian *Ding-an-sich* past-in-itself).

Multiple pasts came into our ken as formerly disenfranchised classes – women, 'people of color', working class, colonial subjects – achieved measures of political standing. Their enhanced status makes them visible to marketers as well as to politicians. Gender, 'settler', 'colonial', slave-quarter, brothel, industrial and other facets of contemporary archaeology may be pursued as moral commitment, but funds must be obtained and results made available: ie, projects and results marketed. That marketing archaeology strongly resembles basic marketing, in identifying niches, creating consumer sense of need or desire, and cultivating brand recognition, should not be surprising; we live in, as Applbaum titles it, the Marketing Era. Ethical archaeology in this world requires care in manufacturing, that is, care to conserve the syntagm and explicate (especially, reflectively, to oneself) the chain of signification between data and interpretation. It requires concern for people affected negatively by exploitation of the data they live with, such as Herzfeld's Cretan people, or campesinos who become *huaqueros* (looters) because it's the only way to make a living (Hollowell-Zimmer 2003:50; see also Luke and Henderson 2006:48). It requires thoughtful and empathetic response to consumers, neither snubbing them nor uncritically falling in with boosterism. In a capitalist world, we too are caught up with marketing ourselves and our products. Multiple pasts are not failures in interpreting 'the' archaeological record; they mirror diversity in the mosaics that are contemporary nation-states. Ethical archaeology tries to proceed within this political reality without sacrificing principles of science.

NOTE

1. One was Winona LaDuke's father, an Anishinaabe who had left his reservation for Hollywood and eventually, calling himself Sun Bear, put on ceremonies for New Age devotees.

REFERENCES

Applbaum, K (2004) *The Marketing Era: From Professional Practice to Global Provisioning*, New York: Routledge

Arnold, B (1990) 'The past as propaganda: totalitarian archaeology in Nazi Germany', *Antiquity* 64, 464–478

Childe, VG (1958) *The Prehistory of European Society*, Harmondsworth, UK: Penguin

Clifford, J (2004) 'Looking several ways: anthropology and native heritage in Alaska', *Current Anthropology* 45, 5–30

Collingwood, RG (1956[1946]) *The Idea of History*, New York: Oxford University Press

Davis, JE (2002) 'Narrative and social movements', in Davis, JE (ed), *Stories of Change: Narrative and Social Movements*, Albany: State University of New York Press

Del Giudice, L and Porter, G (2001) 'Introduction', in *Imagined States: Nationalism, Utopia, and Longing in Oral Cultures*, Logan: Utah State University Press

Eller, C (2000) *The Myth of Matriarchal Prehistory: Why an Invented Past Won't Give Women a Future*, Boston: Beacon Press

Feit, HA (1989) 'James Bay Cree self-governance and land management', in Wilmsen, E (ed), *We Are Here: Politics of Aboriginal Land Tenure*, Berkeley: University of California Press

Fowler, DD (1987) 'Uses of the past: archaeology in the service of the state', *American Antiquity* 52, 229–248

Gibbon, G (1989) *Explanation in Archaeology*, Oxford: Blackwell

Herzfeld, M (1992) 'Metapatterns: archaeology and the uses of evidential scarcity', in Gardin, JG and Peebles, CS (eds), *Representations in Archaeology*, Bloomington: Indiana University Press

Hollowell-Zimmer, J (2003) 'Digging the dirt – ethics and "low-end looting"', in Zimmerman, LJ, Vitelli, KD and Hollowell-Zimmer, J (eds), *Ethical Issues in Archaeology*, Walnut Creek, CA: AltaMira Press

Kehoe, AB (1992) 'The paradigmatic vision of archaeology: archaeology as a bourgeois science', in, Reyman, JE (ed) *Rediscovering Our Past: Essays on the History of American Archaeology*, Aldershot, UK: Avebury

—— (1998) *The Land of Prehistory: A Critical History of American Archaeology*, New York: Routledge

Kennedy, RG (1994) *Hidden Cities: The Discovery and Loss of Ancient North American Civilization*, New York: Free Press

Knarrström, B (2001) *Flint: A Scanian Hardware*, Stockholm: National Heritage Board, Sweden

Kristiansen, K (1981) 'A social history of Danish archaeology (1805–1975)', in Daniel, G (ed) *Towards a History of Archaeology*, London: Thames and Hudson

—— (1985) 'A short history of Danish archaeology', in Kristiansen, K (ed), *Archaeological Formation Processes*, Lyngby: Nationalmuseet

—— (1993) '"The strength of the past and its great might"; an essay on the use of the past', *Journal of European Archaeology* 1, 3–32

Lakoff, G (1987) *Women, Fire, and Dangerous Things: What Categories Reveal About the Mind*, Chicago: University of Chicago Press

Lopez Wario, L (1993) 'De los fragmentos urbanos: revisión de la arqueología en la ciudad de México', paper presented in July in Mexico City, 13th International Congress of Anthropological and Ethnological Sciences

Luke, C and Henderson, J (2006) 'The Plunder of the Ulúa Valley, Honduras, and a Market Analysis for its Antiquities', in Brodie, N , Kersel, MN, Luke, C and Tubb, KW (eds) *Archaeology, Cultural Heritage, and the Antiquities Trade*, Gainesville: University Press of Florida

Malina, J and Vasícek, Z (1990) *Archaeology Yesterday and Today*, Cambridge: Cambridge University Press

Malinowski, B (1954) *Magic, Science and Religion and Other Essays*, Garden City NY: Doubleday

O'Brien, MJ, and Lyman, RL (2001) *Setting the Agenda for American Archaeology: The National Research Council Archaeological Conferences of 1929, 1932, and 1935*, Tuscaloosa: University of Alabama Press

Piggott, S (1981) 'Summary and conclusions', in Daniel, G (ed), *Towards a History of Archaeology*, London: Thames and Hudson

Renfrew, C and Bahn, P (1996) *Archaeology: Theories, Methods, and Practice*, second edition, London: Thames and Hudson

Sassaman, KE (2002) 'Histories by the archaeologist, for the archaeologist', in Tushingham, T, Hill, J and McNutt C (eds) *Histories of Southeastern Archaeology*, Tuscaloosa: University of Alabama Press

Schnapp, A (1996) *The Discovery of the Past: The Origins of Archaeology*, translated by Kinnes, I and Varndell, G, London: British Museum Press. (Original [1993] Paris: Éditions Carré)

Snead, JE (2002) 'The "Western idea": local societies and American archaeology', in Allen, SH (ed), *Excavating Our Past*, Boston: Archaeological Institute of America

Trigger, BG (1984) 'Alternative archaeologies: nationalist, colonialist, imperialist', *Man* 19, 355–370

Watson, PJ (1986) 'Archaeological interpretation', in Meltzer, DJ, Fowler, D, and Sabloff, JA (eds) *American Archaeology Past and Future*, Washington DC: Smithsonian Institution Press

White, HV (1973) *Metahistory*, Baltimore: The Johns Hopkins Press

—— (1987) *The Content of the Form*, Baltimore: The Johns Hopkins Press

CHAPTER 10

'Sustainable' Heritage? Public Archaeological Interpretation and the Marketed Past

Neil Asher Silberman

INTRODUCTION

Public archaeological interpretation has come a long way from earlier eras of unnuanced positivism and full confidence in the objectivity of specialized scholarship. The impact of contemporary social and political ideologies on the choices, emphases, and narratives of archaeological practice is now widely acknowledged (Gathercole and Lowenthal 1989; Kohl and Fawcett 1996; Meskell 1998). Important intellectual attempts have been made to counteract the influence of ethnic nationalism, racism, and colonialism on the practice of public archaeological interpretation, particularly in the realms of site presentation and community education programs (Henson *et al* 2004; Little 2002). For the most part, however, this academic critique has concerned intangible aspects of archaeological interpretation: images, narratives, and commemorative ideologies. Yet over the last 25 years – even as intellectual debates have raged within academia over issues of ideology, narrative construction, and multivocality – the *physical* structures of public presentation at many major archaeological sites have been dramatically transformed.

Governmental authorities and international development agencies have made substantial investments to convert important archaeological and historical sites into 'sustainable' engines of local and regional economic development, in hopes of creating new 'heritage attractions' that will offer local employment opportunities and stimulate interregional tourism and trade (as analyzed by Baram and Rowan 2004 and prescribed by Hutter and Rizzo 1997). Public funding programs like those of the European Commission's Interreg programs and Culture 2000 (DG Education and Culture 2002) and the World Bank's 'Framework for Action in Cultural Heritage and Development in the

Middle East and North Africa' (Cernea 2001) have set standards – and offer substantial economic incentives – for governmental investment in the form, structure and even presentation design of major archaeological sites.

The World Bank has clearly expressed the underlying rationale of the concept of 'sustainable heritage' and outlined its basic political economy:

> By definition, the patrimony represents a vast collection of cultural assets, but these assets also have a huge economic value. Markets only imperfectly recognize this economic value because of insufficient information and inadequate pricing mechanisms. Historically, the economic value of the patrimony's endowments has been given much less attention than its cultural significance. Largely because of this limited recognition, policy makers and planners in developing countries have been little concerned, and little able, to activate and harvest the economic value of their country's patrimony. Bank policy has come to unambiguously recognize this economic value. It holds that the patrimony can become an auxiliary engine for generating economic growth and development'. (Cernea 2001:33)

This vision has, in fact, been put into action. A new trans-national industry has grown up to support the activation and the so-called 'harvesting' of the economic value of heritage resources (Hall and McArthur 1998). Since the bulk of public investment goes into infrastructural improvements at archaeological and heritage sites, and since these require complex project management skills and elaborate presentation technologies not generally within the capacities of local governments or heritage authorities, a network of heritage consultants, multimedia technologists, and exhibit designers compete for lucrative contracts at historical and archaeological sites all over the world.

The result of their efforts at site presentation is the emergence of a distinctive physical form, in which the visitors' centre and multimedia applications are often central elements. Borrowing design concepts from theme parks and interactive museums, site planners now utilize traditional didactic, museum-type text displays only when limited budgets restrict them to the cheapest, no-frills displays. More creative and energetic interpretive solutions, such as interactive applications, computer 3D reconstructions, and Virtual Reality experiences are now almost always utilized in the refurbishing of archaeological sites when the project budget permits (Addison 2003; Seaton and Bennett 1996). Great efforts have been taken to create stunning historical environments with a wide enough range of vivid images and impressions to satisfy almost every visitor's taste (Leask and Yeoman 1999). The practical challenge of the most ambitious heritage development projects thus goes far beyond conveying information about the archaeology and history of the site. In most cases, the operational motivation is not primarily didactic or ideological, but is explicitly economic: By attracting significantly increased numbers of tourists to a particular site, it is assumed that the local economy will benefit by their presence (and their purchasing power). What this usually amounts to – at least in its most successful manifestations – is the creation of venues for carefully processed leisure-time entertainment, structured and marketed with the same modes of tour booking, entrance fees, restaurants, gift shops, and overnight accommodations as other packaged visits of the modern mass tourist industry.

Thus any serious intellectual discussion of the contemporary socioeconomic context of public archaeological interpretation must take this changing market reality into account. While earlier examinations of the social context of archaeological practice have concentrated on the message, the *physical* form and emerging medium of archaeological sites as 'heritage attractions' and their function as sources of even indirect revenue generation is no less important. This paper will attempt to address four basic questions, central to understanding the significance of this phenomenon. What is the place of these new cultural heritage attractions on the contemporary material landscape? What vision of the past do they create in the public (and individual) consciousness? Do they actually produce the economic benefits that their sponsors and funders anticipate? And, finally, what role in this economically driven process do, or should, archaeologists play?

FROM CULTURAL TOURISM TO ENTERTAINMENT

There is, of course, nothing new about archaeological sites being marketed as tourist attractions. From antiquity onwards, there have always been gawkers, gapers, and holiday-makers at the iconic monuments of Europe – Stonehenge, Carnac, the Roman Coliseum, and the Parthenon, just to mention a few. Impressive (and often mysterious) sites of ancient human achievement evoked visitors' feelings of wonder and romantic daydreams of escape from familiar routines and limitations of everyday life. The customs of medieval pilgrimage to the great religious and healing shrines established the basic behaviours that would continue for centuries and indeed to the present: regularized routes, the construction of special visitor accommodations, package tours of important buildings and relics, and a cluster of local economic activities from catering, innkeeping, and guiding, to the sale of souvenirs (Sumption 1975).

By the time of the Grand Tour in the 18th century (Hibbert 1987), the behaviours of traditional religious pilgrimage were merged with a more secular antiquarian fascination. Enlightenment visions of human progress and a romantic longing for ancient grandeur gradually replaced ecclesiastical rituals as the accepted route to communion with the past. Yet the basic behaviours of pilgrimage endured. By the 19th century, mass tourism to archaeological sites throughout Europe and the Middle East, ever more closely linked to local and trans-national transportation systems and marketing networks, created a standardized repertoire of 'must see' antiquarian icons, attractions, and performances, as described in vivid, ethnographic detail in Mark Twain's *The Innocents Abroad* (1869). Yet in this new movement of mass tourism, the profit imperatives of the modern industrial order gradually became central (Kirshenblatt-Gimblett 1998). In the 20th century, as the competition for visitors mounted, public presentations were expanded to include historic re-enactments, reconstructed buildings, national celebrations, and an increasingly wide range of mass-produced souvenirs and memorabilia. In the late 20th century, the theme-park techniques of promotion and niche marketing were added (Bennett 1997). Yet it is a mistake to see the new Information Age 'edutainment' tools of interactivity and Virtual Reality as merely technological enhancements of time-honoured archaeological pilgrimage-and-tourism routines.

In the words of David Lowenthal (2002), the past has become theme park, as different from traditional touristic presentations of ancient monuments as Disneyworld is from a county fair. In the 19th and 20th centuries, the creation of national networks of monuments and protected archaeological sites served as an explicit tool of state-building. They were tangible, landscape-bound visions of common heritage that distinguished the historical identity of a particular country from that of neighbouring and competitor states. Tourism was a method of public education through which distinctive national biographies were conveyed. The new tools of multimedia and elaborate site presentation are still often used to reinforce existing nationalistic messages. There is also an increasing trend toward trans-national messages and 'globalised' interpretation that is hardly less ideological, serving the interests of regional unification and globalization, as in the cases of European Union cultural programs and the UNESCO World Heritage List. Yet the purely economic motivation has become a significant factor in itself: All across the world, in recent decades, archaeological and other heritage sites by the hundreds if not thousands have been valorized, glamorized, and relentlessly merchandized by regions, municipalities, local communities, and even private management companies seeking to attract visitors and the prospects for economic development that they bring (Herbert 1989). In this effort, the raising of visitor revenues – rather than any particular interpretation – is often the chief motivation and the primary index of success.

The phenomenon is especially striking in the Middle East and North Africa, where, despite the continuing conflicts between ethnic groups and nation-states, archaeological sites are increasingly uniform in infrastructure and appearance, funded and developed for their generalized touristic appeal (Silberman 1998). In nations such as Syria, Israel, Jordan, Lebanon, Libya, and Morocco – each still with their distinctive historical-ideological visions – major (usually Roman-period) sites featuring monumental structures, soaring columns, and multimedia experiences have become strikingly uniform, in their use of ancient remains as the stage setting for an enjoyable visitor experience.

The elaborate sites in North Africa and the Middle East, as elsewhere, do not lack a narrative often still bearing messages of national identity, but it is one that is shifting steadily from didactic or rhetorical to experiential – meant to be read primarily with the visitors' emotions and feet. It is carefully and consciously inscribed in the walking paths and in the circulation routes through ruins and exhibit spaces through the painstaking planning of professional (and almost always non-local) site designers, whose expertise has become a prerequisite for every major heritage development project. The visit is conceived as a journey into the past with a beginning, middle and end. Through the generic shaping of the site's space and precise localization of functions, it consists of passage through a series of Goffman-esque 'frames' (Goffman 1974): from the parking lot, through the ticket booth, into the main reception and information area, along the marked or suggested paths of public interpretation with stops at highlighted informational panels and multimedia installations, then to the shop and cafeteria, and then out to the parking lot again. This patterned visitor behaviour has little dependence on the content; sites with such different archaeological and historical significance as Mesa Verde, Knossos, Pompeii, Versailles, and Auschwitz share more than they differ in the layout of visitor facilities and patterned behaviour of visitation that such a layout creates.

That experiential uniformity, I would argue, has far-reaching, yet underappreciated significance. Dean MacCannell (1976) perceptively characterized the function of theme parks, studio tours and heritage visits as a search for 'authentic experience' by work-weary participants in industrialized economies. Since the development of modern heritage sites is now increasingly based on economic considerations, its planners must now contend with the fierce market competition of attracting visitors to heritage sites from other leisure time alternatives like the mountains, the movies or the beach. As a result, the heritage experience has often been tailored to improve the bottom line. The work of Handler and Gable at Colonial Williamsburg (1997) has shown how historical interpretation can be subtly edited to eliminate the kinds of troubling or unpleasant realities that are likely to drive holiday makers away. Finances and balance sheets – far more than official commemorative ideologies – have become the real tyrants in the shaping of 'sustainable' heritage and its interpretive messages. Although this new infrastructural form does not determine the specific content of site presentation, it demands that it be coherent, easy to follow and capable of holding the attention of the widest possible audience. In a word, it enables archaeological sites and other heritage attractions to become part of the 'Experience Economy'.

PUBLIC INTERPRETATION AND THE EXPERIENCE ECONOMY

You do not have to read Neil Postman's scathing jeremiad *Amusing Ourselves to Death* (1985) to know that we live in an age of flashing, shallow and ideologically loaded TV images. Like pieces in a mosaic, they embody a breathless public narrative of conquest and consumption that often controls and reinforces – rather than passively reflects – the consumer economy. In recent years, a particular emphasis has been placed on utilizing video and multimedia to create a wide range of visitor experiences that offer a sense of involvement and interactivity. Beyond computer-based games and searchable databases, there are now elaborate – and sometimes immersive – virtual reconstructions of ancient landscapes and structures (Barcelo *et al* 2000) and the opportunity for visitors to interact with simulated ancient characters from the history of the specific site (eg, Churcher nd). Of course, this interactive element of public interpretation also has a history that stretches far back before the Digital Age. The costumed guides at World's Fairs and early 20th-century open-air museums first challenged the omniscient voice of guide books and text panels. The first-person re-enactors at Colonial Williamsburg and Plimoth Plantation provided visitors with more personalized experiences than the standard guided tour (Silberman 2005). But today, the direct, sensory – rather than merely intellectual or educational – involvement of visitors in public heritage interpretation has become part of an essential marketing strategy.

Indeed it could be argued that this is not an isolated phenomenon but is closely related to changes in the wider economy. Among economic theorists and business strategists, the belief is quickly spreading that experience itself has become a valuable commodity. With the production of manufactured goods now outsourced to regions where the costs of labour are the lowest, and the profitability of secondary services (such as telecommunications, transport, finance, and data processing) likewise suffering from intensive competition, the creation and marketing of consumer experience is an area with the greatest perceived potential for growth (Pine and Gilmore 1999). To achieve this, service providers must distinguish themselves from their competitors by providing a memorable and personalized experience; customers must be courted with the feeling that they are receiving something unique and uniquely designed for them. In this new vision of the 21st-century post-service economy, otherwise routine business transactions are carefully scripted, and events and personalized interactions are staged so as to leave the consumer entertained. Thus, in the ever-expanding range of restaurant chains, shopping malls, and clothing outlets – as well as resorts and tourist attractions – the keys to success, according to the gurus of the Experience Economy (Pine and Gilmore 1998), lay in:

- designing a themed experience
- planting positive cues to elicit pleasant emotions
- eliminating negative cues
- evoking romantic nostalgia through memorabilia
- engaging all five senses in the experience

These are of course the essential components of the theme park experience, but it is now used in the planning of upscale suburbs, gentrified city centres, and restored historic districts – as well as expensively designed and presented archaeological sites. In that sense the past is in danger of becoming just another theme in an expanding experience market. While it could be argued that clothing at Banana Republic would still be as attractive without the 'jungle adventurer' theme – or that food at the Hard Rock Café would be just as tasty without the framed gold records and autographed electric guitars – the point of the Experience Economy is precisely to blur the distinction between product, service, and entertainment (Gottdiener 1997). And that is exactly what the emerging forms of interactive heritage presentation are designed to do so well.

Their goal is to make a visit to a heritage site an unforgettable experience, but what is it exactly that remains so vivid in the visitor's mind? There are clear indications that it is only the memory of the physical experience itself. While sensory effects have been utilized in some sites where national biography remains the main theme (eg, the Wasa Museum in Sweden; the Museum of the History of Catalonia in Barcelona; and the Second Temple Period Archaeological Park and Davidson Exhibition and Virtual Reconstruction Center in Jerusalem) the visitors' reactions are evoked in a carefully planned immersive environment, where impressive and thrilling images are perceived primarily through the senses. It may be legitimate to question whether this mode of apprehension fundamentally alters or transforms the impact of the information conveyed. Embodiment and the social construction of physical sensations has in recent years become a major research interest in a wide range of disciples including archaeology and anthropology (eg, Hamilakis *et al* 2002). Thus, beyond the compilation of attendance numbers and recording of income from admissions and subsidiary sales, the serious analysis of 'embodied' visitor reactions at elaborate, interactive heritage attractions may become an important element of the study of the new physical context of multimedia-aided heritage sites.

A recent study of the use of Virtual Reality to convey archaeological and ethnographic information (Ladeira and Blake 2004) suggests that there may indeed be a clear trade-off between intellectual comprehension and sensory enjoyment. In this study, the test group that was asked to read the information in text form showed significantly higher comprehension of the facts and information presented, while the group that experienced the Virtual Reality version of the same material – presented in a VR environment, with a computer-generated character, of a type increasingly common in digital heritage presentations (eg, Wilkinson *et al* 2004) – showed significantly higher levels of enjoyment and interest, but significantly lower comprehension of the specific information conveyed.

Further study is certainly needed to determine how profoundly the medium of emerging heritage attractions may endanger their value as sources of historical information as well (as also indicated in earlier museum and site studies, eg, Borun 1977; Screven 1975; Shettel 1968; Uzzell 1989). Yet for better or worse the requirements of modern heritage marketing have carefully designed a medium that conscientiously avoids the kinds of subjects or presentation methods that are likely to keep the holiday makers away. No message is effective unless it is, above all, sensorially arresting and emotionally entertaining. But the value of the past is precisely to convey information about other times and cultures, to offer difficult themes for public discussion and serious reflection, a task hardly possible when the goal is to capture a market share of recreational activities. Are we in danger of transforming the past into a theme park and the site into an outlet for McArchaeology? Another important question still remains to be answered: Does this kind of elaborate heritage presentation – even if it is more Hollywood than Heritage – actually provide the economic benefits it claims?

IF YOU BUILD IT, WILL THEY COME?

In an era when public culture budgets are shrinking and cultural institutions of all kinds are being forced to become financially self-sustaining, the viability of preservation and presentation projects are, in the long run, often tied to their success in stimulating economic development – by paid admissions, subsidiary sales of postcards and other museum-shop items, local employment opportunities, and a steady flow of tourist revenue for hotels, shops, and restaurants in the immediate vicinity. It is conceivable, of course, that marketed heritage can succeed by the benchmark of profitability alone. Yet to what extent do these economic benefits trickle down to the inhabitants and associated communities of the heritage sites concerned? The evidence is admittedly anecdotal, yet the pattern – as seen from a contemporary European perspective (Palumbo 2006) and from the particular experience of the Ename Center for Public Archeology in Belgium (Silberman and Callebaut 2006) – is as uniform as it is disheartening for the future of heritage in 21st-century industrial society.

Our experience in European heritage projects has shown that, in the planning stages, if the right balance is not achieved between the contribution of outside professionals and the input from the local community, the preservation project, even if successful, can appear to local residents as an outside imposition – like a shopping mall or private theme park – with solely or mainly economic significance for the political leadership and local business community. If it succeeds, the commercial activity will benefit those investors and public funders with a direct economic stake. Meaningful economic integration into the project by the general public often takes the form of menial service jobs on the site and in the subsidiary commercial establishments. Even the most successful projects can sow resentment among those not immediately benefiting from the economic activity on any meaningful level, and who often suffer directly from the successful site's side effects – a lack of parking, traffic congestion, and disruption of normal routines. It can thus be dismissed as 'someone else's' monument, an alien intrusion not meaningfully integrated into the memories, stories, and attitudes that constitute the entire community's shared identity.

Economic success, with all its social pitfalls, is certainly *not* guaranteed, even though international and regional funding programs continually stress the economic potential of heritage development in marginal areas. Nonetheless, in many cases, particularly in regions where traditional agriculture has collapsed or where industry has fled (leaving historic town centres to deteriorate), the lure of harvested, processed heritage is hard to resist.

Some sites, no matter how meticulously researched and elaborately developed, will never attract large numbers of visitors, for the routes of tourism are exceptionally inflexible, based less on content than on the convenience of nearby highways and airports, the pressures of itinerary planning, and the most comfortable facilities (Hamza 2004). The achievable attendance figures for a potential heritage attraction are limited by its location within the larger marketing networks of the tourist industry. Although the notable recent experience of the Guggenheim Museum in Bilbao, Spain is touted as the model for future development of a formerly neglected area into a focus of thriving cultural tourism, it cannot be uncritically applied to every case where a local government decides or is persuaded to invest public funds in super-sizing a modest, existing monument or archaeological site with the investment in multimedia presentation, obtained either through direct funding or international loans. Despite the attractive offers and funding, the likelihood of energizing local economies through heritage presentation must take into account the harsh calculus of investment costs vs. logically expected return (Briedenhann and Wickens 2004; Palumbo 2006). Although the academic tourism literature is filled with conceptual studies of new formulations like 'co-opetition' among regional attractions (eg, Buhalis 2003), the hard fact of the matter is that, in the absence of detailed market studies and almost always in the absence of enough funds to make such a study before initiating expensive heritage presentation projects, many (most?) local communities' heritage presentation and valorization projects are embarking on what might well be a very dangerous course.

For, in practice, the inspiration for major heritage projects is almost always economic. Whether it is the complex and expensive application process for listing on the UNESCO World Heritage list or the construction of a new visitor centre, local governmental authorities justify their funding applications and budgeting on the idea of local economic development. And they are often encouraged to do so by heritage professionals (with a professional interest in participating in projects) and by scholars who believe that a flow of financing to a particular monument or archaeological site will enhance the possibility of obtaining additional research funds.

If economic targets are not met, the local community eventually bears the brunt of miscalculation. While an elaborately preserved and interpreted site may look perfect to the invited dignitaries and guests on its festive opening day, the invisible hand of the cultural tourism market determines what the future will bring. Although the academic tourism literature is filled with examples and principles for the rationale management of visitor flow at well-known sites and popular attractions, the problem of *inadequate* visitorship (at least to defray the costs of elaborate infrastructures and presentations) remains the single greatest unmet challenge in the realm of 'sustainable' heritage. The novelty of a new site and an energetic public relations campaign may initially create a dramatic rise in visitation, and perhaps spur intensified local investment in subsidiary services such as shops, restaurants, and hotels in the vicinity, yet its natural place in the hierarchy of international and regional tourist routes will have a decisive effect. After the curiosity of local and regional visitors has been exhausted, attendance numbers will rapidly return to their equilibrium level, calling into question the economic strategy that led local officials to invest time, energy and public funds in the heritage project.

To make matters worse, this often occurs precisely at a time when maintenance and security costs will be rising, especially in the case of sites where interpretive technology such as interactive installations and multimedia presentations is used. For a local community to take a leap of faith into the murky waters of the contemporary heritage industry is a serious political risk. Miscalculations about economic sustainability or even viability can only be addressed by extreme measures: either franchising site management to private firms whose concern is still more ruthlessly financial or – even more ultimately destructive to the cause of heritage preservation – namely the investment of yet more public funding in a renovation or extension of the multimedia attractions and experiences to be marketed to visitors at the site.

And so the cycle can grow more and more vicious as the site's position within the hierarchy of tourist destinations clings stubbornly at its point of natural equilibrium. This is not to say that visitation cannot ever be changed for the better, but doing so requires a continuing effort of enormous proportions that may simply not be worth the financial risk for a local community when calculated in terms of investment-and-return (Rousso 2002). As a result there is generally a breaking point, a moment of crisis, when the project that was once was sold as 'sustainable', that is, a self-supporting engine of local economic development, turns out to be anything but that. By the time that unrealistic expectations of increased visitation have failed to materialize and the costs of adequate staffing, maintenance, and regular content updating have soared, its physical state and its once-enthusiastic acceptance by its promoters and the general public has generally changed for the worse. Extensive, detailed statistical studies still need to be carried out to document this process in quantitative terms, yet it is already clear that failed heritage projects are destructive to the contemporary historical landscape. In small and marginal communities under economic stress, heritage – and the political will to preserve and present it – is destroyed in the process. Poorly maintained, or broken and graffiti-covered multimedia kiosks, informational panels, and derelict visitor facilities are the lingering monuments to utterly unsustainable heritage development.

That does not mean that more modest heritage sites do not deserve interpretation, for they each represent a material resource, a constant reminder of the past's ever-presence in the contemporary world. Current heritage practices and new forms of cultural communication programs must be monitored closely and reoriented toward goals in which success lies not only in professional competence, technology and rational planning, but in the creation of lively local institutions – sustainable in the long run not because of how much they make, how they look, or what experiences they provide – but for how effectively they function as centres for common reflection, self-assertion, productive questioning and historical awareness within every community.

A NEW ROLE FOR ARCHAEOLOGISTS?

As archaeologists, we are – or should be – constantly on the watch in our theories and in our research designs for the pervasive influence of contemporary ideologies on our understanding of the past. The decision of the 1st World Archaeological Congress against the participation of apartheid-era South African scholars is just one of the first milestones in a modern history of increasing political activism (Ucko 1987). Struggles over repatriation, indigenous rights, alternative histories, archaeologies of resistance, multivocality, public outreach and community activism are some of the others. The discipline has turned from scholarly preoccupation to serious attempts to trace and understand the various ideological, political and economic pressures that have shaped the structure of the discipline and have moulded its results. The recognition that the ideology of archaeology indeed has a politics, a history, and a social impact has been the subject of endless conferences, monographs, and international academic debates.

Yet our self-congratulation of freeing ourselves intellectually from the pernicious and monolithic antiquarian images of 19th and 20th century racism and nationalism should not blind us to our wider society's tangible structures of representation that have a power all their own. The role of archaeologist as an intellectual within wider society – beyond the confines of specialist study and academic isolation – entails serious obligations and responsibilities (Hamilakis 1999). The flows of international, national, and – increasingly – corporate funding determine not only the physical infrastructure of cultural tourism and historical monuments – but also the research programs, research agendas, and departmental development strategies that are closely connected to them. While professional archaeological organizations issue statements condemning the destruction of antiquities in occupied territory, and disown racist interpretations and patriotic mobilization of archaeological findings that claim to prove the 'priority' of rival claimants to a temple site or olive grove, something else no less powerful and no less potentially pernicious is going on with their willing complicity.

Cultural tourism has constructed a network, a collection, of immovable relics that have become the raw materials for a new kind of profit-driven globalized pilgrimage. All too often, archaeologists, in search of local government good will and research funding, are key players in at least the start of the process. But they rarely ever have the power to control or, seemingly, even recognize their ethical responsibility to sound a note of caution against the seductive representations of the past others create from their work.

If archaeologists – as individuals and as a discipline – are going to have a positive social influence beyond the strictly professional collection of data, they must begin thinking not only of ideology and literary genre, but also of the contemporary economic structures that exploit and endanger the material remains of the past. The reality of archaeology's embeddedness in the trans-national global economy can be neither ignored nor denied. Remaining aloof is hardly an option, since archaeological sites and the permissions to conduct excavations and research about them are dependent on official support. And the building of theme parks continues, with entrepreneurs and presentation firms actively scouting out regional governments, communities, and nations for new heritage attractions. As scholars dedicated to studying and analyzing the material remains of human culture, we must more carefully examine our position within the market forces and capital investment flows that are transforming the historical landscape. We must also engage more critically and directly with the contemporary processes and forms of public archaeological interpretation, lest our reticence or silence allow the myth of 'sustainable' heritage – at least in the economic terms and with the interpretive techniques it is now widely promoted – continue to thrive.

REFERENCES

Addison, L (2003) 'Virtual heritage: technology in the service of culture', in Stephen, NS (ed), *VAST 2001: Virtual Reality, Archeology and Cultural Heritage*, New York: Association for Computing Machinery

Baram, U and Rowan, Y (2004) *Marketing Heritage: Archaeology and the Consumption of the Past*, Walnut Creek, CA: AltaMira Press

Barcelo, J, Forte, M and Sanders, D (eds) (2000) *Virtual Reality in Archaeology*, Oxford: Archaeopress

Bennett, MM (1997) 'Heritage marketing: the role of information technology', *Journal of Vacation Marketing* 3, 272–280

Borun, M (1977) *Measuring the Immeasurable: A Pilot Study of Museum Effectiveness*, Washington: Association of Science-Technology Centers

Briedenhahn, J and Wickens, E (2004) 'Tourism routes for the development of rural areas – vibrant hope or impossible dream?' *Tourism Management* 25, 71–79

Buhalis, D (2003) *eTourism: Information Technology for Strategic Tourism Management*, London: Pearson Educational

Cernea, M (2001) *Cultural Heritage and Development: A Framework for Action in the Middle East and North Africa*, Washington: World Bank

Churcher, G (nd) 'Talking to charismatic agents: general guidelines for conversational characters'. Published on the CHARISMATIC Project website: www.charismatic-project. com/CharismaticAgents.pdf, Accessed 10 Mar 2004

Directorate-General for Education and Culture (2002) *European Funding for the Cultural Sector*, Luxembourg: European Commission

Gathercole, P and Lowenthal, D (eds) (1989) *The Politics of the Past*, London: Routledge

Goffman, E (1974) *Frame Analysis: An Essay on the Organization of Experience*, Cambridge, MA: Harvard University Press

Gottdiener, M (1997) *The Theming of America*, Boulder, CO: Westview Press

Hall, CM and McArthur, S (1998) *Integrated Heritage Management: Principles and Practice*, London: The Stationery Office

Hamilakis, Y (1999) 'La trahison des archeologues? Archaeological practice as intellectual activity in postmodernity', *Journal of Mediterranean Archaeology* 12, 60–79

Hamilakis, Y, Pluciennik, M and Tarlow, S (eds) (2002) *Thinking through the Body: Archaeologies of Corporeality*, New York: Kluwer/Plenum

Hamza, M (2004) 'Tourism-related transport', in *Indicators of Sustainable Development for Tourism Destinations: A Guidebook*, Madrid: World Tourism Organization

Handler, R and Gable, E (1997) *The New History in an Old Museum: Creating the Past at Colonial Williamsburg*, Durham: Duke University Press

Henson, D, Stone, P and Corbishley, M (eds) (2004) *Education and the Historic Environment*, London: Routledge

Herbert, D (1989) *Heritage Sites: Strategies for Marketing and Development*, London: Ashgate

Hibbert, C (1987) *The Grand Tour*, London: Thames Methuen

Hutter, M and Rizzo, I (1997) *Economic Perspectives on Cultural Heritage*, New York: St Martin's Press

Kirshenblatt-Gimblett, B (1998) *Destination Culture: Tourism, Museums, Culture*, Berkeley: University of California Press

Kohl, PA and Fawcett, C (eds) (1996) *Nationalism, Politics and the Practice of Archaeology*, Cambridge: Cambridge University Press

Ladeira, I and Blake, EH (2004) 'Virtual san storytelling for children: Content vs. experience', in Cain, K, Chrysanthou, Y, Niccolucci, F and Silberman, N (eds), *The 5th International Symposium on Virtual Reality, Archaeology and Cultural Heritage*, Aire-la-Ville, Switzerland: Europgraphics

Leask, A and Yeoman, I (eds) (1999) *Heritage Visitor Attractions: An Operations Management Perspective*, London: Cassell

Little, BJ (2002) *Public Benefits of Archaeology*, Gainesville: University Press of Florida

Lowenthal, D (2002) 'The past as a theme park', in Young, T and Riley, R (eds), *Theme Park Landscapes: Antecedents and Variants*, Washington, DC: Dumbarton Oaks Press

MacCannell, D (1976) *Tourist: A New Theory of the Leisure Class*, New York: Schocken Books

Meskell, L (ed) (1998) *Archaeology Under Fire: Nationalism, Politics and Heritage in the Eastern Mediterranean and Middle East*, London: Routledge

Palumbo, G (2006) 'Privatization of state-owned cultural heritage: a critique of recent trends in Europe', in Agnew, N and Bridgeland, J (eds), *Of the Past, for the Future: Integrating Archaeology and Conservation*, Los Angeles, CA: Getty Conservation Institute

Pine, BJ and Gilmore, JH (1998) 'Welcome to the Experience Economy', *Harvard Business Review* July-August 1998, 98–105

—— (1999) *The Experience Economy*, Boston: Harvard Business School Press

Postman, N (1985) *Amusing Ourselves to Death: Public Discourse in the Age of Show Business*, New York: Viking

Rousso, AP (2002) 'The "vicious circle" of tourism development in heritage cities', *Annals of Tourism Research* 29, 165–182

Screven, CG (1975) *The Measurement and Facilitation of Learning in the Museum Environment: An Experimental Analysis*, Washington, DC: Smithsonian Institution Press

Seaton, AV and Bennett, MM (1996) *Marketing of Tourism Products: Concepts, Issues and Cases*, London: Thomson Business Press

Shettel, HH (1968) *Strategies for Determining Exhibit Effectiveness*, Pittsburgh: American Institute for Research

Silberman, NA (1998) 'Promised lands and chosen peoples', in Meskell, L (ed), *Archaeology Under Fire: Nationalism, Politics and Heritage in the Eastern Mediterranean and Middle East*, London: Routledge

—— (2005) 'Monologue, dialogue and autobiography: The future of archaeological narratives', in Callebaut, D and Killebrew, A (eds), *Interpreting the Past: An International Symposium*, Brussels: Flemish Heritage Institute

Silberman, NA and Callebaut, D (2006), 'Interpretation as preservation: rationale, tools, and challenges', in Agnew, N and Bridgeland, J (eds), *Of the Past, for the Future: Integrating Archaeology and Conservation*, Los Angeles, CA: Getty Conservation Institute

Sumption, J (1975) *Pilgrimage: An Image of Mediaeval Religion*, Totowa, NJ: Rowman and Littlefield

Twain, M (1869) *Innocents Abroad, or, the New Pilgrims' Progress*, Hartford, CT: American Publishing Company

Ucko, P (1987) *Academic Freedom and Apartheid: The Story of the World Archaeological Congress*, London: Duckworth

Uzzell, DL (1989) *Heritage Interpretation: The Visitor Experience*, London: Bellhaven Press

Wilkinson, N, Jennings, VJ, Glauert, JRW and Eliott, R (2004) 'A speaking avatar toolkit for cultural heritage applications', in Cain, K, Chrysanthou, Y, Niccolucci, F and Silberman, N (eds), *The 5th International Symposium on Virtual Reality, Archaeology and Cultural Heritage: Short Papers*, Aire-la-Ville, Switzerland: Europgraphics

CHAPTER 11

Contemporary Museum Practice in Cusco, Peru

Helaine Silverman

INTRODUCTION

Museums have become an international phenomenon (Germany 1999; Kinzer 2003; McGuigan and Plagens 2001; Muschamp 1997, 1998; New York Times 2001, 2003; Skidmore College 2001; Szanto 2001), related closely to the global culture industry, itself potentially encompassing contingent issues of colonialism/imperialism (Hitchens 1997), community assertion (Mexican Fine Arts Center Museum 2001), memory (Klein 2001), heritage and tourism (Kirshenblatt-Gimblett 1998), and economic development (Kifner 2000) – with each of these being frequently interconnected to one or more of the others, as in 'heritage and tourism'. Yet Prosler (1998) has correctly observed that critical museum scholarship has largely ignored museums in developing or Third World countries.

I seek to contribute to the strengthening of attention to this neglected area by considering two museums in Cusco, Peru, both dealing with precolumbian Andean civilisation but in very different ways. This chapter is not a museum review. Rather, I seek to unpack the historical, racial, social, local and global influences and contexts that have generated the two museum buildings (their physical and historical locations in Cusco), their collections and their scripts. In so doing, I also interrogate the two museums as repositories of objects used in the construction of national identity for internal consumption (notably in the case of Museo Inka) and external consumption (notably in the case of Museo de Arte Precolombino [MAP]). I consider these two museums as spaces in which elites and non-elites express their ideologies about contemporary Cusco (and Peru) as well as prehispanic society. Ultimately, I seek to explain the museums' exhibitionary scripts within the larger context of Cusco as a major node in the global tourism network, an example of capitalism par excellence.

CUSCO

It is important to first address, albeit briefly, the history and significance of ancient Cusco as the local context for the contemporary city's two archaeology museums. Located in the south highlands of Peru, Cusco was the political capital and preeminent sacred centre of the Inca Empire. Cusco was a glorious urban settlement built of superb cut-stone architecture and composed of majestic palaces, sumptuous temples, noble houses, large plazas and domestic neighborhoods. Inca remains still constitute a visible part of the urban fabric of Cusco, explaining tourist interest.

But Inca remains are not the only pre-modern ones in this bustling provincial city. Upon conquering the Inca Empire in 1532, the Spaniards busily set about remaking the urban, as well as rural, landscape of their new territory. In Cusco they brutally razed many of the great Inca buildings and built atop and around others. Most notably, they transformed the principal Inca public space, Haukaypata, into a proto-typical Spanish plaza. Although international tourism to Cusco is marketed on the basis of the city's Inca past, the socially and physically central Plaza de Armas is a great Colonial Period monument with mere fragments of Inca walls around it. The whole historic district of Cusco is a palimpsest of vanquished Inca grandeur, Spanish secular and religious oppression, Colonial Catholic architectural and artistic creativity, and post-1821 (independence from Spain) Republican and contemporary architecture.

MUSEO INKA

Museo Inka is a public university museum – part of the Museo e Instituto de Arqueología of the Universidad Nacional San Antonio Abad del Cusco. Located one block uphill from the Plaza de Armas (Figure 11.1), the site on which the museum operates has been occupied since Inca times. The actual building in which Museo Inka functions dates to the late 16th century and is one of the most beautiful examples of virreynal architecture in the city (it is the Casa del Almirante). An architectural addition to the Colonial Period mansion and reinstallation of its exhibition as 'Los Inkas del Qosqo' were inaugurated in 1997. The collections for this exhibition are the product of scientific archaeological investigations by Cusqueño and foreign archaeologists over many decades as well as unprovenienced materials donated to the museum from private collections, some of them quite large.

One enters the museum through massive wood doors moving past a larger than life painted wood statue of a powerfully muscled Inca king, setting the tone for the panegyric museum script. From here one

Figure 11.1 Looking up at the Museo Inka, Cusco, Peru. This Colonial Period building is known as the Casa del Almirante.

enters a large courtyard around whose four sides are the ticket office, small library, tiny bookstore, and humble gift shop, as well as two rooms providing an overview of pre-Inca Andean societies. The most noticeable aspect of the courtyard is a group of indigenous backstrap loom weavers in their traditional garments (Figure 11.2). They sell their beautiful textiles through the assistance of an NGO (non-governmental organisation) called Centro de Textiles Tradicionales del Cusco/The Center for Traditional Textiles of Cusco. The presence of these indigenous weavers is congruent with the museum script which emphasises the continuity of Cusco's indigenous population from pre-Inca into Inca times, survival through the brutal Colonial Period, and cultural persistence in subsequent centuries. At the same time, one is reminded of the living displays of the exhibitionary complex (Benedict 1983:43–52; Bennett 1995:59–88; Brown 1994:105–113; Hinsley 1991; Rydell 1999), with the weavers' voluntary presence nevertheless being compelled by the dire economic conditions of the region in which the women live as well as the global tourism industry with whose gaze they are engaged as active agents.

The exhibition script on the second floor deals with the Cusco region. The display is arranged typologically by material (pottery, metallurgy, stone tools, bone, textiles, 'kero' drinking goblets, etc.) and

Figure 11.2 Traditional weavers from the community of Chinchero in the courtyard of Museo Inka, Cusco, Peru.

chronologically by archaeological culture. Because the museum is administered as part of the financially challenged national university, the exhibition is aesthetically and technologically modest in the extreme (Figure 11.3). Nor are the objects on display 'spectacular' since Inca 'art' is somberly geometric and standardised, in contrast to much other precolumbian Andean material culture in Peruvian museums (including the Museo de Arte Precolombino, see below). Indeed, the Cusco region never had a 'great art style', except when conquered (ca. A.D. 600–1100; see Glowacki 2005:117) by the Wari Empire (an earlier polity centred in a highland region farther north), known for its exquisite pottery and textiles. Only with Inca does a 'corporate style' (Moseley 2001:79) develop in the region – a style with an 'ethnically' or 'geopolitically' emblematic iconography and form. But the unembarrassed exhibition of ordinary potsherds, stone tools, food remains and other material aspects of daily life in the precolumbian past is what makes the Museo Inka a fine didactic museum.

The main exhibition script begins with dioramas that show the principal natural environments of the Cusco region and their characteristic subsistence activities. The next area, themed 'Origins', presents the local antecedents to the Incas and ranges over seven thousand years of prehistory until the rise of the Incas. The exhibition script then

Figure 11.3 An example of the typical vitrines in Museo Inka. These are simple wood and glass display cases with standard lighting. Objects are not well displayed in aesthetic terms.

moves into a categorised presentation of the Incas in terms of the different material and ideological aspects of imperial Inca culture, as if following HRAF (Human Relations Area Files) categories. Thus, there are exhibition areas for Inca Herding, Inca Agriculture, Inca Pottery, Inca Architecture, and Inca Religion.

The Inca exhibition leads directly into a section on the Spanish Invasion, which is emphatically labelled and conceived as such. Here there are displays of Colonial Period 'keros' (wood drinking goblets), Colonial-Inca textiles, Inca stone sculptures mutilated by the Spanish extirpators of idolatries, and copies of 17th-century drawings by Felipe Guaman Poma de Ayala that depict Spanish abuse of the indigenous people (the original manuscript is in Copenhagen). The term 'invasion' is used discursively to delegitimise both the Spanish appropriation of native lands and resources as well as to indicate the contamination and overwhelming of native culture. The exhibit directs the visitor to recognise the multifaceted, devastating upheaval in Andean society resulting from the intrusion of the Spaniards. This discourse of invasion stems from the larger ideology of Cusco's municipal government during the mayorship of Daniel Estrada (1990–1995), which aggressively and cogently (in material and discursive forms) attacked the 500th anniversary of Columbus's arrival in the Americas as an invasion.

At the same time, the museum illustrates the survival, transformation and negotiated success of royal Incas under Spanish Colonial rule. A Colonial Period room with its original painted coffered ceiling is furnished with exquisite Colonial carved and shell-inlaid wood furniture, a Colonial woven rug, and a Colonial religious painting. Glazed pottery, including Colonial 'pacchas' (originally an Inca ceremonial form, characterised by a pouring spout or channel for liquid), are also displayed. A brief text states that the Inca nobility lived like Spaniards in this early Colonial Period.

However, neither the noble Incas nor Andean commoners were complacent during the Colonial Period. On exhibit are two major displays addressing the numerous indigenous rebellions in the 17th and 18th centuries in the form of 'art' ('keros' and textiles) and documents of the time. The text explains that 'just because the art was in Spanish style does not mean it dealt with Spanish concerns. It was a period during which … scenes from myths, customs, and history from before the Spanish invasion [were depicted]'. Art, the text explains, was also a form of resistance.

The following room, called Incanismo, visualises the 'increasing cultural value on Tawantinsuyu [Inca Empire] and Inca history' (museum brochure; see discussion in Calvo 1995:82–88) that evolved among Cusco intellectuals in the 19th and 20th centuries. The exhibit includes 19th-century portrait busts and paintings of the Inca emperors and an early 20th-century photograph of a local Cusqueño drama group presenting the Inca drama *Ollantay* (see Chambi 1993:102).

The ethnographic present is illustrated in its own display area with photographs and dioramas of traditional Andean lifeways, such as *campesinos* preparing *chuño* (freeze-dried potatoes), weaving, making ritual offerings to Mother Earth (*Pacha Mama*), and using coca leaf.

Museo Inka is an anthropological museum with an overt political message of empowerment and pride. Its coherent, didactic script makes the museum effective and important in its local context, especially as narrated by local guides and local school teachers. Although the dynamics of prehistoric culture change are not presented (the displays are synchronic snapshots of discrete moments of prehispanic society), the Incas are clearly depicted as the culmination of indigenous cultural development and as continuing into the present day by means of Colonial- and Republican-period transformations. Struggle and resistance to the Spanish and Republican regimes are clearly shown. Cultural continuity is emphasised, albeit with some trace of essentialism in the repeated, unnuanced tropes of 'Andean' and 'Inca' throughout the many texts.

MUSEO DE ARTE PRECOLOMBINO

Museo de Arte Precolombino (or MAP as it calls itself; Figure 11.4) is located one block uphill from Museo Inka (Figure 11.1), in the Plaza Nazarenas, where Cusco's finest hotel, the five-star Hotel Monasterio (built within a Colonial Period monastery and run by Orient Express) functions. Like Museo Inka, MAP was created on a site that had an Inca occupation and on which was subsequently built a fine Colonial mansion, the Casa Cabrera (Figure 11.4). The building was given new life when acquired by the Banco Continental in 1981; it opened as a branch of the private Larco Museum (in Lima) on 22 May 2003, in association with the Banco Continental and AFP Horizonte-Grupo BBVA (a pan-Latin American pension fund) – an association of culture and the museum's money-making potential through insertion into the global tourism industry that is proudly displayed by signage on MAP's front façade (Figure 11.4) and banners on the second floor.

MAP received a tremendous amount of publicity as it prepared to open, in part because its inauguration was timed to coincide with a summit of Latin American presidents that was held in Cusco that year. Also present at the inauguration were many executives from the business

Figure 11.4   Museo de Arte Precolombino (MAP), Cusco, Peru. This Colonial Period building is known as the Casa Cabrera. Note the sponsors' names on the façade under the museum's name.

world who, according to *El Diario del Cusco*, 5 May 2003, 'once more rat-ified their commitment to culture and its preservation, conservation, and promotion/diffusion'. Peruvian President Alejandro Toledo inaugurated MAP at the summit saying, 'We are showing the world our cultural wealth. I am profoundly proud that [we can give to participants] a little of the culture that belongs not only to Peru, but to Latin America … [The region must] look to its past to construct together a new Latin America with more health, education, justice for the poor and culture' (www. terra.com.pe/noticias/cumbre/30523–2.shtml). With this statement, Peru's past was deployed as the sign of Peru's modernity, transnational engagement, and developmental promise for the future. Also, by argu-ing that Peru's heritage belongs not only to the Peruvian nation-state but to a larger Latin America, President Toledo was both defining a zone of historical grounding and contemporary action in the competitive context of American (United States) and European (European Union) power, and echoing the rhetoric of 'universality' that underwrites much heritage dis-course today (see discussion in final section).

MAP displays a select group of 450 exquisite precolumbian objects from the home museum, covering the sweep of ancient pan-Andean creativity. The exhibit moves chronologically with each major archaeo-logical culture within a time period receiving its own room, culmin-ating in separate rooms for spectacular gold, silver and shell jewelry objects. Each room has a carefully chosen wall color that enhances the particular style being showcased. The lighting is dramatic and appro-priate to each specific object. Pieces are well spaced in beautiful vit-rines both within the walls and on pedestals scattered sparingly throughout the rooms (Figure 11.5). Some of the exhibits are particu-larly innovative, indeed breathtaking. MAP is exemplary as a trad-itional art museum-cum-art gallery.

MAP was greeted with exceptional fanfare in the national and local press when it opened. Nevertheless, virtually every published laud-atory remark reveals problematic issues with the museum's concept. Four principal ideas can be distilled from the mutually reinforcing praise appearing in local and national newspapers:

1. MAP is an unproblematic space of enjoyment.
2. Art has universal value and the greatness of precolumbian Peruvian art must be recognised.
3. MAP's exhibition is museographically progressive.
4. MAP promotes the preservation of cultural patrimony.

MAP Is An Unproblematic Space of Enjoyment

But MAP is not enjoyed by the vast majority of Cusqueños. As a pri-vate museum, MAP charges three times more (equivalent to US $6)

Figure 11.5 An example of the beautiful vitrines and display pedestals at MAP (this is the Nasca Gallery). Note the careful lighting of objects and their spacing and presentation as isolated works of art.

than Museo Inka for admission, making it prohibitive for most of the local population. Moreover, the entryway of MAP speaks to its intended public and discourages local visitors: Two guards in suit and tie greet guests at an imposing modernistic ticket counter. In the courtyard beyond the desk are an expensive, trendy restaurant and pricey boutiques (Alpaca 111 sweater store, H. Stern jewelers, along with the museum's own gift shop). The cost of entrance, the guards, and the associated services offered by the museum contravene its purported goal of local relevance; rather, they readily acknowledge their international tourist market.

Art Has Universal Value and the Greatness of Precolumbian Peruvian Art Must Be Recognised

In order to valorise ancient Peruvian material culture as 'great art', MAP argues for the universal appeal of the precolumbian objects on display. The argument is presented implicitly by the decontextualised display of the objects as art. It is presented overtly through the object labels (example, transcribed verbatim from the English text: 'To contemplate these [Nasca] plates elaborated 1,700 years ago makes us reformulate our concept of modernism. We are before timeless beauty, obtained only by the ability of artists that made of painting an excellent way of expression'). It is reiterated by means of a series of quotes from several world-famous artists (Braque, Durer, Gaugin, Kandinsky, Klee, Matisse, Vauxcelles) that are distributed on several walls. Each artist speaks to primitivism and/or universality. For instance, the Paul Klee quote is: 'I wish I was newly born, and totally ignorant of Europe, innocent of facts and fashions, to be almost primitive'.

. The notion of universality has been correctly criticised by scholars. Bourdieu and Darbel (1990), for instance, emphasise that museum competence (aesthetic appreciation, proper behavior) is a cultural (not innate) phenomenon with socially inculcated performances and learned values. Errington (1998:102–117) regards the concept of universality as 'pernicious' and cautions against this view as a 'self-fulfilling prophecy' leading to its trafficking and collecting by the elite art world. Furthermore, MAP's assertion of universality occurs within the transnational capitalism underwriting the museum's operation: Just as the art displayed is said to be equal to that of European artistic masters, so, too, Banco Continental–AFP Horizonte–Grupo BBVA are fully engaged with the modern and developed world; their interest in art (in this case, precolumbian) is an indicator of their commercial viability and cultural modernity.

MAP's repeated textual emphasis of the ancient Peruvian artists as 'primitive' is problematical. As selectively appropriated for use in the museum script, the word 'primitive' reveals an underlying ambiguous racial-cultural assessment of the precolumbian population with implications for the present-day indigenous population. As scripted, 'primitive' furthermore appears to express doubt or frustration concerning Peru's 'progress' toward the modernity within which the European artists enamored of primitivism worked (ie, contemporary primitive art was modern art). Given the elite context of the collection's formation (the Larco family were wealthy, European-descended landholders on the north coast of Peru) as well as its elite context (its underwriters, intended audience, location, building history) in contemporary Cusco, the term 'primitive' is both overt and coded. It perpetuates stereotypes and naturalises structural inequalities in Cusco.

The Exhibition Is Museographically Progressive

Perhaps this is the most shocking of all the statements made in praise of MAP. In its decontextualisation of objects from their respective societies, MAP is reactionary and retrograde. MAP follows a traditional art historical approach, which is to say a historicist presentation, proposing 'an overall distribution of works governed by the factor of period, with the succession of individual galleries being arranged so as to cause the least abrupt chronological transitions' (Bann 1998:235). The objects are hyper-aestheticised by their labels (here is an example from MAP's own English label, faithfully transcribed from the English text: 'Feminine figurines. Nasca. Apogee Epoch, 1–800 A.D. The beauty found in each one is the primitive design and simplicity; obtaining likeable, joyous, feminine figurines, somewhat playful with an absence of adornments that grant them with an evident severity').

The Museum Promotes the Preservation of Cultural Patrimony

The act of collecting is encouraged because there is no explanation of how the collection itself was amassed, or of archaeological method and rationale. MAP conforms to Sherman's (1994:139) scenario of 'a modernist rendition of Quatremére's nightmare, an institution that "protects" art by depriving it of life, flaunting its public role while consecrating a system of value based entirely on private exchange'. The problem with collecting precolumbian material culture ('art') in Peru is that constitutionally the Peruvian state owns the cultural patrimony and only officially authorised archaeological projects are permitted to dig into the subsoil to investigate the remains of that patrimony. Unauthorised excavations are presumably the work of looters with a resultant loss of archaeological context and information about the ancient societies. The display of decontextualised objects in a museum valorises them commercially and incites the desire for possession.

REACTION OF THE PUBLIC TO MUSEO INKA AND MAP

I have commented on Museo Inka and MAP from my biased perspective as an anthropological archaeologist with a real expertise in the Andes, museums and heritage. I see significant differences between the two museums and especially serious deficiencies with MAP. But both museums – whether public or private – seek to receive and engage visitors. An easy way of assessing their degree of success is to read the visitor comments in their guest books. This is exactly what I did in December 2003.

Analysis of visitor comments reveals that the vast majority of remarks are highly positive about both museums. One Scottish couple had visited both museums in the same day and found both to be worthwhile with MAP also being 'beautifully presented'. Museo Inka is frequently described by visitors as 'beautiful', 'interesting', 'fascinating', or 'educational'. At both museums Peruvian visitors express patriotic pride in their past, referring to *nuestros antepasados* ('our ancestors'), though that sentiment is more frequent and effusive at MAP where the spectacular nature of the exhibit is noted repeatedly with exuberant adjectives. Most comments praise MAP's presentation as 'stunning', 'wonderfully displayed', 'very well presented', and the objects are perceived as 'marvelous', 'beautiful', and 'extraordinary' art. Only a handful of comments complain about MAP's museography: insufficient light, deficient texts, poor translations. One unusually astute Limeño criticises MAP's 'lack of dynamism, interactivity, and historical explanations instead of mere artistic criticism – this makes the visit boring for the ordinary tourists who want to know why and how'. Also interesting are the several complaints of a personal nature concerning Museo Inka: The ticket office cannot make change, the bathrooms lack toilet paper, and the guards on the second floor are rude – all of which are valid observations in my experience.

Of course, the use of guest books as a source of information on tourists generates a biased sample: This is a self-selecting group comprised of people who are familiar enough with museums to regard them as worthwhile investments of precious travel time, suggesting an educated cohort. Any visitor's experience in a museum is shaped by his/her own background (eg, Bourdieu and Darbel 1990) as much as by the museum itself (including its larger setting). Far from being passive receptacles, many museum visitors exert a critical eye on what they see – hence the many controversies that have been abundantly documented in the museum literature (eg, Dubin 1999; Henderson and Kaeppler 1997). Guest books themselves can be an enormously powerful venue of resistance, empowerment, and negotiation (or even accord) with a museum/museum script, as explicitly discussed by Truettner (1997:28–29).

Judging from the above examples, the tourist comments on Museo Inka and MAP are both encouraging and discouraging. On the bright side, tourists like the museums. On the down side, most tourists are uncritical about the museums they visit, notably MAP, which is accepted at face value as the art museum it is. If the Museo Inka and MAP guest books are read by the museum directors or staff, the comments contained within will likely prompt no change in the museum scripts, which I regard as especially lamentable for MAP.

CONCLUSION

Museo Inka is a site of postcolonial resistance framed within local archaeological-anthropological discourse. Museo Inka seeks to counteract the necessary displacement of artifacts from their original contexts by providing complementary information in the form of additional wall texts, drawings from Guaman Poma de Ayala, dioramas, photographs, models and so forth. Museo Inka is a passionate voice for entitlement of the local populace of Cusco. It offers a spirited defense for social justice in the city by virtue of its exhibition script that links – in one vast sweep of historical process – the precolumbian societies in the Valley of Cusco, their change under Colonial domination, their transformation during the Independence Movement, the Republican restructuration, and current-day residents.

In contrast, MAP is a site of neocolonialism and reactionary art history. MAP deliberately isolates and decontextualises the objects to achieve their aesthetic recognition and appreciation. Moreover, by presenting the Incas as just one of many ancient Peruvian societies, MAP deterritorialises its own location in Cusco: This museum could be located anyplace. MAP reflects and reinforces the structural inequalities of Peru's history and Cusco's political economy, whereas Museo Inka resists. MAP was created for the upscale global tourism market (including monied Peruvians). Museo Inka, from its inception in 1848 and in its early through present incarnations, has been directed at Cusco's local population, especially the city's primary and secondary school students, and visiting Peruvians. Thus, there are very important class issues at MAP: It is a museum for elite visitors and it is a museum of the ancient elite (the exquisite objects on display were made for consumption by the privileged precolumbian class, an issue never addressed in the exhibition script).

MAP implies a finite end to Andean creativity with the Incas being replaced by the Spanish Colonial regime: end of exhibition (Figure 11.6). As such, MAP conforms to Bann's (1998:237) analysis of the rise of the modern museum: 'For the historically concrete to make an impression, it was necessary for there to be a widespread and pervasive sense of historical loss; that is, the sense that the revolutionary break [in the case of Peru, this would be the Spanish Conquest] had caused a rupture in continuity with the past [and] caused an exactly proportionate need for restitution [ie, display]'. The 21 paintings in MAP's Virreynal Room (Figure 11.6) display Spanish Colonial culture in its most elite and Catholic form; four Colonial Period 'keros' in an easily missed niche are unexplained. MAP deliberately obviates consideration of the descendants of the great prehispanic civilisations – yet they are just outside the museum's doors. MAP's exhibition script purposefully does not link Cusco's inhabitants to their past, thereby denying recognition of Cusquennños as legitimate claimants to physical and narrative space in the museum, let alone the city.

Museo Inka takes the same historical facts and vigorously argues a different position – that despite the trauma of Colonial, Republican and modern oppression, indigenous Andean culture is alive and vibrantly creative. Museo Inka's script explicitly addresses the events, processes and conditions leading to the impoverishment and disenfranchisement of native Andean people still visible today. The presence of Chinchero

Figure 11.6 The Colonial Period in MAP's exhibition script is represented by 21 beautiful paintings of the Colonial Period in an original gallery painted brilliant red.

weavers in Museo Inka's courtyard underscores the connection of Cusco's inhabitants to the past and suggests hope for the present and future of traditional Andean communities through their active participation in the tourism market.

Mitchell (2000) has observed that the hallmark of the modern is the representation process, how history itself is staged or the staging of history. By the very nature of their collections, archaeological museums tend to have a retrospective script and are time affirming. But Museo Inka also mobilises the past for empowerment ('the ordering knowledge produced by museums as a strategy of power' [Sherman 1994:139]) and construction of identity in the present, and it asserts the continued existence of Andean people. In contrast, MAP presents a Romantic elegy to artists of a vanished civilisation.

The interdigitated modernist irony of museums as backward-looking and postcolonial irony of formerly colonised peoples using the quintessential representational device of their colonisers to decolonialise themselves (ie, to become modern is to become like the West and the museum is quintessentially Western and a symbol of the idea of modernity) should not be lost on us. Museo Inka is an integral part of Cusco's project of modernity that strongly implicates an appropriation of the

Inca past (see Silverman 2002). MAP is an integral part of Cusco's post-modern tourist pastiche with its unmoored history and tourist-oriented spectacle (Silverman 2002). It is a matter of emphasis, but with enormously important different outcomes.

Forces of capitalism and globalisation have returned the Casa Cabrera to its former glory and resignified it as a site, once more, of elite privilege and power in its incarnation as MAP. In contrast, the Casa del Almirante has been reconquered by Cusco's dead and living indigenous population through Museo Inka's compelling (though not museographically sophisticated) postcolonial narrative.

This critical analysis of museum practice in Cusco has importance far beyond the particular case studies presented here in three principal ways. First, the scripts of archaeological museums and the outreach these museums promote can be the single greatest contribution of archaeology to people living in the region of their ancient ancestors. This is because of the personal or social validation, political empowerment and potential economic benefits through tourism (albeit grossly unequally distributed) that may be generated. But in Cusco we face a very interesting issue. Museo Inka barely produces enough revenue for its own maintenance. MAP has no such worries since it is a private museum whose operation is funded by strong financial backers. Indeed, in this regard MAP varies significantly from other museums whose creation was deliberately conceived and ordered by local, state or even national governments to jumpstart stagnant urban/regional economies (Kifner 2000; also see discussion by Neil Silberman, this volume).

Second, museums are sites of representation and, potentially, mis-representation. How to rectify negative and inaccurate exhibitions, however, is a very difficult matter requiring lengthy consideration beyond the possibilities of this essay.

Third, and most relevant to the unifying theme of this volume, museums are implicated in 'the structures of a distinctly modern society, most notably the market' (Sherman 1994:125), including the specialised leisure market (Foley and McPherson 2000). As Jean and John Comaroff (2005) have argued, 'The politics of cultural identity appears to have taken on new force with the triumphal rise of neoliberal capitalism ... [Globalization has produced] a subtle shift in the nature of ethnicity: its commodification ... [I]ncreasingly, ethnic groups across the planet are beginning to act like corporations that own a "natural" copyright to their "culture" and "cultural products" – framed in terms, also, of heritage, indigenous knowledge, and intellectual property – which they protect, often by recourse to the law, and on which they capitalise in much the same way as do businesses in the private sector'. Tourism in Cusco (Silverman 2002) and the two archaeology museums discussed here are compelling evidence of the Comaroffs' argument.

Here I have considered only briefly some of the political, economic, social and ethical impacts of the two museum scripts on the nature of local citizenship in Cusco. Cusco – at least its historic centre – is itself an open-air site museum (see Silverman 2002, 2006) and, increasingly, a kind of theme park (see Neil Silberman, this volume). But, whereas Museo Inka was specifically created and recently refurbished for the Cusqueños first and foremost, MAP was overtly designed as an international tourist attraction. As argued in this paper, the two museums present archaeological heritage in very distinct ways and for very different reasons. I would call MAP a form of 'McArchaeology' with its goal 'to capture a market share of recreational activities' and unsettle visitor conscience as little as possible (see Neil Silberman, this volume). In contrast, Museo Inka bravely engages difficult issues of historical depth and social transcendence. In so doing it attempts to convey meaningful information about other times and cultures so as to generate public discussion and serious reflection, a goal McArchaeology eschews. As thousands (potentially hundreds of thousands and even millions) of tourists visit particular museums in Third World/developing countries through the increase of global tourism, it behooves scholars to pay increased attention to how these institutions act and react to their insertion into the transnational capitalist economy, and to that economy's local, national and international agents.

ACKNOWLEDGMENTS

The larger fieldwork project from which this paper resulted was conducted in Cusco in 2003–2004 with an Individual Research Grant from the Wenner-Gren Foundation for Anthropological Research, whose support is gratefully acknowledged.

REFERENCES

Bann, S (1998) 'Art history and museums', in Cheetham, M, Holly, M and Moxey, K (eds), *The Subjects of Art History: Historical Objects in Contemporary Perspectives*, Cambridge: Cambridge University Press

Benedict, B (1983) *The Anthropology of World's Fairs: San Francisco's Panama Pacific International Exposition of 1915*, Berkeley: The Lowie Museum of Anthropology

Bennett, T (1995) *The Birth of the Museum: History, Theory, Politics*, London: Routledge

Bourdieu, P and Darbel, A (1990) *The Love of Art: European Art Museums and Their Public*, Palo Alto: Stanford University Press

Brown, JK (1994) *Contesting Images: Photography and the World's Columbian Exposition*, Tucson: University of Arizona Press

Calvo C., R (1995) *Qosqo: Sociedad e Ideología, Siglo XX*, Cusco: Municipalidad del Qosqo

Chambi, M (1993) *Martín Chambi: Photographs, 1920–1950*, Washington, DC: Smithsonian Institution Press

Comaroff, J and Comaroff, J (2005) 'Ethnicity, Inc.: on the commodification and consumption of cultural identity in the brave new world'. Paper presented at the conference, 'Fetishizing the Free Market: The Cultural Politics of Neoliberlism', *Unit for Criticism and Interpretive Theory, University of Illinois at Urbana-Champaign*, 29–30

Dubin, SC (1999) *Displays of Power: Controversy in the American Museum from the Enola Gay to Sensation*, New York: New York University Press

Errington, S (1998) *The Death of Authentic Primitive Art and Other Tales of Progress*, Berkeley: University of California Press

Foley, M and McPherson, G (2000) 'Museums as leisure', *International Journal of Heritage Studies* 6, 161–174

Germany, L (1999) 'In Houston, a museum that speaks for itself', *The New York Times*, Art & Leisure Section, 31 October

Glowacki, M (2005) 'Dating Pikillacta', in McEwan, GF, *Pikillacta: The Wari Empire in Cusco*, Iowa City: University of Iowa Press

Henderson, A and Kaeppler, AL (eds) (1997) *Exhibiting Dilemmas: Issues of Representation at the Smithsonian*, Washington, DC: Smithsonian Institution Press

Hinsley, CM (1991) 'The world as marketplace: commodification of the exotic at the World's Columbian Exposition, Chicago, 1893', in Karp, I and Lavine, S (eds), *Exhibiting Cultures: The Poetics and Politics of Museum Display*, Washington, DC: Smithsonian Institution Press

Hitchens, C (1997) *The Elgin Marbles: Should They Be Returned To Greece?* London: Verso

Kifner, J (2000) 'Museum brings town back to life: Converted factory is economic catalyst for Massachusetts city', *The New York Times*, 30 May

Kinzer, S (2003) 'Fort Worth Museum frames art in wide open spaces', *The New York Times*, 29 January

Kirshenblatt-Gimblett, B (1998) *Destination Culture: Tourism, Museums and Heritage*, Berkeley: University of California Press

Klein, JM (2001) 'The Jewish Museum, Berlin: amid clutter, at odds with itself', *The Chronicle of Higher Education*, 9 November, B15–17

McGuigan, C and Plagens, P (2001) 'State of the art: it's the age of museums – not the musty kind, but ultramodern showplaces that are betting big on marketing culture to Middle America', *Newsweek*, 26 March, 52–61

Mexican Fine Arts Center Museum (2001) *Grand Opening Celebration* (brochure), Chicago: Mexican Fine Arts Center Museum

Mitchell, T (2000) 'The stage of modernity', in Mitchell, T (ed), *Questions of Modernity*, Minneapolis: University of Minnesota Press

Moseley, ME (2001) *The Incas and Their Ancestors*, London: Thames and Hudson

Muschamp, H (1997) 'The Miracle in Bilbao', *The New York Times Magazine*, 7 September, 54–59, 72, 82

—— (1998) 'Designing museums: often not a lively art', *The New York Times*, 28 June, 32

New York Times (2001) 'Forget the art – it's all about the building', *The New York Times*, 9 December

—— (2003) 'Museums: a special section', *The New York Times*, 27 April 2003

Prosler, M (1998) 'Museums and globalization', in Macdonald, S and Fyfe, G (eds), *Theorizing Museums*, Oxford: Blackwell

Rydell, RW (1999) 'The Chicago World's Columbian Exposition of 1893', in Boswell, D and Evans, J (eds), *Representing the Nation: A Reader. Histories, Heritage, and Museums*, London: Routledge

Sherman, DJ (1994) 'Quatremére/Benjamin/Marx: art museums, aura, and commodity fetishism', in Sherman, D and Rogoff, I (eds), *Museum Culture: Histories, Discourses, Spectacles*. Minneapolis: University of Minnesota Press

Silverman, H (2002) 'Touring ancient times: the present and presented past in contemporary Peru', *American Anthropologist* 104, 881–902

—— (2006) 'The historic district of Cusco as an open-air site museum', in Silverman, H (ed), *Archaeological Site Museums in Latin America*, Gainesville: University Press of Florida

Skidmore College (2001) 'An age of the museum?' Conference held at Saratoga Springs, NY, 6–7 April

Szanto, A (2001) 'Museum building in the Budapest style', *The New York Times*, Arts & Leisure section, 26 August

Truettner, WH (1997) 'For museum audiences: the morning of a new day?', in Henderson, A and Kaeppler, AL (eds), *Exhibiting Dilemmas*, 28–46. Washington, DC: Smithsonian Institution Press

PART 4

ETHICAL FUTURES, EMANCIPATORY ARCHAEOLOGIES: INTRODUCTION

Yannis Hamilakis

While part two questioned some of the common assumptions on ethics and politics in archaeology and part three focused on our ethical and political responsibilities by examining the embeddedness of archaeology within the structures of capitalism, this final section takes an explicitly prospective view. It attempts to answer the question, How are we to construct ethical futures for the discipline and for the broader communities and publics? And how can we combine critique with action in order to start building the conditions for emancipation? As noted in the introduction of this book, several voices in archaeology, anthropology and elsewhere have recently called for ethics to be embedded in practice and in specific contexts. This call can be interpreted in different ways, but the interpretation that many of the contributors in this volume seem to opt for is that of engagement with the material realities of conflict, and the active participation in these conflicts on the side of the people and communities who resist. This is indeed praxis, and not simply practice, in the sense that it combines knowledge, critique and action (*cf* McGuire *et al* 2005). It is theorised practice that attempts to change the world, not simply to understand it. Many of the authors in this section combine archaeology with activism, an often risky venture. It is this activism, combined with theorised practice, that informs their writings here.

Reinhard Bernbeck and Susan Pollock focus on present-day Germany and deliver a powerful critique of assumptions that are normally taken for granted: that archaeology, for example, is by definition a good thing, that the material traces of the past are always a 'positive resource', and that the various groups and communities beyond archaeologists need to share, appreciate and incorporate that resource into their own identities. They thus engage in a subtle and effective critique of the archaeology of identity which, often in its unproblematised form, has dominated much of the theoretical discussion in archaeology for the last 20 years. They remind us that the archaeological past and the archaeological process itself are often the embodiment of oppression and subjugation, and that the material past as a positive identity signifier has very often slipped into commodification. Multicultural diversity and its material signifiers can also mean big business for capital, providing new arenas, new vistas of diversity and variety for audiences to experience, and new markets (*cf* Zizek 1997). Bernbeck and Pollock then turn to their case study and compare two 'sites of memory': the site of the headquarters of the Gestapo during the Nazi period, and the site of the new Holocaust memorial. It is the first site that they find more evocative and effective, an 'open wound' that must remain bare and 'bleeding' to continue its work: to disturb and unsettle, to disrupt the temporality of a present that, as it tends to happen with the Holocaust memorial, memorialises in order to forget (*cf* Forty and Küchler 1999). Archaeology can also mean collective amnesia. The project of the archaeology of perpetrators that Bernbeck and Pollock advocate can contribute to archaeology as a profoundly disturbing experience and practice.

It is this fight against collective amnesia and memorialisation which Ermengol Gassiot and his collaborators join. They have marshalled the whole array of archaeological techniques, from excavation to forensic anthropology, to disrupt the deafening silence on the atrocities committed by the Francoists during the Spanish Civil War. This is not, except indirectly, an archaeology of the perpetrators, but neither is it a conventional archaeology of identity. It is a project 'from below' with little official support, it clashes with the notion of the national reconciliatory consensus, and its tenets have direct implications for the politics of the present: The victims of Franco, his regime and his followers were socialists and others who were fighting to defend the popular republican state. In the era of aggressive neoliberal capitalism, the burials of the defenders of the Republic inevitably bring to the fore ideas of contemporary social justice.

Gassiot and his collaborators see this project as not simply an archaeological but a profoundly political one, a project of praxis that fuses the identity of the researcher with the identity of the activist. This is also the path that the paper by Maggie Ronayne outlines. She describes her experiences in the campaign against the construction of the Ilısu dam in southeast Turkey, a 'development' project that, if realised, will have catastrophic consequences for the primarily Kurdish present-day communities in the area, as well as for the material world, past and present, that forms a significant component of these communities. The Ilısu campaign group and the archaeologists within it have worked *with* the affected communities, not *for* them. Ronayne brings to the fore the role of women, showing very vividly that they will be the ones most affected by the dam, and they are the most vociferous opponents to it, despite the attempts to silence or ignore them; she has shown that gender politics cannot and should not be divorced from the broader economic and political structures within which they are articulated. The Ilısu dam campaign has further shown that while the tradition of professionalisation fetishises the archaeological object or site, often at the expense of the local people and communities, another definition of 'material heritage' is possible: the definition that the affected communities in southeast Turkey have come up with, a definition that archaeologists should take seriously into account: for them, the material heritage is an 'organic wholeness', a 'living relationship between people, past and present' and the material components of their lives. For mothers in particular, their children *are* their heritage, the living agents that connect past and present, without whom sites and artefacts mean nothing. This is a very different definition of heritage from the one adopted by professional organisations and codes of ethics, and the one followed by the archaeologists who rushed to save the 'heritage' of Iraq while many thousands of civilians were being killed all around them (*cf* the Introduction to this book and the chapter by Mourad). Finally, this chapter carries an optimistic message: Battles can be won, and archaeologists can play a key part in contributing to the victories. The Ilısu dam has been stopped for now, but chances are that this will be an ongoing battle for years to come.

This part, and the book as a whole, finishes with the chapter by Dean Saitta, whose starting point is the Ludlow project: a pioneering historical archaeology project that investigates the material memories of the 1914 massacre of Colorado coalminers by the militia employed by the mine owners, during a fierce industrial dispute. This important chapter in US and world labour history has become the focus of an intensive archaeological investigation which started from the outset from the political standpoint: to address class issues in the past and in the present. That this book on archaeology and capitalism finishes with a discussion on class, the largely ignored category in the recent debates on archaeological ethics and archaeological theory (*cf* Duke and Saitta 1998), is indeed very appropriate and telling. Saitta makes clear that the Ludlow Collective is not interested in a project of memorialisation, the mummification of the working-class experience of the early 20th century, which can then be easily co-opted into the body of national narrative, or provide another heritage 'asset' for corporate capitalism. Their project respects and honours the 1914 dead by refusing to create a break between the past and the present; team members are taking part in present-day industrial disputes and strikes. This is an engaged, politically active archaeology, which understands that the ethical is and should be political, and that this means that inevitably archaeologists need to 'take sides'. Saitta suggests that this ethical-political archaeology finds philosophical grounding and further inspiration in the anti-foundationalist ideas of pragmatism, especially as formulated by Richard Rorty.

This part brings the discussion full circle. If official, western archaeology (as suggested in the introduction; *cf* also Kehoe this volume) started as a middle-class project, embedded in the logic of capital and the fetish of commodity, then at the start of the 21st century, using archaeological apparatuses to undermine and fight capitalist modernity with its collective (and selective) amnesia, its aggressive de-territorialisation and commodification of objects, places and human lives, and its apotheosis of middle-class individuality, is perhaps the most fitting, worthwhile and hopeful legacy the discipline can offer.

REFERENCES

Duke, P and Saitta, D (1998) 'An emancipatory archaeology for the working class', *Assemblage* 4 (http://www.shef.ac.uk/assem/4/)

Forty, A and Küchler, S (eds) (1999) *The Art of Forgetting*, Oxford: Berg

McGuire, RH, O'Donovan, M and Wurst, LA (2005) 'Probing praxis in archaeology: the last eighty years', *Rethinking Marxism* 17, 355–372

Zizek, S (1997) 'Multiculturalism, or the cultural logic of multinational capitalism', *New Left Review* 225, 28–51

CHAPTER 12

'Grabe, Wo Du Stehst!' An Archaeology of Perpetrators

Reinhard Bernbeck and Susan Pollock

INTRODUCTION

Archaeology plays an important role in the creation and reinforcement of identities in the present. It generates material remains of past glories that bolster national and ethnic pride, as well as evidence used to support claims for redressing historic and recent wrongs. In these ways, archaeology becomes more than an historical source – it is also a resource, one that can be exploited for its potentials for the present and future. In this paper, we argue that the approach to archaeology as a 'positive resource' is dangerously one-sided, because it sanitises the past. In doing so, it enables empathy and produces a consumable product for late capitalist societies. We argue for a dialectical approach that couples tendencies toward identification with their opposites – a pronounced discomfort with a past that is nonetheless temporally, spatially, and socially close – thereby helping to remove archaeology from its status as a commodity and making it instead a ground for dispute and discord.

THE PAST AS A SOURCE OF IDENTITY: A CRITIQUE

Archaeology pursued in the service of identity building often emphasises the study of groups who are or were subordinated, repressed, and dominated, whether suffering under colonial regimes, military occupations, other forms of state repression, or discrimination on the basis of gender, age, race, or sexuality. There is a growing number of laudable archaeological projects that have taken up the causes of subaltern groups, including those pursuing research on slaves (Singleton 1995), Native Americans under Euro-American colonialism (Lightfoot 2005; Silliman 2004), or striking miners (Ludlow Collective 2000; Saitta, this volume), to name just a few. Archaeologists have often lent their support or at least their approval to uses of the past by the wider public for identity-based purposes. A number of short essays in a recent American Anthropological Association newsletter depict the relationship between past and present as unproblematically positive. Authors discuss struggles over ownership of the past as the ultimate form of identification with the past, but do not question the concept of ownership itself (Chambers 2005; Gleach 2005; Magliocco 2005).

The roots of identity-oriented archaeologies lie in epistemological as well as political disputes. The turn away from a natural science model of archaeology beginning in the early 1980s has brought with it the search for a relevance for archaeological research that goes beyond scientific discovery and scientific knowledge production. Influences from French philosophers since the late 1960s have led to a critique of positivism and its strong tendency to turn anthropological subjects into scientific objects. Althusser analyzed the academic institutions and their inner workings as an 'ideological state apparatus', the primary function of which is the production of consensus (Althusser 1971:142–148), and Foucault (1980:78–108) interpreted academic knowledge as saturated with power. Pushed into a defensive situation, social scientists have sought new approaches that empower their subjects as much as themselves. In archaeology, this has proven difficult, since direct subjects of archaeological research are usually no longer alive. Therefore, an *Ersatz*-subject has been found in those who occupy subject-positions similar to those dominated in the past (for example, women or workers) or descendants of those identified in the archaeological record as oppressed (slaves, the colonised). This search for comparable subaltern groups in the past and the present has paralleled broader academic and societal calls for identity-based politics that draw attention to the specifics of standpoint and experience (Harding 1986).

An archaeology of identity brings with it a number of problems. It contributes to paternalistic endeavors, in which archaeological practice is conceived as being a way to give subaltern groups a voice. Projects typically continue to be conducted on archaeologists' terms: Although the impetus for them may come from members of the public[1], their design, implementation, and final products (especially publications) tend to be under archaeologists' control. Expertise in excavation, analysis, and interpretation of material remains constitutes a body of (semi-secret) knowledge that we bestow on subordinated groups far more often than we learn from (living) others (Pollock, in press). In addition, the attempt at 'giving voice' to those who have been historically silenced does not leave space for subaltern groups to define their own positions. 'Giving voice' implies 'speaking for', a silencing of the already silenced.

A second problem with this kind of archaeology is its tendency to overemphasise the continuity and stability of identity-based groups through time. The anthropological literature is replete with ethnographic studies and theoretical pronouncements that point out that social groups, whether 'cultures', genders, ethnic units, or others, are neither fixed nor bounded entities (Barth 1969; Harrison 1999; cf Gillis 1994). By placing identities at the heart of archaeological projects, we run the risk of creating fictional anchors in the past that serve as stable referents for present problems. The ethical paradox is that such projects may be recognised as unrealistically circumscribed and compact cultural inventions, but the resulting normative renderings of the past are necessary to support presently disenfranchised social groups.

These considerations lead to a third problem: Archaeological narratives of identity may be abused as a justification for the oppression of one group by another in the present. An identity-based archaeology concentrates on producing more or less unidimensional narratives that explore, often in considerable detail, the plight of an oppressed population. However, the generalization of a group's oppression at a specific historical juncture is often placed at the service of subduing others. These processes work through ideological mechanisms such as de-historicisation and universalisation. The archaeologies of India (Bernbeck and Pollock 1996; Ratnagar 2004), Israel (Scham 2001), or Palestine (Yahya 2005) provide ample evidence for this problem.

Finally, identity-based archaeology slips all too easily into the status of a commodity. As the language of many heritage discussions makes clear, when archaeological remains and interpretations are seen primarily as a touchstone for identity claims, the past becomes something to be contested because it may be 'owned'. The notion of the past as possession, whether on a local, national or global ('humanity') level, involves both material remains and knowledge, control over and rights to which become key (Pollock 2005). Competition to control the past may also spawn an industry of replicas, souvenirs and films that in turn contribute to the commodification of the archaeological material itself.

The pursuit of an archaeology of the oppressed serves worthy causes, and as anthropologists and socially and politically engaged individuals we do not wish to detract from attempts to support those who have been oppressed or silenced. However, 'activist archaeology' – an archaeology that explicitly uses the past as a political means to change present social conditions – exhibits a troubling one-sidedness. It neglects the sites, material remains, and narratives about the people whose decisions and actions resulted in the oppression of subdued populations in the first place – the perpetrators. The sites and artifacts that were at the origin of oppression are mostly left unmarked and are avoided, as though focusing on the downtrodden is sufficient to remedy injustice. Those who created inhuman conditions are only rarely portrayed as perpetrators in standard history books: Assyrian kings are depicted as great strategists and sponsors of art (Matthiae 1996), not as experts in extortion, war brutality and torture. Likewise, the US 'founding fathers' gain their appeal as 'freedom fighters' and creators of democracy, rather than as slaveholders.

As a complement to an identity-based archaeology, we advocate an archaeology that focuses on memories that hurt and may therefore have been suppressed or subconsciously hidden: on the perpetrators of injustices. It is a noble goal to give the oppressed a place in history, but that still leaves those responsible for their plight in a neutral, sanitised space, conveniently separated from the structures of repressive power. In a sense, archaeology repeats Hegel's famous and justly criticised master-serf parable (Hegel 1970 [1807]:113–120). Hegel's serf is 'free', because he is not bound to the master in his existence as a human being. Hegel concludes that through his work the serf is independent from the relationship to the master, whereas the master relies entirely for his status on the existence and labour of the serf and is therefore subjected under that relationship. Similarly, archaeologies of identity focus on the exploited as the primary locus of research, turning those who appear weak and powerless into people with agency, with a penchant for resistance and considerable room for negotiation. This image emerges as a consequence of silencing the abusive power of dominant figures and groups.

An archaeology of perpetrators, by contrast, exposes the deeds of people whose actions and decisions contributed to numerous forms of oppression and injustice in the past, people such as dictators, warmongers, or promulgators of racist policies and their followers (cf Hamilakis 2002). It asks where these people made their decisions, and what archaeological traces are left in those places. It enquires as to how those locations and the decisions and actions taken there were connected to a larger public that lived, worked, and, more often than not, accepted persecution and repression. Pursuing archaeological investigations in such locations would not be a celebration of the remains of imperial, colonial, or industrial power, as so often results from heritage-oriented archaeology that focuses on major monuments. Rather, the kind of archaeology we advocate places the spotlight on the unjust and repressive practices carried out by the powerful who lived and worked in these locations, not on the monuments themselves. We contend that an archaeology of perpetrators forms a necessary complement to an identity-oriented archaeology.

TOPOGRAPHY OF TERROR

A project that fits quite closely with the kind of archaeology we are advocating is the excavation and public discussions surrounding the 'Prinz-Albrecht-Gelände' or 'Gestapo-Gelände' in Berlin. The 'Prinz-Albrecht-Gelände' refers to a city block area in central Berlin that was home in Nazi times to the headquarters of the Gestapo, the 'Sicherheitsdienst' of the SS (an internal secret service of the Nazi Party), and the Reichssicherheitshauptamt, together described as the most feared terror institutions of the Third Reich (Rürup 1987:7). The area was originally given its name in 1830 when Prince Albrecht (son of Friedrich Wilhelm III) acquired an 18th-century palace located on the spot. In the 1870s and 1880s, two museums were built nearby as well as the Hotel Prinz Albrecht (Rürup 1987).

In 1934 the Prince Albrecht palace was taken over by the SS. From 1932 on, the hotel was used by Hitler, Goebbels, and other Nazi officials to hold demonstrations. In 1933 the Gestapo occupied the building that previously housed the 'State Applied Art School' (Rürup 1987). Sculptors' studios in the basement were later turned into torture cells for interrogation (Ladd 1997:157). Until the end of the war in 1945, this area remained central to the Nazi apparatus of oppression. During the war, the buildings on the Gestapo-Gelände were bombed, most of them quite badly, although their structures remained partially intact. In the post-war years, the West Berlin government destroyed all the buildings in this city block except for what became the 'Martin Gropius Bau'. The rubble was removed so that nothing would remain on the spot. None of this caused major public reaction, in part because the site ended up right at the border separating East and West Berlin. In the 1950s various city governing bodies made proposals to develop the Gestapo-Gelände for traffic purposes. But once the Berlin Wall was erected in 1961, all such plans were dropped, and the area was used to dump debris from recent construction work. Not even a sign mentioned the former function of the locale.

The Gestapo-Gelände became the subject of renewed interest in the late 1970s and 1980s as part of a wave of increasingly public debates about the appropriate ways to deal with Germany's Nazi past. In 1982 the Berlin government decided that a memorial should be built on the spot. An invitation to submit designs led to prolonged and heated discussions about the appropriate way to engage with the history of Berlin. Some groups, among them the Verein Aktives Museum Faschismus und Widerstand in Berlin (Association for an Active Museum concerned with Fascism and Resistance in Berlin), argued that a memorial for the victims of the Nazis would risk obscuring the deeds of the perpetrators, the bureaucratic terror organisation that had its headquarters on the

Gestapo-Gelände. They further suggested that a memorial would serve to create a sense of closure, ending public debate rather than provoking new questioning (Baumann 1989:1).

On 5 May 1985 the Verein Aktives Museum organised a one-day excavation at the Gestapo-Gelände to symbolically expose its past and to counter the claims of the Berlin Senate that there were no building remains left on the site. The symbolic excavation, which did not include any archaeologists, was undertaken as an act of remembrance, with the goal of making the site an 'open wound', one over which 'grass must never be allowed to grow' (Baker 1990:57–58; Rürup 1987:212). Already in 1983, the Verein Aktives Museum had advocated that Berliners engage with the history of their own localities by excavating: 'Grabe, wo Du stehst!' ('Excavate where you are!') (Baumann 1989:11). As a result of the one-day work at the Gestapo-Gelände and the public discussion it stirred, a full-scale excavation was undertaken in 1986 under the direction of an architectural firm. This project led to the uncovering of foundations and fragments of walls of some of the buildings used by the Nazis as well as one of the torture cells of the Gestapo's in-house prison (Frank 1989). It immediately resulted in the shelving of previous plans for a memorial on the site. Instead, a small barracks was built housing an exhibition called 'Topographie des Terrors' (Topography of Terror). In the course of its construction, more ruins were exposed which were identified as a Gestapo kitchen. The excavated walls remain partly visible, whereas the rest of the site has been left largely undeveloped, with small placards telling visitors what previously existed on the spot (Figure 12.1) (Rürup 1987).

The exhibit 'Topography of Terror' explicitly chose to focus not on those who had suffered in the buildings, but rather on the perpetrators' activities and their widespread net of supporters. Consequently, the coordinators avoided any memorializing, emotional appeal, or didactic authoritarianism. Instead of imposing its message, the accent is on documentation, and the exhibit has succeeded in spurring independent reflection. The focus on documentation of perpetrators has met with hidden resistance by Germans who understand all too well its message, as the barren space and modest exhibit barracks provoked the emotions they intended: shame. On the surface, politicians pretended to aim at transforming the area from a provisional status to a long-term one. The mayor of West Berlin, Eberhard Diepgen, proposed to rebuild the Prince Albrecht palace and use it as a Jewish Museum (Endlich 1989:19–20). This would have amounted to an abuse of Jewish history in order to obliterate the shameful memory connected with the spot. In the end, public discourse among various organizations, foremost among them the Aktives Museum, led to the decision to leave the ruins as they had been found (although in some cases

Figure 12.1 *Topographie des Terrors*: Placards tell viewers about the use of the buildings that stood on this spot in Nazi times. Directly behind the exhibit are remnants of the Berlin Wall. In the background to the right is the building that was the Nazi *Luftfahrtministerium*, later used by the East German government as a ministerial building, after German reunification turned into the *Treuhand* (an institution charged with turning former socialist production units into capitalist businesses), and now a ministerial building of the unified Germany.

covered by glass) but also to keep the remainder of the area as it had been left following the post-war razing of the buildings. As a result, the area is neither neat and clean nor built over; instead, it remains a gap in the urban landscape that provokes passersby and visitors by its unusual sense of non-urban emptiness (Shusterman 1998).

If the attempt at marginalising the memory of perpetrators' deeds at this site failed, another route has been much more successful, namely its insertion in a whole landscape of monuments in Berlin's center. One, the Bendler-Block, provides an interesting contrast to the 'Topography of Terror' site. From its origins in 1914 the Bendler-Block had a military function. It was turned into the ministry of defense in the Weimar republic and was then the headquarters of Hitler's generals, who loyally supported Nazi politics and brutal expansionist wars until nearly the end of the Third Reich. In 1944, however, after a failed assassination attempt against Hitler, four generals were executed in one of the Bendler building's courtyards. In 1954, the Bendler-Block was turned into a symbol of German resistance by means of a permanent exhibit on that subject (Meyer 1999:64–65). Nowadays it serves once again as the ministry of defense of the Berlin Republic. Both the Gestapo-Gelände and the Bendler-Block were primarily spaces where a ruthless staff and their administrators designed extermination and, in the case of the military, ordered the murder of civilians (Jacob 2004). In the post-war decades, these acts of lawlessness in the Bendler-Block have been hidden behind a bombastic show centered on a few perpetrators-turned-resisters, whereas at the Gestapo-Gelände, a conscious effort has been made to emphasise the role of those who committed crimes against humanity.

However, it is another monument, the Memorial for the Murdered Jews of Europe, that is most effective in marginalizing the disquieting memory of Nazi perpetrators and their multitudes of followers (Figure 12.2). This monument had long been in the planning stage. The initial idea for the memorial ran parallel to an embarrassing project of Chancellor Kohl's: the creation of a central monument for the commemoration of dead victims and perpetrators alike at the 'Neue Wache', also in the middle of Berlin near the Brandenburg Gate. Even for many conservatives, this installation could not serve as the central space for solemnly remembering the victims of the Holocaust. A citizens' initiative proposed that there be a central monument solely dedicated to Jewish victims of the Holocaust. A decision by the German parliament made the memorial a reality, despite the vehement opposition of groups such as the Aktives Museum. They argued that as a gigantic objectivation of the Holocaust, the monument would serve to bury memories rather than keep them alive. Others claimed that the hidden rationale for building the memorial was the need for a new, unified German identity and a 'normality' that could only be built on a publicly announced but superficial recognition of past guilt (Kunstreich 1999:32–34).

The construction of the memorial was riddled by scandals, for - example the involvement of the company Degussa, the producer of Zyklon B used in concentration camp gas chambers (Surmann 2003). Nonetheless, the monument has been able to distract attention away from the Topography of Terror exhibit because of its sheer size, its more neutral emplacement, and especially because of its focus on victims with whom one can empathise, rather than on perpetrators. The Holocaust memorial's aesthetically pleasing design also stands in stark contrast to the desolate Gestapo-Gelände (Young 2000:207–216)[2]. Plans from 1989 for a more permanent building for the Topography of Terror exhibit with an added study center were already partly realized, when building was abruptly stopped because of the city government's supposed lack of financial resources. Since December 2004, and coinciding

Figure 12.2   The Memorial to the Murdered Jews of Europe is located in a symbolically central area of Berlin. The memorial consists of more than 2,700 gray, concrete slabs, identical except for their heights and slope of their upper surfaces, with pathways in between the slabs.

with the finishing of the nearby Holocaust Memorial, the already completed parts of the modest building have been *zurückgebaut* ('built back', a euphemism for destruction). Despite – or because of – this apparent setback, the temporary nature of the Topography of Terror exhibit and the fact that there is no long-term solution for it prevent any possibility of closure and keep it in public discussion.

The latest twist in Berlin's memorial landscape is the (illegal) installation of 1,065 wooden crosses near Checkpoint Charlie, one of the gates between East and West Berlin. Each cross stands for a person who was killed at the border of former East Germany. Journalists have already entertained the repugnant comparison between these crosses and the 2,700 stelae at the Holocaust memorial, equating Nazi Germany's millions of victims with East Germany's sporadic violence at its borders. This general propagation of memorials and their explicit spatial connections turn the Berlin Republic's past into a monumental space of deception (Habermas 1999).

Interestingly, despite attempts at diverting attention from the Topography of Terror, it remains a well-known urban space. We think that one of the reasons is that no master plan has ever existed for what was to be done with the space. The recovery of material traces of past perpetrators was a process without a clear end in sight. This is not just true for the work of the members of the Aktives Museum, but also for the public discourse which has accompanied their work and which contrasts with an official political *Erinnerungskultur* (culture of remembering), the major goal of which is to produce convenient *Kranzabwurfstellen* ('places to dump wreaths'), preferably close to the seat of government. Politicians argued that a site was needed to prevent the forgetting of the Holocaust. However, in their push for an immense monument aimed at a clearly bounded, aesthetically elaborate space that would provide a solemn background for symbolic political gestures, they sought a memorial that was separated from the contexts in which ordinary citizens live and work, thus furthering collective forgetting. As pointed out by Young (1993), 'once we assign monumental form to memory, we have to some degree divested ourselves from the obligation to remember' (quoted in Wise 1999:39; see also Gillis 1994).

PERPETRATORS AND ARCHAEOLOGY

The Topography of Terror and its historical background, as well as the context of German *Erinnerungskultur*, may constitute an extreme historical case. However, as Agamben (1998; 2000) has shown in his discussions of the camp as paradigm for the 20th century, the extreme is often in a distinct way indicative of much larger underlying phenomena. The Gestapo-Gelände may fulfill a similarly unique and at the same time symptomatic function as a prototypical space of perpetrators' decision-making and administration. This space is a location of the 'banality of evil' (Arendt 1965).

The potential for an 'archaeology of perpetrators' can be derived from the experiences in Berlin. Our proposal for such an archaeology does not seek to replace other archaeological directions, but rather to complement them by highlighting those areas of the past that are routinely suppressed and often subconsciously censored. We take our inspiration from Walter Benjamin's (1968:256) comment that 'there is no document of civilization which is not at the same time a document of barbarism'. However, his statement glosses over two facets of documents from the past. First, not all material, written and oral witnesses are equally civilised or barbarous. Some show the dark sides of history much more clearly than others. Second, there is a strong tendency to focus on the 'civilised' rather than the 'barbarous' elements of such documents. To counteract this propensity, it is necessary to single out the darker sites of the past and de-emphasise the 'glories' of civilization (*cf* Hamilakis 2002).

Discourse and Positioning

The principal goal of an archaeology of perpetrators is to provoke controversial public discourse. In this respect, it departs from most other archaeologies that aim to create a coherent narrative of the past. The discourses we envision emerging from this kind of archaeology are likely to accentuate two relationships: on the one hand, a critical distance to the past, a kind of Brechtian *Entfremdungseffekt* (alienation effect) that seeks to preclude a desire to identify with characters in narratives about the past; and on the other hand, an uncanny awareness that this distance is unjustified, because one's own forebears or occupiers of similar subject positions were bystanders, if not promoters, of oppression and exploitation in the past. The result is a 'negative identification'. In this way, an archaeology of perpetrators differs from an identity-based archaeology, which promotes positively valued parallels between subject positions in the present and those purported to exist in the past.

The discourses that typify an archaeology of perpetrators will be uncomfortable if not downright painful, replete with defensive statements and attempts to distance oneself from the past. However, collective amnesia and suppression of public knowledge are unlikely to prevail, because material (archaeological) counterarguments are not easily dismissed. The goal of a series of inter-related excavation projects would be to contribute to continuous, controversial public discourses that coalesce into a constantly reworked and problematised history, a 'past that does not pass away'. For example, since the 1960s, there have been almost uninterrupted disputes of this kind in the German public sphere, with the *Historikerstreit* (historians' dispute) and the Walser-Bubis debate among the more recent episodes (Kunstreich 1999:21–34; Piper 1987). Contestation over the past is the best way of keeping memory alive and learning from it (Welzer 1997:124–125). Such archaeological projects will work to expose 'neighborhood sites' where major acts of oppression were committed. Those places are not limited to such obvious spaces as the Gestapo-Gelände or the bunkers underneath the New Chancellery in Berlin (Arnold 2002). They are ubiquitous, and if we as archaeologists cannot identify them, this is in itself a political statement of our unwillingness to recognise Benjamin's dialectical character of past 'civilisations'.

Archaeological Means and Ends

The approach we advocate focuses on the process of doing archaeology, much more than on an end product in the form of site publications, restored buildings, or exhibits. It is not the production of specialist academic knowledge and the accompanying position of authority that is the core of such work, but rather the search for archaeological traces associated with the infliction of injustice, often incorporated in mundane activities such as the clerical tasks of *Schreibtischtäter* ('desk-bound perpetrators'). Tracking down vestiges of these activities will raise fears: Every society has its collectively suppressed, dangerous, and unpacified pasts (Weinrich 2000). Even the act of excavating itself is likely to engender comments that aim at denouncing any specific results. But the beauty of archaeology is that its results are unforeseeable. At any moment, newly discovered evidence can radically alter perceptions of a specific past. Excavation as a central goal and ongoing activity is to be understood in both a metaphorical and a literal sense: of excavating in minds, memories and archives as well as in the ground. The disturbing practice of *exposing* material elements of the past has a corollary in the reevaluation of collective memory through public discourses surrounding the work. In the most successful cases, such discourses will stimulate new projects, as happened in the case of the Gestapo-Gelände.

In an archaeology aimed at exposing perpetrators, there is no real distinction between the means of knowledge production and its ends; they collapse into one another. Knowledge, produced in and through excavation, politicises 'reflexivity at the trowel's edge' (Hodder 1997). Archaeology is no longer an objectified resource to which only some have privileged access. Instead, the discourse surrounding and permeating excavation is the key producer of knowledge. A failed project would result in the acceptance of an excavation's results as authoritative and in no need of reconsideration in a public sphere. Such unfortunate outcomes may be due to the multiple effects of distance and distancing. Bauman (1991:184–197) has noted that feelings of moral responsibility result from social proximity, and the production of distance through mediation and the media is one of modernity's hallmarks that enable acts ranging from crimes to genocide.

Ethically problematic pasts tend to be doubly distant. They are, like all pasts, temporally 'foreign countries', and there is a tendency to elevate them to the quintessentially evil, hermetically sealed off from the present (Broszat 1987:101). It should be the task of archaeology to produce social proximity. Excavations are well-suited for this purpose, because archaeology generally discovers traces of quotidian practices which counter the distancing effects that depict past perpetrators as beings from outer space (Schoenberner in Endlich 1989:53). Discoveries such as the kitchen at the Gestapo-Gelände have the subversive effect of exposing the normalcy of those who committed inhuman acts, providing an ominous continuity and proximity to pasts one would prefer to distance.

An active discourse and engagement with an ongoing excavation on the part of non-archaeologists is most likely to be achieved in the case of locally grounded projects (cf Koonz 1994). It is neither helpful nor desirable to aim for large, centralised projects or overarching national discourses; rather, the goal should be a multiplicity of local projects. As archaeologists, we, too, should have local roots; otherwise, it is too easy for us to maintain a distance to the work and the discourses it produces and for the public to see the results as remote from themselves. For the most part this kind of archaeology will concentrate on recent periods, as this is the best way to begin to engage members of the public in a discourse that touches them. Results of such excavations will be less prone to commodification than other archaeological products. In a capitalist world, the past and its material remains are highly susceptible to claims of ownership, closely linked as they are to the objectifying eye of tourist industries. Even victims' fates can be commodified, as the debate over the Holocaust 'industry' demonstrates (Cole 2000). An emphasis on small-scale, local projects and the centrality of discomfiting discourse work to counteract easy commodification.

The question will arise of what to do with spaces and materials once an excavation is finished. We contend that they should *not* be developed by building museums or monuments, which can all too easily turn sites into tourist destinations, with their accompanying postcards, T-shirts, mugs, and other souvenirs for purchase. Commodification is the ultimate production of social distance, as the lives of past people are turned into objects that can be appropriated by a generalised means of exchange. Museum shops at war memorials or concentration camps transform past actions and suffering into a price tag, comparable to ice cream, a bus trip, or a bottle of shampoo. The production of tourist destinations ensures the erasure of the sites visited, and their meanings are thereby removed from the consciousness of local residents.

Countering Memoricide

Past regimes of domination almost invariably include a double 'memoricide' (for the term, see Weinrich 2000:232). People are silenced by more or less brutal means, ranging from deprivation of education to physical annihilation, and in almost every case, attempts to destroy a group's memory accompany general repression (Gillis 1994; Koonz 1994; Lahiri 2003). Moreover, those in powerful positions also tend to disrupt any memory of the memoricide itself. They are never completely successful, and archaeology can not only restore some of the suppressed collective memories but also the acts that led to their initial destruction. On the other hand, the recovery is never complete, and a nagging feeling of not knowing 'the whole story' will remain. The emphasis on *Auseinandersetzung*, an ongoing process of engaged uncovering, results in an archaeology that is less paternalistic than other archaeologies. Although the initial impetus for projects may continue to come in many cases from archaeologists, who will also provide the expertise needed to implement them, the end products will no longer be in archaeologists' hands but become integrated into the public sphere.

Material memorials objectify memory; they silence by fixing or even halting discourse. Most monuments are 'authoritarian', telling us how we should understand and remember (Cole 2000:146–71; Olesen 2000:68–85; *cf* Gillis 1994:16–17). Using monuments to warn people of former perpetrators is counterproductive in that they tend to reproduce the same authoritarian structures that enabled perpetrators to pursue their goals. It may also make sites attractive to the present-day admirers of the perpetrators (eg, neo-Nazis).

If some kind of marking of a site of perpetration is deemed appropriate, it should, we suggest, be simple and matter-of-fact. Overly aestheticised markers must be avoided, as they tend to draw attention away from the cruelty or degradation which they are supposed to memorialise. A site may be turned into, or left as, a hole or gap in the landscape that catches the attention and provokes comment because of its emptiness, as the Gestapo-Gelände does in Berlin. Alternatively, matter-of-fact memorials may consist of ephemeral markings that encourage frequent change – helping to avoid the inevitable process by which something that is ever-present fades into the background and ceases to be (consciously) seen. Another way to memorialise or otherwise mark a location is to leave a building or monument in a ruined state, as a symbol of destruction and decay.

CONCLUSION

It might be objected that an archaeology of the kind we propose is politically impossible. Although that is undoubtedly so in many places, the example of the Gestapo-Gelände in Berlin demonstrates that it can be realised. Official permission may often be difficult to procure, and an emphasis on the local dimensions of such an archaeology is key to its feasibility. The injunction of the Aktives Museum, 'Grabe, wo Du stehst!' captures both the engagement of people with the places where they live or work as well as the importance of archaeologists working 'in our own backyards'.

We wish to be clear that we are not advocating that an archaeology of perpetrators replace other archaeologies. There are compelling arguments for pursuing projects that focus on subordinated groups, especially in their attempts to assert themselves in relation to dominating forces – for example, the archaeology of the Greenham Common women's peace camps as a counterweight to the declaration of the missile silos as heritage monuments (Marshall 2004). Indeed, we suggest that an archaeology of the kind we propose here should only be pursued after some work has been carried out on those who have suffered from the perpetrators' acts: It is not (yet) appropriate to investigate archaeologically the architects of the Armenian genocide in Turkey, in the absence of research on the victims of those crimes. We do, however, contend that an archaeology of perpetrators can provide a crucial counterweight to identity-based archaeologies. By using our archaeological skills, we can help to interrogate and expose the misdeeds and injustices of the powerful, especially those who lived and worked in our neighborhoods.

ACKNOWLEDGMENTS

We would like to thank the editors for their invitation to contribute to this volume and for their insightful comments on a first version of this paper. We are grateful to Dr. Franziska Lang, who kindly took the two photographs we use in this paper.

NOTES

1. We are aware of the oversimplification implied in the term 'public', especially when used in the unqualified singular (Baram 2005). Nonetheless, we use it here as a shorthand for the sake of convenience.
2. The ethical problems associated with an aestheticisation of the Holocaust have been at the center of a long-lasting philosophical debate (Adorno 1967; Anders 1982; Liessmann 1997).

REFERENCES

Adorno, T (1967) *Prisms*, London: Neville Spearman
Agamben, G (1998) *Homo Sacer*, translated by David Heller-Roazen, Stanford: Stanford University Press
—— (2000) *Means without End: Notes on Politics*, translated by Vicenzo Binetti and Cesare Casarino, Minneapolis: University of Minnesota Press
Althusser, L (1971) *Lenin and Philosophy*, translated by Ben Brewster, New York: Monthly Review Press
Anders, G (1982) *Ketzereien*, Munich: C.H. Beck
Arendt, H (1965) *Eichmann in Jerusalem: A Report on the Banality of Evil*, revised and enlarged edition, New York: Viking
Arnold, B (2002) 'Justifying genocide: archaeology and the construction of difference', in Hinton, AL (ed), *Annihilating Difference: The Anthropology of Genocide*, Berkeley: University of California Press

Baker, F (1990) 'Archaeology, Habermas and the pathologies of modernity', in Baker, F and Thomas, J (eds), *Writing the Past in the Present*, Lampeter, UK: St. David's University College

Baram, U (2005) 'In the public interest: the promise and paradoxes of heritage tourism', Paper delivered at the 70th Annual Meeting of the Society for American Archaeology, Salt Lake City

Barth, F (ed) (1969) *Ethnic Groups and Boundaries: The Social Organisation of Cultural Difference*, Oslo: Universitetsforlaget

Bauman, Z (1991) *Modernity and the Holocaust*, Ithaca: Cornell University Press

Baumann, L (1989) 'Vom Denkmal zum Denkort. Zur Idee eines Aktiven Museums', in *Zum Umgang mit dem Gestapo-Gelände*, Gutachten im Auftrag der Akademie der Künste Berlin, Section II, Berlin: Akademie der Künste

Benjamin, W (1968) *Illuminations*, edited and with an introduction by Hannah Arendt, translated by Harry Zohn, New York: Schocken

Bernbeck, R and Pollock, S (1996) 'Ayodhya, archaeology, and identity', *Current Anthropology* 37(S), S138–142

Broszat, M (1987) *Nach Hitler: Der schwierige Umgang mit unserer Geschichte*, Munich: Oldenbourg

Chambers, E (2005) 'Whose heritage is it?' *Anthropology News*, April 2005, 7–8

Cole, Tim (2000) *Selling the Holocaust*, London: Routledge

Endlich, S (1989) 'Gestapo-Gelände: Entwicklungen, diskussionen, Meinungen, Forderungen, Perspektiven', in *Zum Umgang mit dem Gestapo-Gelände*, Gutachten im Auftrag der Akademie der Künste Berlin, Secion I, Berlin: Akademie der Künste

Foucault, M (1980) *Power/Knowledge*, translated by Gordon, C, Marshall, L, Mepham, J and Soper, K, New York: Pantheon

Frank, R (1989) 'Zur Spurensicherung auf dem Gelände an der ehemaligen Prinz-Albrecht-Straase. Bestand, Veränderungen und Zerstörungen im Dezembr 1988', in *Zum Umgang mit dem Gestapo-Gelände*, Gutachten im Auftrag der Akademie der Künste Berlin, Section III, Berlin: Akademie der Künste

Gillis, J (1994) 'Memory and identity: the history of a relationship', in Gillis, J (ed), *Commemorations: The Politics of National Identity*, Princeton: Princeton University Press

Gleach, F (2005) 'To whom does Pocahontas belong?' *Anthropology News*, April 2005, 8–9

Habermas, J (1999) 'Der Zeigefinger: die Deutschen und ihr Denkmal,' *Die Zeit*, 1 April 1999

Hamilakis, Y (2002) '"The other Parthenon": antiquity and national memory at Makronisos', *Journal of Modern Greek Studies* 20, 307–38

Harding, S (1986) *The Science Question in Feminism*, Ithaca: Cornell University Press

Harrison, S (1999) 'Cultural boundaries', *Anthropology Today* 15(5), 10–13

Hegel, G (1970) *Phänomenologie des Geistes*, Frankfurt a.M.: Ullstein

Hodder, I (1997) '"Always momentary, fluid and flexible": towards a reflexive excavation methodology', *Antiquity* 71, 691–700

Jacob, G (2004) 'Ad Acta', *Konkret* 2, 34–36

Koonz, C (1994) 'Between memory and oblivion: concentration camps in German memory', in Gillis, J (ed), *Commemorations: The Politics of National Identity*, Princeton: Princeton University Press

Kunstreich, T (1999) *Ein deutscher Krieg: Über die Befreiung der Deutschen von Auschwitz*, Freiburg: Ça Ira

Ladd, B (1997) *Ghosts of Berlin: Confronting German History in the Urban Landscape*, Chicago: University of Chicago Press

Lahiri, N (2003) 'Commemorating and remembering 1857: the revolt in Delhi and its afterlife', *World Archaeology* 35, 35–60

Liessmann, K (1997) 'Auschwitz als Vergnügen: Zur kulturellen Ausbeutung der Vergangenheit', in *Kulturkampf: Zensur oder freiwillige Selbstkontrolle?* Hamburg: Konkret Verlag

Lightfoot, K (2005) *Indians, Missionaries, and Merchants: The Legacy of Colonial Encounters on the California Frontiers*, Berkeley: University of California Press

Ludlow Collective (2000) 'Archaeology of the Colorado Coal Field War, 1913–1914', in Buchli, V and Lucas, G (eds) *Archaeologies of the Contemporary Past*, London: Routledge

Magliocco, S (2005) 'Indigenousness and the politics of spirituality', *Anthropology News*, April 2005, 9, 15

Marshall, Y (2004) 'Archaeologies of resistance', Paper presented at the 2004 Chacmool Conference on 'Que(e)rying Archaeology'

Matthiae, P (1996) *La Storia dell' Arte dell' Oriente Antico: I Grandi Imperi*, Milan: Electra

Meyer, U (1999) *Bundeshauptstadt Berlin*, Berlin: Jovis

Olesen, B (2000) 'Truth in 3D: commemoration and historical interpretation at the United States Holocaust Memorial Museum', unpublished MA thesis, Binghamton University

Piper, E (ed) (1987) *'Historikerstreit': Die Dokumentation der Kontroverse um die Einzigartigkeit der nationalsozialistischen Judenvernichtung*, Munich: Piper Verlag

Pollock, S (2005) 'Archaeology goes to war at the newsstand', in Pollock, S and Bernbeck, R (eds), *Archaeologies of the Middle East: Critical Perspectives*, Malden, MA: Blackwell

—— (in press) 'Decolonizing archaeology: political economy and archaeological practice in the Middle East', in Boytner, R and Swartz Dodd, L (eds), *Filtering the Past, Building the Future: Archaeology, Identity, and Change in the Middle East and Southwest Asia*, Tucson: University of Arizona Press

Ratnagar, S (2004) 'Archaeology at the heart of a political confrontation: the case of Ayodhya', *Current Anthropology* 45, 239–259

Rürup, R (ed) (1987) *Topographie des Terrors: Gestapo, SS und Reichssicherheitshauptamt auf dem 'Prinz-Albrecht-Gelände', Eine Dokumentation*, Berlin: Willmuth Arenhövel

Scham, S (2001) 'A fight over sacred turf: who controls Jerusalem's holiest shrine?' *Archaeology* 54(6), 62–74

Shusterman, R (1998) 'Ästhetik der Abwesenheit,' *Lettre International* 43, 30–35

Silliman, S (2004) *Lost Laborers in Colonial California: Native Americans and the Archaeology of Rancho Petaluma*, Tucson: University of Arizona Press

Singleton, T (1995) 'The archaeology of slavery in North America', *Annual Review of Anthropology* 24, 119–140

Surmann, R (2003) Amnesie der Amnesie, *Konkret* 12, 14–15

Weinrich, H (2000) *Lethe: Kunst und Kritik des Vergessens*, Munich: C.H. Beck

Welzer, H (1997) *Verweilen beim Grauen*, Tübingen: Edition Diskord

Wise, M (1999) 'Totem and taboo: The new Berlin struggles to build a Holocaust memorial', *Lingua Franca*, January, 38–47

Yahya, A (2005) 'Archaeology and nationalism in the Holy Land', in Pollock, S and Bernbeck, R (eds), *Archaeologies of the Middle East: Critical Perspectives*, Malden, MA: Blackwell

Young, J (1993) *The Texture of Memory: Holocaust Memorials and Meaning*, New Haven: Yale University Press

—— (2000) *At Memory's Edge*, New Haven: Yale University Press

The Archaeology of the Spanish Civil War: Recovering Memory and Historical Justice[1]

Ermengol Gassiot Ballbè,
Joaquim Oltra Puigdoménech,
Elena Sintes Olives and
Dawnie Wolfe Steadman

INTRODUCTION

On 14 April 1931, after the electoral victory of the anti-monarchical parties, the Second Spanish Republic was declared. This new government promised hope and vindication for numerous sectors of society, as well as agrarian reform, education, improvements in labor conditions in the factories, universal women's suffrage, freedom of political and union association, and the political recognition of the peoples of Galicia, the Basque Country and Catalunya. However, the moderate reforms initiated under moderate leftist M. Azaña ceased when power shifted to right-wing conservatives in 1934 and 1935, a two-year period of reform regression known as the 'Black Biennium'. In October of 1934, popular revolts within Catalunya were brutally repressed, its political autonomy was suspended and members of its government were jailed and deported. In the mining region of Asturias, hundreds of workers were killed and thousands jailed after a revolt of the anarchist and socialist unions. In February of 1936, with the jails full of political prisoners and social reforms paralysed, the Popular Front, a broad-based coalition of leftist parties, won the democratic elections and, again, fresh hope for reforms were laid upon the new Spanish Republic.

On 18 July 1936 several sectors of the army revolted against the new, democratically elected government of the Spanish Republic. These conservative forces counted on the active support of the Falange party (the Spanish version of the Italian and German fascist parties), the Catholic Church, royalists, and other political parties and conservative sectors of society such as business organisations. While the new Spanish Republic was initially unable to restore order, the unions, revolutionary political forces, and the Catalan and Basque nationalist parties confronted a military insurrection that extended over a large portion of Spain. In this context, a broad social revolution was promoted as large industries and estates were collectivized and society was quickly secularised, particularly within public education. Progressive revolutionary governments were formed in Catalunya, the Basque country, and in the national government, that acknowledged the enormous power won by Civil Society. The Civil Society was a secular movement comprised of anti-Fascist committees, workers unions, and so on, that opposed the old ruling alliance of church, nobility and the military.

From the beginning, the military revolt adopted an authoritarian flavour and was similar to the fascist regimes gaining influence in 1930s Europe. In the fascist zones, basic democratic liberties were suppressed and any person considered suspicious of, or in disagreement with, the new regime, including unionists, leftists, schoolteachers and doctors, could be executed[2]. The instructions given by General Mola[3], leader of the revolt, synthesized the philosophy of the repression before his death at the end of 1936:

> [O]ne will consider that the action has to be violent in the extreme to reduce the enemy, who is strong and is well organised, as rapidly as possible. Of course, all leaders of political parties, societies, or unions that do not form part of the Movement will be jailed, and said individuals shall serve as examples so as to quash future rebellions or strikes... Negotiate? Never! This war must end with the extermination of the enemies of Spain...
>
> In this critical moment of the war I have chosen a fight to the death. To the military who have not joined our Movement, we will throw them out without pay. Those that have conducted military operations against us, against the Army, shoot them. If I see my father among the opposing troops I will shoot him... We must sow terror... We must create the sense of absolute power, eliminating without scruples nor hesitation all those that do not think like us. (cit. in Gibson 1986)

There was also violence against the conservatives within the Republican-controlled zones where, during 1936 and the beginning of 1937, numerous clergy and people of the conservative and fascist factions were executed. Nevertheless, in this case it was partly a response to the repression applied in the other areas by the fascists and was never really a well-choreographed strategy by the government. In fact, the government actually tried to stop this popular, spontaneous violence[4].

On 1 April 1939, combat operations in the Iberian Peninsula ended as the fascist army, with the direct support of Germany and Italy and the complicity of most of the European democracies, eliminated the last pockets of Republican resistance. The dictatorship of General Franco, who ascended to power during World War II, began with brutal political repression. The jails were full of political prisoners and the rate of executions was not sufficient to clear them (Juliá *et al* 1999). The extrajudicial executions were reduced after 1939, but the military courts continued dictating death sentences based on the retroactive 'Law of Political Responsibilities'. This law, originally passed in 1934 and reinstated in February 1939, established that all members of the Republican administrations, even at local levels, who did not join the rebellion in 1936 were guilty, paradoxically, of rebellion, high treason, and of participating in the 'Red Terror' against the right. Executions were abundant until after 1943. The number of Spaniards exiled in France, Mexico, the Soviet Union and Argentina surpassed 400,000 (Abellán 1976–1978). The Spanish dictatorship deported several thousand Spaniards to occupied France where they were eliminated in concentration camps. Other expatriates joined the anti-fascist resistance and fought in Dunkirk, on the Russian front, or with the Division Le Clerck of the French Army (Pons 2003). Nevertheless, the defeat of the Axis in World War II did not predicate the fall of the Franco dictatorship, which was seen by some Western countries as a faithful ally against Soviet Communism.

After over 40 years of authoring repression in Spain, General Franco died on 20 November 1975, shortly after ordering the last political executions. Following his coronation, the present king of Spain, Juan Carlos I – who was designated to be heir by Franco – initiated a gradual process of moderate political reforms. One major development was the call for elections in 1977 and the approval of the Constitution in 1978, which integrated a number of opposing political parties and brought them into the national political sphere. Yet the structure of economic power and of important institutions, such as the army, has undergone few profound changes. Another remarkable aspect of post-Francoism has been the pact of silence among the principal Spanish political parties concerning the crimes, still unpunished, of the dictatorship. Thus, over 30 years after Franco's death, there has yet to be an official investigation of the fascist oppression that displayed characteristics of genocide. The platform of adamant forgetfulness has been nearly unscathed until quite recently. It was not until 2005 that the Spanish government participated in a public tribute to the more than 12,000 anti-fascist Spaniards jailed in the concentration camps of the Third Reich.

ANTECEDENTS: ARCHAEOLOGY, RECOVERY OF MEMORY AND PRAXIS

Archaeology can be a tool for recovering the past and promoting a critical vision of the present. A leading edge of this function is its capacity to articulate an understanding of aspects of the past with specific interests of certain communities or social sectors in a process of dialogical engagement, or praxis (Gassiot and Palomar 2000; Leone and Potter 1999; McGuire *et al* 2005). The objective is generally to foment, through the knowledge of past facts, an analysis of present situations intended to guide public actions and develop civil rights. A secondary function contemplates actions from archaeology that agree, in its specific objectives, with the purpose of certain movements or social initiatives. One example is American indigenous archaeology and the debates on the repatriation of archaeological remains (*cf* Nicholas and Hollowell, and Bauer *et al*, this volume). Another is the creation, since the 1980s, of teams of specially trained archaeologists, anthropologists and historians who document systematic violations of human rights. The seminal case of the latter example is the development of the Argentine Forensic Anthropology Team (EAAF) in 1984, whose work has exposed the political crimes of the Military Junta (1976–1983) (Cohen 1992; Doretti and Snow 2003; Joyce and Stover 1991). The EAAF has provided new lines of evidence that expose past crimes against humanity by recovering the bodies of victims and meticulously documenting proof of torture and murder. In the last two decades, forensic human rights teams have opened mass graves in Guatemala, Argentina, Bosnia, Rwanda, Sierra Leone, Ethiopia, and dozens of other countries (Steadman and Haglund 2005). These actions have often been carried out under the auspices of national or international bodies[5], or are supported by non-governmental organisations (NGOs).

Spain, during both the pro-Franco dictatorship and the later democratic phase, has been condemned to forgetting the thousands of missing and assassinated persons during the Civil War and the immediate postwar period. In the early 1940s, in the 'Causa General'[6], the crimes that happened during the war in the Republican zone were documented and magnified by the dictatorship. However, silence and censorship veils the disappearances and executions of those repressed by Francoism. The situation has changed relatively little, despite subsequent democratic governments. In the 1980s, archival research led to the compilation of lists of politically motivated killings (for example, Juliá *et al* 1999; Solé i Sabate 1985). Nevertheless, these lists were not always exhaustive (Espinosa 2002), since the Francoist repression did not always use written registries. It is also very difficult to break the silence of the witnesses who are still alive yet fearful. Further, many of the graves of victims were buried in areas now covered by highways or destroyed by other processes of urbanisation.

Only in 1995 did Spain begin to develop a framework to document the archaeological vestiges of the political repression of Francoism, within the movement of more general processes of recovering historical memory (Echevarría 2005; Fuentes 2005; Menéndez 2005). The general characteristics of this effort and the current problems we face include:

1. In nearly all cases, initiatives have been promoted by social movements, organised by different associations for the recovery of historical memory.
2. Perhaps with the exception of only the almost secret excavation of a grave on behalf of the Catalan government in 2004 (as yet unpublished), none of the activities have included the participation of public administrations above the municipality level. On the contrary, upper governmental echelons have created obstacles to the investigations[7].
3. The responses to legal requests during these investigations have been unbalanced. In no case have courts approved or promoted the investigations and, once they have received notification of an interment, only rarely give legal recourse by permitting exhumations and analyses.
4. The participation of archaeologists and physical anthropologists has, by and large, been in service to the various associations for the recovery of memory. However, scientific institutions, such as public universities, have participated little in these initiatives (see below). Therefore, most of the archaeologists involved are not connected to established research centers in Spain but rather are public archaeologists.
5. With some exceptions, the archaeologists and physical anthropologists who participate in these initiatives belong to the generation of grandchildren of those involved in the Civil War and are too young to have experienced the dictatorship. On the other hand, many of them have some type of commitment to social movements, leftist political organizations, or citizen initiatives beyond their professional activity.

THE PARTICIPATION OF THE UNIVERSITIES IN THE RECOVERY OF HISTORICAL MEMORY IN CATALUNYA

The recovery of historical memory of the Civil War continues to be a pressing subject for political administrations as well as for academia. Diverse initiatives in the last two years have introduced hope for change. In the first place, the pressure of public opinion has forced the Spanish government to create an Inter-Ministerial Commission to initiate investigations, although the extent of their long-term dedication is currently uncertain. Equally, autonomous governments, such as that of Catalunya, have reaffirmed their commitment to this issue, although words have not always translated into actions. Secondly, archaeologists and anthropologists from universities are slowly answering the call and beginning to excavate mass graves to document the physical remains of the Civil War. Private groups or individuals initially accomplished this type of activity. One of the first actions in Catalunya was the recovery of an antiaircraft shelter in the Gracia district of Barcelona. Community members and historians joined forces with prehistory students from the Universitat Autónoma de Barcelona in 1999. In the summer of 2005, the Catalan municipality of Camarassa and a group of archaeologists from the University of Barcelona sponsored an excavation of the trenches of the front lines of 1938, which happen to be located in a late Iron Age site.

Both examples reflect the increasing involvement of archaeologists with ties to public universities. However, the participation has been limited to the efforts of private groups of investigators, motivated by an ethical and political conscience but with little support from their places of employment. The institutional involvement of the universities and research centers has been initiated gradually over the past two years. Again, the initiative has created a framework for collaboration through the Civil Society with associations for the recovery of memory, which, with the mediation of some scientific investigators, have proposed collaborative agreements with Catalan universities. Although these agreements have facilitated institutional support for activities such as the excavation of graves, there has been little legal regulation by local governments and on no occasion have governments offered economic incentives to facilitate the work.

Currently, the Association for the Recovery of Historical Memory of Catalunya (ARMHC) and the Department of Prehistory at the Universitat Autónoma de Barcelona (UAB) are pushing one of the main initiatives for the recovery of historical memory by excavating mass graves. Forensic anthropologists from the State University of New York, Binghamton (SUNY-Binghamton) in the United States and a team of molecular geneticists from the UAB have joined this effort. This collaboration formally commenced with the signing of an agreement in February of 2004 with the goal of forming scientific teams that can take part in research toward the recovery of historical memory.

Why Use Archaeology to Recover Memory?

Two interests melded as a result of the collaboration between the UAB and the ARMHC. Investigators from the UAB had already established archaeological programs with social and political implications in other countries, such as Nicaragua (Gassiot et al 1997; Gassiot and Palomar 2000) and in the previously mentioned Gracia district of Barcelona. They believe that as a social science, archaeology offers a means to critically rethink the social conflicts of the present through knowledge of the past, and the processes of contradiction and change, and can therefore affect political action. The ARMHC, on the other hand, hoped that agreements with scholarly institutions would provide scientific rigour to the tasks of recovering and vindicating collective memory. To this end, the investigator from Binghamton University has provided methodological training in forensic archaeology and anthropology for the Spanish scientists.

The primary goal of the Catalan archaeologists is to establish a place for archaeology and scientific research in the civil movement for the recovery of historical memory in Spain. Such a program will bolster the denunciation of fascism in Europe as well as other parts of the world. This initiative is made possible by the existence of citizen mobilization with specific objectives, independent of political institutions. Our task as archaeologists and anthropologists is subordinate to these objectives (in this case, the critical recovery of memory), even as we adopt an activist role by introducing elements of dialogue. Thus, the incorporation of university researchers introduces new players into a movement already marked by a plurality of actors, including relatives of the disappeared, political activists, and followers of recent and local history, and that promises to form a very strong identity. Our participation is founded on the premise that the push for the recovery of historical memory has existed for some time, yet this movement must now include archaeological involvement. We also recognise that archaeological participation often incorporates ethical or political motivations. All of this creates an amalgam of objectives that mark the timeline of our activities. The limitation of space here forces us to synthesise them in a very schematic form as follows:

General Scope of the Historical Analysis

Here we have established two lines of inquiry:

a. To contribute, with the addition of a new range of data (from archaeological and anthropological investigations, as well as recovered oral memory), to the analysis of Francoist repression. Far from understanding it as a precise or spontaneous and reactive fact, the Franco regime was designed as a repressive machine that employed the physical destruction of the political and intellectual opposition and used fear as a weapon to control the base of Franco's political power. A sample of its success in this sense is that it has been the only European fascist regime that survived the year 1945, and that its memory today still generates mixed feelings of ideological submission and fear. In addition, the study of the Franco regime allows the understanding of a model which, to a great extent, was followed by the Latin American dictatorships of the 1970s and 1980s.
b. To stimulate a reflective analysis of the process of the Spanish political transition to present conditions, where, surprisingly, many pillars of the Franco regime are still effective, due to historical amnesia. Vestiges of the regime still infiltrate the government and the structure of local economic and political power in many places.

Specific Scope of the Historical Analysis

In our investigations we hope, first of all, to provide quantitative and qualitative data on the repressive acts on the basis of the recovered empirical information found from excavations, anthropological analyses, and information retrieved from archives and oral interviews. For example, in any given context we ask: Who was assassinated? How did the murders take place? How did these events influence life in local communities? Secondly, these investigations will seek the restitution of the memory of the victims, often denigrated publicly for almost 70 years, and the causes by which they fought and were executed. The recovery of the bodies and their return to living relatives brings this process into the most intimate sphere of the lives of family and friends. Finally, obtaining this information with a solid empirical base will aid in proving the existence of repressive acts that, according to present national and international law, are criminal. In this sense it is worth emphasising that many of the assassinations were never investigated nor is there an official report of death, a fact that turns the assassinated people into 'disappeared'. This will allow these crimes to be legally defined as murder and judged as such today. Although some atrocities occurred 70 years ago and prosecutions will be unlikely in many cases, by establishing the illegality of many different documented cases of murder we hope to achieve the legal and economic restitution of the victims and the sentencing, in at least moral terms, of the assassins. Successful prosecution will support the creation of a truth commission in Spain that can promote an ample process of historical revision and determination of responsibilities, as has already occurred in countries as different as Argentina and South Africa.

Structural Scope

One of the central aspects of the collaboration of American investigators is to produce Catalonian specialists in forensic anthropology and archaeology. This is a new area of research in Spain (forensic research has been a tradition of medicine, not anthropology) and is based on the willingness of anthropologists and archaeologists to receive additional specialised training. Therefore, in the first stage of the joint project among ARMHC, UAB and Binghamton University, one of the primary efforts has been to define an investigative protocol that integrates the roles of each specialty (eg, archaeology, forensic anthropology, genetics, historical research). An important concern to tackle is the 'illusion of DNA' – the assumption that genetic testing, which is generally very expensive, is the only way of identifying victims, and that such tests are applicable in all cases. This belief has caused a number of cases investigated in Spain to lack the rigour required in the forensic recovery and documentation of the archaeological sites (Menéndez 2005). Improper techniques or collection procedures make it impossible to reconstruct perimortem events or observe antemortem conditions, such as fractures, that could lead to identification. In order to solve this problem, it is necessary to educate national specialists by collaborating with foreign institutions and researchers. This process of institutional collaboration should also be understood in the context of the social movements previously discussed.

Actions Realized

The program designed by the UAB and ARMHC with the collaboration of Binghamton University has already celebrated its second anniversary. During this time a close collaboration has emerged between the academic centres and civil society organised around the recovery of memory. In the first stage of this joint effort, the initiatives have centered upon securing a methodology based on historical research, archaeology, anthropology, and genetics, a process that has required much training. Our efforts at this stage must also overcome the public administration's disqualifications of, and lack of commitment to, the archaeological recovery of Civil War graves on the basis of a lack of economic resources for an exhaustive program of documentation.

The education process has been carried out via lectures and training seminars and at two archaeological interventions. The first of these, promoted by the association 'Forum for Memory', took place in June and July 2004 in Santaella, Andulusia, and formed the nexus of collaboration among UAB-ARMHC and Binghamton University. We wanted to participate in an initiative administrated by an organization with previous experience in this type of research, so that we could understand the specific types of problems these efforts incur, from not only the anthropological and archaeological perspectives but also the social, judicial, and historiographic aspects. In the excavations carried out in the municipality of Santaella, we documented a mass grave containing 17 men shot by the Falange party in 1936. The skeletal analysis has been completed (Steadman *et al* 2007) and the DNA analysis is ongoing. These investigations could not have been carried out without the economic resources and political support of the 'Forum for Memory'.

In the second investigation, we initiated a three-week excavation at a cemetery in Olesa de Montserrat in November 2004. UAB and ARMHC, with the collaboration of Binghamton University, carried out the excavations. The previously developed investigative protocol was implemented and it now serves as a model for future investigations. Unfortunately, none of the excavated skeletons corresponded to the known assassinated victims and we determined that the mass grave (or graves) is likely beneath a mausoleum constructed in the 1980s. Nevertheless, the initiative allowed us to present to the public and to the Catalan government a full field project and defined research program, as well as conjoining activism with history by working with relatives and the local government of Olesa.

CONCLUSIONS

The work in Spain has barely begun. The resistance to fascism and the social revolution during the Spanish Civil War have been referred to almost romantically by progressive people in many countries of the world. In contrast, within Spain the silence imposed by the dictatorship and the subsequent democratic governments has encouraged the public to forget one of the cruelest and most passionate moments of our history. Also, this silence has perpetuated the lack of historical justice towards the victims of one of the bloodiest episodes of political repression in our country. Surviving family members can only cling to the story of the murder of their father, sister or grandparent. Paradoxically, today there are still monuments in many towns in Spain to the executioners and those who ordered the massacres. Over 30 years later, the democracy has still not come to terms with the victims or publicly condemned the crimes of fascism. Nevertheless, for many years different sectors of society have united with the common objective of reversing this situation and opening the door of the past by giving dignity to those who suffered through the dictatorship by promoting, through the memory of those who died, the values of democracy, freedom and social justice. The story that we have told here speaks to how we as archaeologists and anthropologists have integrated ourselves into this struggle. It is a fight that, by dignifying the dead, returns them, in a certain way, to life.

NOTES

1. Translated from the Spanish by Dr Peter J. McCormick and Dr Amy Sellin (Fort Lewis College); the translation was approved by the authors.
2. At the beginning of the war, in some places the fascist army systematically shot 10% of the population, as a way of eliminating opponents and extending fear throughout the population.
3. General Mola, *Instrucción Reservada n°1*, July 1936, Archivo General Militar de Ávila.
4. The recent work by Espinosa (2003) is overwhelming. It discusses the advance of Franco's army between Seville and Badajos, an initial Republican zone with a population of 434,000 people. Those killed by the leftists numbered 243. The repression by the right amounted to 6,610 dead, a conservative figure in the opinion of this chapter, as numbers were derived solely from archives.
5. For example, see the 1993 United Nations resolution at: http://www.unhchr.ch/Huridocda/Huridoca.nsf/0/1ac96d31dfba63478025676600391d27?Opendocument.
6. A so-called exhaustive report on the victims of Republican violence during the war, promoted by the dictatorship, was published by Lama (1943). It was usual to exaggerate their numbers (eg, Espinosa 2002; Juliá 1999).
7. For example, in Catalunya the Directorate of Cultural Patrimony has, to date, refused to grant permission of excavation of mass graves.

REFERENCES

Abellán, JL (ed) (1976–1978) *El Exilio Español de 1939* (6 volumes), Madrid: Taurus

Cohen, M (1992) *Tumbas Anónimas: Informe sobre la Identificación de Restos de Víctimas de la Represión Ilegal*, Buenos Aires: Catálogos Editora

Doretti, M and Snow, C (2003) 'Forensic anthropology and human rights: the Argentine experience', in Steadman, DW (ed), *Hard Evidence: Case Studies in Forensic Anthropology*, Upper Saddle River, NJ: Prentice-Hall

Echevarría, F (2005) 'La guerra civil en la memoria o la memoria recuperada de l'oblit', *L'Avenç* 299, 31–33

Espinosa, F (2002) *La Columna de la Muerte*, Barcelona: Crítica

Fuentes, A (2005) 'Exhumació i arqueología forense: els afusellats a Villamayor de los Montes (Burgos)', *L'Avenç* 299, 28–30

Gassiot, E and Palomar, B (2000) 'Arqueología de la praxis: información histórica de la acción social. El caso de la Unión de Cooperativas Agropecuarias de Miraflor, Nicaragua', *Complutum* 11, 87–99

Gassiot, E, Palomar, B, Estévez, J and Zurro, D (1997) 'Archaeology without frontiers: co-operation between UAB (Spain) and UNAN (Nicaragua)', Paper presented at the Third Annual Meeting of European Association of Archaeologists, Ravenna, 24–28 September

Gibson, I (1986) *Queipo de Llano: Sevilla, Verano de 1936. Con las Charlas Radiofónicas Completas*, Barcelona: Grijalbo

Joyce, C and Stover, E (1991) *Witnesses from the Grave: The Stories Bones Tell*, Boston: Little, Brown

Juliá, S (co-ord.), Casanova, J, Solé i Sabaté, JM, Villaroya, J and Moreno, F (1999) *Víctimas de la Guerra Civil*, Madrid: Temas de Hoy

Lama, JM (1943) *Causa General: La Dominación Roja en España*, Madrid: Ministerio de Justicia

Leone, MP and Potter, PB (eds) (1999) *Historical Archaeologies of Capitalism*, New York: Kluwer/Plenum

McGuire, RH, O'Donovan, M and Wurst, LA (2005) 'Probing praxis in archaeology: the last eighty years', *Rethinking Marxism* 17, 355–372

Menéndez, X (2005) 'La recuperació de la memoria: estat de la qüestió a Catalunya', *L'Avenç* 299, 34–39

Pons, E (2003) *Republicanos Españoles en la Segunda Guerra Mundial*, Madrid: La Esfera Libros

Solé i Sabaté, JM (1985) *La Repressió Franquista a Catalunya 1938–1953*, Barcelona: Edicions 62

Steadman, DW and Haglund, W (2005) 'The scope of anthropological contributions to human rights investigations', *Journal of Forensic Science* 50, 23–30

Steadman, DW, Sintes, E, Oliart, C and Bauder, JM (2007) *Forensic Anthropological Investigation of 22 Skeletons Recovered from Spanish Civil War Mass Graves in the La Guijarrosa and Santaella Cemeteries, Santaella, Spain*, Binghamton: Department of Anthropology, Binghamton University

CHAPTER 14

The Culture of Caring and Its Destruction in the Middle East: Women's Work, Water, War and Archaeology

Maggie Ronayne

INTRODUCTION

In response to the onslaught of US-led globalisation[1] and of its wars, the defence by communities of their lives, livelihoods, culture and heritage is key to opposing and eventually ending this destruction. While it is an important task for archaeologists and other profession-als to report to the public in all available media the destruction wrought by large-scale development projects and war, what is also demanded of us is that we work out with communities how our skills and information can be of use to them in their self-defence organising. Once we embark on this work, it is necessary to evaluate it carefully: How productive can we expect this work to be and how productive is it proving? What are the obstacles that may be preventing a genuine collective mutuality? That is, how much has the professional learnt about making what s/he knows accessible, and have the efforts of the grassroots been adequately strengthened thereby? And of course, how much has the professional learnt, not only about the issue in con-tention (the threat posed by dams in Turkey, for example) but also about the subject (archaeology, for example)?

In fact, the relationship between the grassroots movement for sur-vival and archaeologists is not easy; nor is such a link often even attempted. It has to be worked out collectively. The usual training archaeologists receive does not teach us how to do this work on the job, so to speak. Despite theory classes and discussions about the politics of the past, our universities continue to teach us to prioritise the artefact, the site and, in recent decades, the landscape, over the lives of those who are often the inheritors of the culture and history we are studying or trying to salvage (cf Hamilakis, this volume). In common with other professionals, we are trained to see ourselves above grassroots people directly concerned with preserving culture and heritage, whether we have signed on to join that hierarchy or not.

In Western countries most archaeologists are low-paid contract workers in developer-led archaeology, while those who place the material into interpretative frameworks and determine the structures and principles of the profession are the permanently employed minority in the universities, government departments, museums and company management (see also Walker and McGuire 1999; Everill, this volume). In the Third World the hierarchy extends further, with local labourers paid Third World wages to dig for archaeologists, many of whom are from a dominant ethnic group in the area or from the West. This hierarchy between archaeologists and grassroots people and within archaeology itself is a key obstacle to archaeologists' productive participation in developing the movement for survival which is deeply connected, if not one, with the movement against cultural destruction.

The best way I know to deal with these obstacles in my own work is to get them out in the open and find out from those affected by large-scale development projects what they think is needed from an archaeologist. As a result of my involvement with campaigns to stop the Ilısu Dam and other, similar projects in Turkey, and from the experience of grassroots women's organisations in both the Global South and North[2], my archaeological work prioritises grassroots people and their demands. My academic work always begins from women's experience and women's cultural work, which comes from my deep involvement with and commitment to the grassroots women's movement. Here I want to look at why it is so vital to prioritise women's case against the dam. How much does each cultural destruction depend on bypassing women to succeed? And whom does it attack? It is a contention of this article that we gain useful knowledge, including theory and ethical principles, in working within these struggles. After seven years of involvement with Ilısu and other campaigns, my own understanding of how to work as an archaeologist is completely altered and is still developing. I could not have received this education from any book, which is not to attack books but to reprioritise the people active outside universities and companies, for which book knowledge becomes a political instrument.

THE ILISU DAM AND THE GAP DEVELOPMENT PROJECT

The State water agency of Turkey, the DSI, is the developer for the Ilısu dam, a €1.8 billion hydroelectric project on the River Tigris and the lynchpin of dams on the river (Figure 14.1). It is opposed by a number of campaigns and communities in the region as well as in Europe. This opposition, to which my work contributes, caused the collapse of the consortium of European and Turkish companies planning

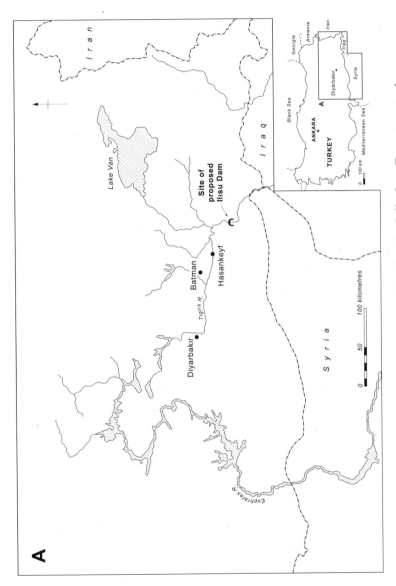

Figure 14.1 Location of the Ilısu dam on the river Tigris. Map by A. Gallagher, Department of Archaeology, NUI Galway.

to build it in 2001/2002. The consortium had been seeking export credit to underwrite project costs from a number of European governments and possibly the US, with the British government potentially a key creditor. Though various – usually vague – benefits have been claimed for Ilısu, the destination of the electricity has never been made clear; it is said to be for industry in western Turkey like other such projects. Despite the victory over the previous consortium, a new group of companies is restarting the project, including VA Tech (Austria), Alstom (Switzerland) and Züblin (Germany), not least because of competition for business in the water and energy sectors as a result of the US-led war on Iraq. All the more reason, then, to set out some lessons learned last time.

If built, the dam would flood over 300 square km in the Kurdish region of Turkey, displacing up to 78,000 people – nomads, villagers and residents of the town of Hasankeyf. The dam is part of the Southeast Anatolia Development Project (Turkish acronym GAP) and central to much wider tensions and potential water wars in the Middle East and Western Asia (Dolatyar and Gray 2000; Marsh undated). The use of such dams and control of water-flow as a lever of power has been a feature of regional politics in recent decades. GAP is said to be one of the biggest regional development projects in the world, involving 90 dams and 60 hydroelectric power plants on the Tigris, Euphrates and other rivers (KHRP et al 2002:16).

Work by local campaigners, the Department of Archaeology, National University of Ireland, Galway and fact-finding delegations by European NGOs have documented how the Ilısu dam would result in severe poverty, illness, break-up of families and communities, environmental pollution, cutting off of water-flow to downstream communities in Syria and Iraq, and immense cultural destruction (Cornerhouse et al 2001; Diyarbakır Bar Association 2001; Ilısu Dam Campaign et al 2001; KHRP 1999; Ronayne 2002, 2005; Save Hasankeyf Platform 2000). Thousands of archaeological, cultural and historical sites would be submerged by Ilısu's reservoir, including most of the historic town of Hasankeyf (for details of sites and dates, see Algaze 1989; Algaze et al 1991; Kitchen 2000; Kitchen and Ronayne 2001; Save Hasankeyf Platform 2000; Tuna et al 2001; Tuna and Velibeyoğlu 2002). Located at the point where the Silk Road once crossed the Tigris, the town has a number of upstanding medieval remains including a citadel, mosques, mausolea, a probable 12th-century ruined bridge and many caves. It has great cultural significance for a variety of people, first of all its residents, as a Muslim pilgrimage site and for many Kurdish people the world over. Ilısu would also be built in an area which has importance for understanding the interface between Neanderthals and *Homo sapiens sapiens*, was one of the first areas in the world where communities domesticated plants and animals, and has been a frontier zone for empires, including the Roman and Assyrian Empires. People from the region regularly say that it is not only Kurdish history that will be submerged but the heritage of the whole of humanity. Independent investigations have found haphazard and flawed consultation on project plans with some affected communities, and none at all with many others (see, for example, Ilısu Dam Campaign *et al* 2001; Ronayne 2005). According to women affected by the dam and women's organisations, they are the least consulted but the most opposed to the project (Ronayne 2005:22–26). Yet women's opposition to Ilısu and other dams and why they are opposed has been hidden.

Women's Work, Water and War

The region where Ilısu would be built, the predominantly rural Southeast, is one of the most impoverished in Turkey. A small minority of landlords who are often also religious and political (including tribal) leaders own the vast majority of land, so GAP plans for irrigation and electricity generation cannot benefit the majority (McDowall 2000b). Land reform to change this unequal distribution has never been part of the GAP programme. The burden of poverty and the resulting work falls most heavily on women. Women carry out most of the basic unwaged subsistence work in bearing and caring for large numbers of children; but, also, a substantial part of their work in the villages – and this is true for most women in the global South – involves growing the family's food, livestock management, and other work to make the land, and resources on it, productive. Women and children are also responsible for fetching water. This work is hardly ever officially recognised and there is no evidence that it has been considered in planning or compensation processes for Ilısu. According to women and their organisations, within the family and community structures prevalent in the Kurdish region, supported by the practical actions of the State, religious institutions and landlords, the entitlement of women to ownership of land is non-existent; despite legal reforms on paper, they do not generally inherit land or property (Ronayne 2002:38, 118; 2005:24–25; see also Aydin 1986:162, 166). The rate of illiteracy in the southeast is high for both women and men but it is noticeably higher for women (GAP-RDA 1994). Many older women in particular speak only Kurdish, making communication with Turkish officials about the dam very difficult if not impossible. Kurdish women's organisations say that there are always arguments within families since the women in particular do not want to move (knowing what they will face) but it is the men who are always asked to sign the forms for expropriation of land and resettlement, and it is they who receive any compensation (Ronayne 2005:25).

GAP has been created and carried out in a war zone. Until recently, the region where Ilısu would be built was under emergency rule. Since 1984, as a result of armed conflict between the Turkish State and the PKK (Kurdistan Workers' Party), an estimated 3,000 to 4,000 villages in the region were evacuated and many destroyed (McDowall 2000a:440); approximately three million people were forced to flee their homes to live in slums in the cities of the region or in western Turkey (KHRP *et al* 2003:13). Over 30,000 people have died (*ibid* and McDowall 2000a:442); some families have lost several members. This has been the background for widespread abuses on the part of the security forces, including village destructions, torture, rape and other sexual torture against women in particular, extra-judicial killings and 'disappearances' (*ibid* and McDowall 2000a:440–441). Most of the internally displaced population still live in desperate conditions. Displaced women and their organisations have outlined how families were broken up after the forced move to the cities. They speak of children lost on the way, severe levels of hunger and malnutrition, soaring mother-and-infant illness and mortality rates (see also Göç-Der 2002), 20 to 30 people crowded into one or two small rooms or sheltering under tarpaulins, child labour, children running away or hooked on drugs or glue sniffing, women's suicides when they cannot take care of their children as they did in the villages (Ronayne 2002:120), and women's sex work in order to feed families (Ronayne 2005:25). Many family members, particularly men, have migrated to western Turkey and beyond to look for work. All the women agreed that whether the displacement is the result of war or dams, these are the conditions that women and all of those in their care face.

The findings of the World Commission on Dams support their view in showing that within communities affected by large dams, women have paid the highest price (WCD 2000:114–116). Following a ceasefire by the PKK in 1999, emergency rule was lifted in 2002 but people still suffer from its effects, and now from the war on Iraq. There has been a return to conflict in the region since June 2004. GAP does not address the impact of conflict or the legacy of the many decades of aggression against Kurdish people; many would see it as an extension of that conflict. An issue people regularly raise is that there are several evacuated villages in the Ilısu reservoir area, but if built, the dam would flood them and permanently remove the possibility of the villagers' return. Some improvements of the security situation have taken place since 2002, but women speak of the continuing threat of rape, and other sexual torture and harassment such as strip searches by the security forces (Ronayne 2005:112–114). These well-known tactics divide women from men and create a climate of violence, which women say contributes to high levels of domestic violence and murder.

This background and the risks women in particular face are entirely relevant to the question of cultural heritage and the Ilısu dam. Archaeologists could not hope to halt the project by focusing solely on ancient sites or opposing in isolation; those we all look to for information on the extent of the impact and for direction in opposition to the dam are women and men from the reservoir area and close by, who have lived through war and face this destruction. The threat to their physical safety and the lack of free speech must be seen as undermining their opposition to the project, including its cultural impact. This makes it easier to see why saving archaeological sites might not be their chief priority. At the same time, the cultural damage the dam would do can be incorporated into people's concerns. In fact, what women have had to say about their children, their work, their villages and their opposition to war became central to grasping the cultural impact of Ilısu.

ACCOUNTABILITY: THE BASIS FOR THE ARCHAEOLOGICAL CASE AGAINST ILISU

The impact of Ilısu on cultural heritage has been the focus of much controversy. From 2000 to 2002 I worked (with Dr Willy Kitchen, an archaeologist based in Britain) on a voluntary basis as advisor on cultural heritage to the Ilısu Dam Campaign, the pressure group set up to target British government involvement in the project. However, most of our work was undertaken independently or by means of the World Archaeological Congress, including a review of the Environmental Impact Assessment Report for Ilısu (Kitchen and Ronayne 2001), submissions to the governments considering support for the project, talks at public meetings, work with Kurdish communities in Europe, and other initiatives. (For an outline and evaluation of what we did and the process we used, see Ronayne 2006a).

Accountability to the people affected by the dam in the reservoir area, those already internally displaced by conflict and those Kurdish people who had fled to Europe and beyond, required that we first ask people what their demands were in relation to the dam, how they would be impacted, what culture would be destroyed, what might result from our visits/reports and what they wanted from us as archaeologists. The necessary follow-up was to evaluate that information in the light of what we knew, or thought we knew, and work out how to present our information to people affected by the dam, and both their views and ours to the public, reporting back and consulting with them to make a case together against the project. International planning guidelines for large infrastructure projects (by the Organisation for Economic Co-operation and Development [OECD] and World Bank, for example) contain requirements or, more weakly, recommendations to consult with affected communities and especially 'vulnerable groups', which as a rule explicitly includes women. This also means consultation about cultural impact and significance assessment – to whom culture and heritage are important and why. These guidelines are rarely if ever adhered to in practice; the purpose in using them is to make visible that even by standards the developers themselves have agreed to, finding out what different sectors of communities want and in particular taking the needs of women into account is considered necessary or at least recommended. Professional standards in archaeology provided similar support, such as the ICOMOS 1990 Charter for the Protection and Management of Archaeological Heritage, and the principles and code of ethics of the World Archaeological Congress (WAC), though there tends to be a much stronger requirement to consult with Indigenous communities and seek their informed consent than with others (a measure of the success of the Indigenous movement's pressure on archaeology); for example, there is little or nothing about taking women's views into account.

But for two archaeologists to attempt a new relationship with the communities was not going to have a great impact on its own. There was a need to seek widespread support across the profession for an archaeological case against the dam, informed by this accountability, particularly in countries where governments were considering financial support, and focusing on Britain as the leading potential creditor. A key tactic was to gain the support of professional organisations. From 1999 to 2004, I worked within the World Archaeological Congress (I sat on the executive board), to direct WAC's campaign against Ilısu and other such projects. WAC position statements during this campaign on the role of archaeologists were and are still useful as a reference point for what is considered 'professional' in such circumstances. Commenting on the collapse of the Ilısu consortium, WAC noted:

> Professional processes, for archaeologists, do not begin with salvage excavations and budgets for them. Rather the priority must be full and fair consultation to establish the economic, cultural and social rights of all the women, children and men affected by such projects. They must be the ones to decide the basis on which their heritage and cultural forms may or may not be used, moved or studied. In situations where that cannot occur – and Southeast Turkey is a clear example of this – there are cultural heritage grounds for halting a dam project (WAC 2001b).

The Ilısu dam as a Tool for Cultural and Other Ethnic Cleansing

Accountability to and consultation with affected communities and most especially with women began to reveal for the first time the true extent of cultural destruction. In a number of ways, it showed that it would be a mistake to focus only on calls to rescue ancient sites. For example, much of the public outcry over the dam focused on the potential flooding of Hasankeyf, partly because it has great cultural significance for a variety of people and partly because the British government, followed by others, made it a condition of providing credit that the developer should 'preserve as much of the archaeological heritage of Hasankeyf as possible'. But none of the affected communities and local campaigners I have spoken with support the archaeological salvage works in advance of Ilısu, undertaken under the auspices of the Turkish State by teams from Turkish, European and US universities, though some could not say so publicly because they need work on the excavations. As local campaigners, the Hasankeyf Volunteers, said, '[W]e kept telling them they cannot transport the whole city to some other place. Because Hasankeyf is a whole, you cannot fracture it, you cannot cut it into pieces, there is an organic wholeness there' (interview, June 2001). It is not that people do not understand the value of excavations in revealing the historical reality, particularly in a region where there is a long history of repression of people, their culture and history. It is that they see the archaeological work as facilitating the continuation of the dam.

It became clear that the long history of genocide and repression against the Kurdish people and other ethnic groups such as Armenians, including the cleansing of the diversity of culture from the reservoir area, had to form part of archaeological considerations. This cultural cleansing is not the only or even (in the case of some of the dams) the main purpose of the development, but it is an expedient result for a State that has a long history of forced assimilation and which continues to deny the existence of Kurds and others. This tactic, fed by secular Turkish nationalism, is defended by the powerful and independent Turkish military. For example, from 1915–1916, 'about one million Armenians perished' (McDowall 2000a:104), a genocide Turkey continues to have difficulty acknowledging. I have been shown the location of a historical Armenian presence in the Ilısu reservoir area; only an independent investigation could say what it might reveal of these early 20th-century events. No full set of statistics is available but it is estimated that over 30 million people of Kurdistan inhabit several countries in Western Asia and the Middle East, carved up into different states after World War I. Since the foundation of the Turkish state in 1923, there has been severe repression of the Kurdish population, including forced displacement on a large scale, military campaigns and massacres, forced assimilation via the school system, and bans on the Kurdish language, in addition to the methods of the recent conflict already noted (Kendal 1993; McDowall 2000a:184–213 and 395–454). Those who have attempted to speak and write about this, people from the communities, lawyers, journalists and scholars (some of them Turkish), have been imprisoned for long periods (Kendal 1993:76; McDowall 2000a:ix, 409–10, 424, 452). There have been improvements particularly since 2002, but there is still no substantive freedom of expression. Culture and history are key elements in the struggle for economic and social change and for free expression in the Kurdish region.

Again, there is physical evidence in recent Kurdish history of repression, massacre and struggle, which Ilısu would submerge. There is also evidence it would submerge past and current practices of diverse communities from traditions within Islam, Christianity and other religions. Any assessment worth its name would need to consider such evidence, the removal of access rights and the termination of religious practices that the dam would cause. There are a number of claims to ancient heritage in the Ilısu reservoir area, and people have also raised issues concerning much more recent heritage. Whatever the truth of any of those claims, they must be acknowledged. There is no indication that such impact and people's concerns have been considered properly or (in some cases) at all; given the political climate in the region and the history described above, they are not likely to be addressed. The World Archaeological Congress (2001a) has noted that the question of people's right to have access to and express their culture and heritage is recognised in various standards, and commented that 'the Ilısu dam would have amounted to a form of ethnic cleansing in which governments and companies would have been complicit' (WAC 2001b).

People from the region feel strongly about the recent history of conflict in the area. Women spoke most clearly about what is at stake, showing that the dam would cover over evidence of crimes by the security forces, such as village destructions from the 1990s and possibly graves of the disappeared. One displaced mother, who every Saturday demonstrates with other mothers for peace and the demand to know where their disappeared children are, put things in perspective:

> Yes, Hasankeyf is our history but the essence of our history was our children. We have no geography any more, no towns and cities. We have nothing left. Our children were our history (interview, June 2001).

That is, the children are the inevitable inheritors and the continuation of the history of that region, and without them, history is destroyed.

It is not that the mothers of the disappeared are unconcerned with the submerging of archaeological sites and cultural places; rather, they are making a case against the dam by exposing the low value accorded to the lives of themselves and their children, and therefore to Kurdish culture and society. This orientation from women led me as an archaeologist to uncover information on the potential existence of such graves in the reservoir area, to raise my findings publicly, and to highlight the implications to potential backers of the dam. The historian David McDowall speaks of mass graves near Siirt, which is one of the provinces within which the reservoir of Ilısu lies (McDowall 2000a:425). Human rights lawyers and activists have confirmed that mass graves of unknown persons have been found in recent years in areas close to Ilısu (interview with Human Rights Association, Batman branch, August 2004). Archaeologists in Turkey confirm that such graves could well exist in the reservoir area but also point out that it is impossible for any archaeologist to investigate or excavate them professionally, independently and safely; the State does not permit it (Ronayne 2006b:84). So I felt that the appropriate archaeological response in this case was to expose these facts and demand, together with the women, that they be addressed.

But it is not only justice that the women want; their concern is with the survival of culture. The issue of return to villages from which people were displaced in the 1990s is fundamental to this question. It is one of the chief demands of the movement for peace in the region. Displaced women speak about recovering the way of life, mutual support, capacity to grow food to feed their children, and the knowledge of how to live that life; women still resident in the reservoir area say they do not want to leave, despite living in what is once more effectively a war zone (Ronayne 2005:71 *passim*).

Women's Case for Survival and Against Cultural Destruction

The strongest case against the cultural destruction that would be caused by the dam is the one made by women. This is because women, as chief carers for families and communities, are able to spell out most clearly what displacement and the loss of the land means. When asked to outline these impacts as they see them, women respond that it is never only a question of the dam, and they explain the cultural impact of Ilısu with reference to what they face in war, conditions in the slums of the cities, the loss of children, and the break-up of the social and cultural framework they had worked hard to build in their home villages. As one displaced woman put it: 'the building of dams means the evacuation of villages by other means' and 'war doesn't just mean to kill a person with a weapon. If you cut down the trees or kill a culture that's war'. The most effective way to kill culture, including the knowledge of what went before, is to destroy the human beings through whose relationships and works culture survives.

Often invisible and unvalued, the work of building and maintaining community is done primarily by women, in the work of giving birth to and caring for their children and everyone in the household or village. This is a key means by which culture is shaped, transmitted, defended and changed. In fact, not only individuals and communities but also the acts and relationships of which they and their culture are comprised can only live by and through this biological, manual and mental work. What is culture without that work? The opposition of women to the dams and the targeting of women for particular kinds of repression should be understood in this context. A multi-racial network of grassroots women in Europe explain it, in a letter to support the movement for water and life in Bolivia:

> As homes, livelihoods and communities are destroyed due to lack of access to water or when they are lost under the waters of a dam, it is women who do the work of survival of the community and of its cultural roots. While much lip service is paid to 'culture', the reality is trampled on. Yet what is culture, if not the unique relationships each community has developed, in order to pass on and extend what it has learnt for its survival and its pursuit of happiness. And protecting such culture, based in the history of our struggles, is first of all the work of women. (Global Women's Strike 2003)

The point made is that this culture work, whether it is in Africa, Latin America, Europe or Kurdistan, is not simply a matter of defending static tradition and custom or even guarding the living body of song, sacred artefacts, dance and so on, but is comprised of living relationships between people, past and present. Within these relationships the knowledge needed for survival is gathered, remade, passed on. This knowledge is lost or becomes useless in the forced move to the cities, because of everything the women have said they face after such a move. Their defence of these relationships, their struggle to hold onto memory and place and return to rebuild their lives in the villages from which they were forced out, is not superstition but a respect for the strategies of survival, sometimes miraculous in the circumstances that their ancestors and they themselves have worked out. It is their own value and their connection with their past that they are defending. Once this is considered, it is easier to see why not only archaeological salvage work, but anthropological and ethno-archaeological studies designed to rescue fragments of this knowledge, would not be of use to the living communities opposing the dam, those who want to return and those still in the reservoir area who do not want to leave.

THE DIFFERENCE ACCOUNTABILITY MAKES: AN ARCHAEOLOGIST DRAWS SOME LESSONS FROM ILISU

The case I have outlined here, based on what women in particular have said, proved to be a headache for the governments and companies, especially when resoundingly endorsed by the World Archaeological Congress (whose statements on the dam I drafted). It is not my contention that this work was the sole reason for the victory over the last consortium, which was the achievement of a movement composed of a wide range of communities, individuals and professionals in Turkey and Europe, some working together and some independently. But it is my view that women's opposition and the accountable working relationship developed between archaeologists and affected communities, particularly with women, made a vital contribution to halting dam construction last time and to concessions the new consortium of companies has already had to make.

For example, it proved vital in altering the basis for opposition to Ilısu on cultural heritage grounds. Having previously boxed off the 'archaeology angle' as mainly the site of Hasankeyf, both the EU governments and NGOs raising concerns widened their assessment of cultural impacts following our campaigning, the WAC letters and my subsequent reports. The British government replied to Professor Martin Hall, then president of WAC, requesting permission to circulate the first WAC letter to other export credit agencies and governments (WAC 2001a); this letter, a review by Dr Kitchen and myself of the project's Environmental Impact Assessment (EIA) and my subsequent work became key reference points on cultural heritage and Ilısu. So much so that the revised EIA (IEG 2005) the new consortium has produced (the old EIA with spin) borrows liberally from this work, particularly regarding the need to assess recent heritage and contemporary culture in the area. This success is because the work expressed an accountable relationship between professional archaeologists and grassroots communities, enabling it to spell out clearly the archaeological considerations that support opposition to the project by villagers, residents of Hasankeyf and other local campaigners. That accountability enabled us to draw out the connections between ancient sites, more recent sites, and the people alive and making culture in the area today who are their first inheritors. Thus the true extent of the dam's cultural impact began to be considered and this consideration began from the presentation of the views, experience and demands of the communities directly affected. As archaeologists, we spoke with far more power as a result of the connection with the communities and other campaigners; and they in turn were more powerful with our support.

This connection focused on and now takes as its starting point the culture of caring which is mainly women's labour, and it is a theme developed and extended in my reports in recent years. This fact above all has made it more difficult for governments and other potential supporters to accept any plan by the dam builders to limit the cultural heritage grounds to salvaging a small percentage of Hasankeyf or covering the costs for rescue archaeology at a few other sites. It was not and still is not realistic to suppose that costs and technical difficulties of salvage archaeology for Ilısu could be a serious lever to halting a €1.8 billion project. Then again, no one was under any illusions that the dam builders cared for the preservation of culture and women's or anyone's work to defend it. But the strategy of the dam's backers and planners has always been to treat the involuntary resettlement, environmental consequences and cultural heritage separately, thereby dividing and narrowing each case. This was thwarted last time by the coming together of those sectors of people who are expected to remain divided, and by making public women's opposition to the destruction of their life's work of building and maintaining communities – the greatest cultural destruction – and their case for the survival of culture. This case has been the most hidden; yet as the case for the valuing of every human life and caring for that life, it is the most powerful. Particular claims on benefits to women have been made in the context of GAP dams, so making public what women had to say, bringing archaeology's case together with their case and ensuring it was heard, makes the dam more difficult to justify as a 'cultural and social development project'. Again, the value of the strategy worked out among women villagers, the Global Women's Strike and myself is reflected in the latest round of project documents. Where previously women were almost completely invisible, they now go to great lengths to focus on women; some women reported being consulted for these documents for the first time ever and attribute that to our collective work. Of course these 'consultations' were inadequate and women are granted visibility only as victims, their enormous cultural contribution hidden. This is our next battle. But the acknowledgment of women is another victory and undermines the documents.

Maintaining those connections, however, is not easy. The work needed to accurately reflect the voices and demands of grassroots communities has been a struggle. The case against the dam outlined here is not acceptable to some within and beyond archaeology, particularly not a case made on the basis of what grassroots women have said. There can be no doubt that many archaeologists involved with rescue projects would agree that the priority is the lives of human beings, and that they are personally opposed to what such mega-projects destroy in the name of development. But the realities and the economics of salvage archaeology demote this priority, rendering professionals charged with saving the past accountable in the first instance to developers and governments responsible for destroying it (*cf* Everill, this volume). Archaeologists working on the salvage projects or providing impact assessments, concerned as I have no doubt they are with preventing destruction, are in the pay of the developer, in this case the Turkish State and the companies. Or, as with the university teams from other countries, are working under the State's auspices and require its permission in order to conduct fieldwork. This lack of independence undermines the surveys, impact assessments and salvage excavation. In that sense, archaeologists doing that work are embedded with the destroyers of culture and heritage. In a case like that of southeast Turkey, the history of war and cultural cleansing in the region, as well as the continuing climate of repression and threat of torture, make the implications of their involvement all the more serious. As archaeologists themselves acknowledge, addressing issues such as mass graves is impossible.

Thus, Ilısu illustrates the use of setting down some basic principles for how archaeologists can work. But on the other hand, attempts to theorise a set of ethics or even a broad framework from abstract first principles are of limited use. If these codes of ethics and practice are not written from experience in these movements and in collaboration with communities, they will contain abstractions which can throw people off the scent of pursuing people's original objectives in their struggles. The approach outlined here seemed the only effective way to go, if we as professionals were not to be drawn into supporting what we said we were opposing. It also found support in the grassroots of the profession in the UK and Ireland, students and low-paid field archaeologists. Through opposition to the dam and stating their intention to refuse to work on any salvage projects for it, these colleagues were also able to highlight their own case for wage rises and better conditions (see Anonymous 2001). This illustrates an important point: Archaeologists who want to take this approach need to develop a collectivity among ourselves, also in order to cross internal hierarchies in our profession.

Ilısu shows that while saving archaeological sites may not be the priority for survival movements, these are movements against cultural destruction; communities, beginning with women, in defending their lives, livelihoods and homes are also defending cultural heritage. In the case of Ilısu, archaeological salvage projects (among other things) have been prioritised over consultation with affected communities or coherent resettlement plans; the dam builders have valued ancient artefacts and sites over the people who live in the reservoir area now, or who lived there in the very recent past, often the inheritors of that ancient history and culture. Our training as archaeologists also teaches us to value the object and deny the social relationships it embodies, relations both past and present. In *Capital*, Marx (1990:163–177) called it the fetishism of commodities. In other words, we are trained to facilitate capital and so our seemingly natural but in fact altogether social 'instinct' when confronted with threatened destruction is to propose survey and excavation or, at best, a campaign focused on saving sites, without first checking whether these tactics and instruments are appropriate. To do otherwise requires undoing a lot of that training and, among other things, may involve refusing some kinds of work, crossing accepted boundaries of disciplines and resisting the tendency to treat communities as objects of study.

This does not mean abandoning all we know; Ilısu shows that archaeological skills, used in a different way, can be even more relevant and creative. A referee for this paper commented that 'the activist stance to prevent the dam's construction [is] dominant in this article and the archaeology project [is] underdeveloped'. This is only true if you believe archaeology and the movement to change the world for the better to be mutually exclusive, and archaeology to be defined by a limited technical set of tasks involving observing, measuring and removing material culture. In the case of Ilısu, I have not excavated sites, following the direction of affected communities who rightly view such work as preparing the way for the dam. But I have used what I know as an archaeologist to say what is significant and what culture would be lost – in reviews of impact assessments, submissions to governments, public meetings, media work and so on. Neither does this rule out survey and excavation as useful tools in other circumstances or even in the Ilısu area at some future point, should the political situation change, eg, families are desperate to find graves of their disappeared loved ones, but this sort of excavation is currently not possible due to repression and military control. This approach has offered me a way forward in archaeology which is independent of developers, governments and political parties. I have not reported here on the detail of the archaeology of many periods affected by the dam or the technical difficulties of assessment and salvage; this has been presented in many of our reports and documents over the years and most of those are publicly available. I have focused on what I believe is urgent for archaeologists to know and which we rarely read about in the textbooks and journals – how as a professional, and specifically as an archaeologist, I worked with grassroots communities, and how we made our case together. That *is* the archaeological project – one that made a significant contribution to halting a destructive dam last time and will continue to develop, including as part of the opposition to GAP and the latest attempt to build Ilısu.

CONCLUSION

When as archaeologists we facilitate a development, it is not just sites that are destroyed or have to be salvaged by record; people's lives, livelihoods and well-being are at stake. When women defend the culture of caring and when their struggle can be publicised (no easy thing, since governments and the media rarely want to hear of women), there is every chance of stopping such a project as the Ilısu dam. If the dam gets stopped, then archaeological sites as well as everything else we can call culture is saved. The support of archaeologists strengthens women's case and vice versa. On the other hand, if archaeologists campaign on the basis of time and money to salvage ancient sites only, prioritising these for preservation, money may well be given for salvage or parts of some sites are preserved (as in the case of the Aswan High Dam in Egypt), but in almost every case the destructive project goes ahead, destroying community, culture and many other sites. So involvement on the latter basis not only limits the sort of victory achievable by the women for everyone, but can also be instrumental in the defeat of the movement against the dam.

The victory last time on Ilısu is just one example of many. Similar campaigns with which I worked forced the withdrawal of companies from the Yusufeli dam project in northeast Turkey (Hildyard *et al* 2002). In Bolivia, an enormous Indigenous movement – where women are, as ever, in the majority – ousted Bechtel corporation from the city of Cochabamba where it had tried to privatise the water supply. Not only did that movement make clear that they were fighting for their very survival, but it also showed that the fight was about stopping the destruction of their culture and beliefs. So battles can be won, destruction halted, and when professionals are accountable to grassroots movements and work with them, we all move forward.

ACKNOWLEDGMENTS

Thanks are due to the following: the communities and their organisations affected by Ilısu and other dams and/or displaced by war who have organised meetings to inform me on a number of occasions; Nick Hildyard of Cornerhouse for information and advice on large dam projects; the International Free Women's Foundation, Netherlands for assistance with consultation of Kurdish women in Europe; Selma James, international co-ordinator of the Global Women's Strike, for comments on the text and direction on women's work of community and culture; Dr W.H. Kitchen, Institute for Lifelong Learning, University of Sheffield who undertook archaeological campaign work on Ilısu with me; the Kurdish Human Rights

Project for assistance with trips to the region; Professor John Waddell, Department of Archaeology, National University of Ireland, Galway for supporting this work in various practical ways; Professor Martin Hall, Deputy Vice Chancellor of the University of Cape Town and former president of WAC for facilitating the WAC campaign on Ilısu.

NOTES

1. I am aware there is academic discussion of globalisation and archaeology, the role of developer-led archaeology in that context, and related subjects. This paper, rather than addressing those discussions, is trying to present some lessons learned in the course of actively opposing globalisation's effects.
2. The author has worked for a number of years in the Global Women's Strike, a grassroots women's network, independent of political parties, in over 60 countries worldwide, the majority in the Global South. For further information on the Strike, see www.globalwomenstrike.net.

REFERENCES

Anonymous (2001) 'Archaeologists green ban', *Rescue News* 85, 8

Algaze, G (1989) 'A new frontier: first results of the Tigris-Euphrates archaeological reconnaissance project, 1988', *Journal of Near Eastern Studies* 48, 241–281

Algaze, G, Breuninger, R, Lightfoot, C and Rosenberg, M (1991) 'The Tigris-Euphrates archaeological reconnaissance project: a preliminary report of the 1989–1990 seasons', *Anatolica* 17, 175–240

Aydin, Z (1986) *Underdevelopment and Rural Structures in Southeastern Turkey: The Household Economy in Gisgis and Kalhana*, London: Ithaca

Cornerhouse Research, Ilısu Dam Campaign, Kurdish Human Rights Project, Friends of the Earth, Berne Declaration, Campaign an Eye on Sace, Pacific Environment, World Ecology, Economy and Development (2001) *Review of EIAR for the Ilısu Dam and HEPP*, London: Kurdish Human Rights Project and Cornerhouse

Diyarbakır Bar Association (2001) 'An Assessment on the Ilısu Dam and HEPP Environmental Assessment from a Legal Point of View', submission to the UK government, Diyarbakır and London: Diyarbakır Bar Association and Cornerhouse *et al*

Dolatyar, M and Gray, TS (2000) *Water Politics in the Middle East: A Context for Conflict or Co-operation?* London: Macmillan

Göç-Der (2002) *Research and Solution Report on the Socio-Economic and Socio-Cultural Conditions of the Kurdish Citizens Living in the Turkish Republic Who are Forcibly Displaced Due to Armed Conflict and Tension Politics: The Problems They Encountered Due to Migration and Their Tendencies to Return Back to the Villages*, Istanbul: Göç-Der

GAP Regional Development Administration (GAP-RDA) (1994) *Status of Women in the GAP Region and Their Integration to the Process of Development*, Ankara: GAP

Global Women's Strike (2003) 'Letter to the Minister of Justice of Bolivia on the water protests in Cochabamba and the killing of a protestor', www.allwomencount.net

Hildyard, N, Griffiths, H, Le Verger, M and Godinot, S (2002) *Damming Indictment: How the Yusefeli Dam Violates International Standards and People's Rights*, London: Amis de la Terre, Cornerhouse, Friends of the Earth, France Libertés, Kurdish Human Rights Project and Ilısu Dam Campaign

IEG (Ilısu Environment Group) (2005) *Ilısu Dam and HEPP: Environmental Impact Assessment Report Update*, 31 July 2005

Ilısu Dam Campaign, Kurdish Human Rights Project, Cornerhouse, World Economy Ecology and Development, Eye on SACE Campaign and Pacific Environment Research Centre (2001) *If The River Were A Pen...The Ilısu Dam, The World Commission on Dams and Expert Credit Reform*, London: Kurdish Human Rights Project

Kendal (1993) 'Kurdistan in Turkey' in Chaliand, G (ed) *A People Without a Country: The Kurds and Kurdistan*, translated by M Pallis, New York: Olive Branch Press

Kitchen, WH (2000) 'The Ilısu dam archaeological surveys: chronology, sites under threat, methodological limitations and pointers to further research', unpublished document produced for the Ilısu Dam Campaign

Kitchen, WH and Ronayne, M (2001) *The Ilısu Dam Environmental Impact Assessment Report: Review and Critique*, www.nuigalway.ie/archaeology. Summarised in *Public Archaeology* 2, 101–116

KHRP (Kurdish Human Rights Project) (1999) *The Ilısu Dam: A Human Rights Disaster in the Making*, London: KHRP

KHRP, Cornerhouse, Ilısu Dam Campaign (2002) *Downstream Impacts of Turkish Dam Construction on Syria and Iraq*, London: Kurdish Human Rights Project

KHRP, Göç-Der and Human Rights Association (2003) *Internally Displaced Persons: The Kurds in Turkey*, London: Kurdish Human Rights Project

Marsh, N, undated 'Water wars', UK Defence Forum, www.ukdf.org.uk/ts5.htm

Marx, K (1990) *Capital Volume 1*, London: Penguin

McDowall, D (2000a) *A Modern History of the Kurds*, London: I.B. Taurus

—— (2000b) 'Ilısu: the economic and social context', www.Ilısudamcampaign.net

Ronayne, M (2002) *The Ilısu Dam: Displacement of Communities and Destruction of Culture*, London: KHRP, National University of Ireland, Galway, Cornerhouse, Ilısu Dam Campaign

—— (2005) *The Cultural and Environmental Impact of Large Dams in Southeast Turkey*, London: KHRP and National University of Ireland, Galway

—— (2006a) 'Archaeology against cultural destruction: the case of the Ilısu dam in Southeast Turkey', *Public Archaeology* 5(4), 223–236

—— (2006b) *The Ilısu Dam: A Monument to Barbarism: Review of the EIAR Update for the Ilısu Dam in the Kurdish Region of Turkey*, available at www.nuigalway.ie/archaeology and www.globalwomenstrike.net

Save Hasankeyf Platform (2000) 'The lost city of Hasankeyf and the protection of Hasankeyf/Ilısu dam', campaign document, Turkey

Tuna, N, Öztürk, J and Velibeyoğlu, J (eds) (2001) *Salvage Project of the Archaeological Heritage of the Ilısu and Carchemish Dam Reservoirs Activities in 1999*, Ankara: METU TAÇDAM

Tuna, N, and Velibeyoğlu, J (eds) (2002) *Salvage Project of the Archaeological Heritage of the Ilısu and Carchemish Dam Reservoirs Activities in 2000*, Ankara: METU TAÇDAM

Walker, M and McGuire, R (1999) 'Class confrontations in archaeology', *Historical Archaeology* 33, 159–183

WAC (World Archaeological Congress) (2001a) Correspondence between Professor Martin Hall and the UK government, 16th January 2001, 2nd May 2001 published as 'The Ilısu dam: WAC protests to the British government', *Public Archaeology*, 50–56

—— (2001b) 'Withdrawal of Support for Ilısu Dam Project', Press Statement, 14 November, www.nuigalway.ie/archaeology

WCD (World Commission on Dams) (2000) *Dams and Development*, London: Earthscan

CHAPTER 15

Ethics, Objectivity and Emancipatory Archaeology

Dean J. Saitta

Part of the challenge facing an ethical and socially responsible archaeology is to square traditional, time-honored commitments to 'objective' scholarly inquiry with the politically interested motivations of an emancipatory archaeology. Emancipatory archaeology has been defined in different ways (eg, Duke and Saitta 1998; Layton 1989; Leone and Preucel 1992; Wilkie and Bartoy 2000). In the view taken here, emancipatory archaeology is dedicated to expanding the conversation about what it means to be human by illuminating variation in the forms and consequences of social relationships that have organized human life across time and space. By 'expanding' I mean taking archaeological knowledge to audiences – native peoples, the working poor – who historically have had little use for archaeology as traditionally practiced. The organizational variation at issue in this conversation is, of course, contingent; that is, it is shaped by time, place and circumstance. Things could always have turned out differently. Emancipatory archaeology aims, through its conceptual frameworks and public outreach initiatives, to foster critical thought about the determinants of *contemporary* lived experience in hopes of impelling positive social change. Emancipatory archaeology is an archaeology of hearts and minds; it is a moral as well as scientific enterprise.

The challenge of an emancipatory archaeology is especially profound as concerns study of the very recent, 20th-century past. Here, capitalist relationships are known to lay behind the differential distributions of wealth and poverty observable in the material record. Thus, investigation of this past inevitably involves us in contemporary cultural critique. In this paper I describe how the ethics of objective inquiry and the ethics of an engaged, emancipatory archaeology come together in research on the 1913–1914 Colorado Coal Field Strike. This episode constitutes perhaps the best example of open class warfare in American history. It began when 90% of Colorado Fuel and Iron Company coal miners left the shafts and their company town homes for makeshift tent colonies on the Colorado prairie in September 1923. One of Colorado's largest employers, CF&I produced coking coal for blast furnaces that supplied rails for the expanding American transportation network. The miners were striking for higher wages and safer working conditions, among other concerns. The strike climaxed when the Colorado militia, in a last ditch effort to break the strike, attacked the Ludlow tent colony on 20 April 1914. The so-called Ludlow Massacre claimed the lives of 25 people, including two women and 11 children. The events of 1913–1914 have powerful, continuing symbolic importance in contemporary struggles between Capital and Labour. I detail how archaeology at Ludlow contributes to this political struggle while broadening our scientific understanding of American labour history.

A PRAGMATIST ETHIC

The Colorado Coal Field War Archaeological Project is dedicated to producing new knowledge of American labour history, disseminating this knowledge to multiple audiences, and engaging working class interests as a way to educate for social change (Ludlow Collective 2001). Participants in this work come to it for a variety of reasons and with a variety of expectations (Walker and Saitta 2002; Wood 2002a). My particular involvement in this work is informed by pragmatist philosophical commitments. As formulated by John Dewey nearly 90 years ago, pragmatism turns from the 'problems of philosophy' to the 'problems of men' (Dewey 1917). It applies itself less toward knowing or 'getting things right' (in terms of capturing some final transcendental truth) than toward living or 'making things new' (Rorty 1989). For pragmatists, making things new requires that we improve our ability to respond to the views, interests and concerns of ever larger groups of diverse human beings; to expand the scope of who counts as 'one of us' (Rorty 1989, 1999).

I take pragmatism as seamlessly dovetailing with the dialectical thrust of a critical archaeology (Saitta 1989), and with the kind of sensibility that equips us for using our craft (*sensu* Shanks and McGuire 1996) to address human needs. Pragmatism does so without abandoning time-honored and still useful concepts of truth, experience, and testing. Instead, it reformulates these concepts in a way more sensitive to meeting human need. In so doing, it responds more directly – and perhaps more coherently and honestly – to the widespread consensus that archaeological work occurs in a political context, and that we must therefore be aware of how the results of our inquiries are used within that context. A brief summary of these core commitments follows.

The first core pragmatist commitment is to an antifoundational notion of truth – the idea that there are no fixed, stable grounds on which knowledge-claims can be established. Truth is not an accurate reflection of something non-human (Rorty 1998); rather, it is a matter of intersubjective consensus among human beings, one mediated by currently available theories, methods, and data. This notion produces a warrant for aggressively experimenting with theory and method in order to arrive at true beliefs. Experimentation is crucial for improving and expanding the conversation between and among interested parties of scientists and citizens. It is the vitality of this conversation that moves archaeology and its constituencies toward the sorts of 'usable truths' that can serve human need.

The second core commitment is to the idea that truth-claims must be evaluated against a broader notion of experience. Specifically, they must be evaluated in terms of their concrete consequences for life today – for how we want to *live* as a pluralistic community. Instead of simply asking whether a claim about the past is empirically sufficient in light of available data, pragmatism asks *what difference the claim makes to how we want to live*. What are the implications of theoretical claims from evolutionary archaeology, interpretive archaeology, Marxist archaeology or, indeed, any other current framework for understanding society and history for how we think about, and how we might intervene in, human social life? To what extent does a truth-claim expeditiously meet the human needs at stake in, say, reburial or repatriation controversies; ie, to what extent does it facilitate putting human souls to rest and human minds at ease? 'Experience', in this view, is relational, interactive, and creative; it acknowledges our status as social and historical beings; it is genuinely reflexive (Kloppenberg 1996). Defining experience in this way means that we must subsume the usual realist 'criterial' rationality for judging truth-claims (ie, criteria emphasizing logical coherence and correspondence between theory and data) under something that is still broadly criterial but much more qualitative and humanistic.

A third commitment is to a particular notion of 'testing', specifically as it relates to the evaluation of truth-claims produced by different standpoints, perspectives, and cultural traditions. Especially germane to archaeology these days are those truth-claims that divide scientific and various 'descendant community' knowledges of the past, including indigenous, immigrant, working class, and other 'folk' knowledges. In contrast to the mainstream scientific view where competing ideas are tested against each other in light of the empirical record, pragmatism stipulates that we test the ideas of other cultures and descendant communities by 'weaving' them together with ones we already have (Rorty 1989). Testing is a matter of interweaving and continually reweaving webs of belief so as to increasingly expand and deepen community and, perhaps, create new fields of possible action

(Rouse 2003:101). It prescribes a 'measured relativism' (Appleby *et al* 1994) that balances a commitment to evaluation with the parallel belief that cultural pluralism is our best recipe for civil cohesion (Menand 1997:xxviii).

The specter of objectivity haunts these core pragmatist commitments. What does objectivity mean in this context? The notion of objectivity embraced by pragmatists, as alluded to above, is one that Megill (1994) describes as *dialectical*. Dialectical objectivity takes a particular stance toward the subjectivity of the knower. Whereas other kinds of objectivity seek either to exclude subjectivity (*absolute* objectivity) or contain it (*disciplinary* objectivity), dialectical objectivity adopts a positive attitude toward subjectivity. Subjectivity is seen as indispensable to the constituting of objects, as necessary for objectivity. As Heidegger (1927) notes, objects first become known to us through action in the world. Knowing is thus acting, and human acting is always acting in company (Fabian 1994). These arguments close the loop to a concept of 'objective truth' as a matter of intersubjective consensus (solidarity) among human beings, rather than as a matter of accurate reflection of something non-human.

This pragmatist notion of objectivity differs from 'realist' notions that are widely embraced in contemporary archaeology. Realist objectivity stipulates that there is an independent reality, that alternative accounts map it differently and that, while hope and bias complicate the picture, systematic exploration of similarity and difference can establish credible knowledge-claims and produce more complete understandings of the past. Binford (1982) in his defense of middle range theory, characterized this kind of objectivity as 'operational objectivity'. This qualified notion of objectivity is today invoked by archaeologists across the paradigmatic spectrum. Thus, processualists embrace 'mitigated objectivity' (Clark 1998), contextualists 'guarded objectivity' (Hodder 1991), and feminists 'embodied objectivity' (Wylie 1995).

The rub is that such notions of objectivity, no matter how well qualified, might not be best for regulating a more democratic, civically engaged archaeology. Zimmerman (2001) argues that within archaeology there is no clear epistemology for 'coalescing' descendant community and mainstream scientific understandings of the past. Others have also advocated a rethinking of epistemology now that previously disenfranchised groups have places at the table (eg, Schuldenrein 1999). The democratic practice of archaeology, like that of history, still lacks a philosophical grounding that is compatible with its affirmations (Appleby *et al* 1994). Kitcher's (2001) so-called 'modest realism' moves us a bit closer, although it still qualifies objectivity little differently than the other realisms at work across the sciences.

Alternatively, pragmatism's ideals better dovetail with those indigenous epistemologies that are concerned with living as well as knowing (Saitta 2003). Pragmatism's commitment to 'testing' the beliefs of other cultures by interweaving and continually reweaving them with beliefs that we already have is clearly in keeping with Watkins's (1998) sensible suggestion, offered in response to Clark (1998), that we settle differences between scientific and indigenous knowledges by finding a 'path between trees', rather than by bulldozing the forest or circumventing it altogether. The navigational guide in these encounters is something fully human – wider, deeper, stronger, and better community – rather than some independent object that we seek to accurately represent in theory.

In summary, pragmatism emphasizes ways of living instead of rules for knowing, the 'weaving together' of knowledges instead of their 'validation against' experience, and the social utility of narratives instead of the absolute truth of laws and theories. These governing ideals neither forsake reality, nor undermine the possibilities for learning, nor capitulate to relativism. Pragmatism subsumes Enlightenment criterial rationality and nomothetics to more humanistic – but no less explicit and compelling – regulative ideals. In so doing, it converges with the epistemologies of subaltern groups – native peoples, working classes – for whom the social causes and consequences of scientific knowledge-claims can be of great concern. This in turn promises a more collaborative and democratic, and less authoritarian, archaeology.

At the same time, pragmatism usefully breaks with *both* the analytical and continental philosophical traditions that so many have found wanting as underpinnings for the theoretical and applied aspects of processual and postprocessual archaeology, respectively. The desirable outcome of pragmatism's advocacy of these particular notions of truth, experience, and testing is stronger community – richer and better human activity – rather than some singular, *final* truth about the past or some imagined 'more comprehensive' or 'more complete' account of history. The loyalty in pragmatism is to other human beings struggling to cope, rather than to the realist hope of getting things right; moral and ethical progress is viewed as an expansion in the number of people among whom unforced agreement can be established through free and open encounters (Rorty 1991).

Pragmatism's ethical imperatives overlap with those enunciated by scholars seeking an ethical archaeology (eg, contributors to Lynott and Wylie 2000). These include the need to be self-conscious of one's subjectivity, accountable for one's presuppositions and claims, and responsive to the various constituencies having an interest in the past. Pragmatism's ethical imperatives especially resonate with Martin Hall's (2004) redefinition of ethics as 'principles of engagement' whereby we, as contributors to public knowledge, use our knowledge to serve the public good – whatever we take 'public good' to mean. Whether these ethical principles are best theorized as universal or situational is a matter of debate. I lean toward Rorty's (2001) position that community-building is best served by situationalism or, in his terms, 'ethnocentrism': that there is more to be gained by replacing the Enlightenment rationalist commitment to universal moral obligations with the rather more modest idea that we – as Westerners, intellectuals, archaeologists, or whatever – merely have some instructive and possibly persuasive stories to tell that might help to build trust across the boundaries that divide us from others. In the next section, I consider how archaeology in the Colorado Coal Fields is contributing to such wider ethical and emancipatory goals.

EMANCIPATORY PRACTICE

Archaeologists have always been ambivalent about applying their knowledge in political or emancipatory projects. Even with today's widespread awareness that our work is political, the activist strain in archaeology is at risk of disappearing as the more pointedly critical concepts used by archaeologists to understand the past – power, hierarchy, class, and so on – are appropriated and domesticated by those lobbying for allegedly more 'scientific' approaches. Several commentators have recently worried about how such appropriations blunt archaeology's critical/activist edge (eg, Thomas 2000).

Elsewhere, I have considered the dulling effects of theories that describe subject societies with concepts that rest on a foundational belief in continuous rather than categorical variation; eg, descriptions of ancient societies as 'small-scale', 'middle range', 'transegalitarian', 'intermediate', and 'heterarchical' (Saitta 2005b). Such terms are held by some to better capture organizational variety and/or address the 'classificatory ambiguity' (Neitzel and Anderson 1999) of archaeological cultures. The rub for the activist scholar, however, is that these concepts do not assign a distinctive ontological status to the subject societies of interest. They neither highlight specific causal powers that can focus comparative work, nor do they engagingly explain to our varied public constituencies exactly *how* the present is different from the past. We need something stronger, with a sharper critical edge, for capturing and comparing organizational differences across time and space, and for fostering the kinds of critical self-consciousness about contemporary lived experience that can impel broader interest, engagement, and change.

Historical archaeology is one pursuit that has provided a concrete touchstone for action, given recent arguments establishing capitalism as a central analytical focus (Delle *et al* 2000; Leone 1995; contributors to Leone and Potter 1999; Little 1994; Matthews *et al* 2002; Orser 1996; Paynter 1988). A focus on capitalism foregrounds social divisions and conflicts – around class, power, ethnicity, gender – and their embodiment in material culture. This approach has balanced inquiry and produced more complete accounts of the past. Just as importantly, it has encouraged self-consciousness about the social value and political utility of archaeology (Leone 1995). Contributors to Leone and Potter (1999), for example, take an explicitly activist approach to their subject matter. They are concerned that their scholarship illuminate capitalism in ways that can demystify its operation, if not actually help to transform it. This orientation offers new possibilities for connecting archaeology to contemporary life and for diversifying archaeology's public audience, even as we struggle with the forms that our activism and advocacy should take.

The Colorado Coal Field War Archaeological Project looks to extend this emerging tradition and set of scholarly and political commitments. The scholarly goal of the project is to fill in what 'official' Western history leaves out; namely, a better understanding of the existential concerns and strategies of men in the mineshafts and women and children in the home. Official Western histories, when they address this episode in American industrial relations, focus on famous people, events, and the organizing activities of the United Mine Workers union. We have only anecdotal information about the everyday lives and relationships of the ethnically diverse population – 24 different languages were spoken in the southern Colorado coal fields – that comprised the labour force. Archaeology can flesh out their side of the story, address official history's blind spots, and help produce a fuller understanding of cultural and historical process on the Western frontier.

McGuire (2004) and Saitta (2005a) detail some of the project's contributions so far. The main research questions focus on (1) whether the distribution of ethnic groups in the tent colony duplicated or departed from the ethnic segregation of the company towns; (2) how striking families supported themselves, given minimal strike relief and siege-like conditions; and (3) to what extent coal camp life changed and/or improved following the strike. The Ludlow excavations provide the strike context, and we are excavating in pre- and post-strike contexts at the Berwind coal camp above Ludlow, from which many of the Ludlow colonists came. We are looking to test documentary accounts of life in the coal camps and tent colonies as well as investigate other ways – unrecorded by history – in which miners might have been coping with their circumstances.

The archaeological contexts have good integrity and abundant remains. The assemblages at Ludlow – clothing, jewelry, children's toys, bullets, cartridges – speak to a hurried, catastrophic abandonment on the day of the massacre. Complete excavation of one tent platform and its associated artifacts (including a crucifix and a button inscribed with the words *Societa Alpinisti Tyrolesi*) suggest an Italian Catholic ethnic identity. This gives us confidence that the ethnic organization of the camp is knowable. Other data suggest that miners may have been consciously striving to actively preserve ethnic identity. Preliminary analysis of ceramic remains from one cellar at Ludlow suggests that workers were resisting 'Americanizing' influences in turn-of-the-century immigrant life that elsewhere were expressed by the embracing of a Victorian order in foodways and associated material culture (Gray 2005).

Data on daily subsistence comes from several deep features including a privy, trash pit, and several cellars. Dietary remains reveal an enormous reliance on canned foods, much more than what we see in working-class contexts at Berwind. Much of this canned food is undoubtedly Union-supplied. At the same time, some features contain lots of evidence for home canning, such as mason jars. This implies access to local farmers or gardens for fresh vegetables and fruit. Similarly, cow bones showing up in Ludlow deposits – combined with the fact that they represent inferior cuts of meat – may suggest supply from local ranchers. Additional faunal analysis may disclose patterns of meat-sharing within the tent colony. In general, our current data from deep features suggest worker strategies consistent with Labour's commitment to using *place* – understood as social ties of kin and community that link workers to family and friends employed in local business, health care, and law enforcement – as a way to offset Capital's greater command of *space* through control of markets, telegraph, railroad, and other technologies (Harvey 1996).

Comparisons of the Ludlow assemblage with pre- and post-strike deposits at the nearby coal camp of Berwind reveal some interesting changes in household strategy over time. Wood (2002b) shows how working-class women in the company towns were able to raise whole families on miner's wages that would not even feed two people. Trash dating before the strike contains lots of tin cans, large cooking pots, and big serving vessels. Families took in single male miners as boarders to make extra income, and women used canned foods to make stews and soups to feed them. After the strike the companies discouraged boarders but the wages still remained very low. The tin cans and big pots disappear from the trash, to be replaced by canning jars and lids, and the bones of rabbits and chickens. Women and children who could no longer earn money from boarders instead produced food at home to feed the family. It remains to be seen whether post-strike contexts suggest an overall improvement in worker living conditions over time.

Coal Field archaeology is thus producing some promising leads for reconstructing Labour's strategies in Western coal towns and striker tent colonies. We hope to conduct future fieldwork at the Colorado militia camp located several hundred meters southwest of the Ludlow colony, so as to conduct the 'archaeology of perpetrators' advocated by Pollock and Bernbeck (this volume). However, landowner permission to excavate at the militia camp has thus far been denied. The work conducted in other contexts, however, has added to the historical understanding of events gained through written documents.

At the same time – and in keeping with the ethical prescriptions of a pragmatist view – we are using these findings to engage contemporary communities and issues in southern Colorado and in the United States. We see our work as a form of political action sensitive to working-class histories and interests. In the last decade, many historical archaeologists have advocated that we should work directly with local groups having an intimate connection to the historical sites that we study (eg, LaRoche and Blakey 1997; Spector 1993; Wilkie and Bartoy 2000).

In southern Colorado we make a distinction between Ludlow's *descendants* and *descendant community* (McGuire and Reckner 2002). Ludlow's descendants are principally middle-class Anglos. Their parents participated in the great social mobility of the 1950s and 1960s. Today they are teachers, lawyers, businesspeople, managers and administrators, and they are scattered across the United States. They share an identity as descendants of the massacre but they do not form a community, either in the sense that they live near each other or as members of an organization or club. The descendants' memories are familial and personal. Their interest in our work stems from a concern to establish or re-establish a connection to their familial past and/or to see to it that their family's role in this past is properly honored. We have aided descendants in locating graves so that stones could be raised to family members who died in the massacre, and by correcting errors in documentation or labels on photos in historical archives.

Ludlow's *descendant community* is the unionized working people of southern Colorado. They include many descendants of people who participated in the strike, but the vast majority of them have no familial connection to the events of 1913–1914. A minority of them are ethnic Whites (Italians and Eastern Europeans) but the majority are Chicanos. It is this population that maintains the monument and organizes the annual memorial service that has been held at the site every June since 1918. Indeed, this long commemorative tradition is evidenced by one of the more evocative artifacts produced by our excavation, a bent, rusted wreath stand from a past memorial service that we recovered from a trash-filled, still-undated privy. Although the last unionized mine in the area closed in 1997, the descendant community is still actively involved in union struggles. Many of the everyday realities that provided context for the Ludlow Massacre – workplace danger, corporate greed, chronic tension between Capital and Labour – are still with us. The memorial service is a national event for the union and an opportunity to address contemporary issues facing organized labour.

Workers in a variety of industries in southern Colorado closely identify with, and draw inspiration from, the events at Ludlow. Since the project began, employees of Las Animas County and health-care workers at Mt. San Rafael Hospital in Trinidad have unionized. Both groups chose the union of their fathers and uncles, the United Mine Workers of America. The lifespan of the project has also coincided with a steelworkers strike at the Oregon Steel plant in Pueblo, Colorado, about 75 miles north of Ludlow. Oregon Steel is the direct corporate descendant of the Colorado Fuel and Iron Company. The steelworkers struck to end forced overtime and thus reclaim one of basic rights that were at issue in 1913, the eight-hour workday. The steelworkers made Camp Ludlow a powerful symbol of their struggle. We participated in the struggle by joining steelworkers on the speaker's platform at the annual Ludlow memorial service and at their union hall in Pueblo.

We also engage a number of other public constituencies. Our work has been featured in numerous local and regional newspaper articles and on Colorado Public Radio. In these contexts we remind citizens that the workplace rights we enjoy and take for granted today were won via struggle and paid for in blood. This has elicited numerous invitations to speak to various groups and societies across the political and ideological spectrum, from the Daughters of the American Revolution, to the Rocky Mountain Explorers Club, to the American Federation of Labour – Congress of Industrial Organization's Union Summer programs. We have taken the project into Colorado schools, in the form of a middle school classroom history trunk intended to enlighten an even younger generation about Colorado's significant labour history, and through the University of Denver's 'Reach Out DU' classroom lecture program.

We have worked with the Colorado Endowment for the Humanities to educate teachers interested in weaving Colorado's labour history into middle and high school curricula. We involve Ludlow's descendant community in this activity. This community understands that writing the past has consequences, and it has a keen interest in how it is presented. The 'vernacular' or 'folk' histories of this community often differ from official history (Bodnar 1992). Vernacular histories emphasize the militia's role in starting the shooting on 20 April. They implicate the militia in many more atrocities against colonists on the day of the massacre, and count many more casualties in the conflict. They suggest, for example, that additional bodies were secretly removed from Ludlow by the militia after the assault and subsequently deposited in unmarked graves on the Colorado prairie. These histories also conflict with the 'critical' histories that we activist-scholars write about Western industrialization and its human cost. Vernacular history has intellectual as well as considerable emotional appeal. Thus, developing pedagogies that negotiate between and among vernacular, official and critical histories is a real challenge. However, it is one that must be met in order to deepen the public's appreciation of the past, enhance archaeology's contemporary relevance, and build alliances for change.

Our project is also contributing in more publicly visible ways to community building in the Colorado coalfields. Labour history sites are generally neglected in America's commemorative landscape (Foote 1997). Mindful of this lacuna, we produced a three-sided interpretive kiosk for the Ludlow site that described the history, archaeology, and legacy of the events that transpired there. We followed this up with a smaller historical marker for Berwind, modeled on the Corazon de Trinidad ('Heart of Trinidad') markers that celebrate Santa Fe Trail history in downtown Trinidad. The Berwind marker emphasizes the role played by Colorado's immigrants in the making of the Industrial West. We have just completed an interpretive trail for the Ludlow Massacre site to replace the original kiosk, a feature that updates the story told by archaeology and locates the Ludlow drama in a wider landscape. These interpretive materials offer 'counter-classic' narratives to balance the triumphal, mythic narratives that have long informed Western public history. Their location at a site like Ludlow that functions so powerfully as a 'living' memorial creates pressure and incentive to update when appropriate, lest they succumb to the kind of ossification or 'Disneyfication' of history that increasingly has come to characterize other kinds of public commemorative efforts (Silberman, this volume).

CONCLUSION

Colorado Coal Field War scholarship employs theory and method that is common to much contemporary archaeological practice. This scholarly work is producing some promising leads for fleshing out working-class agency and history in a region long dominated by mythic narratives of rugged individualism, frontier conquest, and national progress. What most distinguishes our project is its unapologetic activist and emancipatory dimension. This public outreach work is informed by a pragmatist ethos emphasizing the expansion of conversation and community. Ours is one of the few archaeological projects in the United States that speaks to the historical struggles of, and also directly to, working-class people. We are building an archaeology that we hope working people will relate to both emotionally and intellectually.

This raises the question of exactly *how* this archaeological work is emancipatory. Yolanda Romero, president of UMWA Local 9856 Women's Auxiliary, captured a bit of it with her observation about the meaning of excavated artifacts from the Ludlow tent colony:

> Until now, we've only known what we've seen in photographs. But to see a real thing, an item that a person actually handled, really brings those people and that time to life… [W]orkers today are still fighting for some of the same protections the Ludlow miners wanted. People should know how far we've come and how far we still have to go. (UMWJ 1999)

This observation takes on added salience in the aftermath of several mining accidents in Alabama, Kentucky and West Virginia that claimed the lives of over 30 miners in the first few months of 2006. Archaeological work at Ludlow thus illustrates that the coal mining past is, in many ways, still present. For this, our work is earning considerable approval and support from citizens closest to the history of Ludlow. The United Mine Workers of America now count us among their union brothers and sisters (Butero 2005) and always reserve a spot on the speaker's platform for us at the annual Ludlow memorial service. There is still much to do however, to build the kind of trust and shared 'observational language' that is required, if archaeological work is to contribute meaningfully to emancipatory projects in the community.

We have also worked, through educational channels and public history initiatives that enrich an impoverished commemorative landscape, to reach a broader audience that has never heard of the Ludlow Massacre and that has missed, or misunderstood, the history of US labour conflict and its powerful legacy. Whether these wider audiences will be convinced of Ludlow's significance in the human struggle for workplace freedom and dignity remains to be seen. For the moment we content ourselves with the knowledge that we're politically engaged – that we're 'in the game', to quote Hall (2004) – and the belief that our activities are cultivating an audience for archaeological work while simultaneously justifying archaeology's existence as an enterprise that serves the public good.

REFERENCES

Appleby, J, Hunt, L and Jacoby, M (1994) *Telling the Truth About History*, New York: W.W. Norton

Binford, L (1982) 'Objectivity – explanation – archaeology, 1981', in Renfrew, C, Rowlands, M, and Segraves, B (eds), *Theory and Explanation in Archaeology*, New York: Academic Press

Bodnar, J (1992) *Remaking America: Public Memory, Commemoration, and Patriotism in the Twentieth Century*, Princeton: Princeton University Press

Butero, B (2005) Remarks at the Ludlow Memorial rededication service, 5 June 2005

Clark, G (1998) 'NAGPRA, the conflict between science and religion, and the political consequences', *Society for American Archaeology Bulletin* 16, 22

Delle, J, Mrozowski, S and Paynter, R (eds), (2000) *Lines That Divide: Historical Archaeologies of Race, Class, and Gender*, Knoxville: University of Tennessee Press

Dewey, J (1917) 'The need for a recovery of philosophy', in Dewey, J, Moore, AW, Brown, HC, Mead, GH, Bode, BH, Stuart, HW, Tufts, JH, and Kallen, HM (eds), *Creative Intelligence: Essays in the Pragmatic Attitude*, New York: Henry Holt

Duke, P and Saitta, D (1998) 'An emancipatory archaeology for the working class', *Assemblage* 4 (On-line journal located at http://www.shef.ac.uk/~assem)

Fabian, J (1994) 'Ethnographic objectivity revisited: from rigor to vigor', in Megill, A (ed), *Rethinking Objectivity*, Durham: Duke University Press

Foote, K (1997) *Shadowed Ground: America's Landscapes of Violence and Tragedy*, Austin: University of Texas Press

Gray, A (2005) *Contested Ideals: Cultural Citizenship at the Ludlow Tent Colony*, Master's thesis, Department of Anthropology, University of Denver

Hall, M (2004) Keynote Address, Contemporary and Historical Archaeology in Theory Conference, Leicester

Harvey, D (1996) *Justice, Nature and the Geography of Difference*, Oxford: Blackwell

Heidegger, M (1927) *Being and Time*, San Francisco: Harper

Hodder, I (1991) 'Interpretive archaeology and its role', *American Antiquity* 56, 7–18

Kitcher, P (2001) *Science, Truth, and Democracy*, Oxford: Oxford University Press

Kloppenberg, J (1996) 'Pragmatism: an old name for some new ways of thinking?' *The Journal of American History* 83, 100–138

LaRoche, C and Blakey, M (1997) 'Seizing intellectual power: the dialogue at the New York African Burial Ground', *Historical Archaeology* 31, 84–106

Layton, R (ed) (1989) *Conflict in the Archaeology of Living Traditions*, London: Unwin Hyman

Leone, M (1995) 'An historical archaeology of capitalism', *American Anthropologist* 97, 251–268

Leone, M and Potter, P (eds) (1999) *Historical Archaeologies of Capitalism*, New York: Plenum Publishers

Leone, M and Preucel, R (1992) 'Archaeology in a democratic society: a critical theory perspective', in Wandsnider, L (ed), *Quandaries and Quests: Visions of Archaeology's Future*, Carbondale, IL: Center for Archaeological Investigations

Little, B (1994) 'People with history: an update on historical archaeology in the United States', *Journal of Archaeological Method and Theory* 1, 5–40

Ludlow Collective (2001) 'Archaeology of the Colorado coal field war, 1913–1914', in Buchli, V and Lucas, G (eds), *Archaeologies of the Contemporary Past*, London: Routledge

Lynott, M and Wylie, A (eds) (2000) *Ethics in American Archaeology*, Washington, DC: Society for American Archaeology

Matthews, C, Leone, M and Jordan, K (2002) 'The political economy of archaeological cultures', *Journal of Social Archaeology* 2, 109–134

Megill, A (1994) 'Introduction: four senses of objectivity', in Megill, A (ed), *Rethinking Objectivity*, Durham: Duke University Press

Menand, L (1997) 'An introduction to pragmatism', in Menand, L (ed), *Pragmatism*, New York: Vintage

McGuire, R (2004) 'Colorado coalfield massacre', *Archaeology* 57, 62–70

McGuire, R and Reckner, P (2002) 'The unromantic West: labor, capital and struggle', *Historical Archaeology* 36, 44–58

Neitzel, J and Anderson, D (1999) 'Multiscalar analyses of middle-range societies: comparing the late prehistoric Southwest and Southeast', in Neitzel, J (ed), *Great*

Towns and Regional Polities in the Prehistoric American Southwest and Southeast, Albuquerque: University of New Mexico Press

Orser, C (1996) *A Historical Archaeology of the Modern World*, New York: Plenum Press

Paynter, R (1988) 'Steps to an archaeology of capitalism', in Leone, M and Potter, P (eds), *The Recovery of Meaning: Historical Archaeology in the Eastern United States*, Washington, DC: Smithsonian Institution

Rorty, R (1989) 'Science as solidarity', in Lawson, H and Appignanesi, L (eds), *Dismantling Truth: Reality in the Postmodern World*, New York: St. Martin's Press

—— (1991) *Objectivity, Relativism, and Truth*, Cambridge: Cambridge University Press

—— (1998) *Achieving Our Country: Leftist Thought in Twentieth Century America*, Cambridge, MA: Harvard University Press

—— (1999) *Philosophy and Social Hope*, New York: Penguin

—— (2001) 'Justice as a larger loyalty', in Festenstein, M and Thompson, S (eds) *Richard Rorty: Critical Dialogues*, Oxford: Blackwell

Rouse, J (2003) 'From realism or antirealism to science as solidarity', in Guignon, C and Hiley, D (eds), *Richard Rorty*, Cambridge: Cambridge University Press

Saitta, D (1989) 'Dialectics, critical inquiry and archaeology', in Pinsky, V and Wylie, A (eds), *Critical Traditions in Contemporary Archaeology*, Cambridge: Cambridge University Press

—— (2003) 'Archaeology and the problems of men', in Van Pool, T and Van Pool, C (eds), *Essential Tensions in Archaeological Method and Theory*, Salt Lake City: University of Utah Press

—— (2005a) 'Labour and class in the American West', in Loren, S and Pauketat, T (eds), *North American Archaeology*, Oxford: Blackwell

—— (2005b) 'Dialoguing with the ghost of Marx: mode of production in archaeological theory', *Critique of Anthropology* 25, 27–35

Schuldenrein, J (1999) 'Charting a middle ground in the NAGPRA controversy: secularism in context', *Society for American Archaeology Newsletter* 17, 22

Shanks, M and McGuire, R (1996) 'The craft of archaeology', *American Antiquity* 61, 75–88

Spector, J (1993) *What This Awl Means: Feminist Archaeology at a Wahpeton Dakota Village*, Minneapolis: Minnesota Historical Society Press

Thomas, J (2000) 'Reconfiguring the social, reconfiguring the material', in Schiffer, M (ed) *Social Theory in Archaeology*, Salt Lake City: University of Utah Press

UMWJ (1999) 'Lest we forget: Ludlow Project puts massacre in spotlight', *United Mine Workers Journal*, March-April, 12–13

Walker, M and Saitta, D (2002) 'Teaching the craft of archaeology: Theory, practice, and the field school', *International Journal of Historical Archaeology* 6, 199–207

Watkins, J (1998) 'Native Americans, Western science, and NAGPRA', *Society for American Archaeology Bulletin* 16, 23

Wilkie, L and Bartoy, K (2000) 'A critical archaeology revisited', *Current Anthropology* 41, 747–778

Wood, M (2002a) 'Moving toward transformative democratic action through archaeology', *International Journal of Historical Archaeology* 6, 187–198

—— (2002b) 'A house divided: changes in women's power within and outside the household, 1900–1930', in O'Donovan, M (ed), *The Dynamics of Power*, Carbondale: Center for Archaeological Investigations

Wylie, A (1995) 'Epistemic disunity and political integrity', in Schmidt, P and Patterson, T (eds), *Making Alternative Histories: The Practice of Archaeology and History in Non-Western Settings*, Santa Fe: School of American Research

Zimmerman, L (2001) 'Processing the past: interacting with descendent communities', paper presented at the 2001 Society for American Archaeology meeting, New Orleans

About the Contributors

ERMENGOL GASSIOT BALLBÈ finished his doctoral thesis in 2001 on an economic analysis of hunter and gatherer populations. He is now an associate professor of the Department of Prehistory at the Universitat Autònoma of Barcelona. His professional trajectory has centered on praxis and archaeology on one hand, and on the other, the study of the processes of social territorial exploitation and its long-term evolution. In relation to the first aspect, he has coordinated an archaeological training project in Nicaragua and researched archaeology and the formation of historical identity within farmer organizations in northern Nicaragua. In Catalunya he has promoted lines of archaeological investigations with local museums and institutions. With respect to the second aspect, he has co-directed investigations on the Atlantic coast of Nicaragua and in the Pyrenees. Finally, since 2002 he has promoted in Catalunya the participation of the academic world in the recovery of historical memory, particularly of the fight against fascism. His mailing address is: Department of Prehistory, Autonomous University of Barcelona, Edifici B, Bellaterra 08193, Barcelona (SPAIN); email: ermengol.gassiot@uab.es.

ALEXANDER A. BAUER is a Lecturer at Princeton University, where he teaches a seminar on 'Cultural Heritage Law and Policy', and is currently working with Stephen Urice on an interdisciplinary text for this emerging field. He received his Ph.D. in anthropology from the University of Pennsylvania, with a dissertation entitled 'Fluid Communities: Maritime Interaction and Cultural Identity in the Bronze Age Black Sea'. In 2005, he was made editor of the *International Journal of Cultural Property*, now published by Cambridge University Press. Beyond cultural heritage issues, his research interests include the Bronze Age of the Near East and Eurasia, ancient trade and exchange, and archaeological theory, particularly regarding the use of semiotics in archaeological interpretation. His mailing address is Princeton Writing Program, Princeton University, South Baker Hall, Princeton, NJ 08544, USA; email: abauer@princeton.edu.

REINHARD BERNBECK is Professor of Anthropology at Binghamton University, with a specialty in the archaeology of the Middle East. He has taught at the Freie Universität Berlin, and has directed and participated in field projects in Syria, Jordan, Turkey, and Iran. His particular research interests include historiography and historical materialism. Among his publications are *Theorien in der Archäologie* (1997) and the co-edited book *Archaeologies of the Middle East: Critical Perspectives* (with Susan Pollock, 2005). His mailing address is Department of Anthropology, Binghamton University, Binghamton, NY 13902, USA; email: rbernbec@binghamton.edu.

PHILIP DUKE is a Professor of Anthropology at Fort Lewis College, Durango, Colorado, where he has taught since 1980. He is a Fellow of the

Society of Antiquaries. Until recently, his professional work has been conducted on the archaeology of western North America, and he is the author of, among other publications, *Points in Time: Structure and Event in a Late Northern Plains Hunting Society*, and co-editor of *Beyond Subsistence: Plains Archaeology and the Postprocessual Critique*. He also works with the Ludlow Collective at the site of the 1914 Ludlow massacre near Trinidad, Colorado. His research interests include public archaeology and repatriation issues, and currently he is investigating the nexus between the construction of the Minoan Bronze Age and contemporary tourism on Crete. His latest book *The Tourists Gaze, the Cretans Glance: Archaeology and Tourism on a Greek Island* has just been published by Left Coast Press. His mailing address is Department of Anthropology, Fort Lewis College, Durango, CO 81301, USA; email: duke_p@fortlewis.edu.

PAUL EVERILL holds a doctorate from the University of Southampton. He has been actively involved in archaeological fieldwork since 1989 and studied for his undergraduate degree at Saint David's University College, Lampeter, Wales between 1991 and 1994. Following the completion of his Masters degree at Southampton, he worked full-time in commercial, developer-funded archaeology which later inspired his Ph.D. – an ethnographic study of British contract archaeology. The results of his 'Invisible Diggers' project are beginning to have an impact on the profession. In October 2004 he became a founding member and secretary of a national 'Diggers' Forum', which was set up as a 'special interest group' within the 'Institute of Field Archaeologists' to help improve the working lives of professional archaeologists in the UK. Since completing his Ph.D. in 2006 he has been employed by the Southampton City Council Archaeology Unit, and also co-directs an independent research excavation in the former Soviet republic of Georgia. His mailing address is: 91 Stokes Court, The Dell, Southampton, Hampshire, SO15 2PR UK; email: paul@everill.net.

PEDRO PAULO A. FUNARI is Professor of Historical Archaeology, Campinas State University, Brazil, and a research associate at Illinois State University (USA) and Barcelona University (Spain). Born in Brazil, Funari has a B.A. in history, M.A. in social anthropology, and a Ph.D. in archaeology. He is co-editor of *Historical Archaeology, Back from the Edge* (London: Routledge, 1999) and *Global Archaeological Theory* (New York: Plenum, 2005), among others; a member of the editorial board of several leading journals, such as *Journal of Material Culture, International Journal of Historical Archaeology, Public Archaeology* and *Arqueología Suramericana*; referee of such journals as *Current Anthropology* and *American Anthropologist*; and consultant editor of the *Encyclopaedia of Historical Archaeology* (London: Routledge, 2002). A committed engaged archaeologist, Funari has been senior South American representative at the World Archaeological Congress (1994–2002) and acting WAC Secretary (2002–2003). He organized the first International Conference on Archaeological Theory in South America in

1998, a WAC-sponsored meeting. His mailing address is: Departamento de História, IFCH/UNICAMP, Caixa Postal 6110, Campinas, 13081–970, SP, Brazil; email: ppfunari@uol.com.br.

YANNIS HAMILAKIS is Senior Lecturer at the University of Southampton and has taught at the University of Wales Lampeter (1996–2000) and the Autonomous University of Barcelona (2005). He has held a number of research fellowships, most recently a residential scholarship at the Getty Research Institute, Los Angeles (2005–2006). He sits on a number of editorial boards of journals and book series, including the *Journal of the Royal Anthropological Institute, Archaeologies: The Journal of the World Archaeological Congress, Research in Archaeological Education*, and the *WAC Research Handbooks in Archaeology* (published by Left Coast Press). His research interests include the politics of the past, critical pedagogy, the archaeology of the consuming body, the archaeology of the bodily senses and the prehistory of the Aegean. His most recent books are, *The Nation and its Ruins: Antiquity, Archaeology and National Imagination in Greece* (Oxford University Press, 2007), and *Archaeology and European Modernity: Producing and Consuming the 'Minoans'* (co-edited with N. Momigliano; Padova: Aldo Ausilio, 2006). He is currently working on a book on the archaeology of the senses for Cambridge University Press, co-edits a special issue of the journal *History and Memory*, and conducts archaeological ethnography on the island of Poros, Greece, as part of the Kalaureia Research Project. His mailing address is: Archaeology, School of Humanities, University of Southampton, Southampton SO17 1BJ, UK; email: y.hamilakis@soton.ac.uk.

JULIE HOLLOWELL is a cultural anthropologist coming out of Indiana University's innovative Archaeology and Social Context Program. She is currently a Killam Fellow at the University of British Columbia and a Research Associate with Indiana University's Center for Archaeology in the Public Interest. Julie co-edited *Ethical Issues in Archaeology* (with LJ Zimmerman and KD Vitelli) and recently co-authored *Ethics in Action: Case Studies in Archaeological Dilemmas* with Chip Colwell-Chanthaphonh and Dru McGill, her fellow organizers of the Society for American Archaeology's annual Ethics Bowl. She currently serves as co-chair of the World Archaeological Congress (WAC) Committee on Ethics and as series co-editor (with George Nicholas) of the WAC Research Handbooks in Archaeology (Left Coast Press). Her research interests focus on archaeological ethnography; intellectual property issues in cultural heritage; subsistence digging and the antiquities market; and the repatriation of knowledge, materials and research directives to source communities. Her mailing address is: Department of Anthropology, University of British Columbia, 6303 NW Marine Dr, Vancouver, V6T 1Z1, Canada; email: jjh@indiana.edu.

ALICE BECK KEHOE retired in 1999 as Professor of Anthropology, Marquette University, where she taught since 1968. Among her publications are the widely used textbook, *North American Indians: A Comprehensive Account*; *The Ghost Dance: Ethnohistory and Revitalization*; the introductory anthropology textbook, *Humans*; *The Land of Prehistory: A Critical History of American Archaeology*, and *America Before the European Invasions*. Her current academic interests include American Indians and history of archaeology. Recent research includes ethnographic fieldwork in an Aymara Indian village in Bolivia, historical research at the Institute for Advanced Studies in the Humanities, Edinburgh University, and continued collaboration with the Piegan Institute and Blackfeet Community College on the Blackfeet Reservation, Montana. In these researches she combines participant observation with archival and academic research to contextualize data in their societal and historical situations. Her mailing address is: 3014 N. Shepard Ave, Milwaukee, WI 53211–3436, USA.

SHANEL LINDSAY completed her Ph.D. at Northeastern University School of Law, and has served as a clerk for Judge Mark S. Coven in Quincy District Court in Quincy, Massachusetts and for the Massachusetts Supreme Court. She was awarded her B.A. in anthropology from the University of Pennsylvania in 2003, and her intellectual interests include the emerging areas of cultural rights and intellectual property in the new millennium; email: lindsay.sha@neu.edu.

RANDALL MCGUIRE has a B.A. in anthropology from the University of Texas in Austin (1974) and an M.A. (1978) and Ph.D. (1982) in anthropology from the University of Arizona. Since 1982, he has been on the faculty of Anthropology at Binghamton University, Binghamton, New York. He is currently a Professor of Anthropology. His research interests include the prehistory of the Southwest, and 19th- and 20th-century class relations in the United States. He is the author or co-author of 10 books or monographs and over 95 articles or book chapters. He has received a total of 18 research grants from the National Science Foundation, the National Geographic Society and the Colorado Historical Society. In the spring of 1999, he was a Fulbright Teaching Fellow at the Universitat Autònoma de Barcelona in Spain. In 2002, the American Anthropological Association gave him the McGraw-Hill AAA Award for Excellence in Undergraduate Teaching of Anthropology. He is working with the Ludlow Collective at the site of the 1914 Ludlow massacre near Trinidad, Colorado. He and Elisa Villalpando of the Centro INAH de Sonora, in Hermosillo, Sonora have studied the Trincheras Tradition of northern Sonora, Mexico, for the last 25 years. His most recent book, *Archaeology as Political Action*, is in press with the University of California Press. His mailing address is: Department of Anthropology, Binghamton University, Binghamton, NY 13902, USA; email: rmcguire@binghamton.edu.

TAMIMA ORRA MOURAD is a historian, museum specialist and archaeologist, currently researching the socio-political history of the development and application of theories and methods in Near Eastern archaeology. She is a Ph.D. student at the Institute of Archaeology-UCL, sponsored by CAPES (scholarship agency of the Brazilian Ministry of Education). Her research is focused on the role of knowledge in Near Eastern archaeology, in colonial and nationalist settings, and as promoter of ethnic and religious conflicts in both national and international scale. In the course of her research, she has found an ongoing necessity to point out alternatives to former roles archaeologists have played, strongly believing that archaeology should incorporate – aside from its academic and scientific vocations – the social role of promoting tolerance and peace. Her mailing address is: Institute of Archaeology, University College, London, 31–34 Gordon Square, London WC1 0PY, London; email: t.mourad@ucl.ac.uk.

GEORGE NICHOLAS is Professor of Archaeology, Simon Fraser University, Burnaby, British Columbia, Canada. He was founding director of Simon Fraser University's Indigenous Archaeology Program in Kamloops (1991–2005). Since moving to British Columbia in 1990 from the United States (he remains an American citizen), he has worked closely with the Secwepemc and other First Nations, and directed a community-based, community-supported archaeology program on the Kamloops Indian Reserve for 16 years. His research focuses on the archaeology and human ecology of wetlands, early postglacial land use, intellectual property rights and archaeology, Indigenous archaeologies, and archaeological theory, all of which he has published widely on. He is the editor of the *Canadian Journal of Archaeology* and series co-editor (with Julie Hollowell) of the World Archaeological Congress' *Research Handbooks in Archaeology* (Left Coast Press). His mailing address is: Department of Archaeology, Simon Fraser University, 8888 University Drive, Burnaby, V5A 4X9, Canada; email: nicholas@sfu.ca.

SUSAN POLLOCK is Professor of Anthropology at Binghamton University. She lived for two years in Berlin while a Research Fellow of the Alexander von Humboldt-Stiftung. She specializes in archaeology of the Middle East and has conducted fieldwork in Iran, Turkey and Iraq. Her research contributes to studies of political economy, ideology and representation, and archaeology in the media. Her publications include *Ancient Mesopotamia: The Eden That Never Was* (1999) and the co-edited book *Archaeologies of the Middle East: Critical Perspectives* (with Reinhard Bernbeck, 2005). Her mailing address is: Department of Anthropology, Binghamton University, Binghamton, NY 13902; USA; email: bg9711@binghamton.edu.

JOAQUIM OLTRA PUIGDOMÉNECH is a graduate student in history, specializing in prehistoric archaeology, at the Universitat Autònoma of Barcelona. In 2002 he earned a scholarship from the Spanish government for his Ph.D. research project, 'Food production and consumption in the south east of the Iberian peninsula between 1500 and 900 cal ANE'. He also works with Ermengol Gassiot at a prehistoric site in the Pyrenees (northeast Iberian Peninsula). Oltra applies GIS, faunal analysis and topography to his archaeological research. His mailing address is: Department of Prehistory, Autonomous University of Barcelona, Edifici B, Bellaterra 08193, Barcelona (SPAIN); email: joaquim.oltap@uab.cat.

ELENA SINTES OLIVES received her B.A. in history in 2001 and is currently a graduate student in the Department of Prehistory at Universitat Autònoma of Barcelona. She has participated in several excavations and skeletal analyses of historic and prehistoric archaeological sites on Balearic Island and in the Iberic Peninsula. Her research interests focus on understanding ancient social organisation through the study of their skeletons. Her current work is an analysis of skeletal collections from two prehistoric collective burials in Menorca. She has participated in two mass grave excavations from the Spanish Civil War. Her mailing address is: Department of Prehistory, Autonomous University of Barcelona, Edifici B, Bellaterra 08193, Barcelona (SPAIN); email: elenasintes@hotmail.com.

ERIKA M. ROBRAHN-GONZÁLEZ is research associate at Campinas State University and at the Archaeological and Ethnological Museum/University of São Paulo, Brazil. Born in Brazil, Robrahn-González has a B.A. in history, an M.A. in social anthropology and a Ph.D. in archaeology. Running her own archaeological firm, she has been conducting archaeology projects for more than 20 years, with special focus on central and western Brazil. Currently, her interests include public archaeology and social approaches to sustainable development, as well as ethnoarchaeology, especially with indigenous groups. She has published extensively in the areas of conceptual and strategic aspects of transdisciplinary social-ecology research, and cultural heritage management. She is co-editor of different journals and a member of the Ethical Commission in the Brazilian Archaeological Society. Her mailing address is: Alamada Alemanha 479, Residencial Euroville, Granja Viana. Carapicuiba/São Paulo, Brasil, 06355–465; email: arqueo@ terra.com.br.

CHARLES RIGGS received his Ph.D. in 1999 in anthropology from the University of Arizona. His area of expertise is in Southwest archaeology with emphases on prehistoric architecture, migration, GIS-based approaches, public education, Native American collaboration, and cultural resource management. Prior to joining the anthropology faculty at Fort Lewis College, Dr. Riggs worked for a number of years in cultural resource management, serving as a project director and as head of the mapping department for a leading Southwestern cultural resource management firm. His experience in Southwest archaeology includes fieldwork or research in southern California, New Mexico and throughout Arizona. Dr. Riggs' dissertation, entitled *The Architecture of Grasshopper Pueblo*, was published by the University of Utah Press in 2001. He has served as the Anthropology Department's faculty mentor for the Mesa Verde National Park internship program since 2003. His mailing address is: Dept. of Anthropology, Fort Lewis College, Durango, CO 81301, USA; email: riggs_c@fortlewis.edu.

MAGGIE RONAYNE, Lecturer in Archaeology at the National University of Ireland, Galway, has also taught at the Universities of Southampton and Oxford (UK) and at University College Cork (Ireland), where she first studied. She has done fieldwork in Ireland, Scotland, Wales and France, often teaching on training excavations. From 1994 to 2003 she served on the World Archaeological Congress executive board. Her expertise is on cultural destruction in war and by large development projects, highlighting the essential work of women in creating and defending culture. This orientation is informed by her involvement in the Global Women's Strike, a network of grassroots women in over 60 countries, autonomous of political parties. She is Ireland Strike coordinator. She is author/editor of a number of books and articles, including *The Cultural and Environmental Impact of Large Dams in Southeast Turkey*. Her mailing address is: Department of Archaeology, National University of Ireland-Galway, Galway, Ireland; email: maggie.ronayne@nuigalway.ie.

DEAN J. SAITTA is a professor in the Department of Anthropology at the University of Denver. He is co-Principal Investigator of the Colorado Coal Field War Archaeological Project. He has worked at DU since 1988, teaching archaeology, evolutionary anthropology and urban studies. He is the author of numerous articles on North American archaeology and the philosophy of archaeology. He is co-author of *Denver: An Archaeological History*, and is currently writing a book for scholarly and popular audiences entitled *The Archaeology of Collective Action*. In 1998 he won the University Scholar-Teacher of the Year award, and from 2000 to 2003 he served as University Professor of Social Science. He is a past member of the Board of Directors of the Colorado Endowment for the Humanities, Executive Committee of the Colorado Council of Professional Archaeologists, and editorial board of the journal *Rethinking Marxism*. He is currently president-elect of the University of Denver Faculty Senate. His mailing address is: Department of Anthropology, University of Denver, Denver, CO 80208, USA; email: dsaitta@du.edu.

NICK SHEPHERD is a Senior Lecturer in the Centre for African Studies at the University of Cape Town. He has published widely on issues of archaeology and society in South Africa and the politics of archaeology in Africa, including the award-winning essay 'Heading South, Looking North: Why We Need a Post-Colonial Archaeology'. In 2005–2006 he was based in the WEB DuBois Institute at Harvard University as a Mandela Fellow. He is founder editor of *Archaeologies: Journal of the World Archaeological Congress*. Current projects include an edited volume, *Desire Lines: Space, Memory and Identity in the Post-Apartheid City* (Routledge, 2007) a second volume, *Borderlands: Indigenous Archaeologies in Southern Africa* (AltaMira Press, forthcoming), and a book on archaeology and society in South Africa. His mailing address is: Centre for African Studies, University of Cape Town, Private Bag, Rondebosch 7701, South Africa; email: shepherd@humanities.uct.ac.za.

NEIL ASHER SILBERMAN is director of the Ename Center for Public Archaeology and Heritage Presentation in Belgium. A former Guggenheim Fellow and a graduate of Wesleyan University in the US, he served as a contributing editor for *Archaeology* magazine and is a frequent contributor to other archaeological and general-interest periodicals. His books include *The Bible Unearthed* (with Israel Finkelstein, Free Press 2001); *Heavenly Powers* (Penguin Putnam 1998); *The Message and the Kingdom* (with Richard A. Horsley, Putnam 1997); *The Archaeology of Israel* (with David A. Small, Sheffield 1995); *Invisible America* (with Mark P. Leone, Holt 1995); *The Hidden Scrolls* (Putnam 1994); *Between Past and Present* (Holt 1989); and *Digging for God and Country* (Knopf 1982). Mr. Silberman has been on the staff of the Ename Center since 1998, consulting on heritage policy and working on projects in archaeology and heritage interpretation in Belgium, The Netherlands, France, Germany, Jordan, and Israel. His mailing address is: Ename Center for Public Archaeology and Heritage Interpretation, Abdijstraat 13–15, 9700 Oudenaarde, BELGIUM; email: neil.silberman@enamecenter.org.

HELAINE SILVERMAN is a professor in the Department of Anthropology at the University of Illinois at Urbana-Champaign. She received her Ph.D. in anthropology from the University of Texas at Austin in 1986. She conducted various archaeological projects on the south coast of Peru between 1983 and 1996, focusing on the interplay of political organization, ritual practice, and expressions of identity among the Paracas and Nasca peoples of this region. In addition to numerous articles, she is the author of *Cahuachi in the Ancient Nasca World* (1993), *Ancient Andean Art: An Annotated Bibliography* (1996), *Ancient Nasca Settlement and Society* (2002) and *The Nasca* (2002, written with Donald A. Proulx). She has edited/co-edited four volumes dealing with Andean archaeology (*Andean Archaeology*, 2004; *Andean Archaeology I: Variations in Sociopolitical Organization*, 2002; *Andean Archaeology II: Art, Landscape and Society*, 2002; *Andean Archaeology III: North and South*, 2006) and another treating mortuary landscapes (*The Space and Place of Death*, 2002). Currently she is studying archaeological tourism and the construction of local and national identities in Peru. Her mailing address is: Department of Anthropology, University of Illinois, 109 Davenport Hall, Urbana, IL 61801, USA; email: helaine@uiuc.edu.

DAWNIE WOLFE STEADMAN received her Ph.D. from the Department of Anthropology at the University of Chicago in 1997. A skeletal biologist, Steadman conducts research in both North American bioarchaeology as well as forensic anthropology. She became a Diplomate of the American Board of Forensic Anthropology in 2005. She worked with the Argentine Forensic Anthropology Team in Buenos Aires in 1991 and was the Training Coordinator for the Physicians for Human Rights Cyprus Project in 1999. Since 2004 she has served as a forensic training consultant for the archaeologists and physical anthropologists at the Universitat Autònoma of Barcelona. Her mailing address is: Department of Anthropology,

Binghamton University, SUNY, P.O. Box 6000 Binghamton, NY 13902–6000, USA; email: osteo@binghamton.edu.

STEPHEN K. URICE is an Associate Professor of Law at the University of Miami School of Law. He also serves as director of the Project for Cultural Heritage Law and Policy. Dr. Urice earned his doctoral degree in art history at Harvard University; his dissertation focused on an early Islamic site in Jordan where he directed excavations and a research project from 1979 until 1987. The results of that project were published as *Qasr Kharana in the Transjordan* (American Schools of Oriental Research, 1987). On completion of his law degree at Harvard, he practiced in New York and Los Angeles. His mailing address is: University of Miami School of Law, P.O. Box 248087, Coral Gables, FL 33124–8087, USA; email: surice@law.miami.edu.

INDEX

green
press
INITIATIVE

Left Coast Press Inc. is committed to preserving ancient forests and natural resources. We elected to print *Archaeology And Capitalism* on 30% post consumer recycled paper, processed chlorine free. As a result, for this printing, we have saved:

3 Trees (40' tall and 6-8" diameter)
999 Gallons of Wastewater
402 Kilowatt Hours of Electricity
110 Pounds of Solid Waste
216 Pounds of Greenhouse Gases

Left Coast Press Inc. made this paper choice because our printer, Thomson-Shore, Inc., is a member of Green Press Initiative, a nonprofit program dedicated to supporting authors, publishers, and suppliers in their efforts to reduce their use of fiber obtained from endangered forests.

For more information, visit www.greenpressinitiative.org